THE HEROIC LEGEND OF
ARSLAN

STORY BY
YOSHIKI TANAKA

MANGA BY
HIROMU ARAKAWA

11

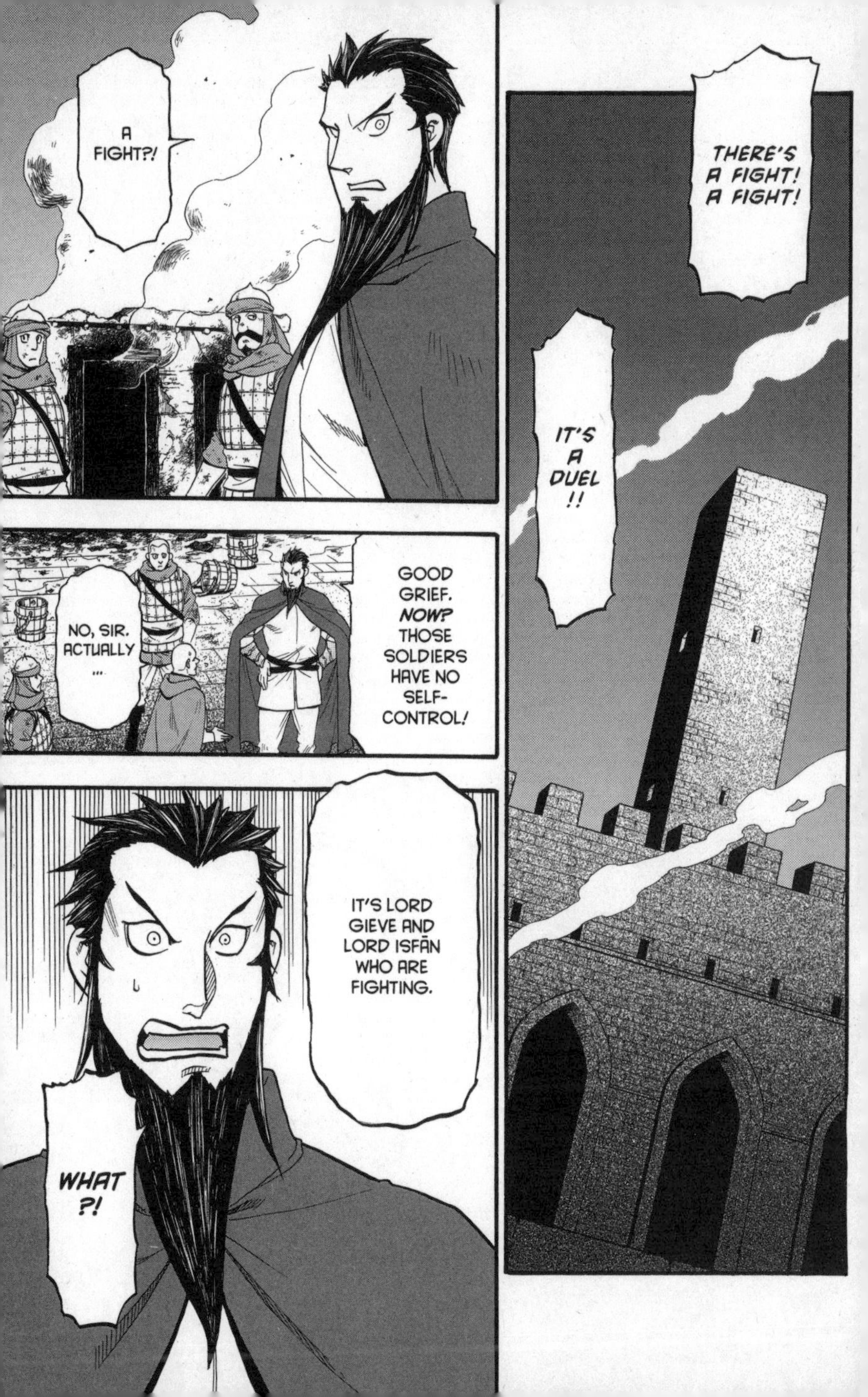
THERE'S A FIGHT! A FIGHT!
IT'S A DUEL!!
A FIGHT?!
GOOD GRIEF. *NOW?* THOSE SOLDIERS HAVE NO SELF-CONTROL!
NO, SIR. ACTUALLY ...
IT'S LORD GIEVE AND LORD ISFĀN WHO ARE FIGHTING.
WHAT?!

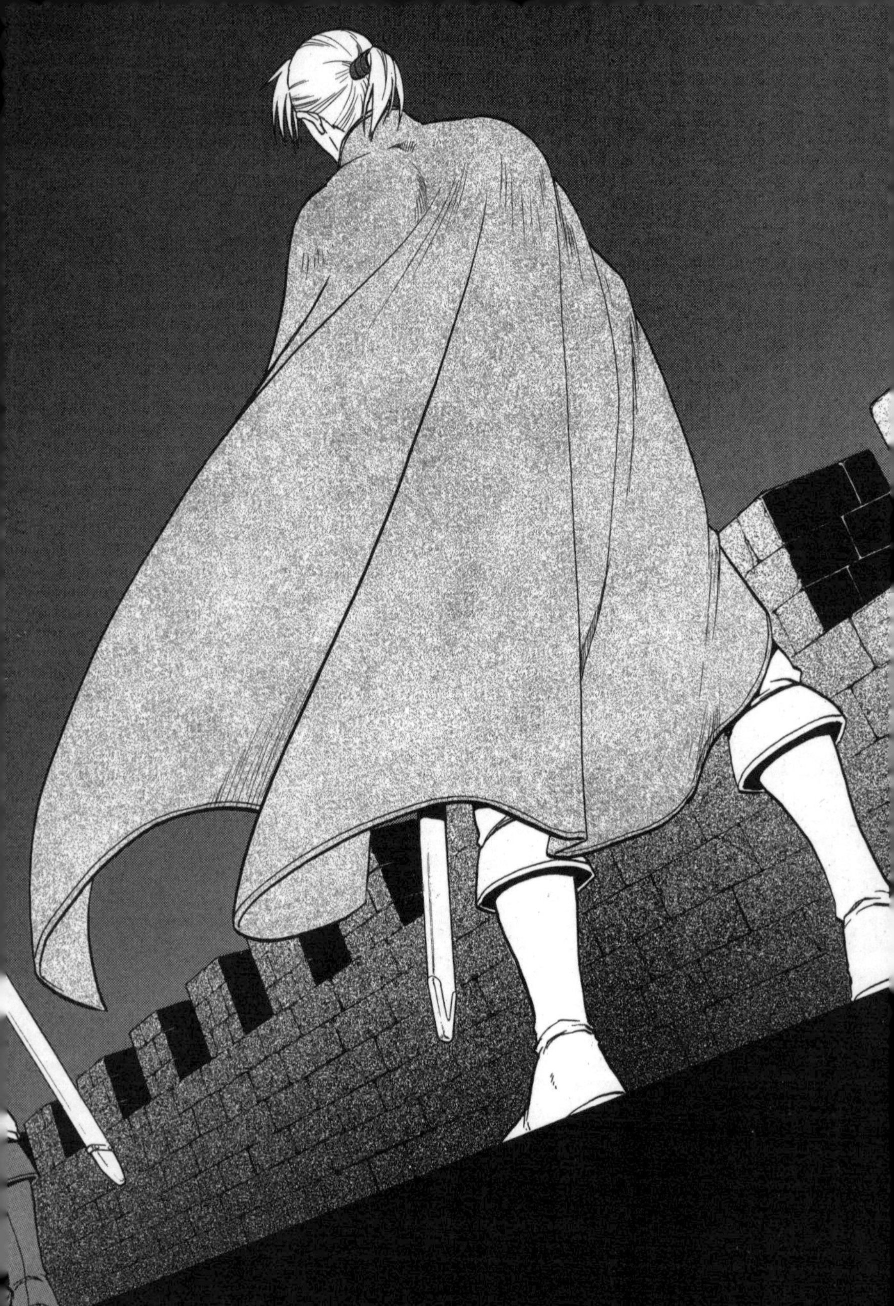

Chapter 65: The Wolf's Wrath

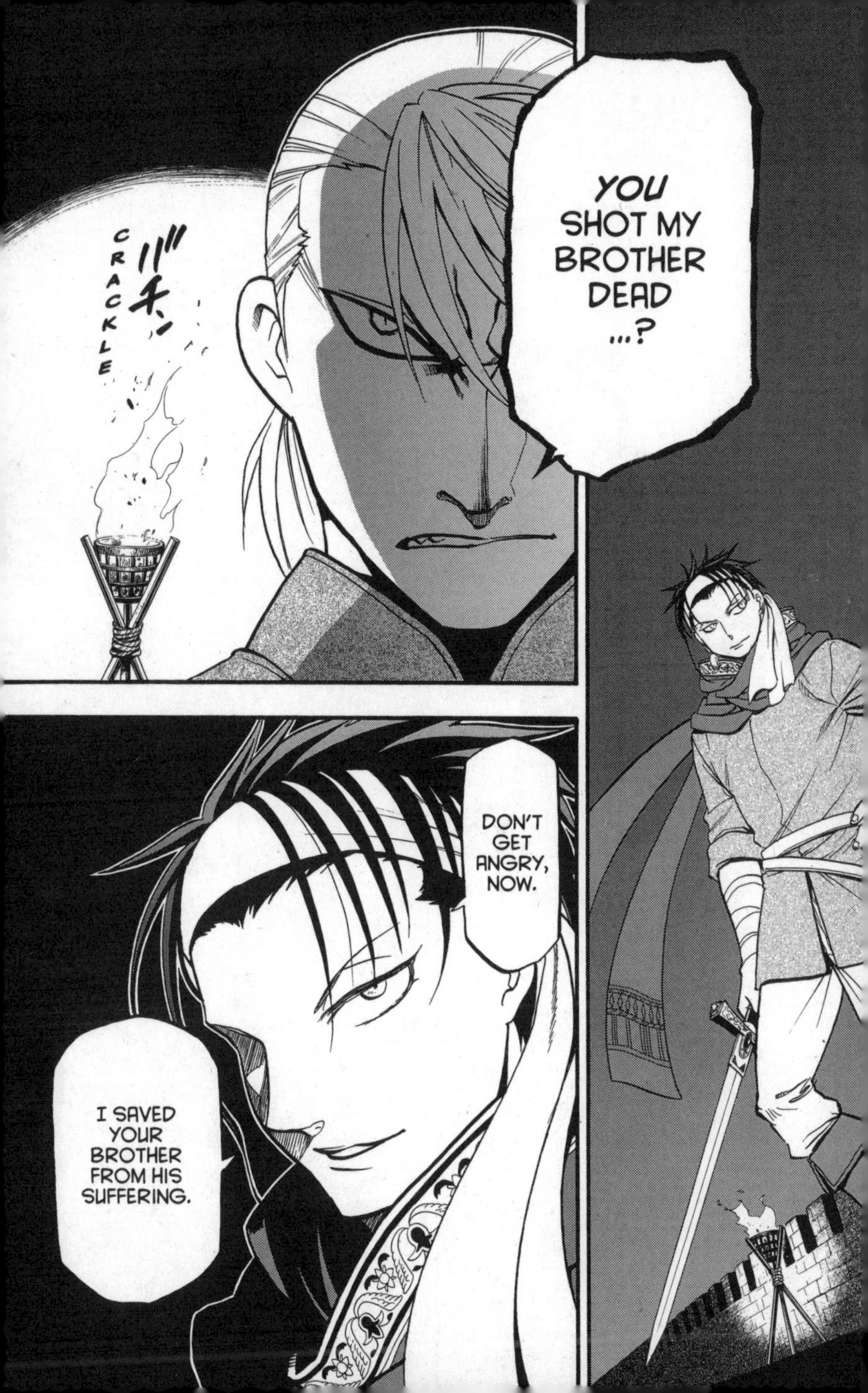
YOU SHOT MY BROTHER DEAD ...?
バチン
CRACKLE
DON'T GET ANGRY, NOW.
I SAVED YOUR BROTHER FROM HIS SUFFERING.

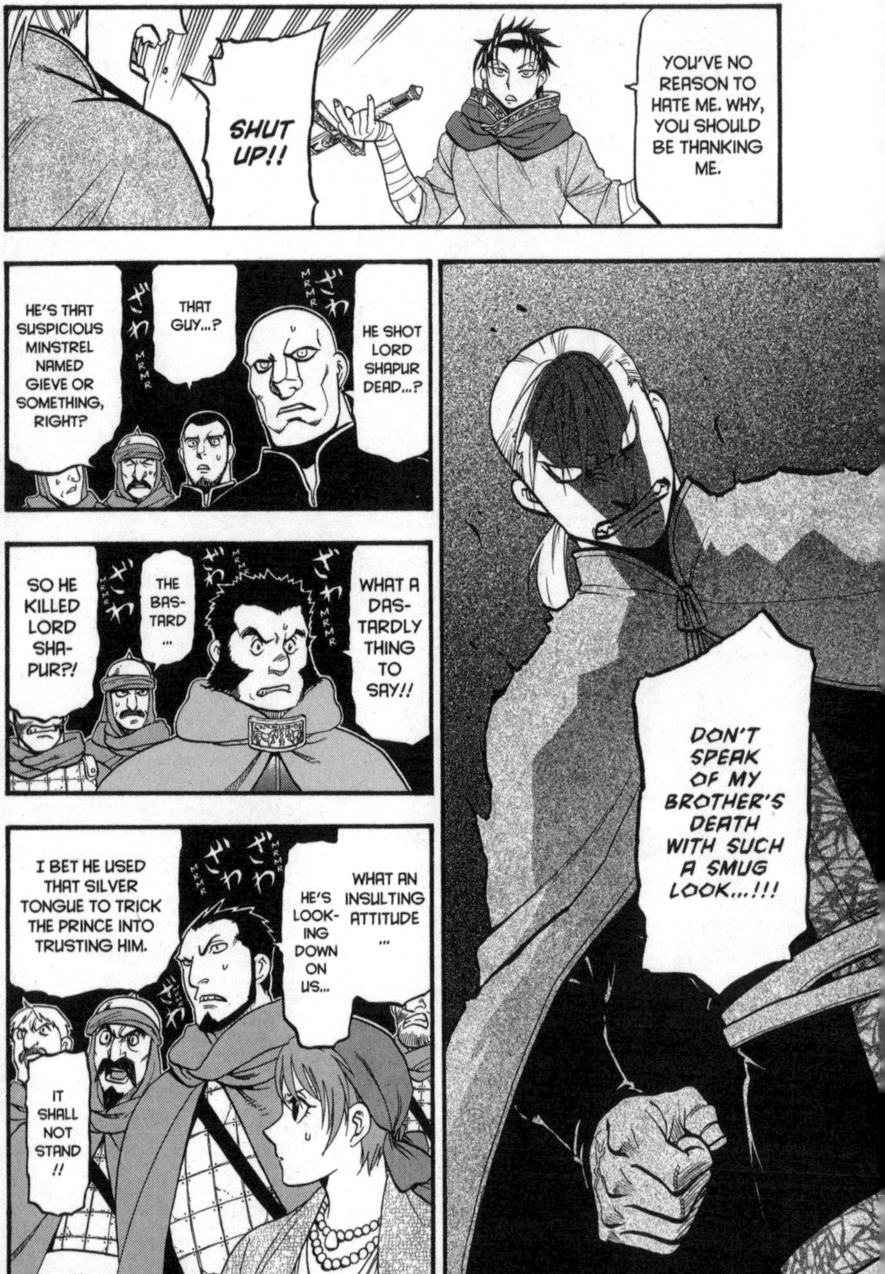
YOU'VE NO REASON TO HATE ME. WHY, YOU SHOULD BE THANKING ME.
SHUT UP!!
DON'T SPEAK OF MY BROTHER'S DEATH WITH SUCH A SMUG LOOK...!!!
ざわ MRMR
HE SHOT LORD SHAPUR DEAD...?
THAT GUY...?
ざわ MRMR
HE'S THAT SUSPICIOUS MINSTREL NAMED GIEVE OR SOMETHING, RIGHT?
ざわ MRMR
WHAT A DASTARDLY THING TO SAY!!
ざわ MRMR
THE BASTARD...
ざわ MRMR
SO HE KILLED LORD SHAPUR?!
ざわ MRMR
ざわ MRMR
WHAT AN INSULTING ATTITUDE...
HE'S LOOKING DOWN ON US...
I BET HE USED THAT SILVER TONGUE TO TRICK THE PRINCE INTO TRUSTING HIM.
IT SHALL NOT STAND!!

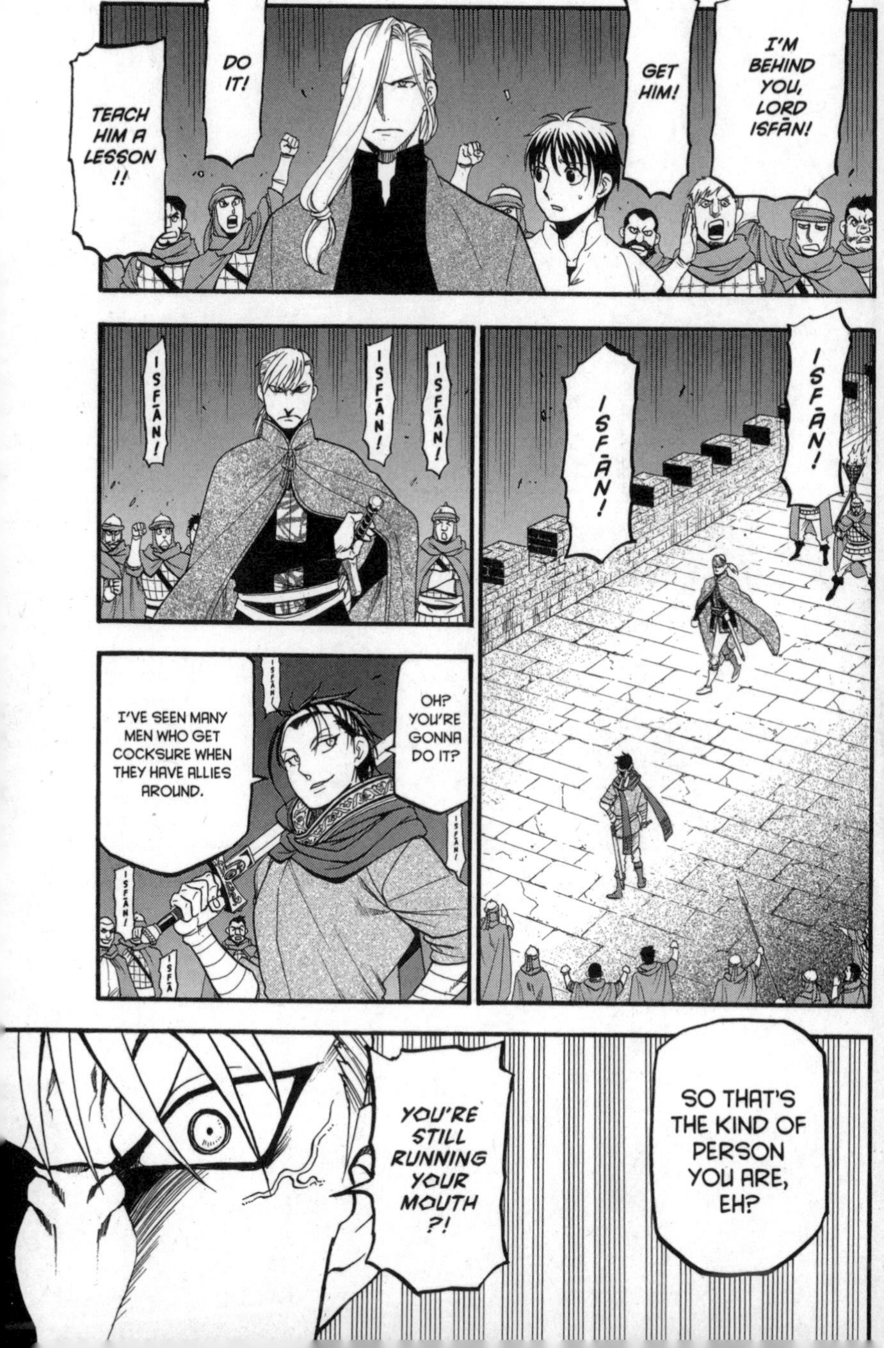
I'M BEHIND YOU, LORD ISFĀN!
GET HIM!
DO IT!
TEACH HIM A LESSON!!
ISFĀN!
ISFĀN!
ISFĀN!
ISFĀN!
ISFĀN!
OH? YOU'RE GONNA DO IT?
I'VE SEEN MANY MEN WHO GET COCKSURE WHEN THEY HAVE ALLIES AROUND.
SO THAT'S THE KIND OF PERSON YOU ARE, EH?
YOU'RE STILL RUNNING YOUR MOUTH?!

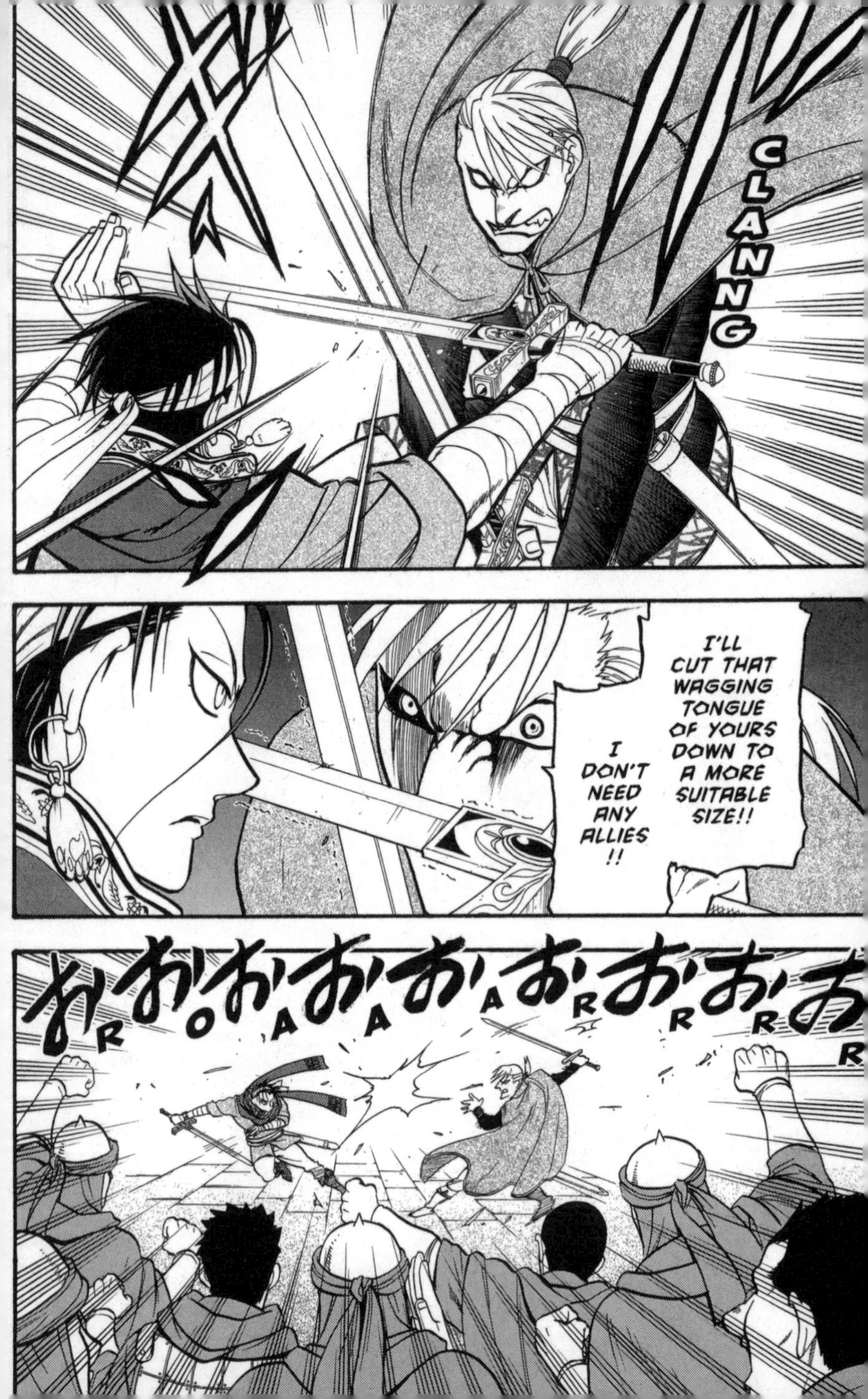
CLANNG
I'LL CUT THAT WAGGING TONGUE OF YOURS DOWN TO A MORE SUITABLE SIZE!!
I DON'T NEED ANY ALLIES!!
ROAARRRR

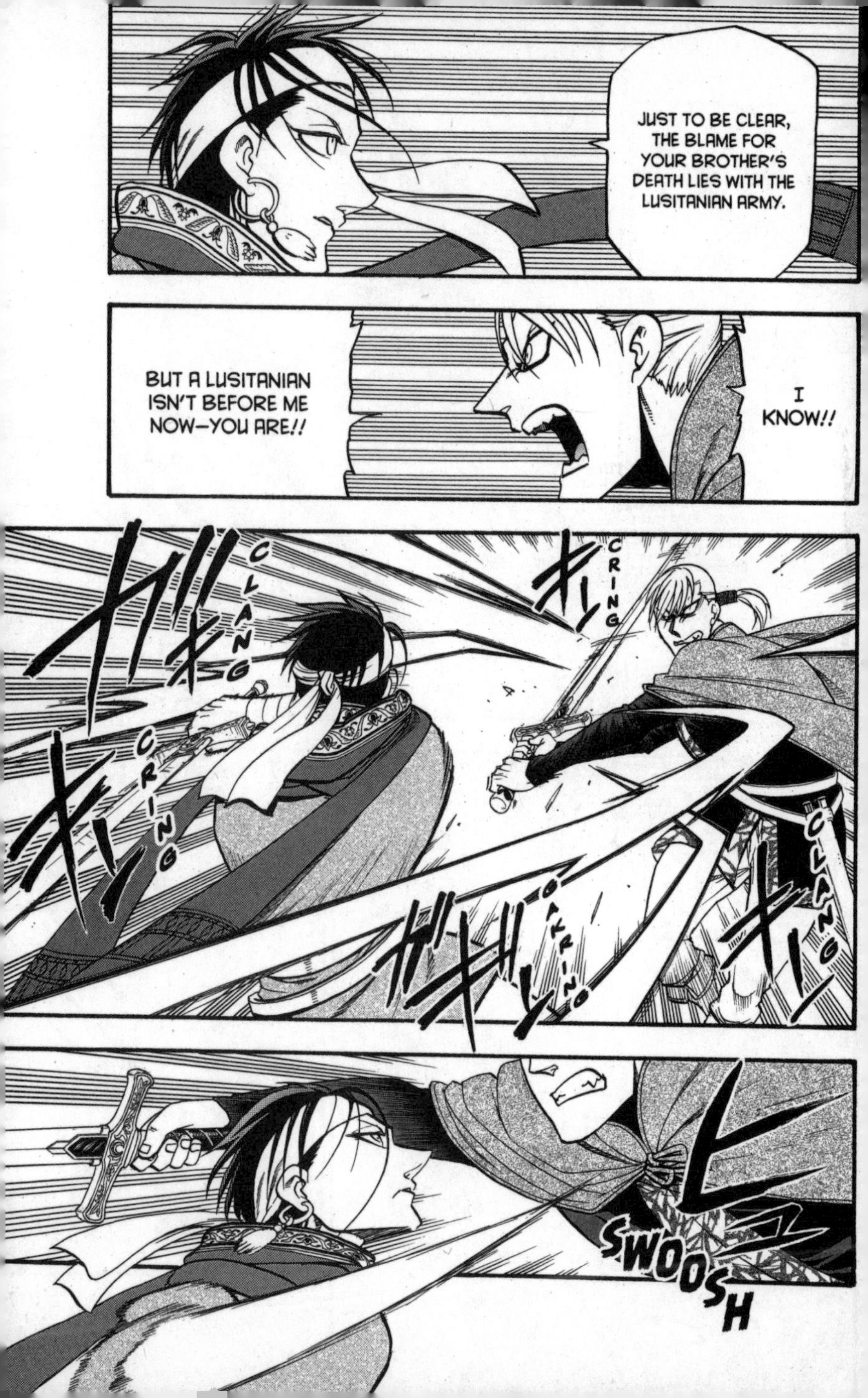
JUST TO BE CLEAR, THE BLAME FOR YOUR BROTHER'S DEATH LIES WITH THE LUSITANIAN ARMY.
I KNOW!!
BUT A LUSITANIAN ISN'T BEFORE ME NOW—YOU ARE!!
CRING
CLANG
GAKRING
CLANG
CRING
SWOOSH

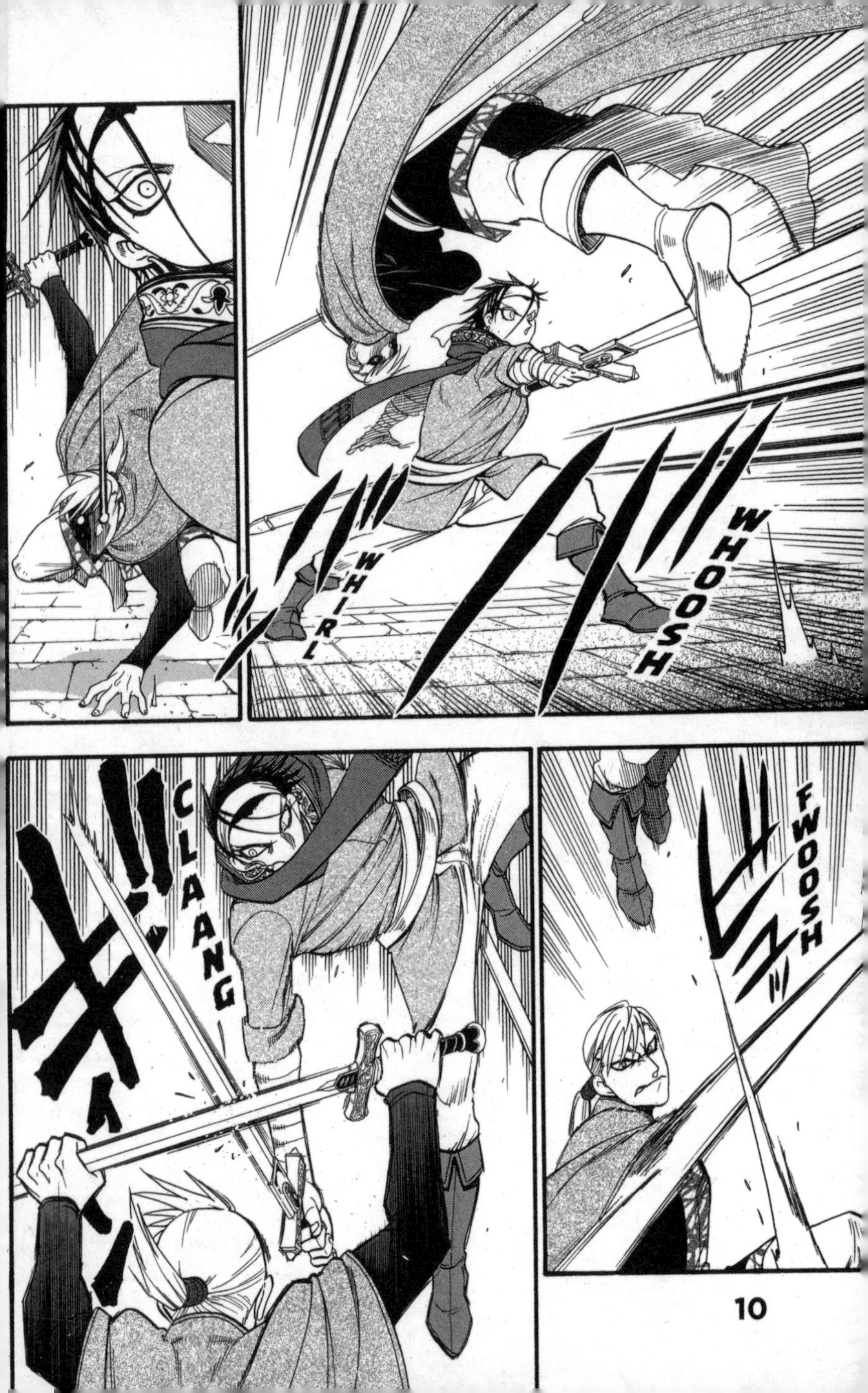
WHOOSH
WHIRL
FWOOSH
CLAANG

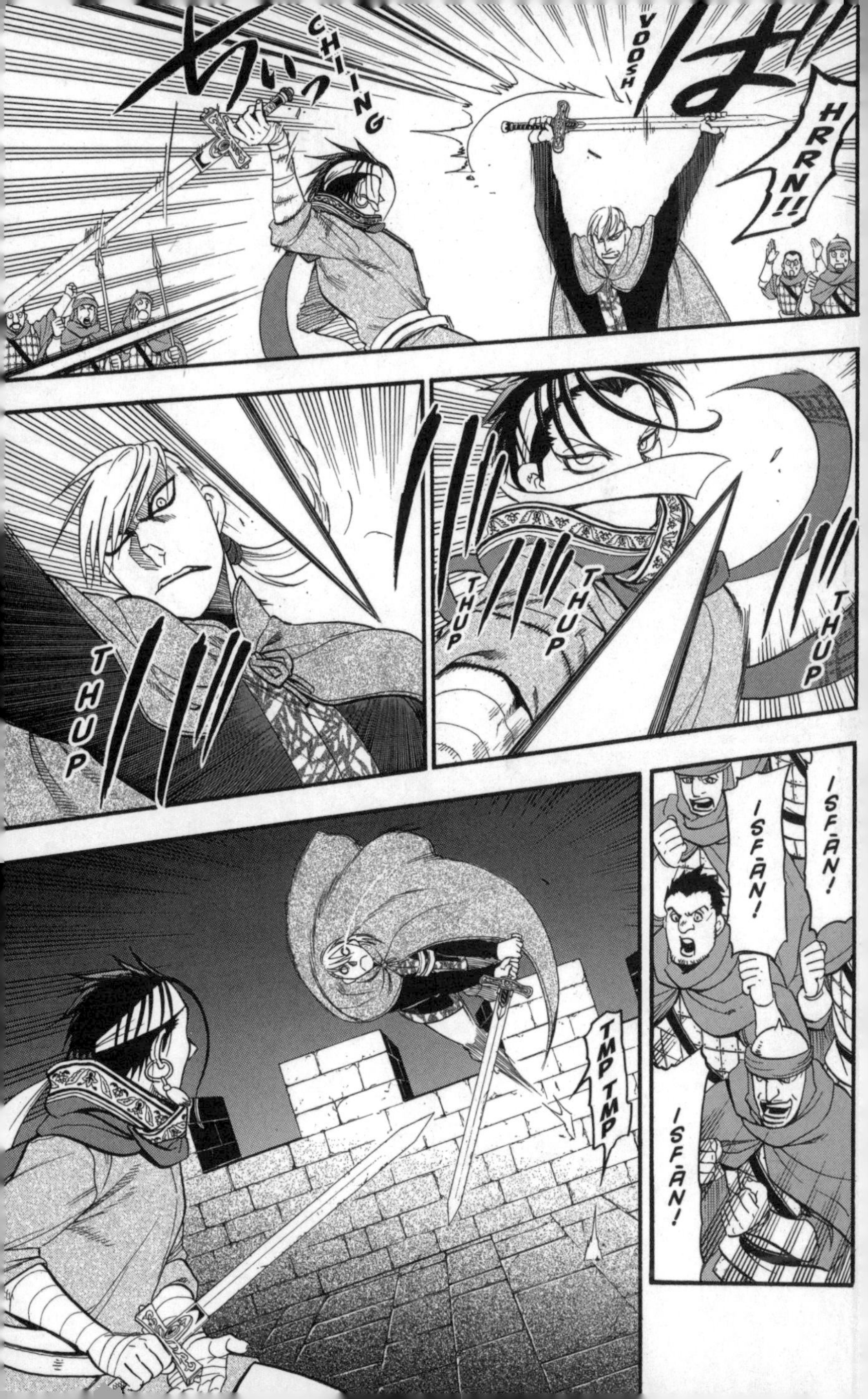
HRRN!!
VOOSH
CHIING
THUP
THUP
THUP
THUP
ISFĀN!
ISFĀN!
ISFĀN!
TMP TMP

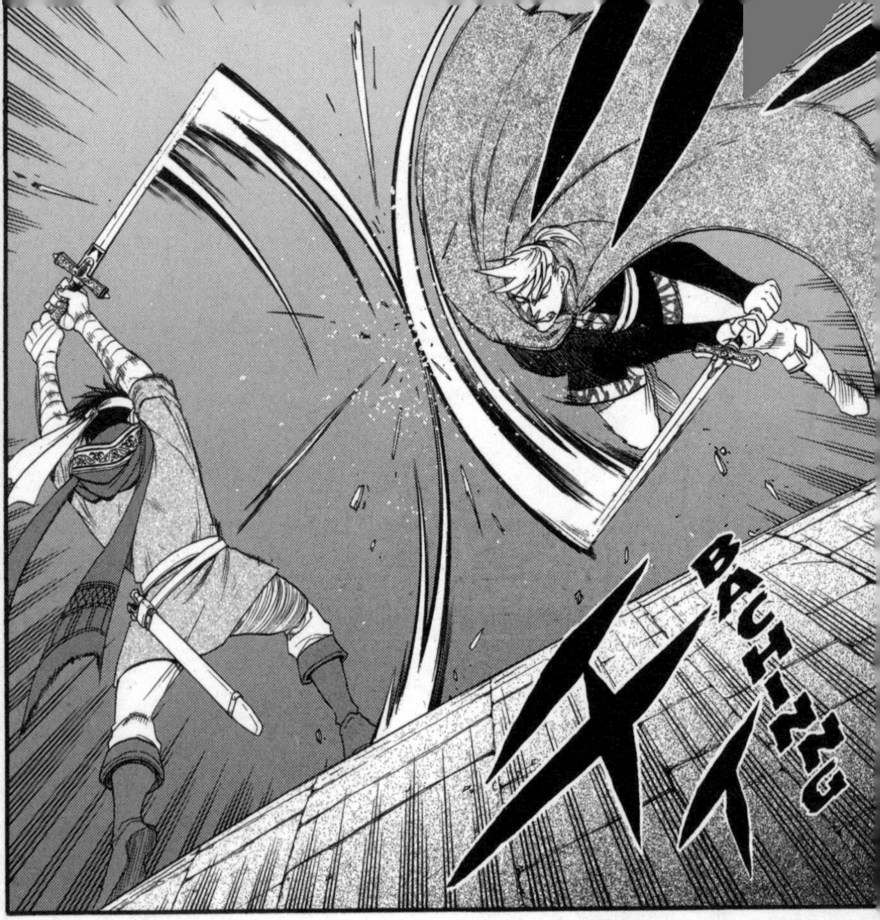
BAUHZZU
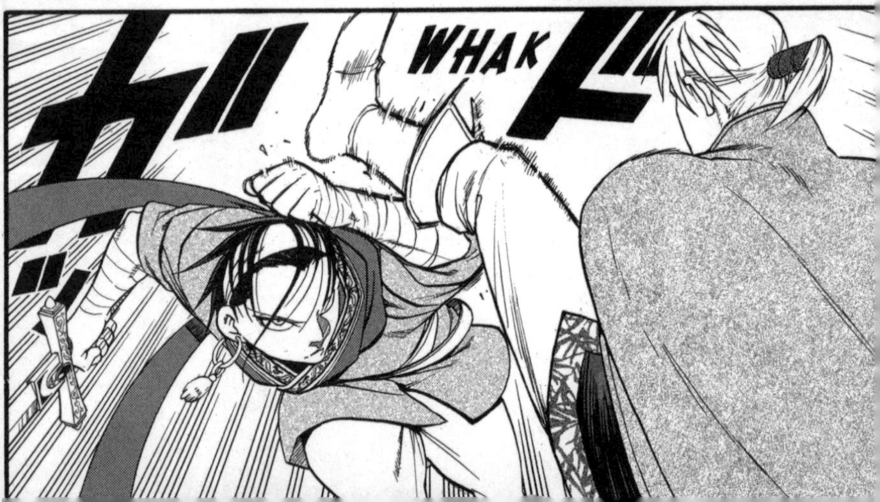
WHAK

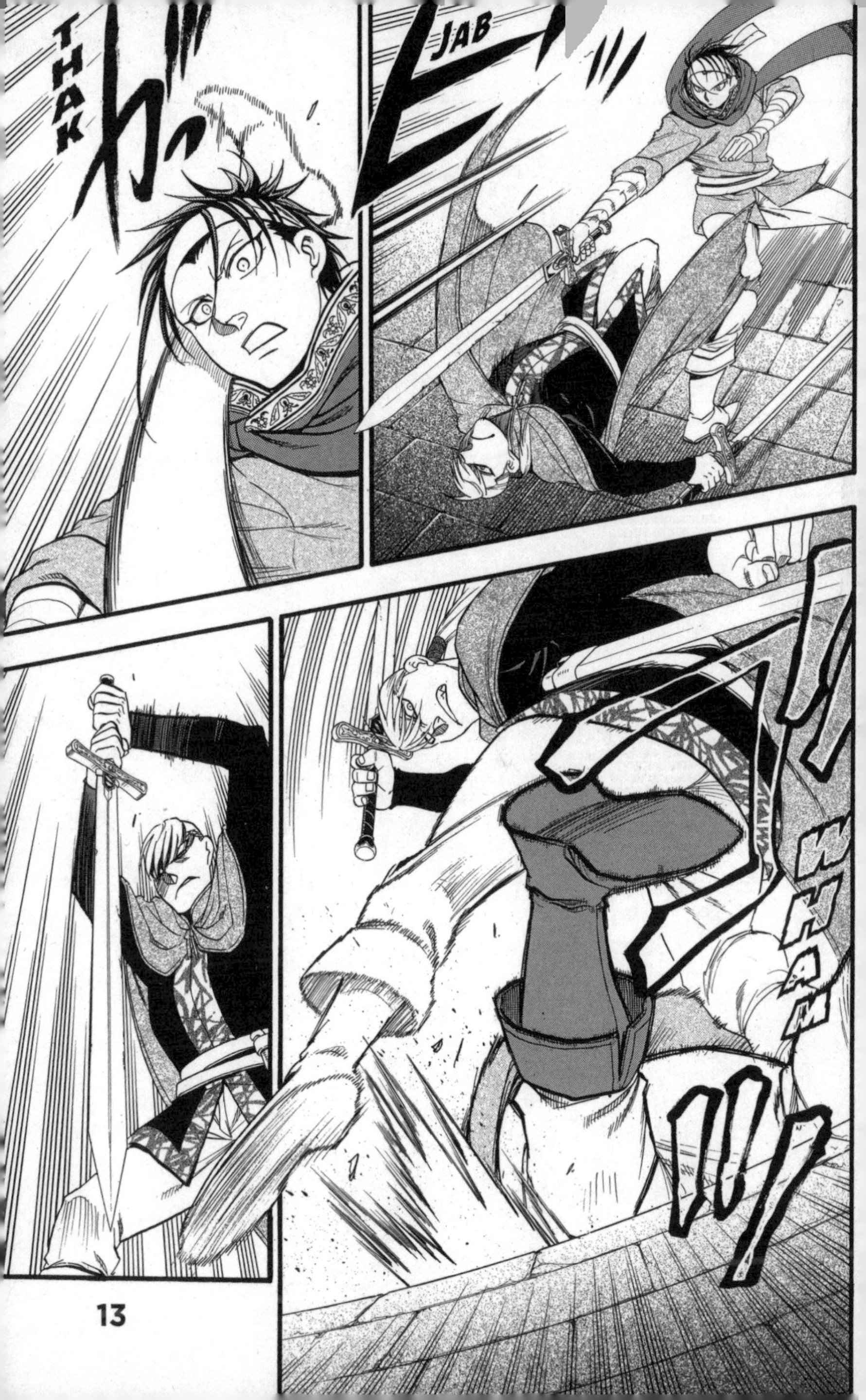
JAB
THAK
WHAM

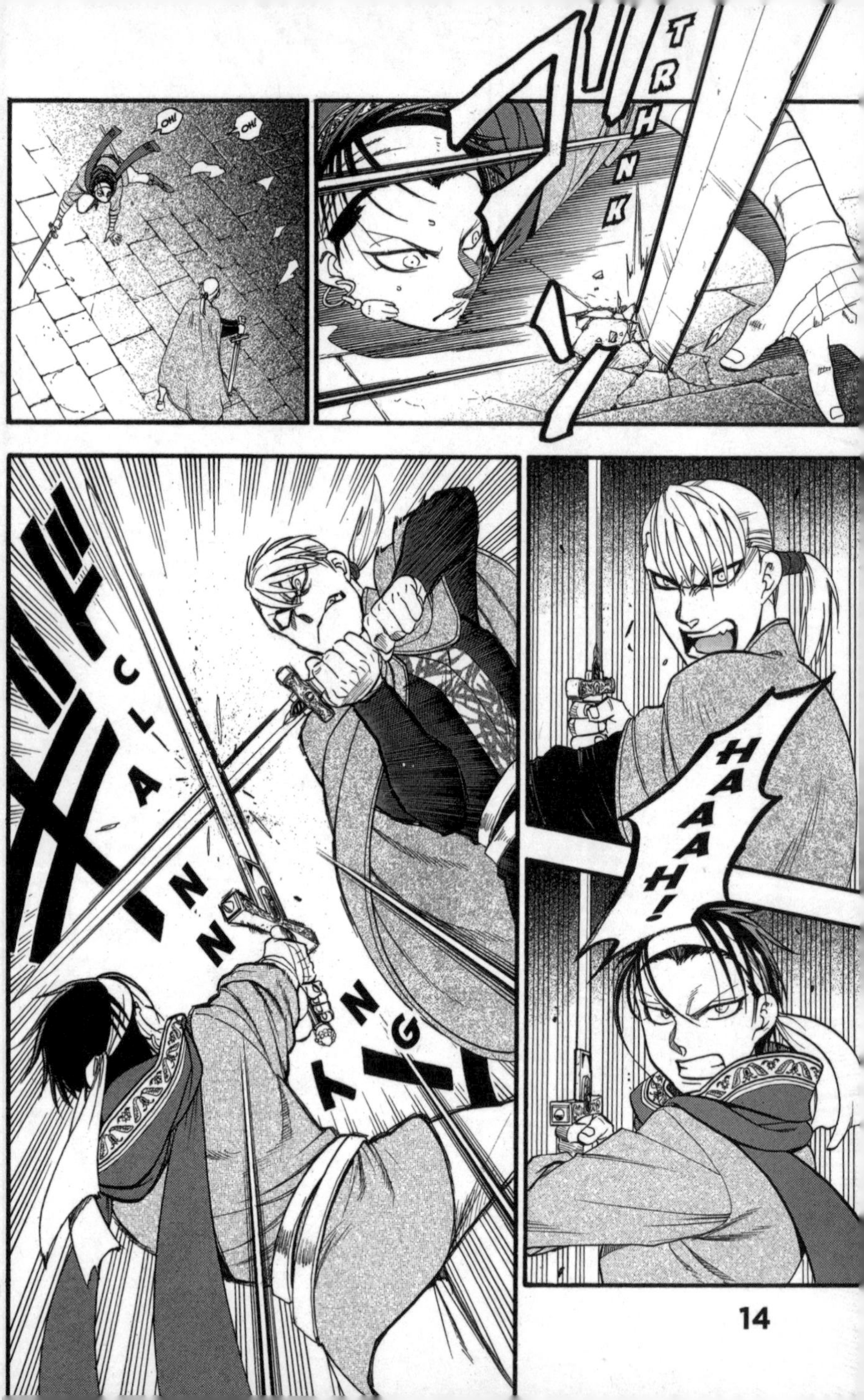
TRHNK
OW!
OW!
HAAAAH!
CLANNG

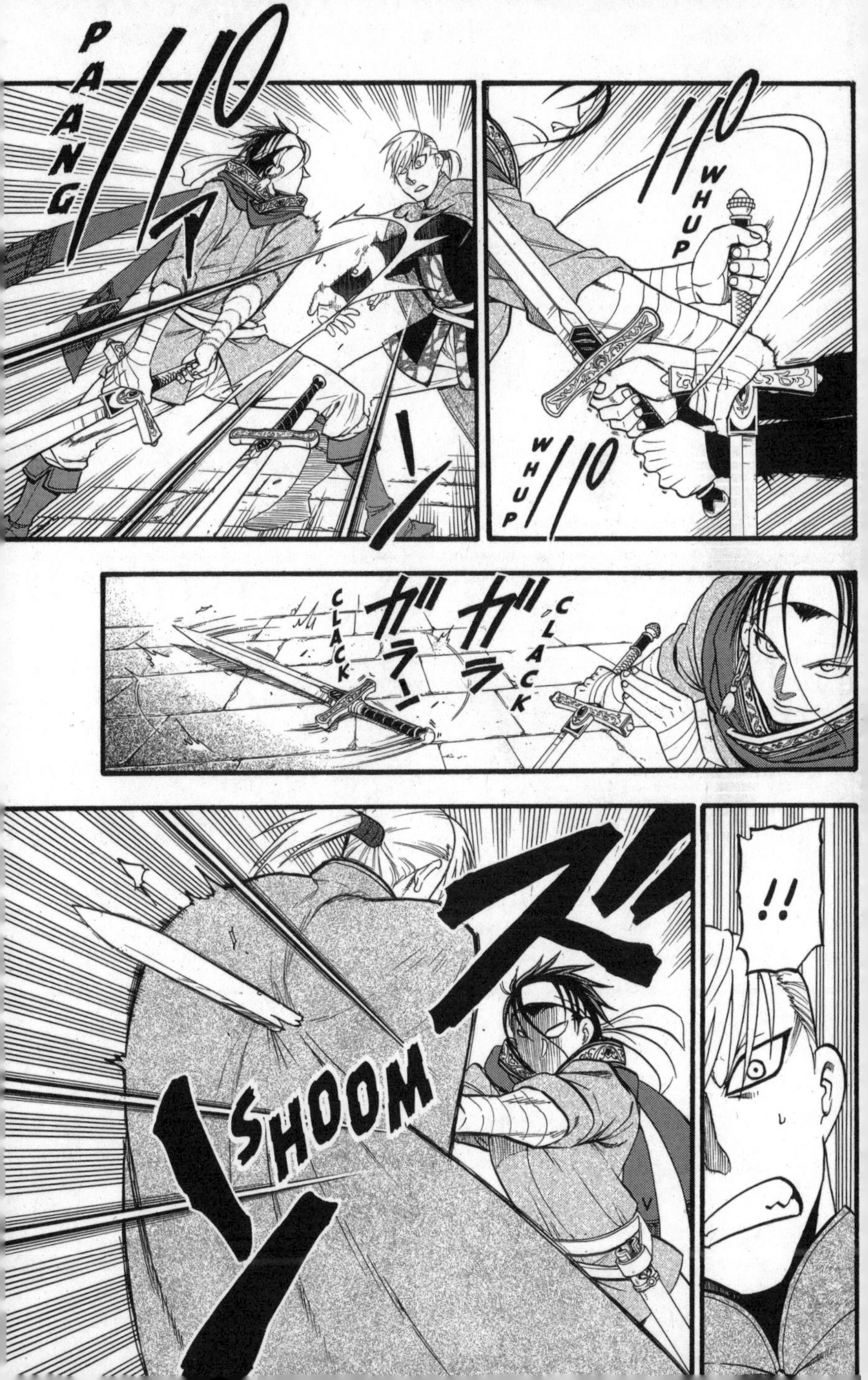
WHUP
WHUP
PAANG
CLACK
ガラ
ガラーン
CLACK
!!
SHOOM

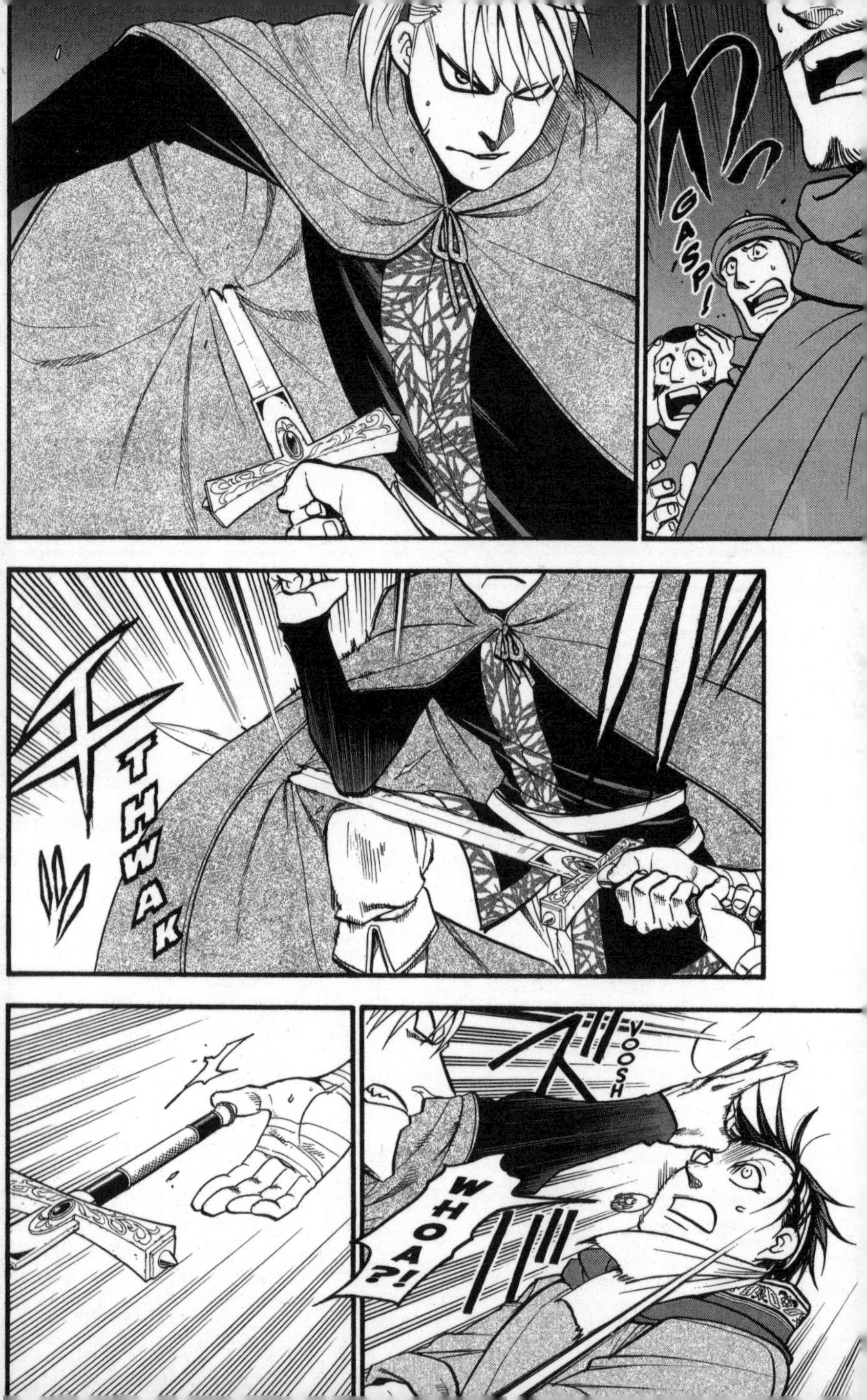
GASP!
THWAK
VOOSH
WHOA?!

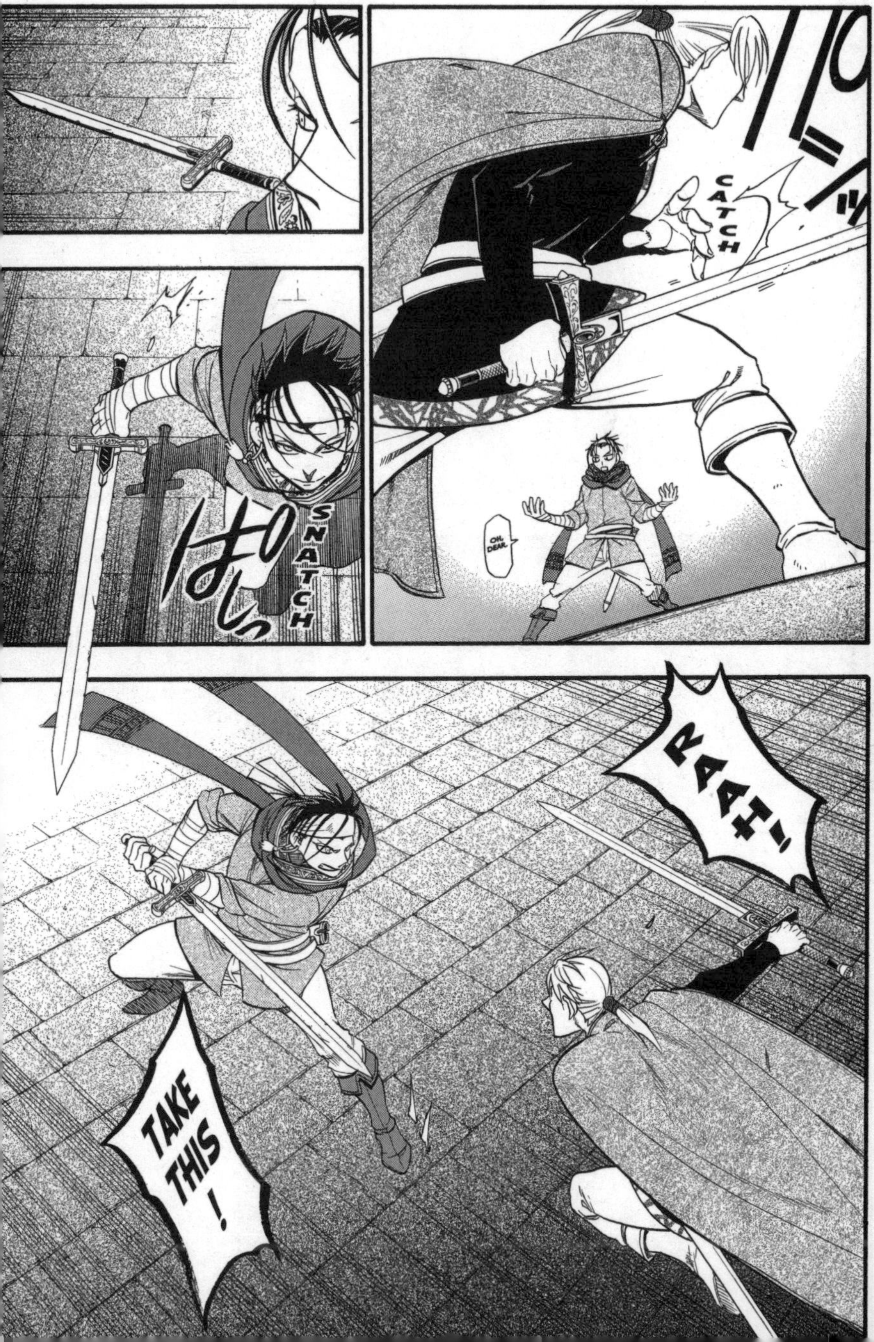
CATCH
OH, DEAR.
SNATCH
RAAH!!
TAKE THIS!

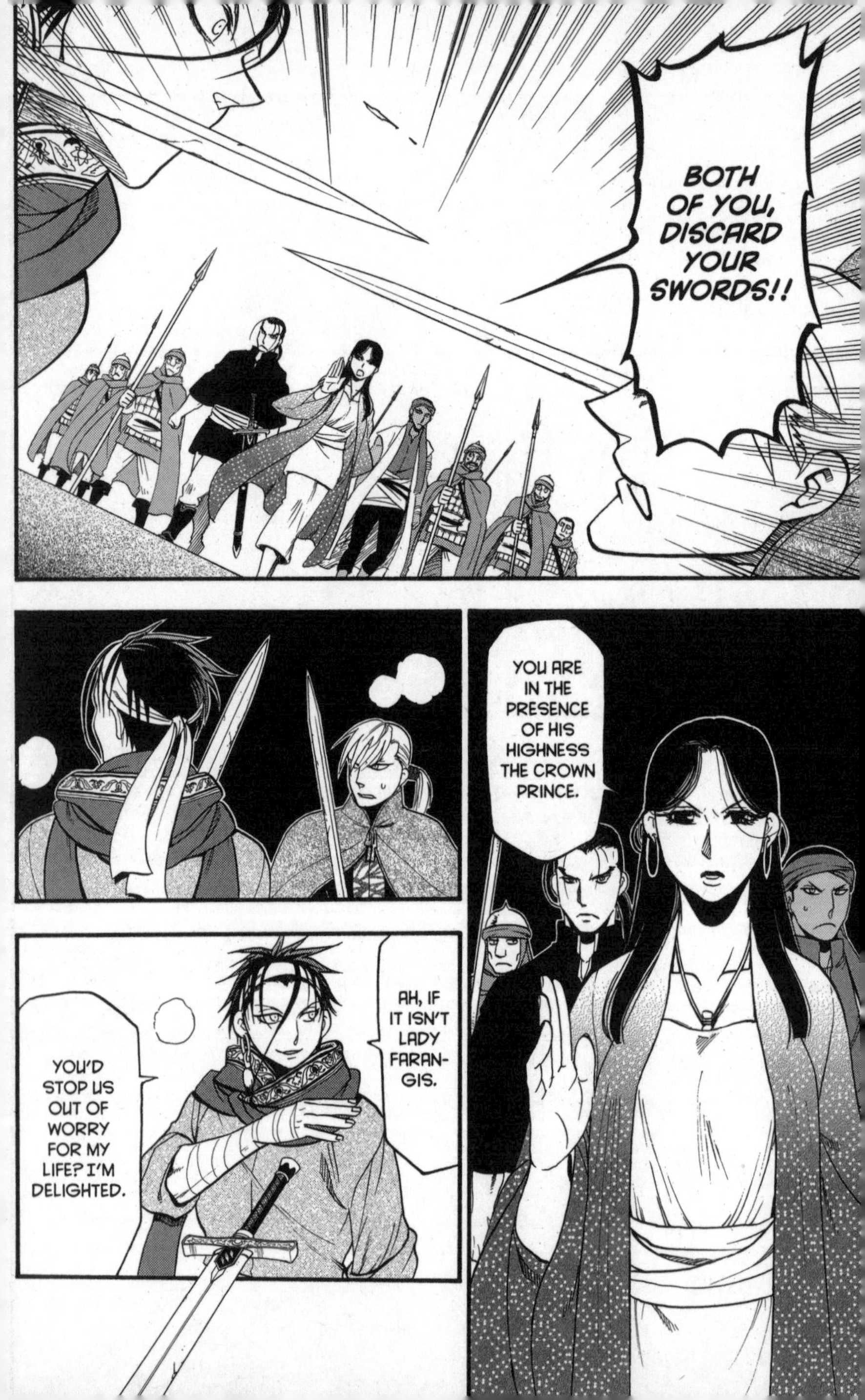
BOTH OF YOU, DISCARD YOUR SWORDS!!
YOU ARE IN THE PRESENCE OF HIS HIGHNESS THE CROWN PRINCE.
AH, IF IT ISN'T LADY FARAN-GIS.
YOU'D STOP US OUT OF WORRY FOR MY LIFE? I'M DELIGHTED.

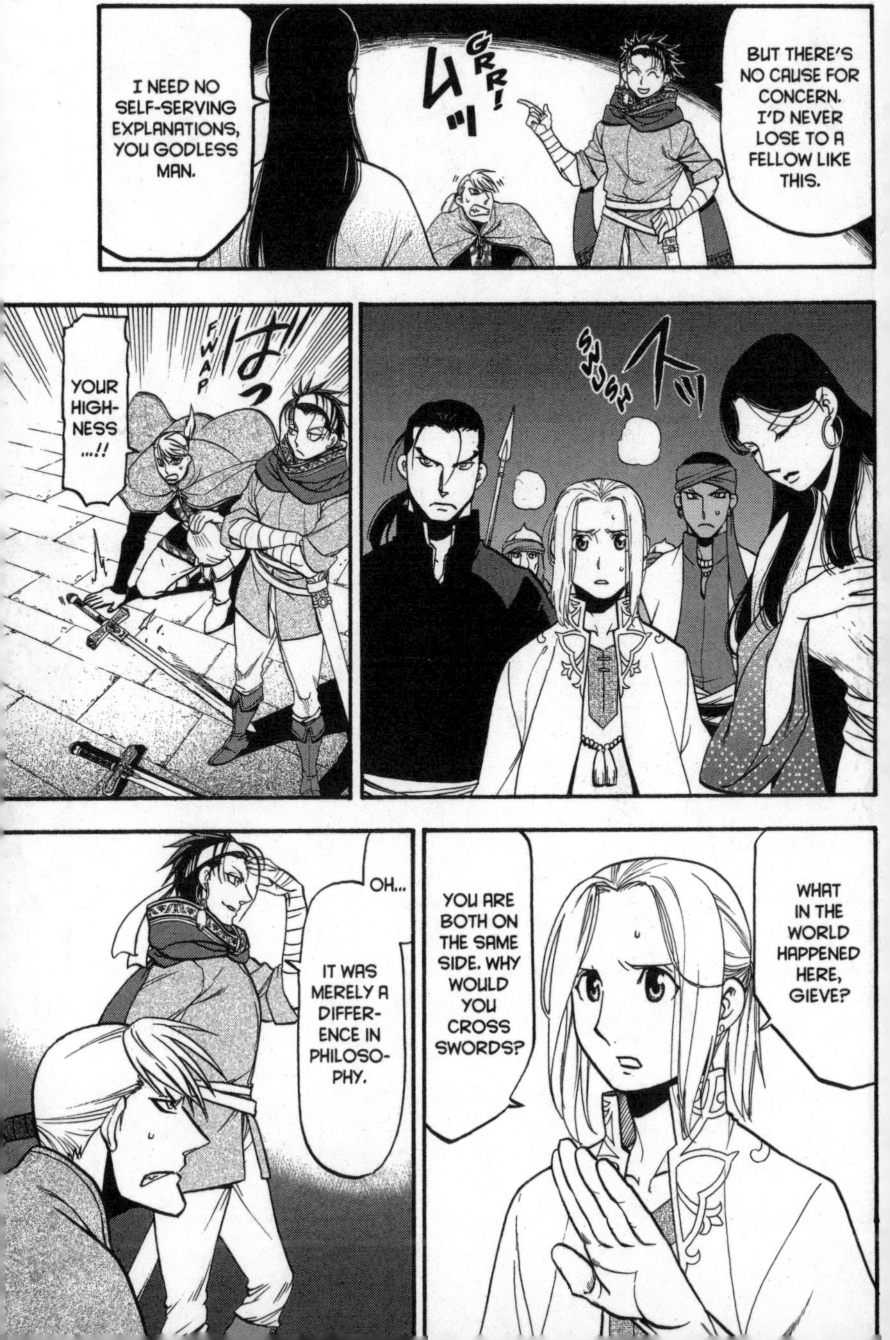
BUT THERE'S NO CAUSE FOR CONCERN. I'D NEVER LOSE TO A FELLOW LIKE THIS.
ムッ
GRR!
I NEED NO SELF-SERVING EXPLANATIONS, YOU GODLESS MAN.
スッ
SWISH
ばっ
FWAP
YOUR HIGHNESS...!!
WHAT IN THE WORLD HAPPENED HERE, GIEVE?
YOU ARE BOTH ON THE SAME SIDE. WHY WOULD YOU CROSS SWORDS?
OH...
IT WAS MERELY A DIFFERENCE IN PHILOSOPHY.

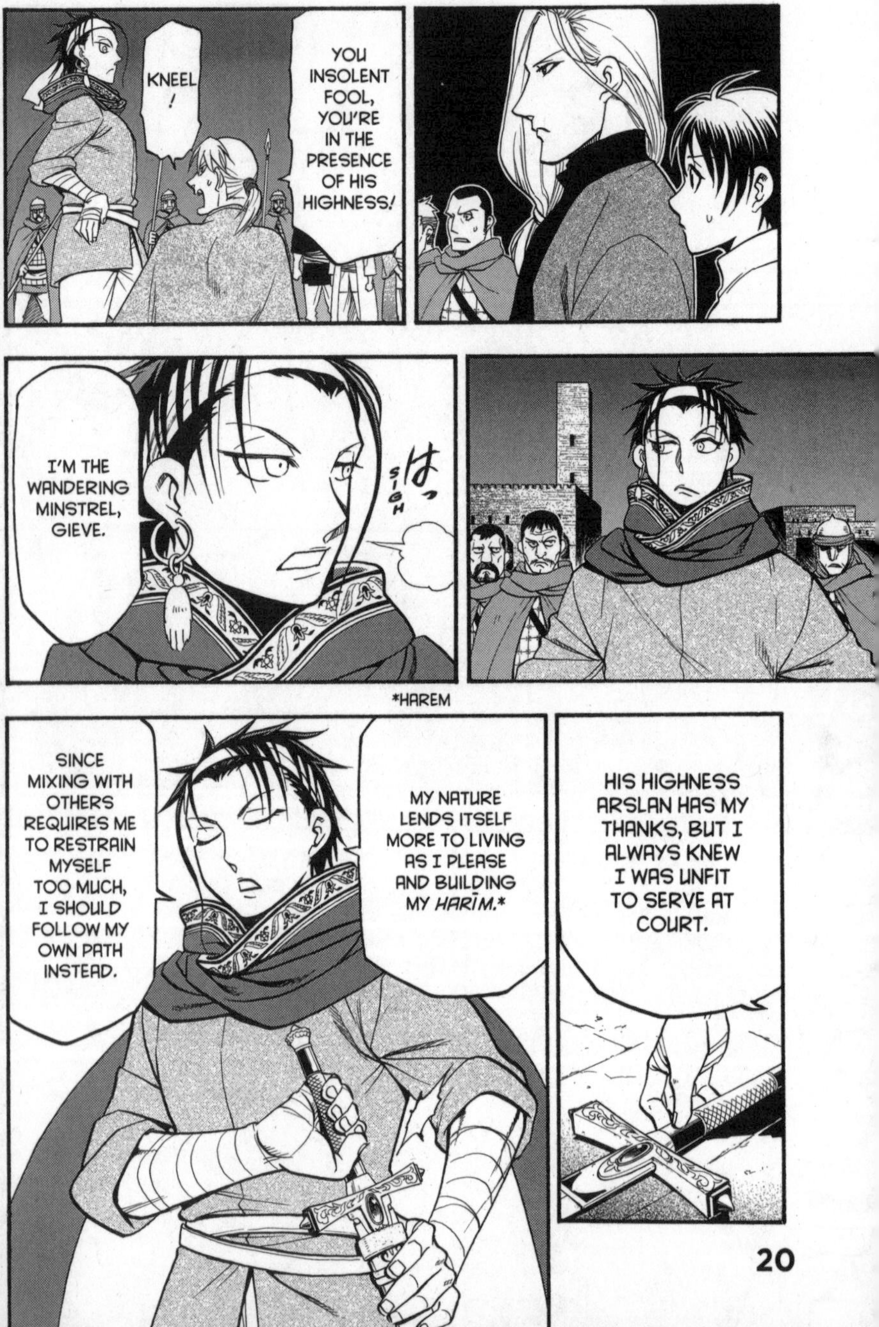
YOU INSOLENT FOOL, YOU'RE IN THE PRESENCE OF HIS HIGHNESS!
KNEEL!
SIGH
I'M THE WANDERING MINSTREL, GIEVE.
HIS HIGHNESS ARSLAN HAS MY THANKS, BUT I ALWAYS KNEW I WAS UNFIT TO SERVE AT COURT.
MY NATURE LENDS ITSELF MORE TO LIVING AS I PLEASE AND BUILDING MY *HARĪM.**
SINCE MIXING WITH OTHERS REQUIRES ME TO RESTRAIN MYSELF TOO MUCH, I SHOULD FOLLOW MY OWN PATH INSTEAD.
*HAREM

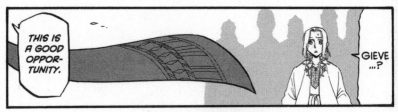

THIS IS A GOOD OPPORTUNITY.

GIEVE ...?

WITH THIS, I'LL BE LEAVING YOUR EMPLOY, YOUR HIGHNESS.

STAY WELL.

GIEVE?!

THE HEROIC LEGEND OF
ARSLAN

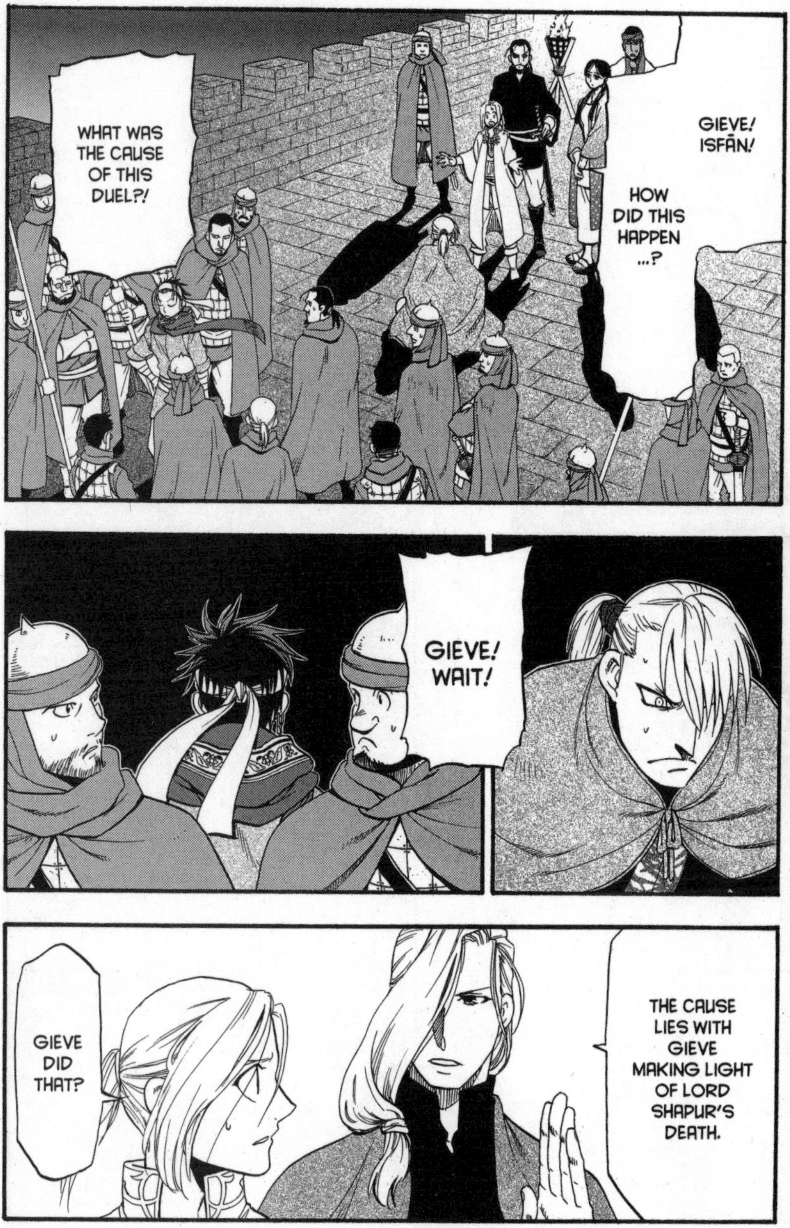
GIEVE! ISFĀN!
HOW DID THIS HAPPEN ...?
WHAT WAS THE CAUSE OF THIS DUEL?!
GIEVE! WAIT!
...
THE CAUSE LIES WITH GIEVE MAKING LIGHT OF LORD SHAPUR'S DEATH.
GIEVE DID THAT?

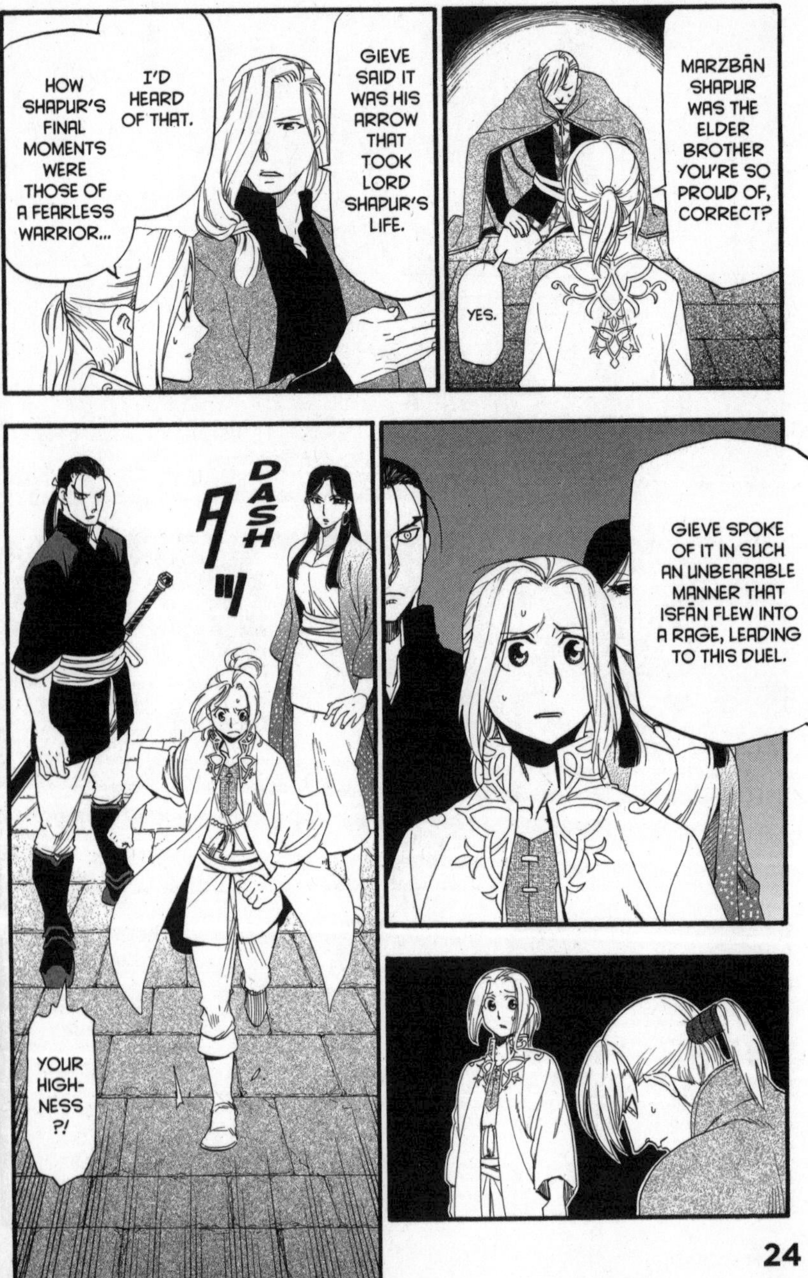
MARZBĀN SHAPUR WAS THE ELDER BROTHER YOU'RE SO PROUD OF, CORRECT?
YES.
GIEVE SAID IT WAS HIS ARROW THAT TOOK LORD SHAPUR'S LIFE.
I'D HEARD OF THAT.
HOW SHAPUR'S FINAL MOMENTS WERE THOSE OF A FEARLESS WARRIOR...
GIEVE SPOKE OF IT IN SUCH AN UNBEARABLE MANNER THAT ISFĀN FLEW INTO A RAGE, LEADING TO THIS DUEL.
DASH
YOUR HIGHNESS?!

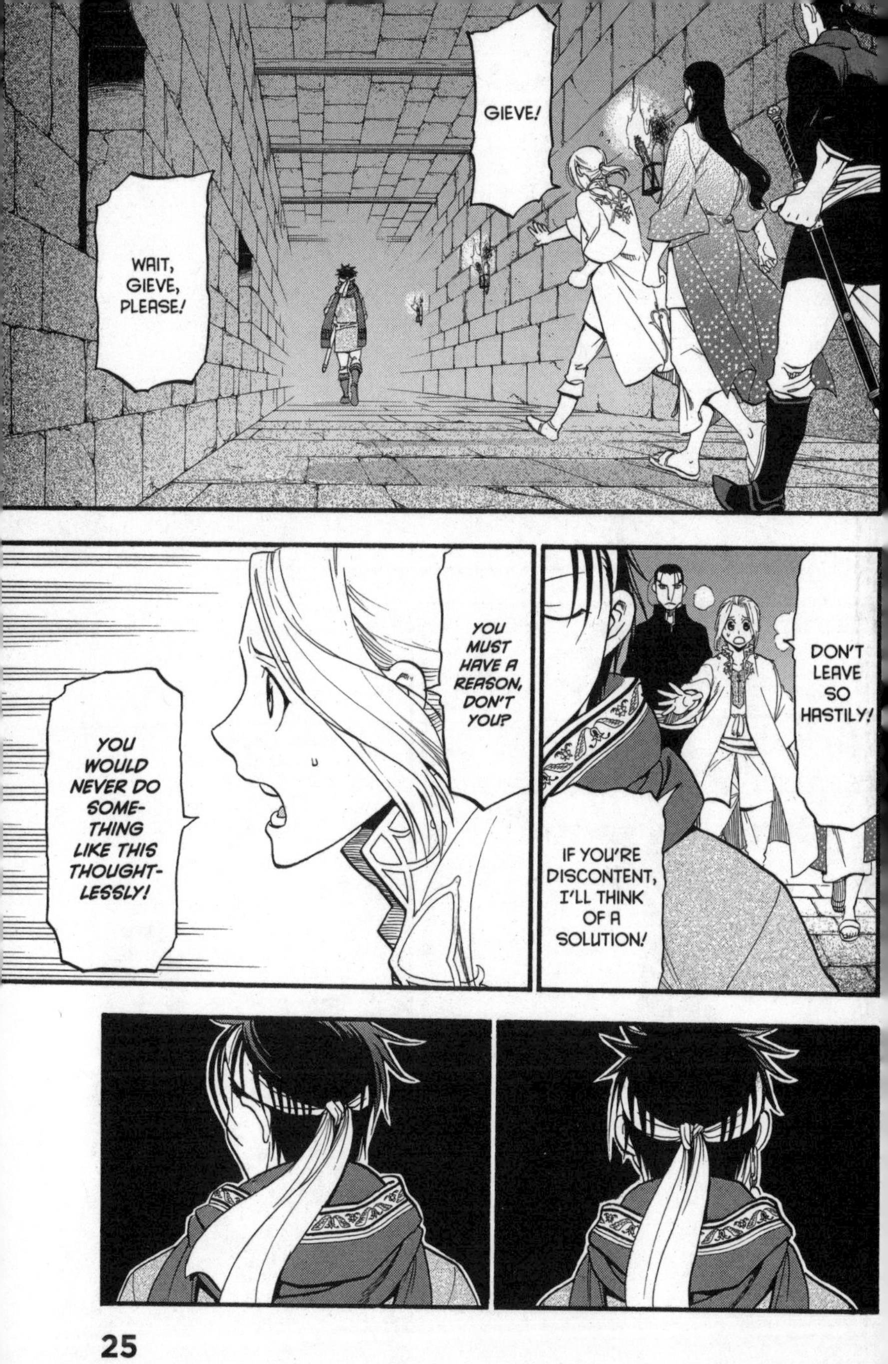
GIEVE!
WAIT, GIEVE, PLEASE!
DON'T LEAVE SO HASTILY!
IF YOU'RE DISCONTENT, I'LL THINK OF A SOLUTION!
YOU MUST HAVE A REASON, DON'T YOU?
YOU WOULD NEVER DO SOMETHING LIKE THIS THOUGHTLESSLY!

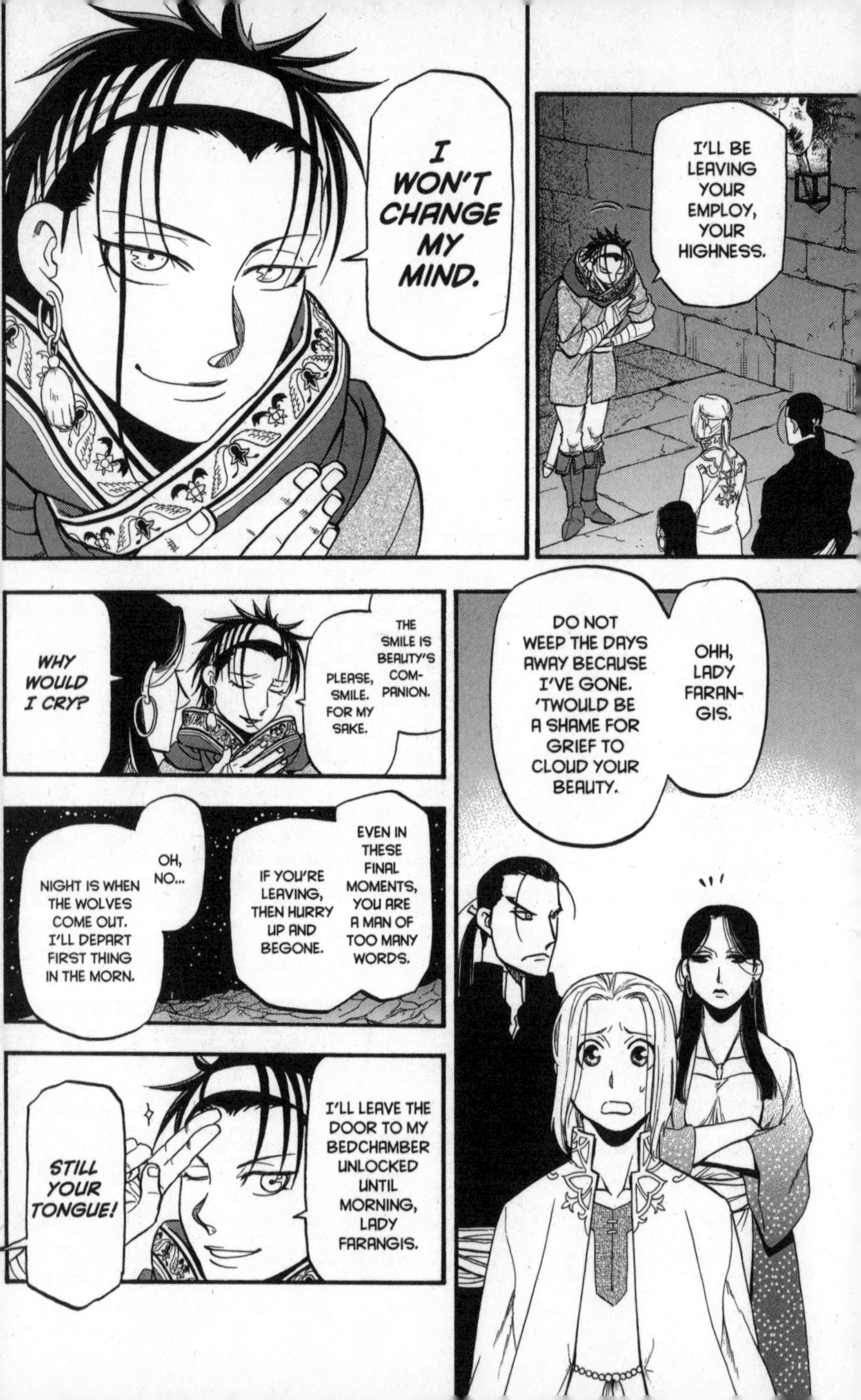
I'LL BE LEAVING YOUR EMPLOY, YOUR HIGHNESS.
I WON'T CHANGE MY MIND.
OHH, LADY FARANGIS.
DO NOT WEEP THE DAYS AWAY BECAUSE I'VE GONE. 'TWOULD BE A SHAME FOR GRIEF TO CLOUD YOUR BEAUTY.
THE SMILE IS BEAUTY'S COMPANION.
PLEASE, SMILE. FOR MY SAKE.
WHY WOULD I CRY?
EVEN IN THESE FINAL MOMENTS, YOU ARE A MAN OF TOO MANY WORDS.
IF YOU'RE LEAVING, THEN HURRY UP AND BEGONE.
OH, NO...
NIGHT IS WHEN THE WOLVES COME OUT. I'LL DEPART FIRST THING IN THE MORN.
I'LL LEAVE THE DOOR TO MY BEDCHAMBER UNLOCKED UNTIL MORNING, LADY FARANGIS.
STILL YOUR TONGUE!

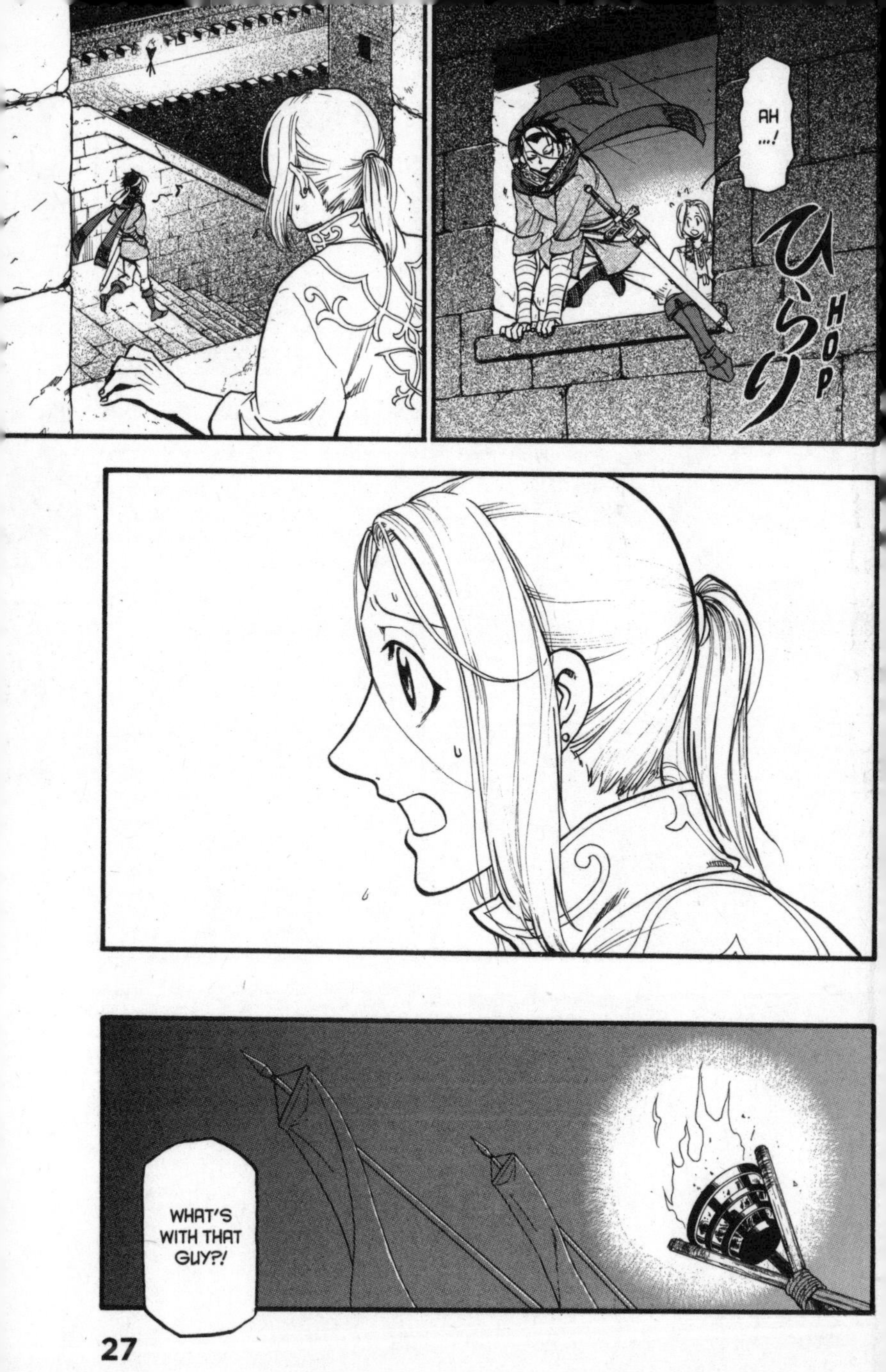
AH ...!
ひらり
HOP
WHAT'S WITH THAT GUY?!

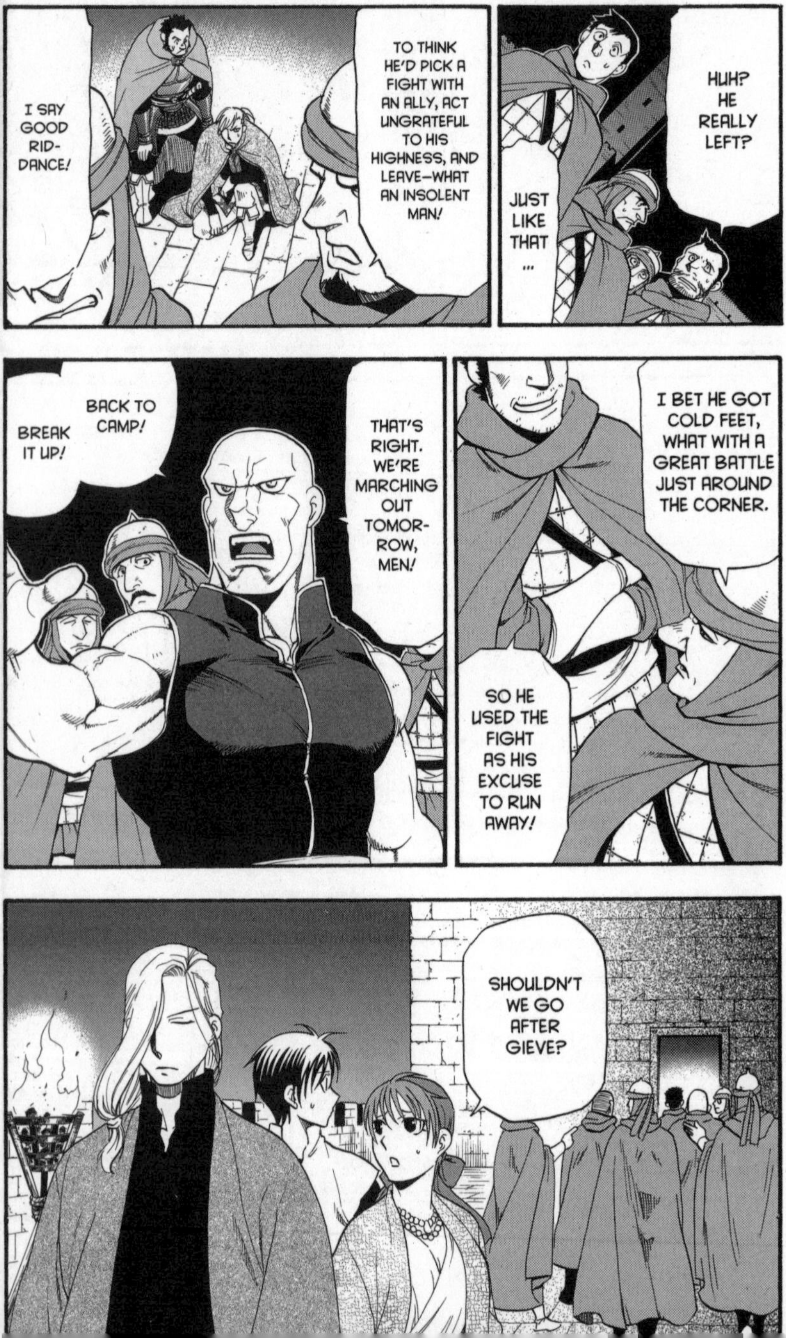
HUH? HE REALLY LEFT?
JUST LIKE THAT ...
TO THINK HE'D PICK A FIGHT WITH AN ALLY, ACT UNGRATEFUL TO HIS HIGHNESS, AND LEAVE—WHAT AN INSOLENT MAN!
I SAY GOOD RID-DANCE!
I BET HE GOT COLD FEET, WHAT WITH A GREAT BATTLE JUST AROUND THE CORNER.
SO HE USED THE FIGHT AS HIS EXCUSE TO RUN AWAY!
THAT'S RIGHT. WE'RE MARCHING OUT TOMOR-ROW, MEN!
BACK TO CAMP!
BREAK IT UP!
SHOULDN'T WE GO AFTER GIEVE?

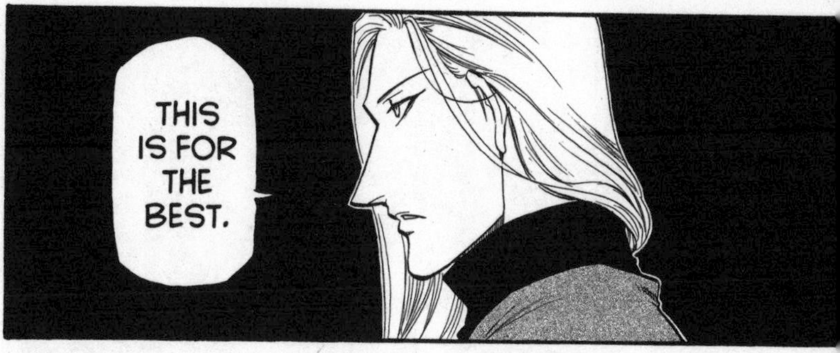
THIS IS FOR THE BEST.

Chapter 66: A Poem of Parting

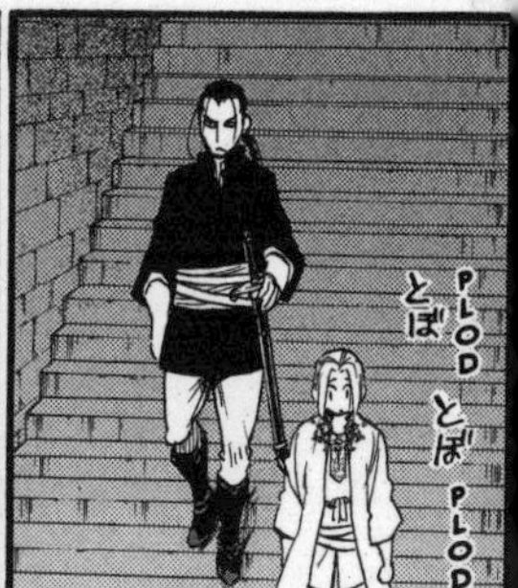
とぼ PLOD
とぼ PLOD

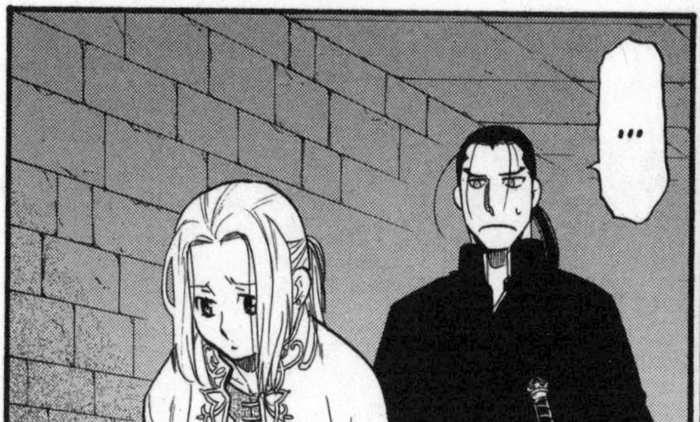
...

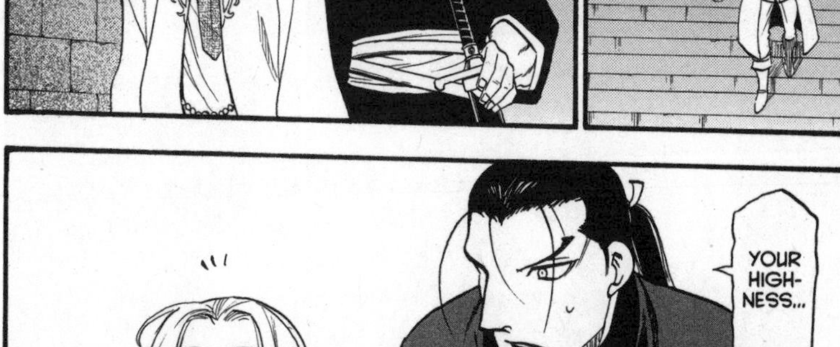
YOUR HIGH-NESS...

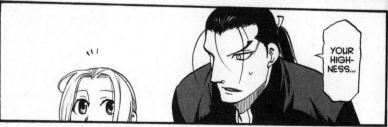

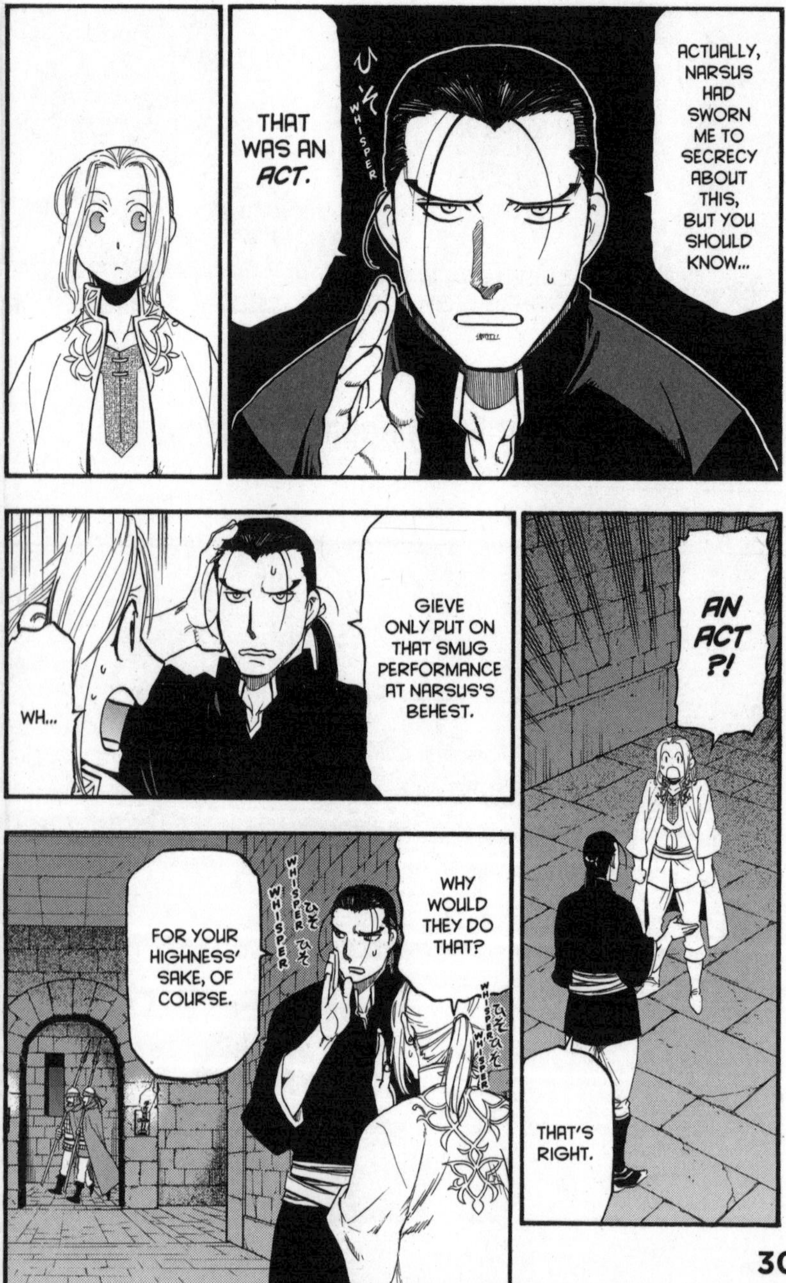
ACTUALLY, NARSUS HAD SWORN ME TO SECRECY ABOUT THIS, BUT YOU SHOULD KNOW...
ひそ WHISPER
THAT WAS AN ACT.
AN ACT?!
THAT'S RIGHT.
GIEVE ONLY PUT ON THAT SMUG PERFORMANCE AT NARSUS'S BEHEST.
WH...
WHY WOULD THEY DO THAT?
ひそ ひそ WHISPER WHISPER
FOR YOUR HIGHNESS' SAKE, OF COURSE.
ひそ ひそ WHISPER WHISPER

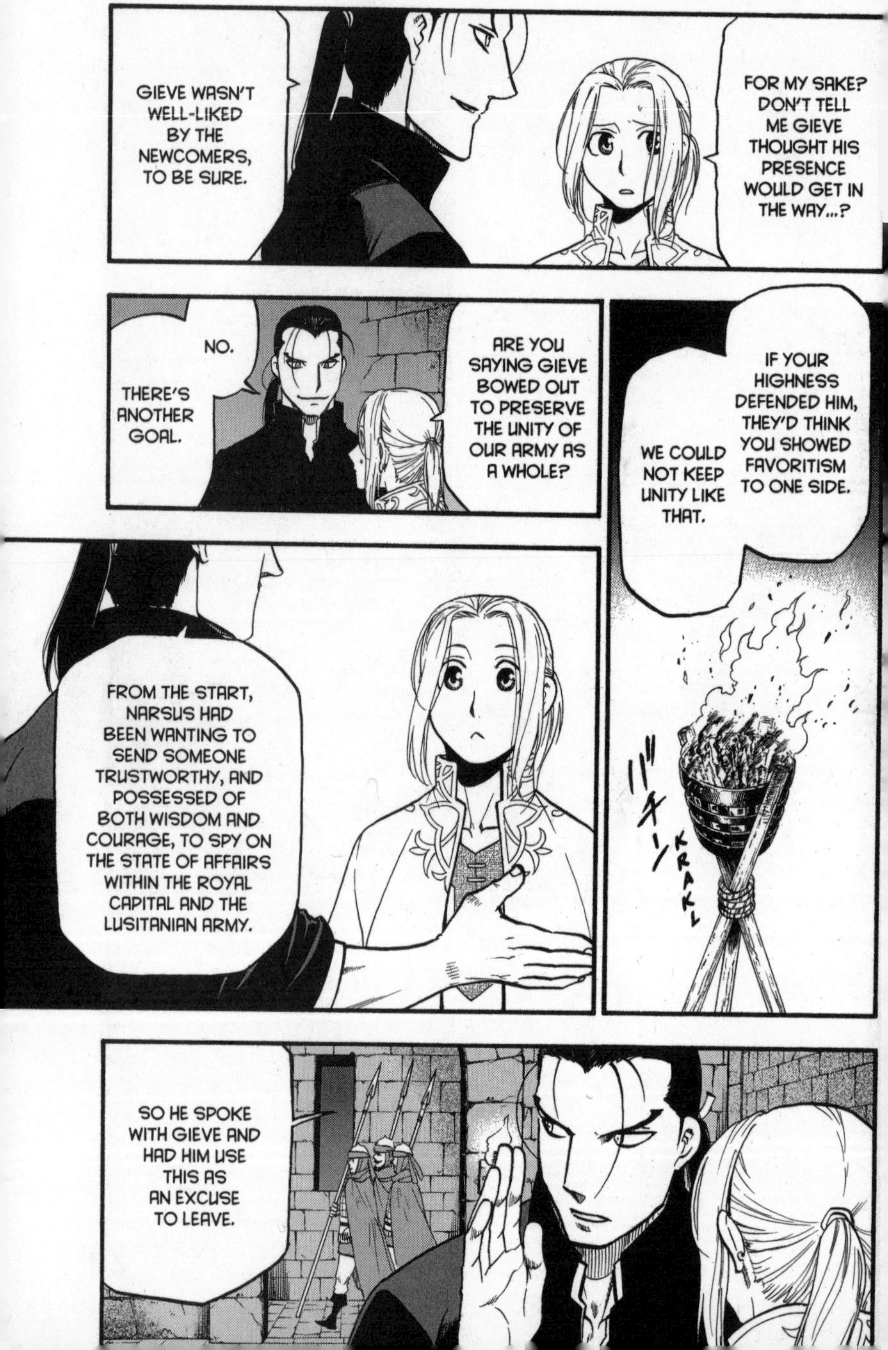
FOR MY SAKE? DON'T TELL ME GIEVE THOUGHT HIS PRESENCE WOULD GET IN THE WAY...?
GIEVE WASN'T WELL-LIKED BY THE NEWCOMERS, TO BE SURE.
IF YOUR HIGHNESS DEFENDED HIM, THEY'D THINK YOU SHOWED FAVORITISM TO ONE SIDE.
WE COULD NOT KEEP UNITY LIKE THAT.
KRAK
ARE YOU SAYING GIEVE BOWED OUT TO PRESERVE THE UNITY OF OUR ARMY AS A WHOLE?
NO.
THERE'S ANOTHER GOAL.
FROM THE START, NARSUS HAD BEEN WANTING TO SEND SOMEONE TRUSTWORTHY, AND POSSESSED OF BOTH WISDOM AND COURAGE, TO SPY ON THE STATE OF AFFAIRS WITHIN THE ROYAL CAPITAL AND THE LUSITANIAN ARMY.
SO HE SPOKE WITH GIEVE AND HAD HIM USE THIS AS AN EXCUSE TO LEAVE.

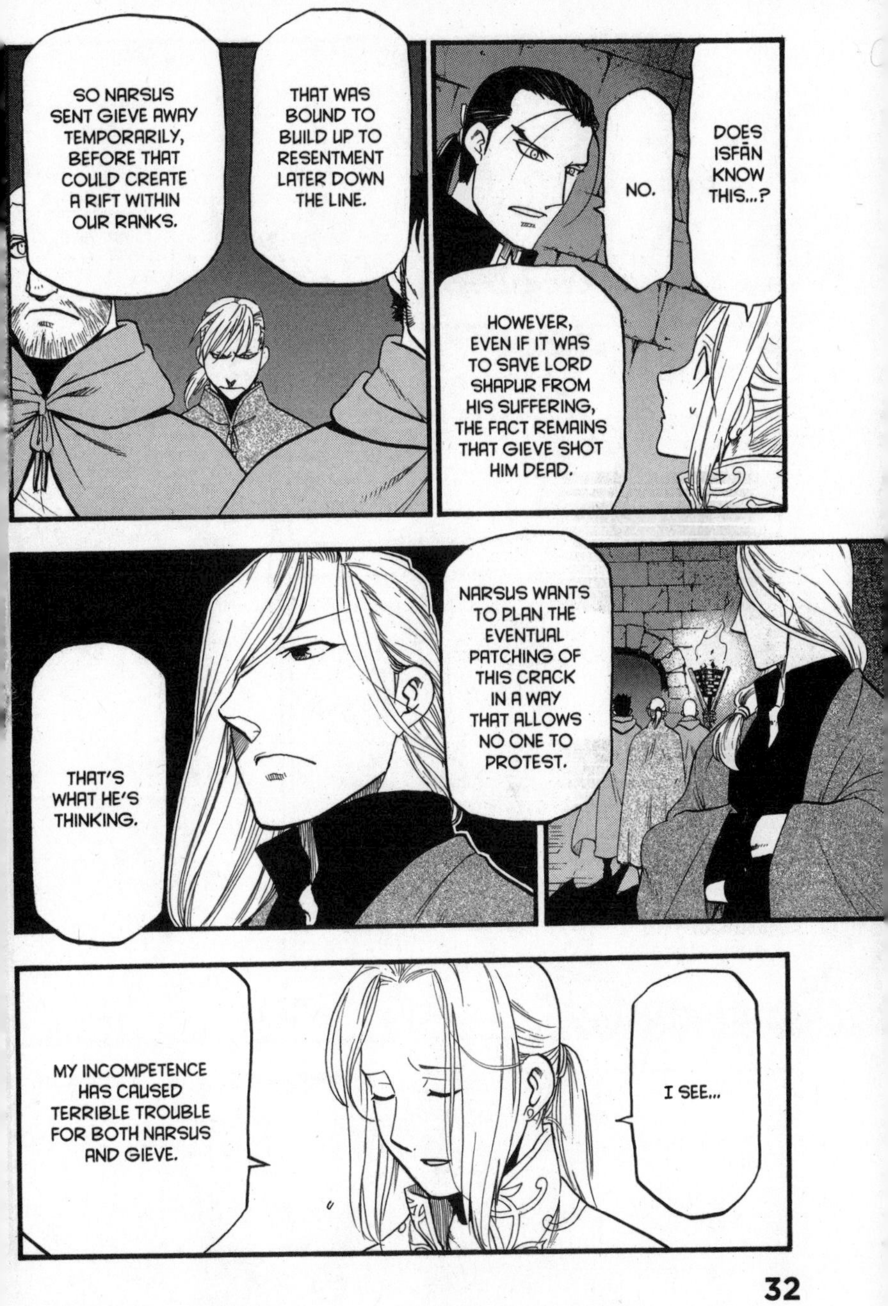
DOES ISFĀN KNOW THIS...?
NO.
HOWEVER, EVEN IF IT WAS TO SAVE LORD SHAPUR FROM HIS SUFFERING, THE FACT REMAINS THAT GIEVE SHOT HIM DEAD.
THAT WAS BOUND TO BUILD UP TO RESENTMENT LATER DOWN THE LINE.
SO NARSUS SENT GIEVE AWAY TEMPORARILY, BEFORE THAT COULD CREATE A RIFT WITHIN OUR RANKS.
NARSUS WANTS TO PLAN THE EVENTUAL PATCHING OF THIS CRACK IN A WAY THAT ALLOWS NO ONE TO PROTEST.
THAT'S WHAT HE'S THINKING.
I SEE...
MY INCOMPETENCE HAS CAUSED TERRIBLE TROUBLE FOR BOTH NARSUS AND GIEVE.

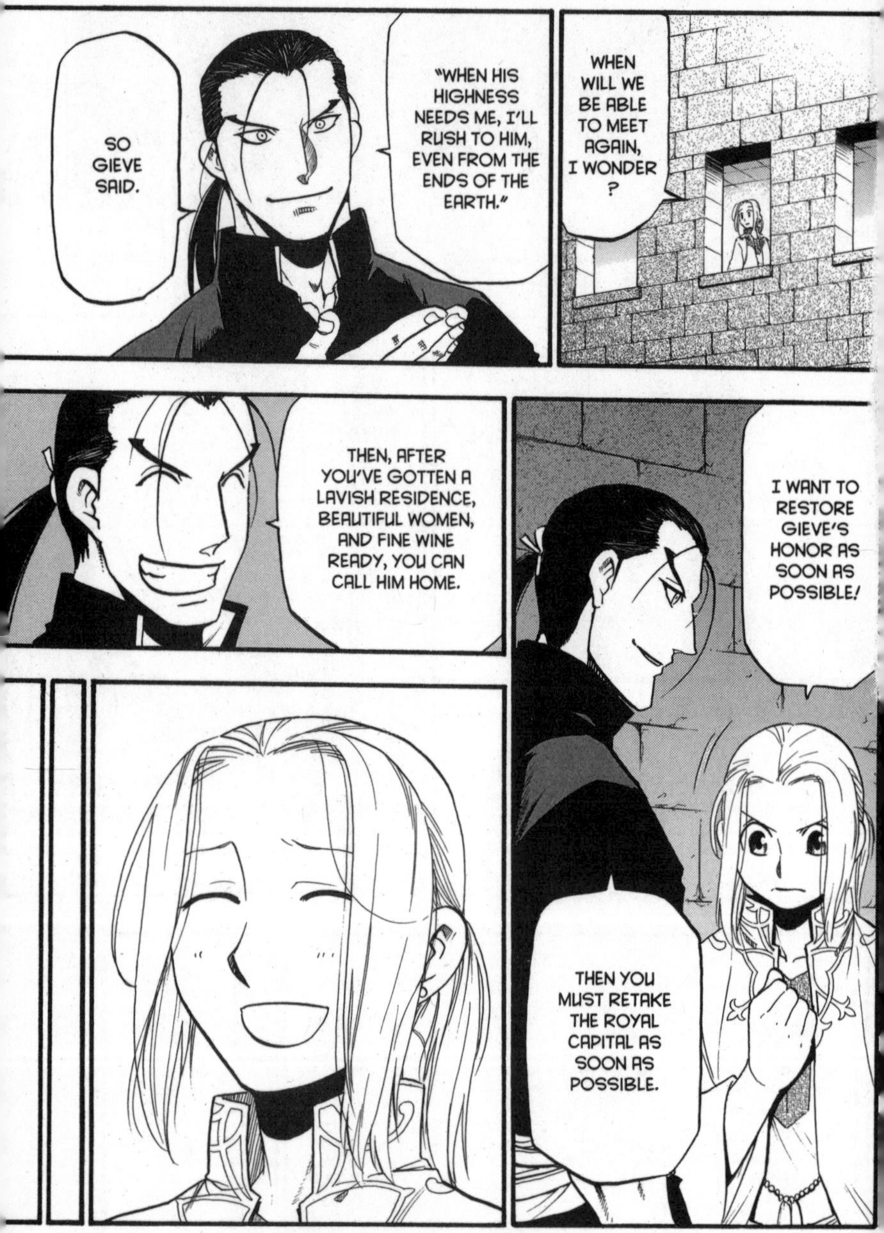
WHEN WILL WE BE ABLE TO MEET AGAIN, I WONDER?
"WHEN HIS HIGHNESS NEEDS ME, I'LL RUSH TO HIM, EVEN FROM THE ENDS OF THE EARTH."
SO GIEVE SAID.
I WANT TO RESTORE GIEVE'S HONOR AS SOON AS POSSIBLE!
THEN YOU MUST RETAKE THE ROYAL CAPITAL AS SOON AS POSSIBLE.
THEN, AFTER YOU'VE GOTTEN A LAVISH RESIDENCE, BEAUTIFUL WOMEN, AND FINE WINE READY, YOU CAN CALL HIM HOME.

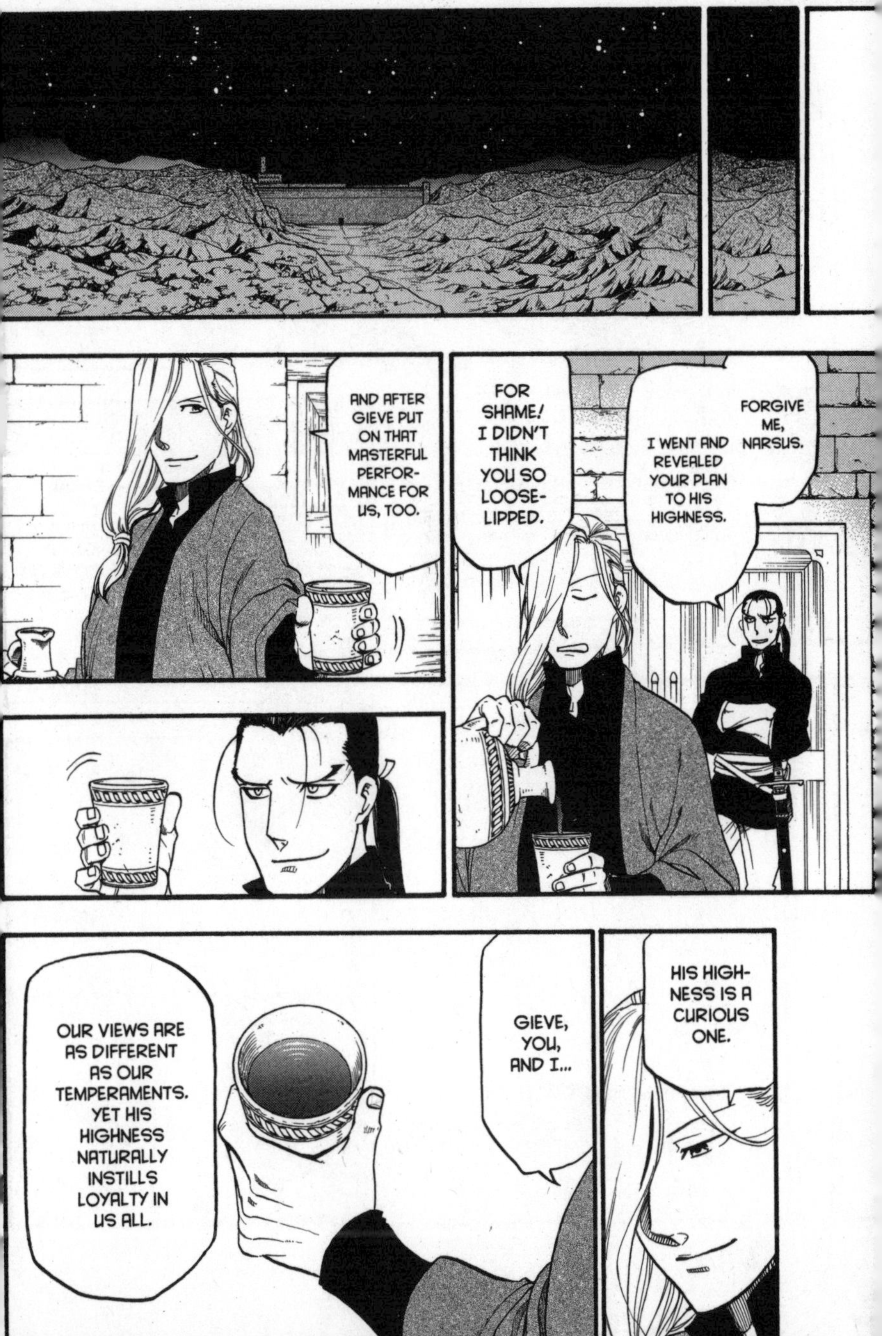
FORGIVE ME, NARSUS.
I WENT AND REVEALED YOUR PLAN TO HIS HIGHNESS.
FOR SHAME! I DIDN'T THINK YOU SO LOOSE-LIPPED.
AND AFTER GIEVE PUT ON THAT MASTERFUL PERFORMANCE FOR US, TOO.
HIS HIGHNESS IS A CURIOUS ONE.
GIEVE, YOU, AND I...
OUR VIEWS ARE AS DIFFERENT AS OUR TEMPERAMENTS. YET HIS HIGHNESS NATURALLY INSTILLS LOYALTY IN US ALL.

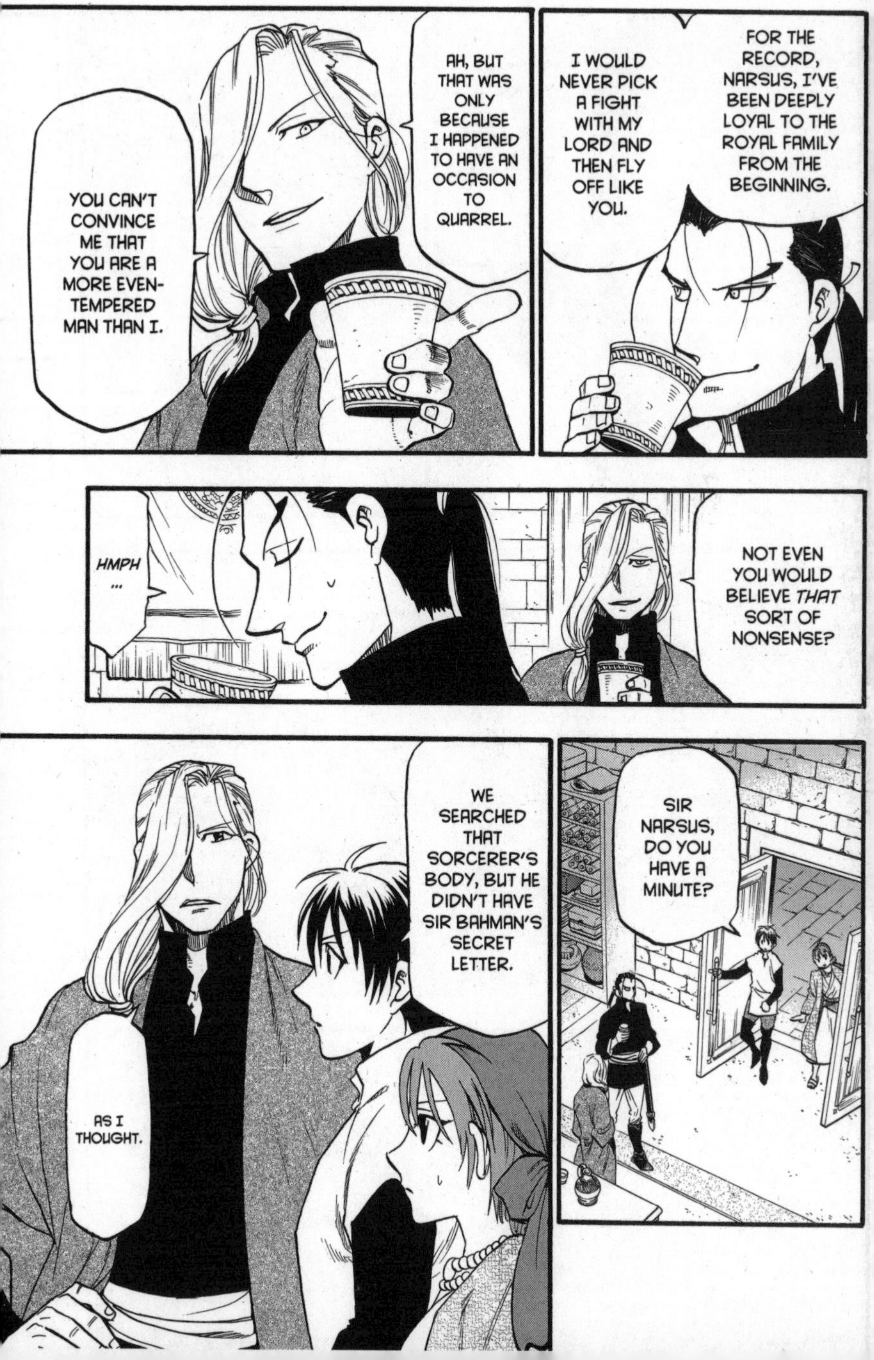
FOR THE RECORD, NARSUS, I'VE BEEN DEEPLY LOYAL TO THE ROYAL FAMILY FROM THE BEGINNING.
I WOULD NEVER PICK A FIGHT WITH MY LORD AND THEN FLY OFF LIKE YOU.
AH, BUT THAT WAS ONLY BECAUSE I HAPPENED TO HAVE AN OCCASION TO QUARREL.
YOU CAN'T CONVINCE ME THAT YOU ARE A MORE EVEN-TEMPERED MAN THAN I.
NOT EVEN YOU WOULD BELIEVE *THAT* SORT OF NONSENSE?
HMPH...
SIR NARSUS, DO YOU HAVE A MINUTE?
WE SEARCHED THAT SORCERER'S BODY, BUT HE DIDN'T HAVE SIR BAHMAN'S SECRET LETTER.
AS I THOUGHT.

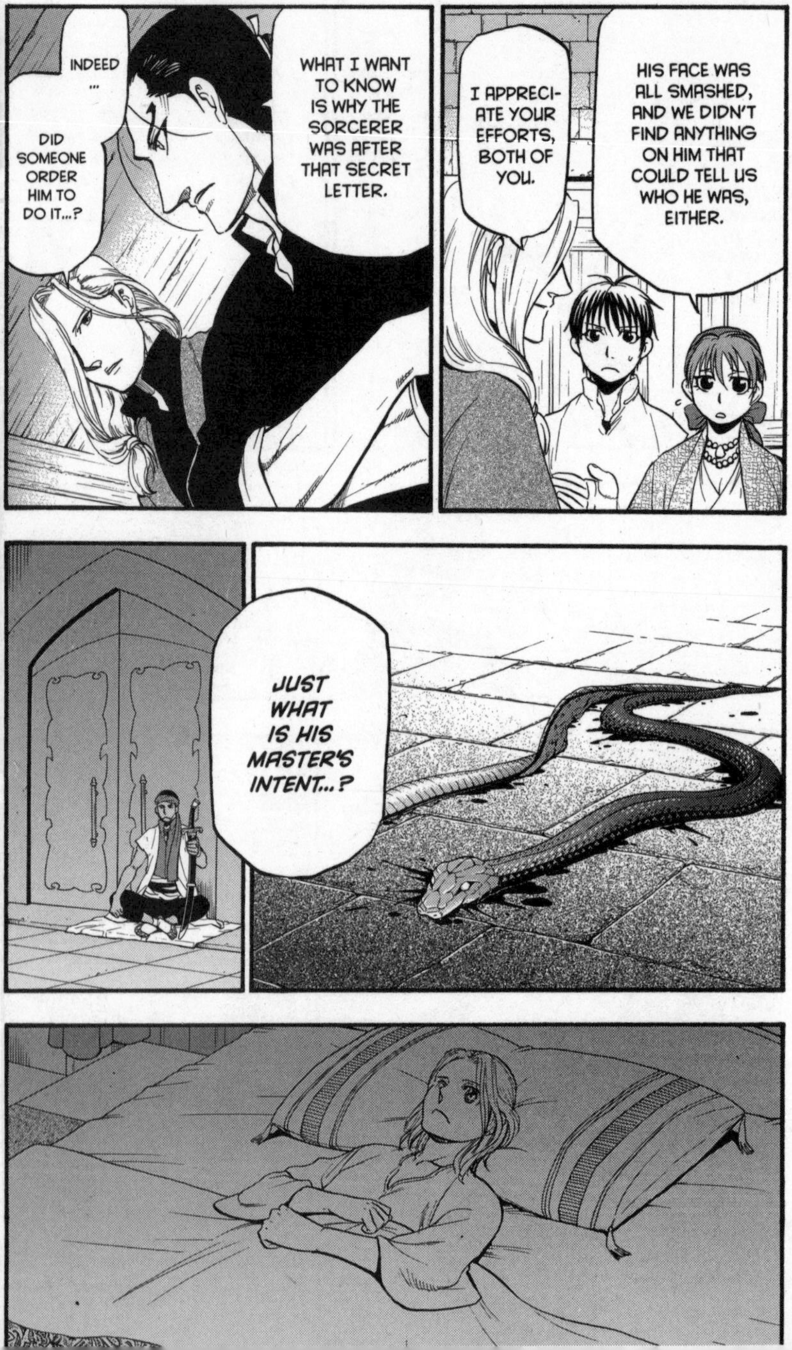
HIS FACE WAS ALL SMASHED, AND WE DIDN'T FIND ANYTHING ON HIM THAT COULD TELL US WHO HE WAS, EITHER.
I APPRECIATE YOUR EFFORTS, BOTH OF YOU.
WHAT I WANT TO KNOW IS WHY THE SORCERER WAS AFTER THAT SECRET LETTER.
INDEED ...
DID SOMEONE ORDER HIM TO DO IT...?
JUST WHAT IS HIS MASTER'S INTENT...?

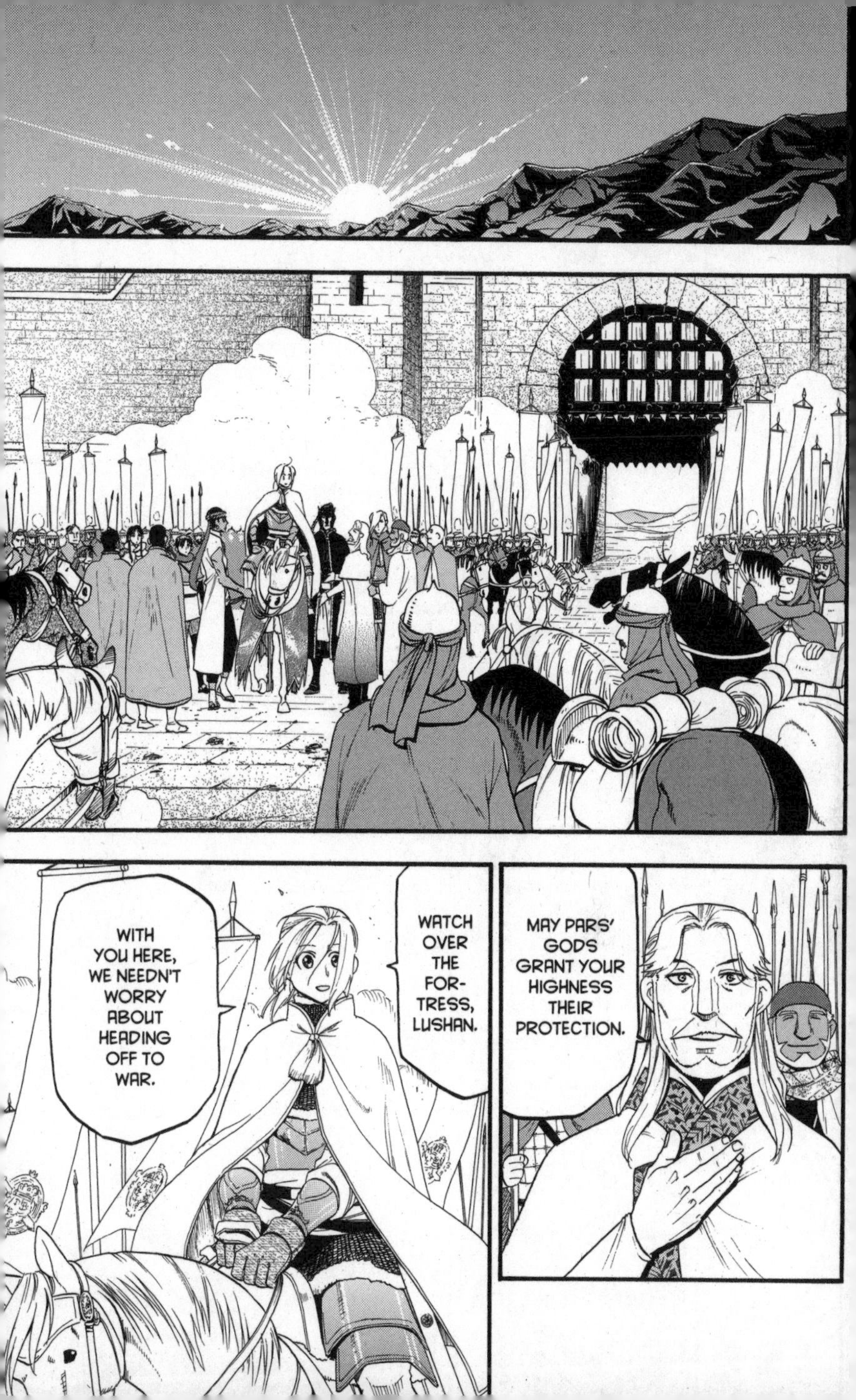
MAY PARS' GODS GRANT YOUR HIGHNESS THEIR PROTECTION.
WATCH OVER THE FOR-TRESS, LUSHAN.
WITH YOU HERE, WE NEEDN'T WORRY ABOUT HEADING OFF TO WAR.

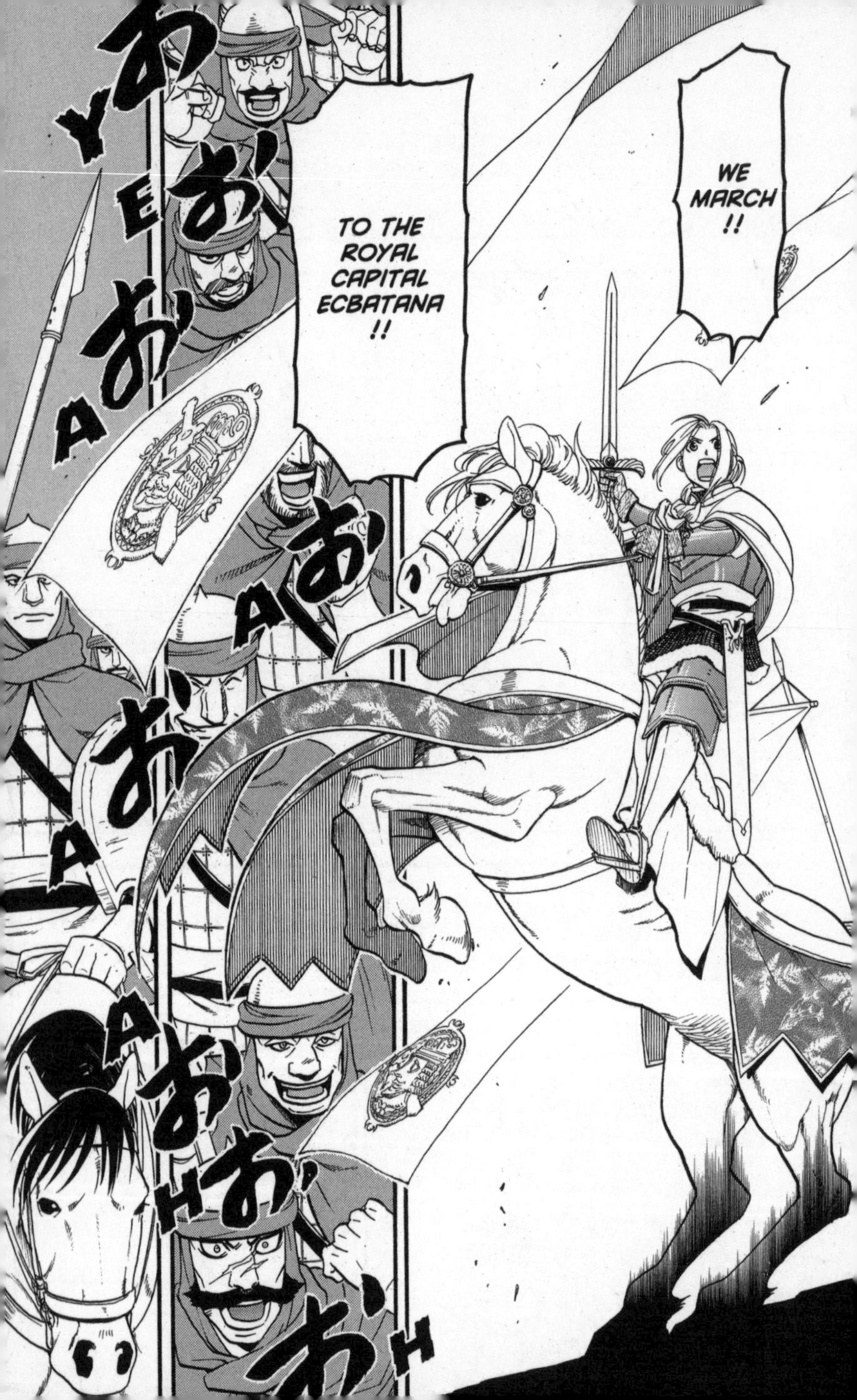
WE MARCH !!
TO THE ROYAL CAPITAL ECBATANA !!

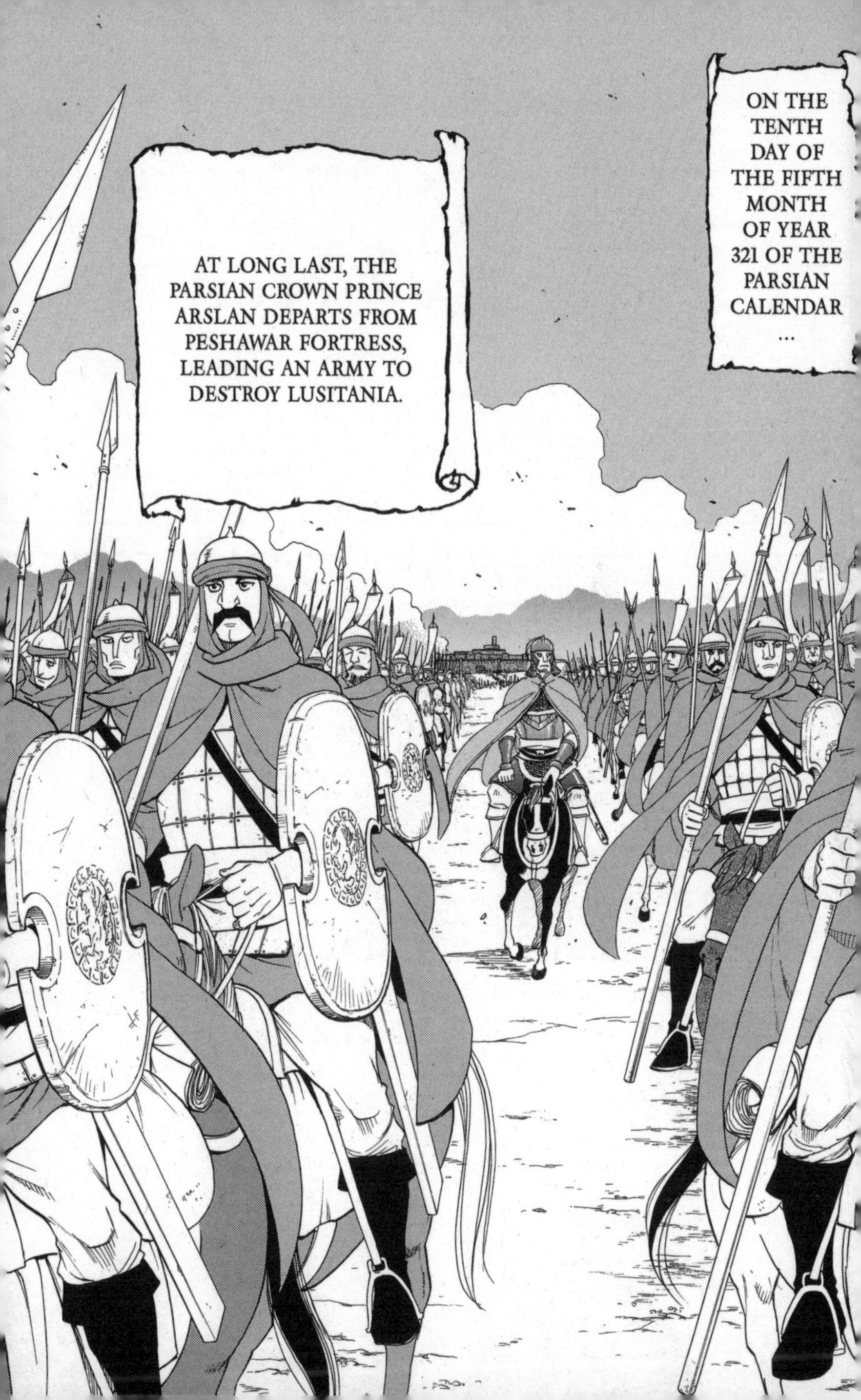
ON THE TENTH DAY OF THE FIFTH MONTH OF YEAR 321 OF THE PARSIAN CALENDAR ...
AT LONG LAST, THE PARSIAN CROWN PRINCE ARSLAN DEPARTS FROM PESHAWAR FORTRESS, LEADING AN ARMY TO DESTROY LUSITANIA.

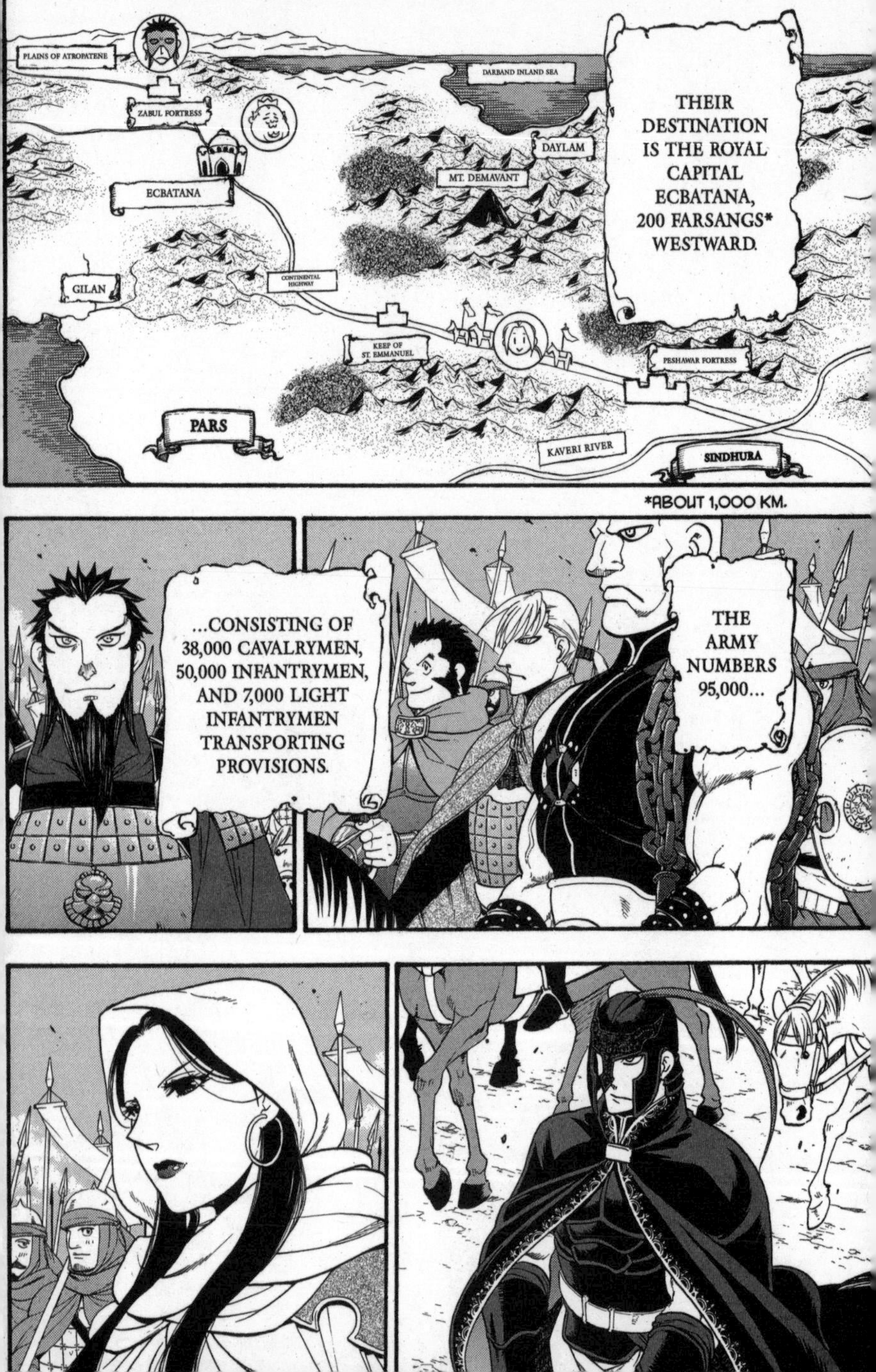
THEIR DESTINATION IS THE ROYAL CAPITAL ECBATANA, 200 FARSANGS* WESTWARD.
DARBAND INLAND SEA
PLAINS OF ATROPATENE
ZABUL FORTRESS
DAYLAM
MT. DEMAVANT
ECBATANA
CONTINENTAL HIGHWAY
GILAN
KEEP OF ST. EMMANUEL
PESHAWAR FORTRESS
PARS
KAVERI RIVER
SINDHURA
*ABOUT 1,000 KM.
THE ARMY NUMBERS 95,000...
...CONSISTING OF 38,000 CAVALRYMEN, 50,000 INFANTRYMEN, AND 7,000 LIGHT INFANTRYMEN TRANSPORTING PROVISIONS.

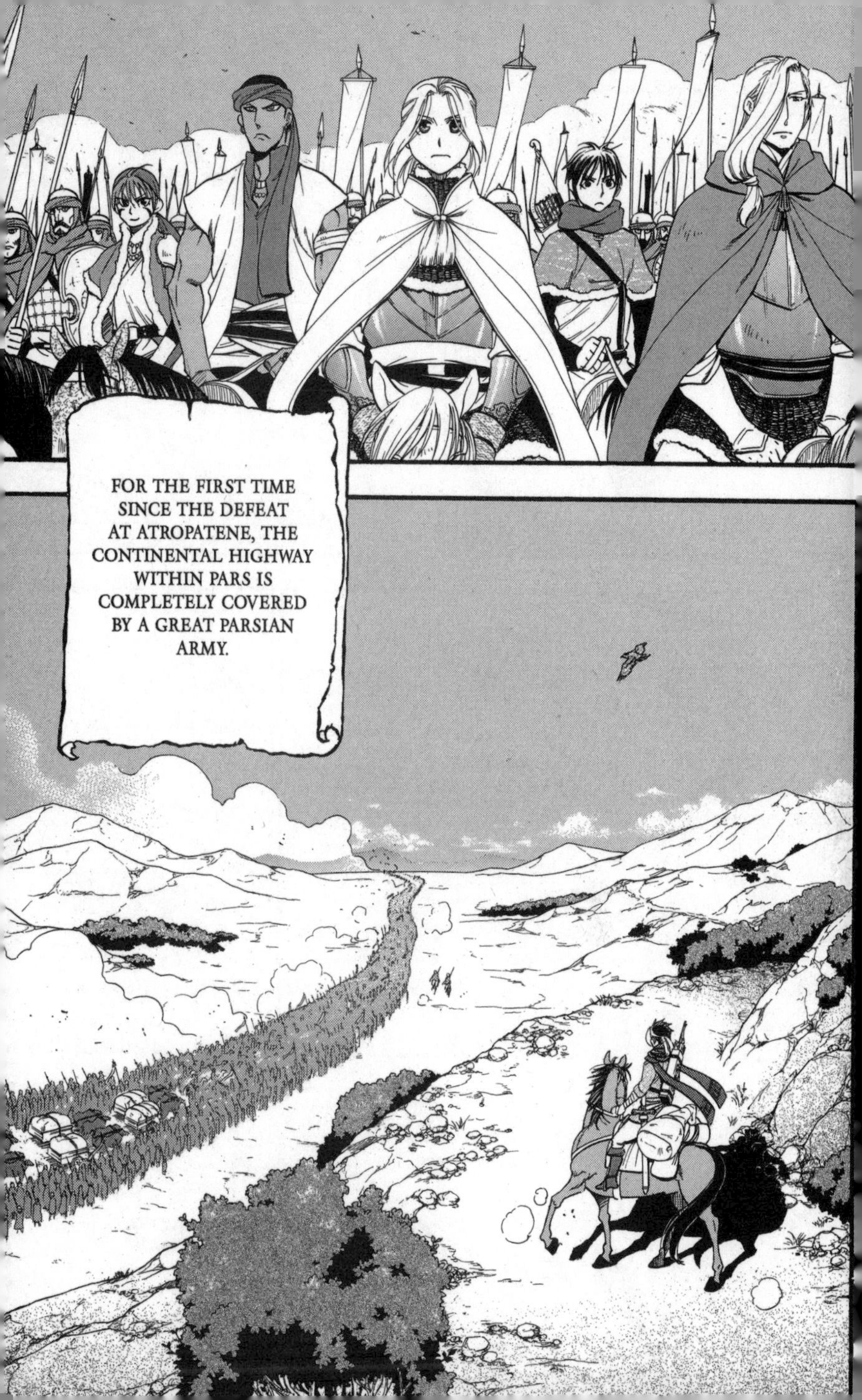
FOR THE FIRST TIME SINCE THE DEFEAT AT ATROPATENE, THE CONTINENTAL HIGHWAY WITHIN PARS IS COMPLETELY COVERED BY A GREAT PARSIAN ARMY.

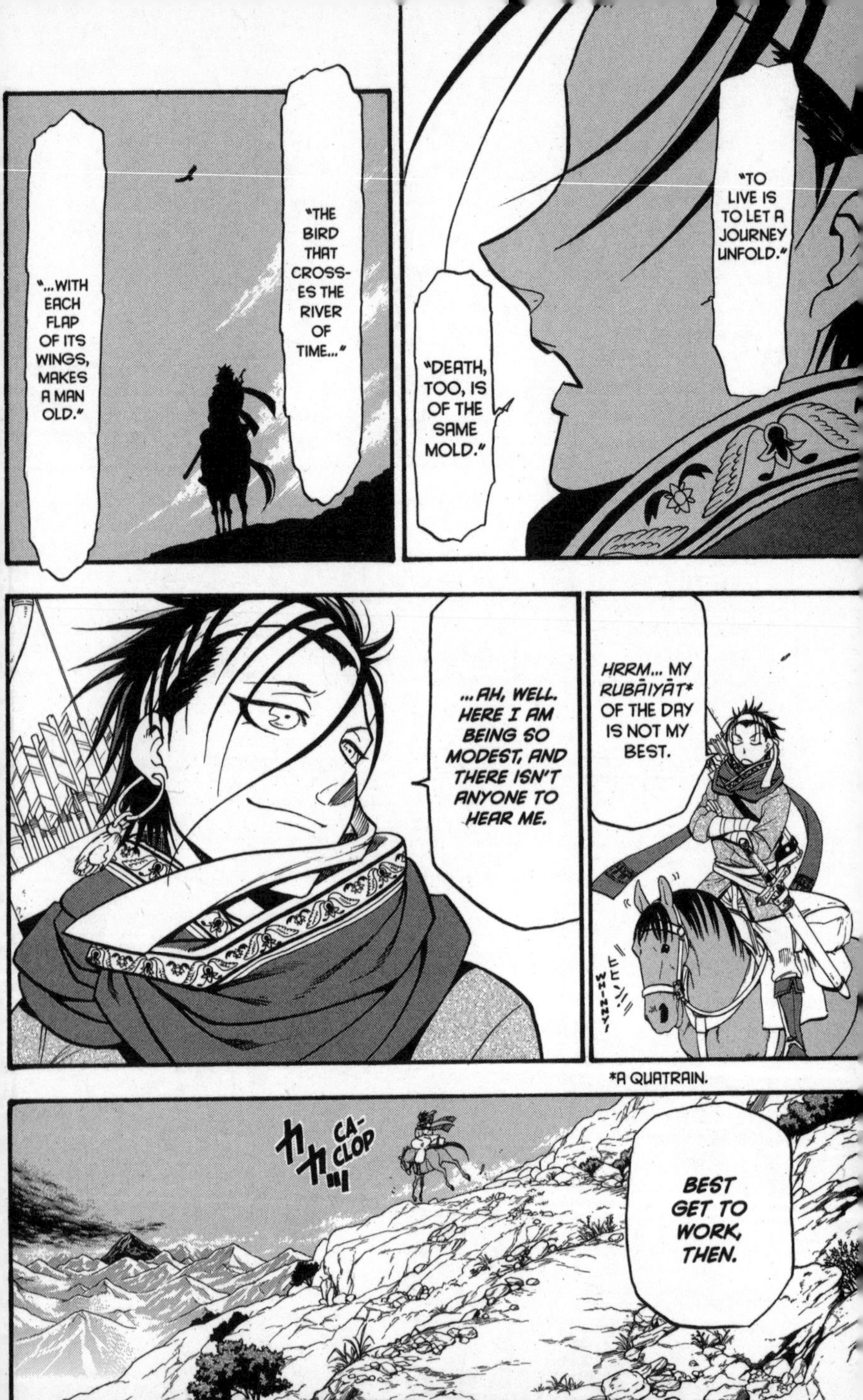
"TO LIVE IS TO LET A JOURNEY UNFOLD."
"DEATH, TOO, IS OF THE SAME MOLD."
"THE BIRD THAT CROSS-ES THE RIVER OF TIME..."
"...WITH EACH FLAP OF ITS WINGS, MAKES A MAN OLD."
HRRM... MY RUBĀIYĀT* OF THE DAY IS NOT MY BEST.
WHINNY!
...AH, WELL. HERE I AM BEING SO MODEST, AND THERE ISN'T ANYONE TO HEAR ME.
*A QUATRAIN.
BEST GET TO WORK, THEN.
CA-CLOP

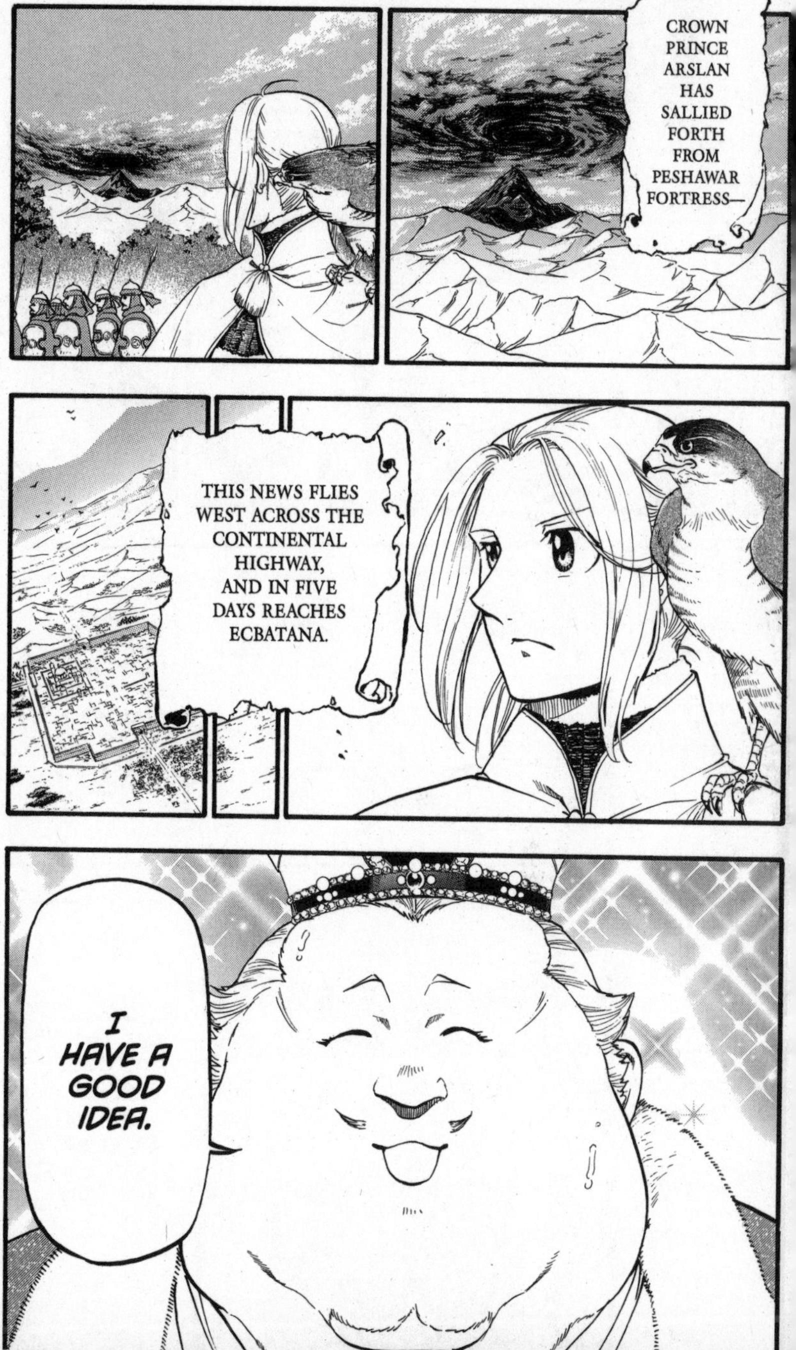
CROWN PRINCE ARSLAN HAS SALLIED FORTH FROM PESHAWAR FORTRESS—
THIS NEWS FLIES WEST ACROSS THE CONTINENTAL HIGHWAY, AND IN FIVE DAYS REACHES ECBATANA.
I HAVE A GOOD IDEA.

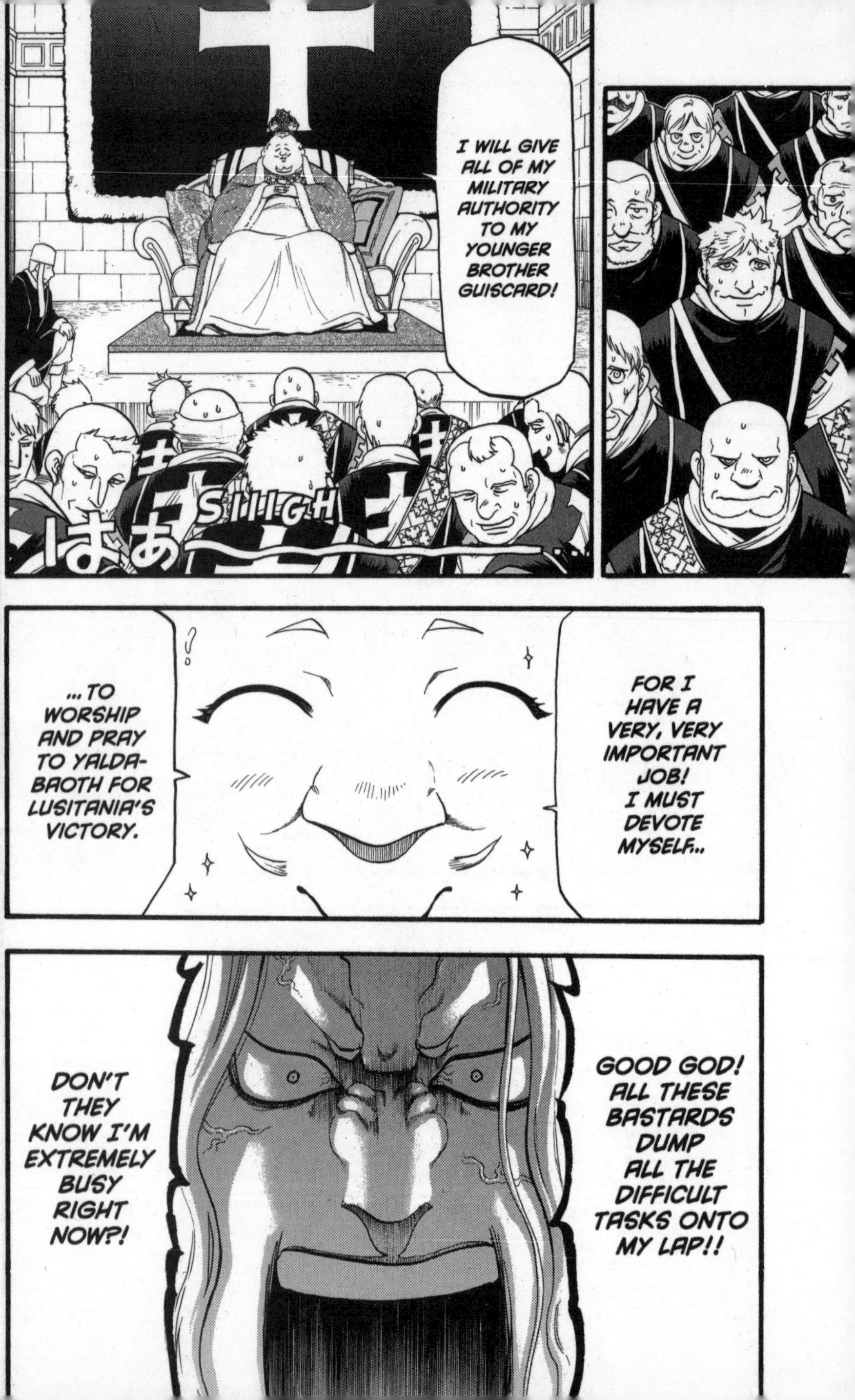
I WILL GIVE ALL OF MY MILITARY AUTHORITY TO MY YOUNGER BROTHER GUISCARD!
SIIIGH
はあ
FOR I HAVE A VERY, VERY IMPORTANT JOB! I MUST DEVOTE MYSELF...
...TO WORSHIP AND PRAY TO YALDA-BAOTH FOR LUSITANIA'S VICTORY.
GOOD GOD! ALL THESE BASTARDS DUMP ALL THE DIFFICULT TASKS ONTO MY LAP!!
DON'T THEY KNOW I'M EXTREMELY BUSY RIGHT NOW?!

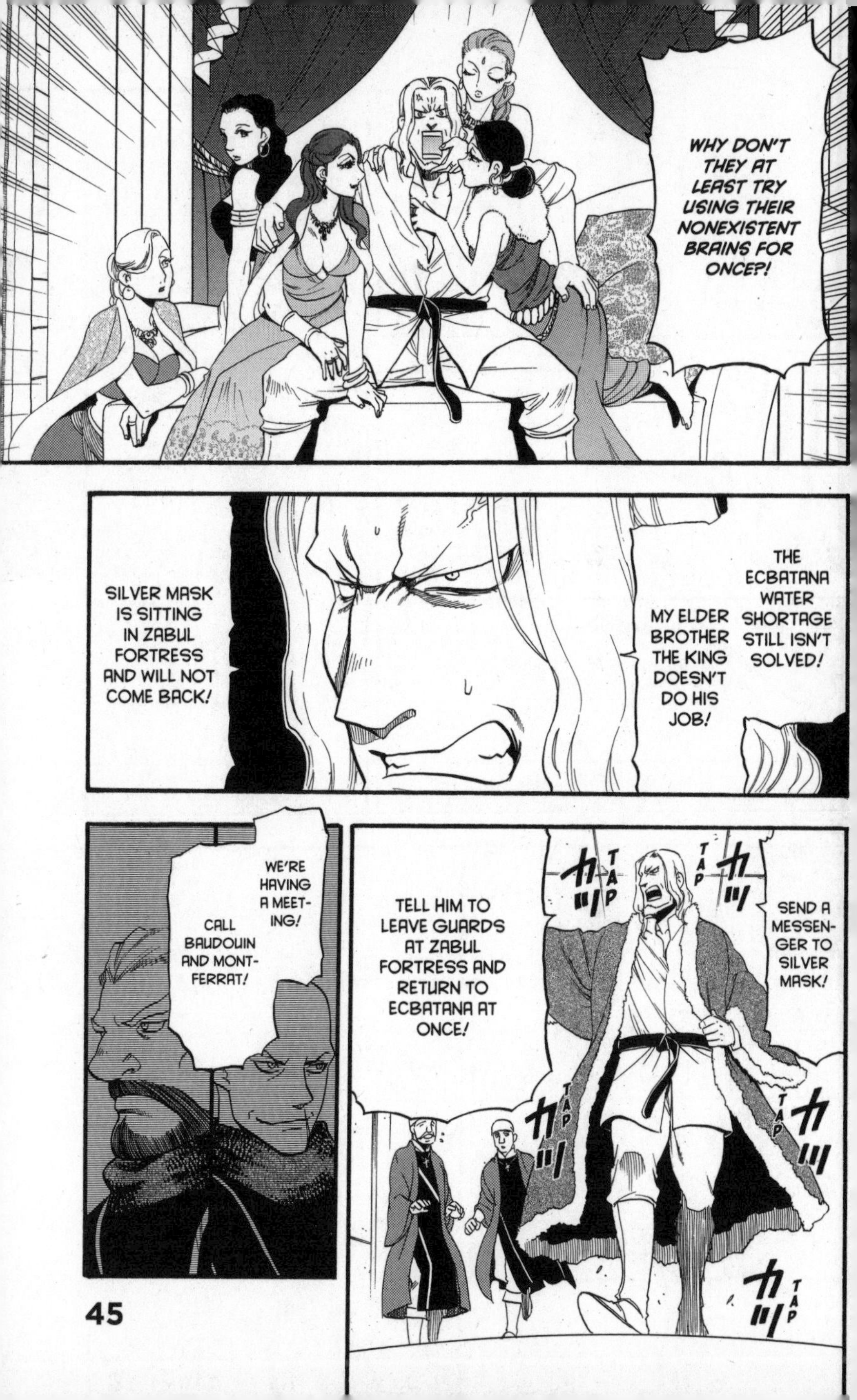
WHY DON'T THEY AT LEAST TRY USING THEIR NONEXISTENT BRAINS FOR ONCE?!
THE ECBATANA WATER SHORTAGE STILL ISN'T SOLVED!
MY ELDER BROTHER THE KING DOESN'T DO HIS JOB!
SILVER MASK IS SITTING IN ZABUL FORTRESS AND WILL NOT COME BACK!
カッ TAP
カッ TAP
SEND A MESSEN-GER TO SILVER MASK!
TELL HIM TO LEAVE GUARDS AT ZABUL FORTRESS AND RETURN TO ECBATANA AT ONCE!
カッ TAP
カッ TAP
カッ TAP
WE'RE HAVING A MEET-ING!
CALL BAUDOUIN AND MONT-FERRAT!

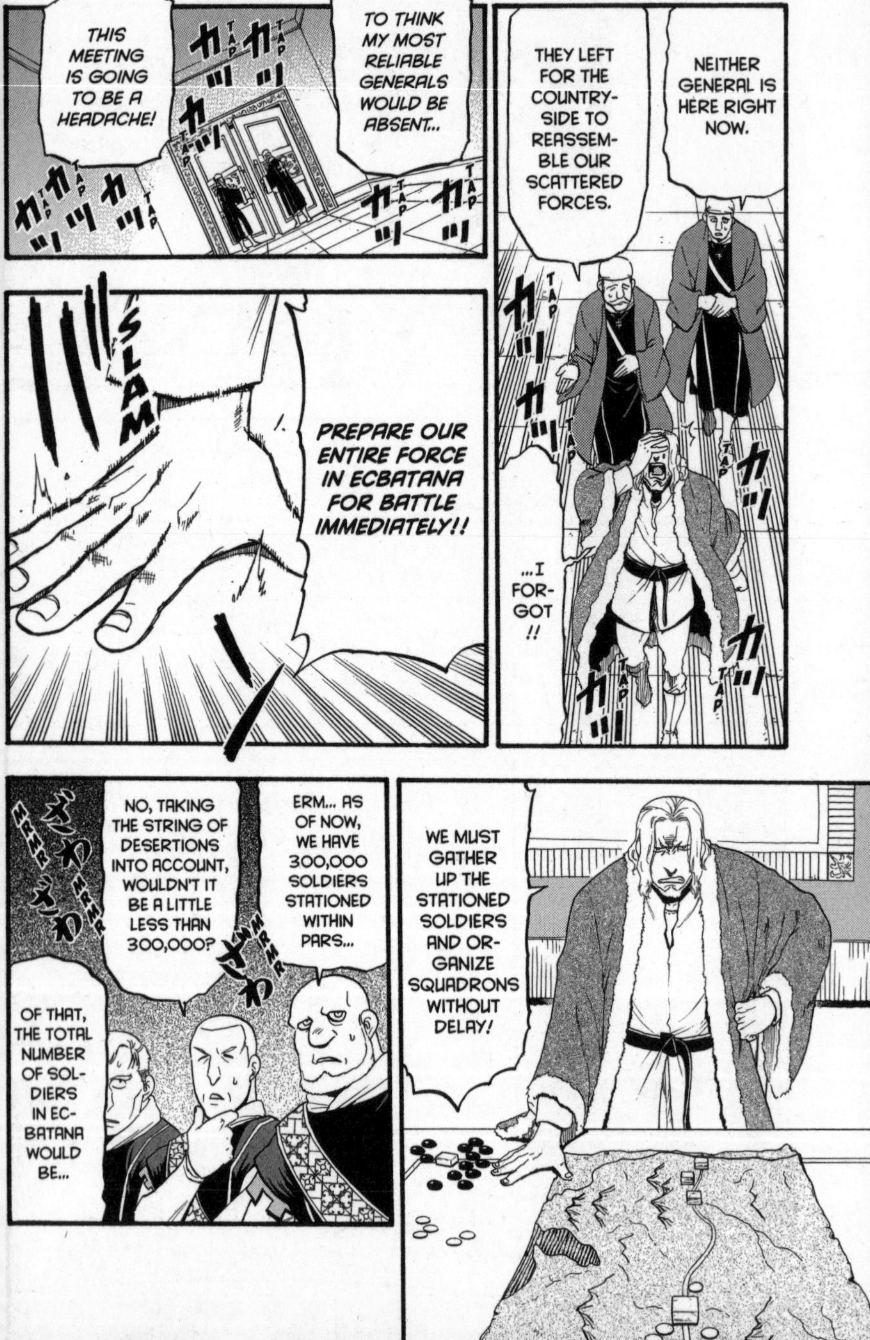
NEITHER GENERAL IS HERE RIGHT NOW.
THEY LEFT FOR THE COUNTRY-SIDE TO REASSEM-BLE OUR SCATTERED FORCES.
TAP TAP TAP TAP TAP
...I FOR-GOT!!
TO THINK MY MOST RELIABLE GENERALS WOULD BE ABSENT...
TAP TAP TAP TAP TAP TAP TAP TAP
THIS MEETING IS GOING TO BE A HEADACHE!
SLAM
PREPARE OUR ENTIRE FORCE IN ECBATANA FOR BATTLE IMMEDIATELY!!
WE MUST GATHER UP THE STATIONED SOLDIERS AND OR-GANIZE SQUADRONS WITHOUT DELAY!
ERM... AS OF NOW, WE HAVE 300,000 SOLDIERS STATIONED WITHIN PARS...
MRMR
NO, TAKING THE STRING OF DESERTIONS INTO ACCOUNT, WOULDN'T IT BE A LITTLE LESS THAN 300,000?
MRMR MRMR
OF THAT, THE TOTAL NUMBER OF SOL-DIERS IN EC-BATANA WOULD BE...

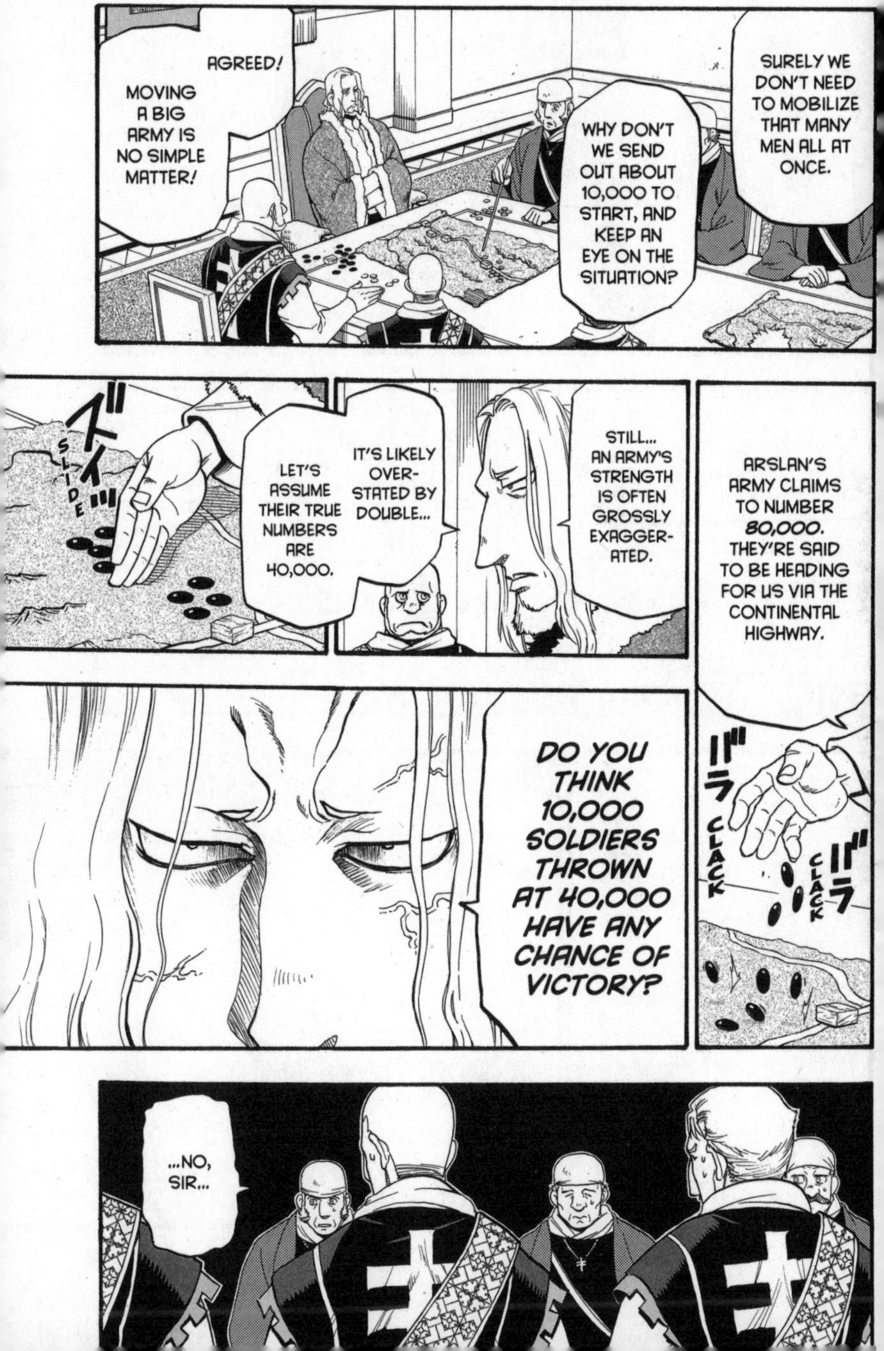
SURELY WE DON'T NEED TO MOBILIZE THAT MANY MEN ALL AT ONCE.
WHY DON'T WE SEND OUT ABOUT 10,000 TO START, AND KEEP AN EYE ON THE SITUATION?
AGREED!
MOVING A BIG ARMY IS NO SIMPLE MATTER!
ARSLAN'S ARMY CLAIMS TO NUMBER 80,000. THEY'RE SAID TO BE HEADING FOR US VIA THE CONTINENTAL HIGHWAY.
STILL... AN ARMY'S STRENGTH IS OFTEN GROSSLY EXAGGER-ATED.
IT'S LIKELY OVER-STATED BY DOUBLE...
LET'S ASSUME THEIR TRUE NUMBERS ARE 40,000.
SLIDE
CLACK
CLACK
DO YOU THINK 10,000 SOLDIERS THROWN AT 40,000 HAVE ANY CHANCE OF VICTORY?
...NO, SIR...

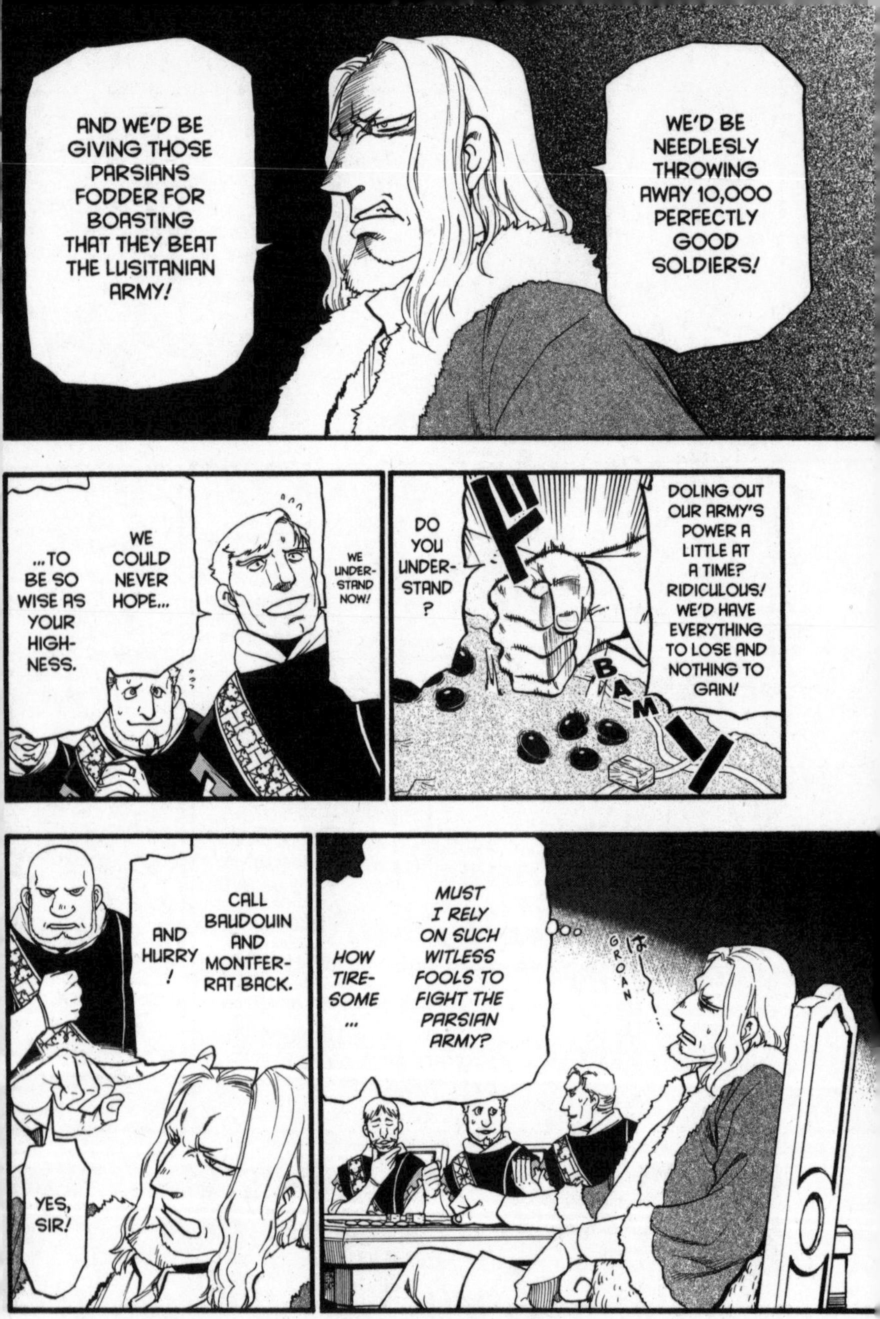
WE'D BE NEEDLESLY THROWING AWAY 10,000 PERFECTLY GOOD SOLDIERS!
AND WE'D BE GIVING THOSE PARSIANS FODDER FOR BOASTING THAT THEY BEAT THE LUSITANIAN ARMY!
DOLING OUT OUR ARMY'S POWER A LITTLE AT A TIME? RIDICULOUS! WE'D HAVE EVERYTHING TO LOSE AND NOTHING TO GAIN!
DO YOU UNDERSTAND?
BAM
WE UNDERSTAND NOW!
WE COULD NEVER HOPE...
...TO BE SO WISE AS YOUR HIGHNESS.
GROAN
MUST I RELY ON SUCH WITLESS FOOLS TO FIGHT THE PARSIAN ARMY?
HOW TIRESOME...
CALL BAUDOUIN AND MONTFERRAT BACK.
AND HURRY!
YES, SIR!

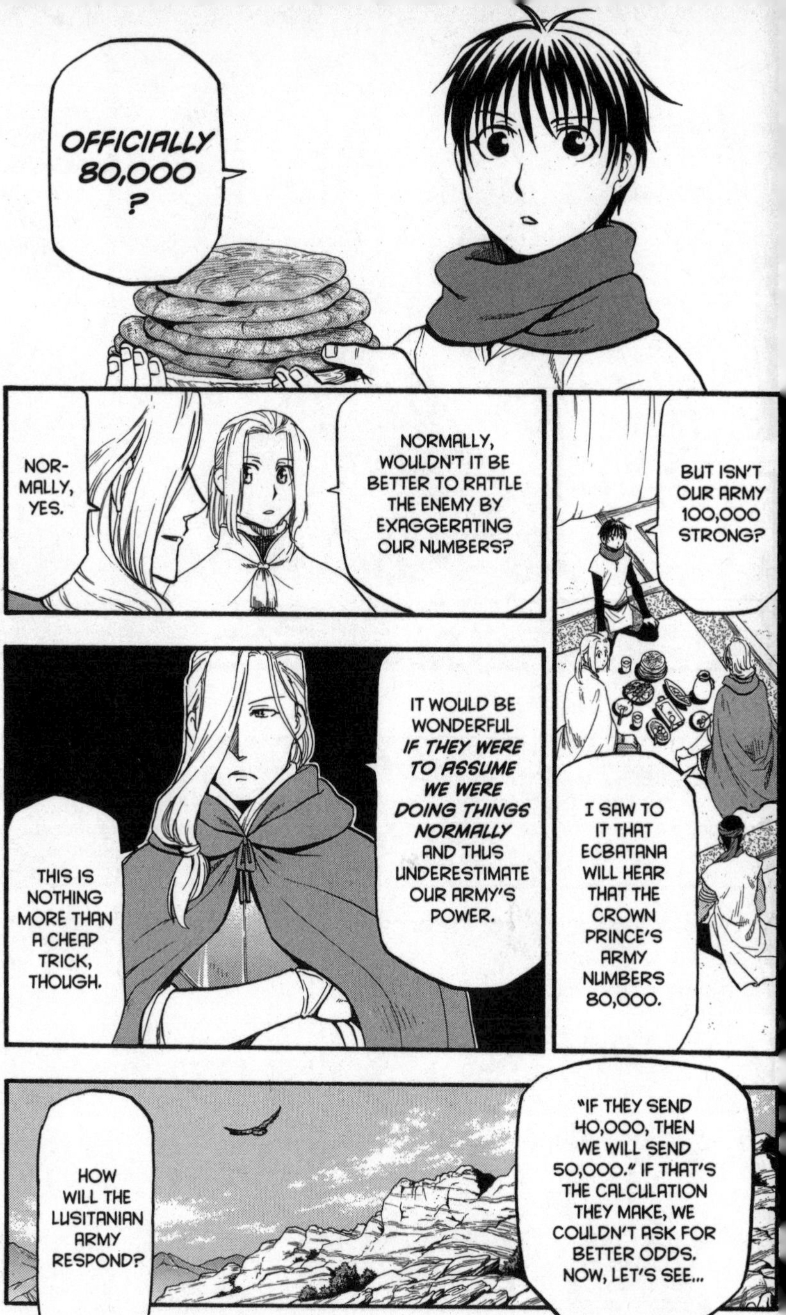
OFFICIALLY 80,000?
BUT ISN'T OUR ARMY 100,000 STRONG?
I SAW TO IT THAT ECBATANA WILL HEAR THAT THE CROWN PRINCE'S ARMY NUMBERS 80,000.
NORMALLY, WOULDN'T IT BE BETTER TO RATTLE THE ENEMY BY EXAGGERATING OUR NUMBERS?
NOR-MALLY, YES.
IT WOULD BE WONDERFUL *IF THEY WERE TO ASSUME WE WERE DOING THINGS NORMALLY* AND THUS UNDERESTIMATE OUR ARMY'S POWER.
THIS IS NOTHING MORE THAN A CHEAP TRICK, THOUGH.
"IF THEY SEND 40,000, THEN WE WILL SEND 50,000." IF THAT'S THE CALCULATION THEY MAKE, WE COULDN'T ASK FOR BETTER ODDS. NOW, LET'S SEE...
HOW WILL THE LUSITANIAN ARMY RESPOND?

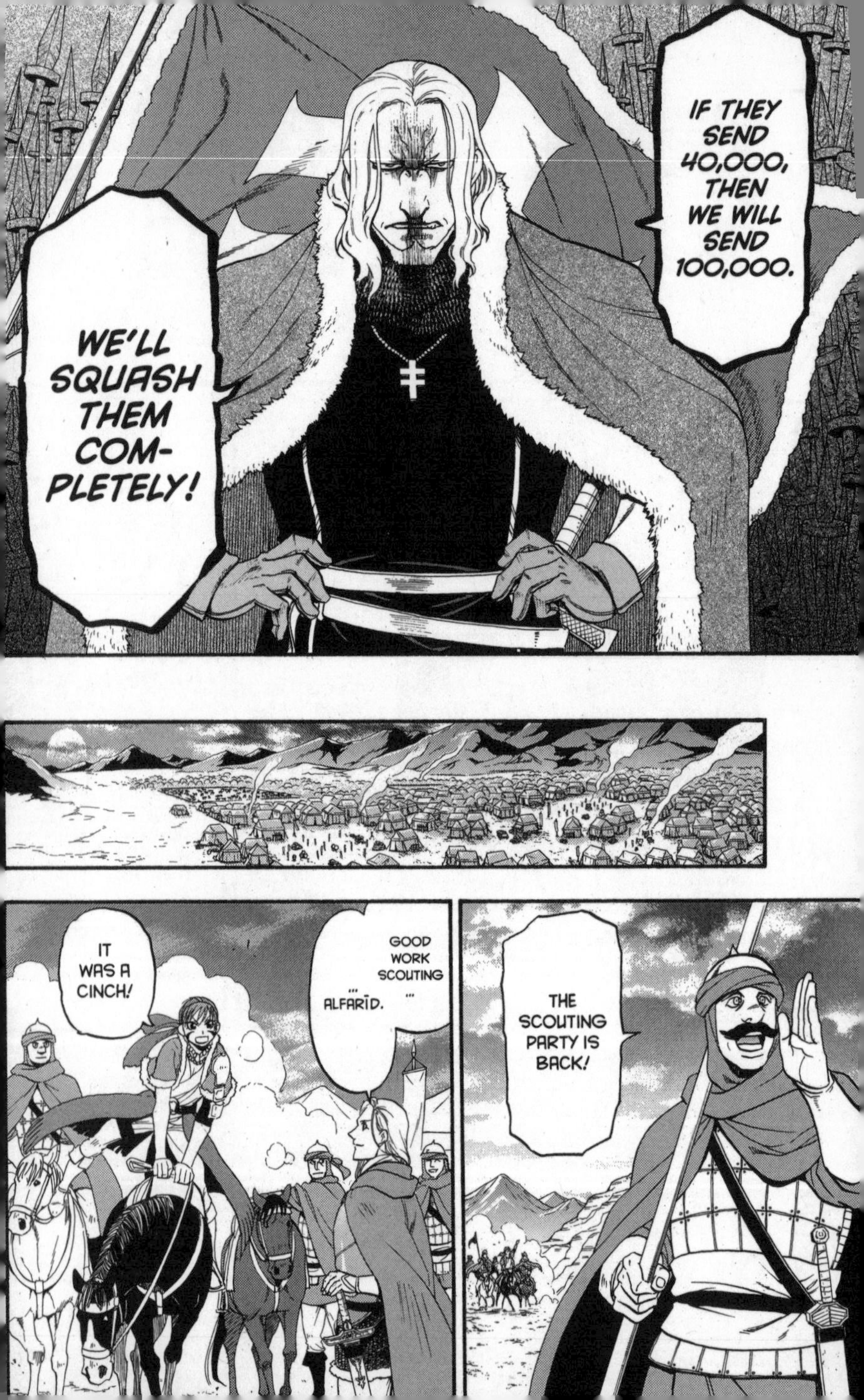
IF THEY SEND 40,000, THEN WE WILL SEND 100,000.
WE'LL SQUASH THEM COM-PLETELY!
THE SCOUTING PARTY IS BACK!
GOOD WORK SCOUTING ... ... ALFARĪD.
IT WAS A CINCH!

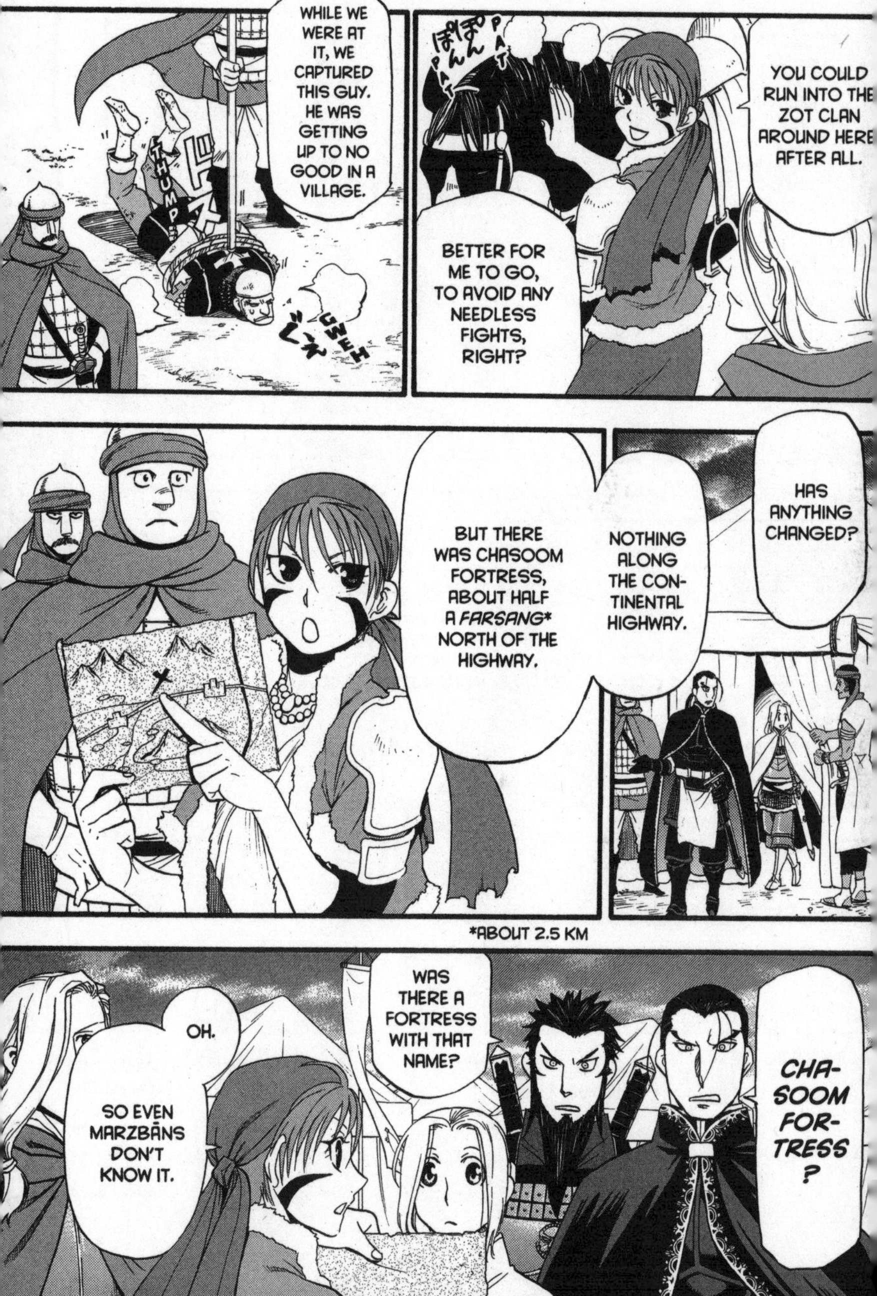
YOU COULD RUN INTO THE ZOT CLAN AROUND HERE AFTER ALL.
PAT PAT
BETTER FOR ME TO GO, TO AVOID ANY NEEDLESS FIGHTS, RIGHT?
WHILE WE WERE AT IT, WE CAPTURED THIS GUY. HE WAS GETTING UP TO NO GOOD IN A VILLAGE.
THUMP
GWEH
HAS ANYTHING CHANGED?
NOTHING ALONG THE CON-TINENTAL HIGHWAY.
BUT THERE WAS CHASOOM FORTRESS, ABOUT HALF A *FARSANG** NORTH OF THE HIGHWAY.
CHA-SOOM FOR-TRESS?
WAS THERE A FORTRESS WITH THAT NAME?
OH.
SO EVEN MARZBĀNS DON'T KNOW IT.

*ABOUT 2.5 KM

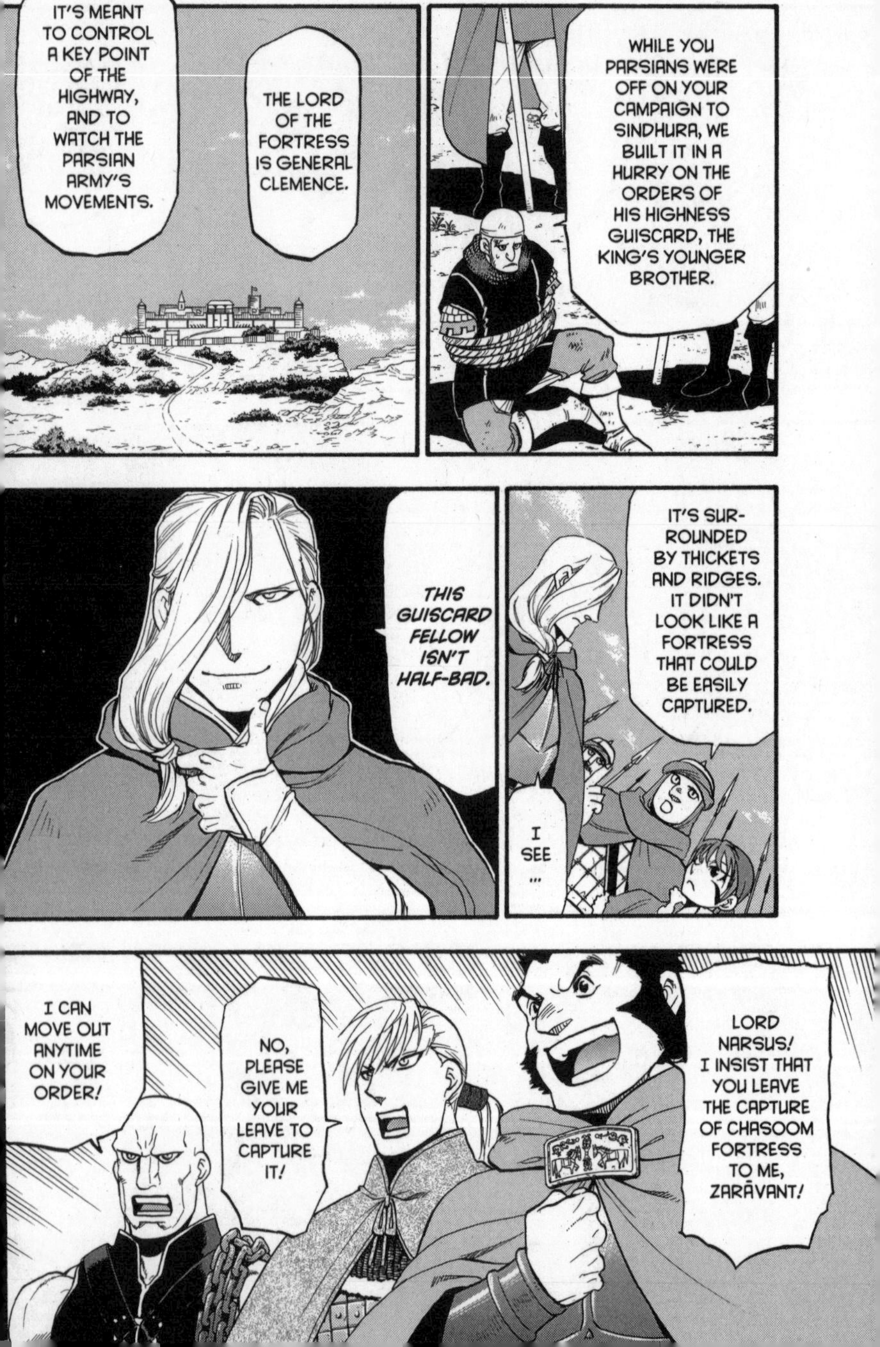
WHILE YOU PARSIANS WERE OFF ON YOUR CAMPAIGN TO SINDHURA, WE BUILT IT IN A HURRY ON THE ORDERS OF HIS HIGHNESS GUISCARD, THE KING'S YOUNGER BROTHER.
IT'S MEANT TO CONTROL A KEY POINT OF THE HIGHWAY, AND TO WATCH THE PARSIAN ARMY'S MOVEMENTS.
THE LORD OF THE FORTRESS IS GENERAL CLEMENCE.
IT'S SUR-ROUNDED BY THICKETS AND RIDGES. IT DIDN'T LOOK LIKE A FORTRESS THAT COULD BE EASILY CAPTURED.
I SEE ...
THIS GUISCARD FELLOW ISN'T HALF-BAD.
LORD NARSUS! I INSIST THAT YOU LEAVE THE CAPTURE OF CHASOOM FORTRESS TO ME, ZARĀVANT!
NO, PLEASE GIVE ME YOUR LEAVE TO CAPTURE IT!
I CAN MOVE OUT ANYTIME ON YOUR ORDER!

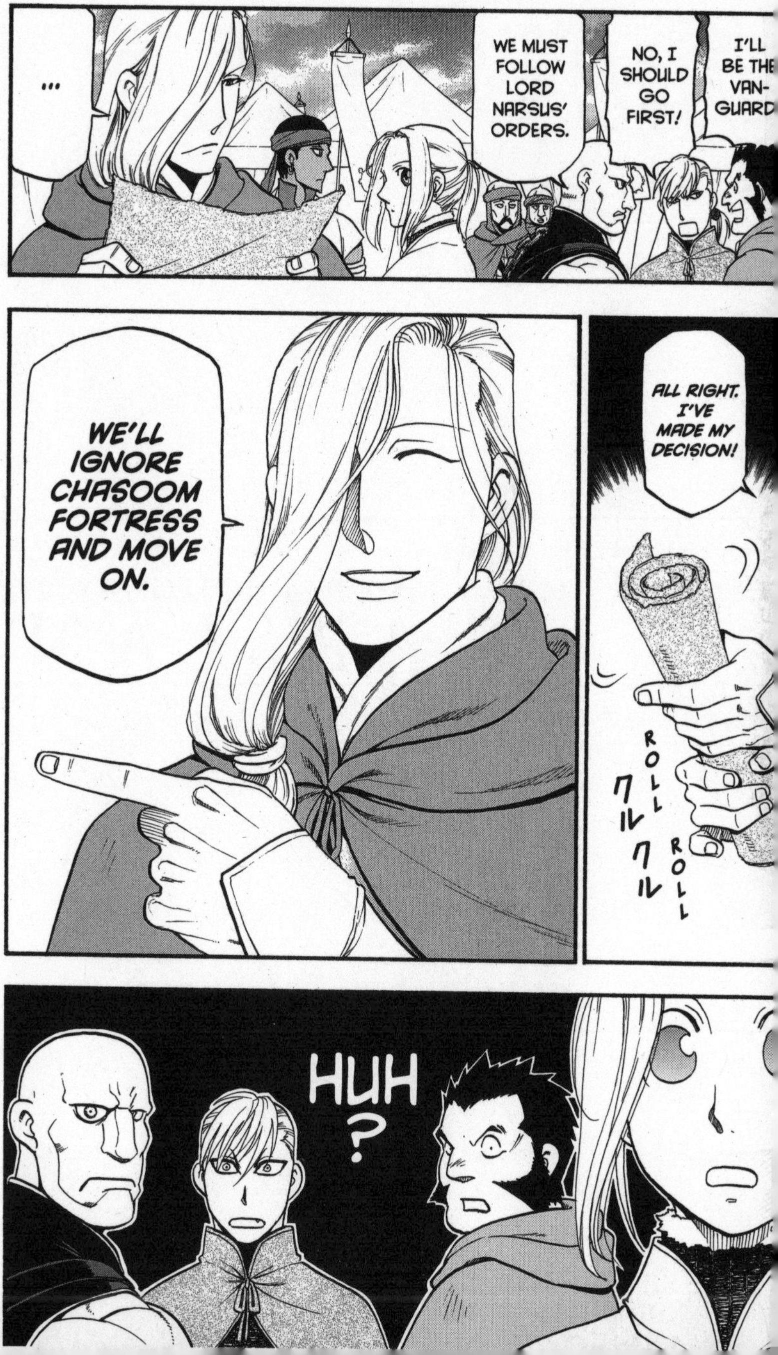
I'LL BE THE VAN-GUARD
NO, I SHOULD GO FIRST!
WE MUST FOLLOW LORD NARSUS' ORDERS.
...
ALL RIGHT. I'VE MADE MY DECISION!
ROLL ROLL
クル クル
WE'LL IGNORE CHASOOM FORTRESS AND MOVE ON.
HUH?

THE HEROIC LEGEND OF
ARSLAN

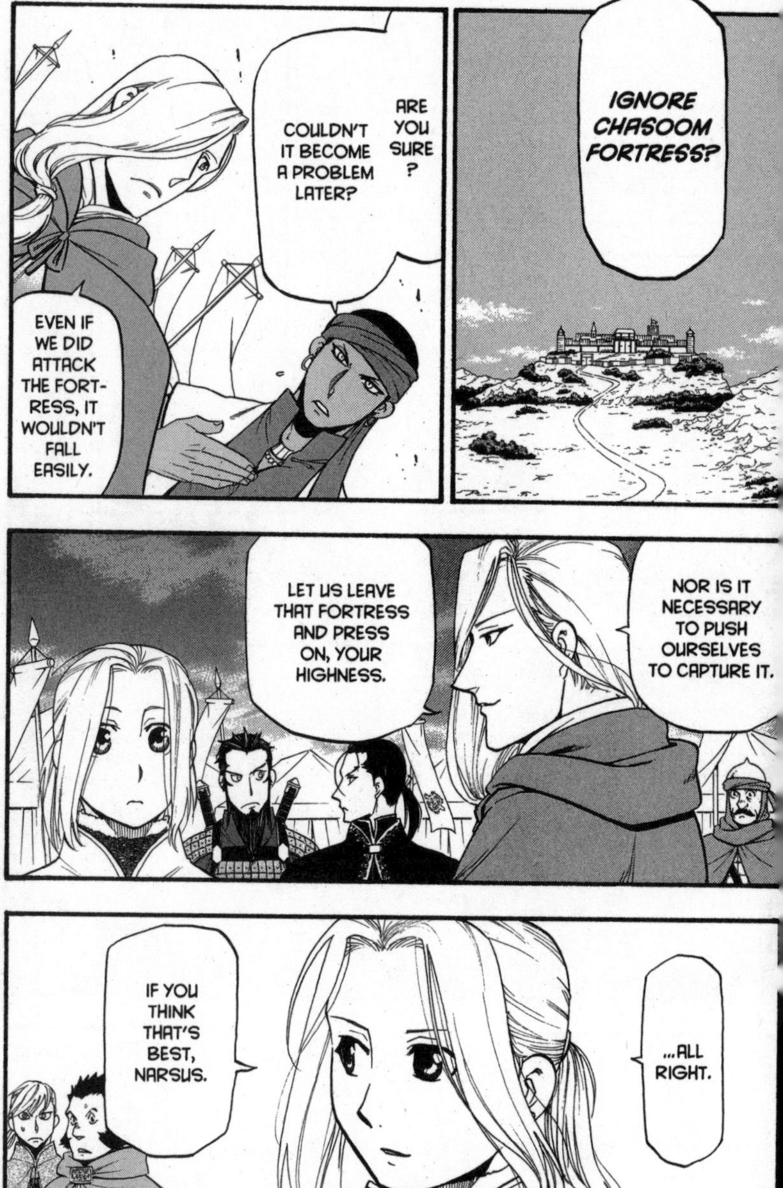
IGNORE CHASOOM FORTRESS?
ARE YOU SURE?
COULDN'T IT BECOME A PROBLEM LATER?
EVEN IF WE DID ATTACK THE FORTRESS, IT WOULDN'T FALL EASILY.
NOR IS IT NECESSARY TO PUSH OURSELVES TO CAPTURE IT.
LET US LEAVE THAT FORTRESS AND PRESS ON, YOUR HIGHNESS.
...ALL RIGHT.
IF YOU THINK THAT'S BEST, NARSUS.

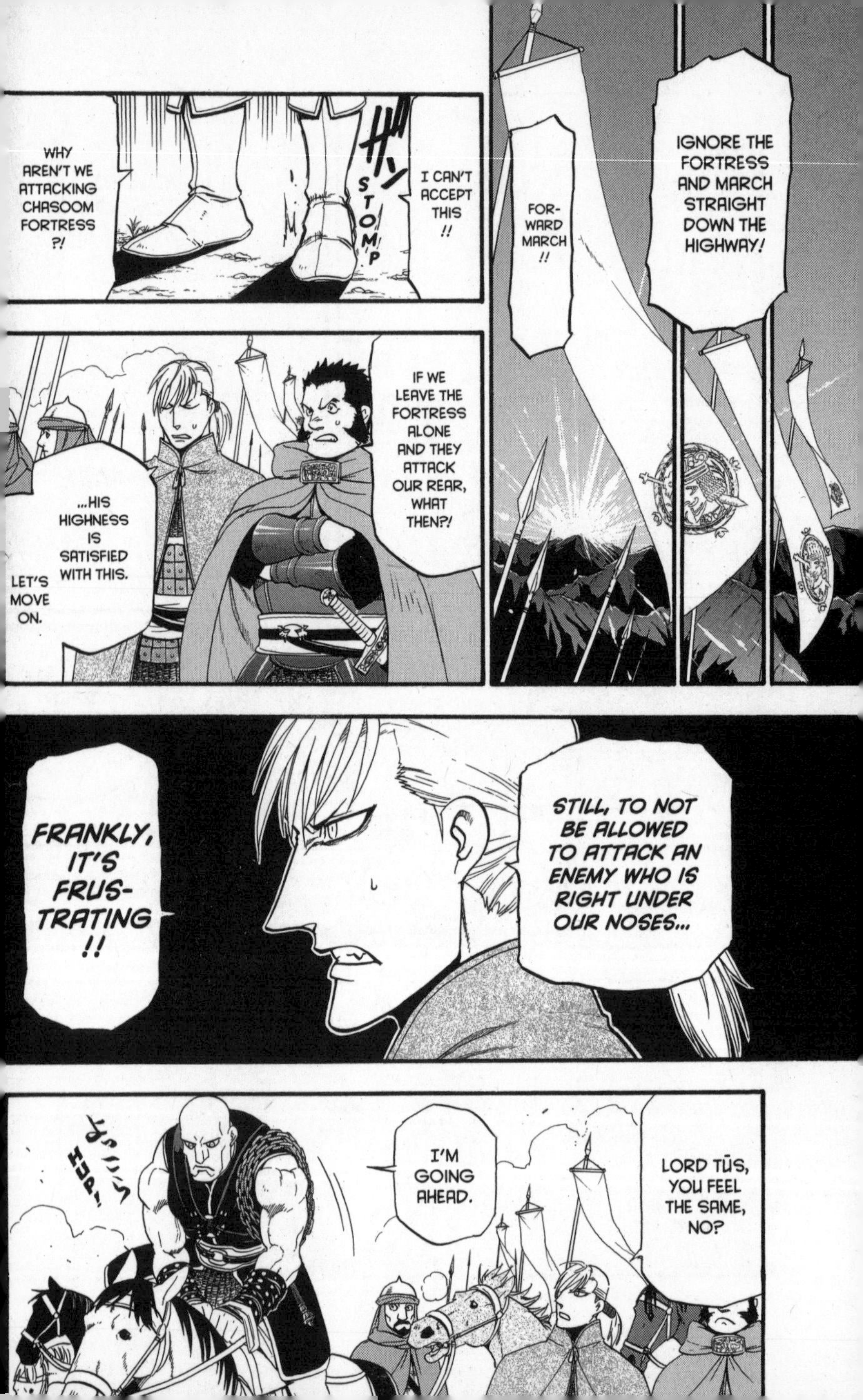

IGNORE THE FORTRESS AND MARCH STRAIGHT DOWN THE HIGHWAY!
FOR-WARD MARCH!!
I CAN'T ACCEPT THIS!!
STOMP
WHY AREN'T WE ATTACKING CHASOOM FORTRESS?!
IF WE LEAVE THE FORTRESS ALONE AND THEY ATTACK OUR REAR, WHAT THEN?!
...HIS HIGHNESS IS SATISFIED WITH THIS.
LET'S MOVE ON.
STILL, TO NOT BE ALLOWED TO ATTACK AN ENEMY WHO IS RIGHT UNDER OUR NOSES...
FRANKLY, IT'S FRUS-TRATING!!
LORD TŪS, YOU FEEL THE SAME, NO?
I'M GOING AHEAD.
HUP!

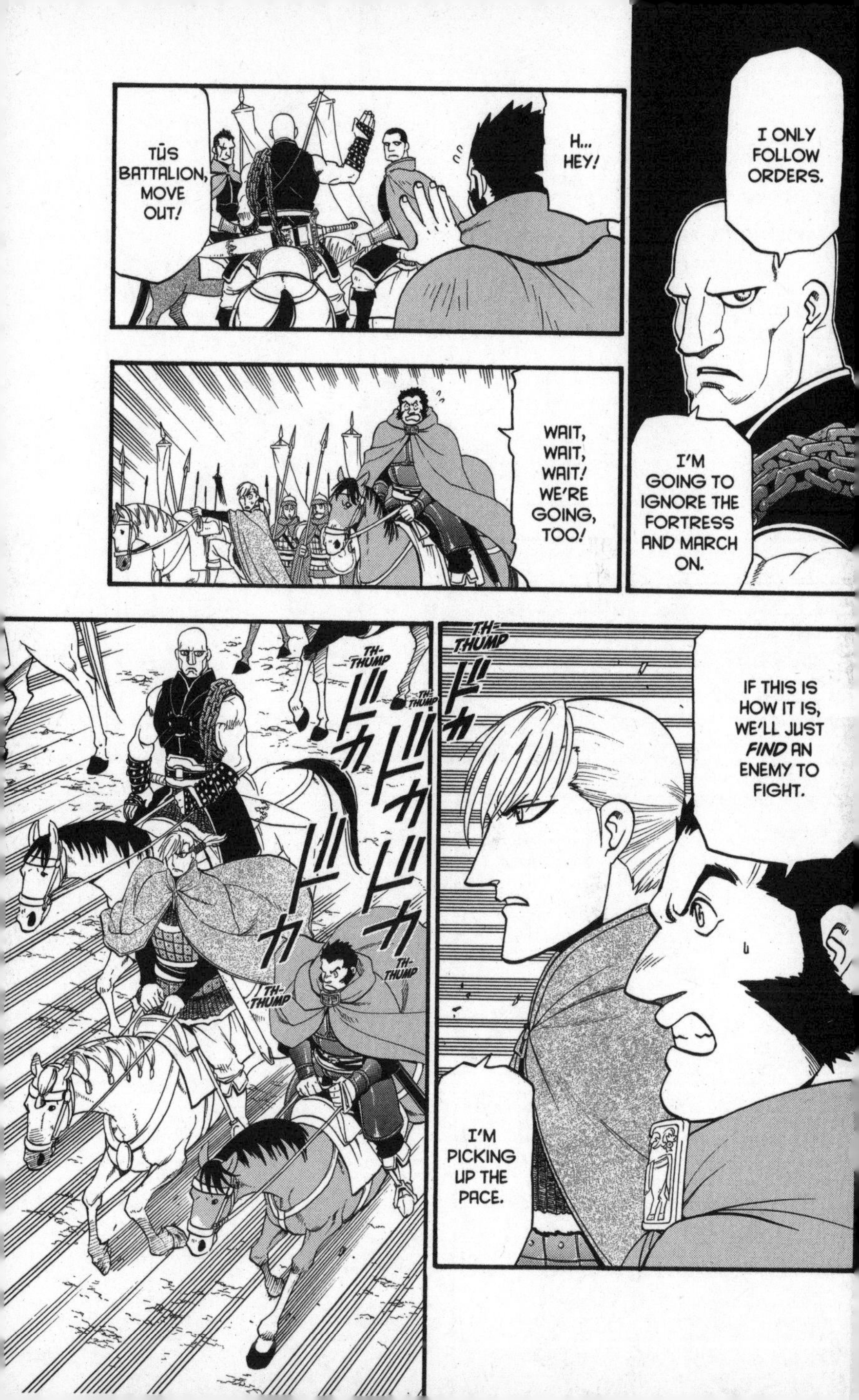
I ONLY FOLLOW ORDERS.
I'M GOING TO IGNORE THE FORTRESS AND MARCH ON.
H... HEY!
TŪS BATTALION, MOVE OUT!
WAIT, WAIT, WAIT! WE'RE GOING, TOO!
TH-THUMP
IF THIS IS HOW IT IS, WE'LL JUST *FIND* AN ENEMY TO FIGHT.
I'M PICKING UP THE PACE.
TH-THUMP
TH-THUMP
TH-THUMP
TH-THUMP

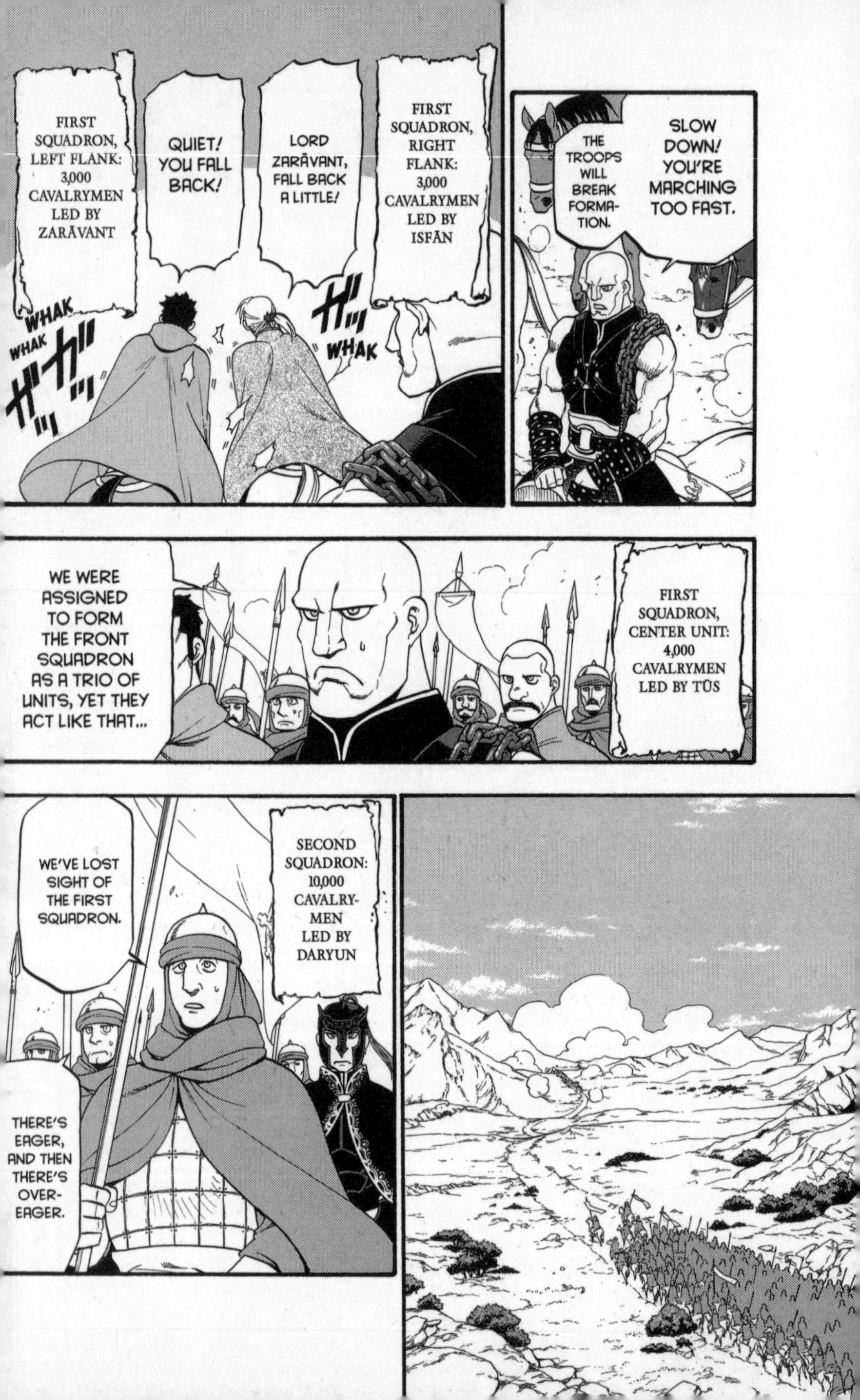
SLOW DOWN! YOU'RE MARCHING TOO FAST.
THE TROOPS WILL BREAK FORMATION.
FIRST SQUADRON, RIGHT FLANK: 3,000 CAVALRYMEN LED BY ISFĀN
LORD ZARĀVANT, FALL BACK A LITTLE!
ガッ
WHAK
QUIET! YOU FALL BACK!
FIRST SQUADRON, LEFT FLANK: 3,000 CAVALRYMEN LED BY ZARĀVANT
WHAK WHAK
FIRST SQUADRON, CENTER UNIT: 4,000 CAVALRYMEN LED BY TŪS
WE WERE ASSIGNED TO FORM THE FRONT SQUADRON AS A TRIO OF UNITS, YET THEY ACT LIKE THAT...
SECOND SQUADRON: 10,000 CAVALRYMEN LED BY DARYUN
WE'VE LOST SIGHT OF THE FIRST SQUADRON.
THERE'S EAGER, AND THEN THERE'S OVER-EAGER.

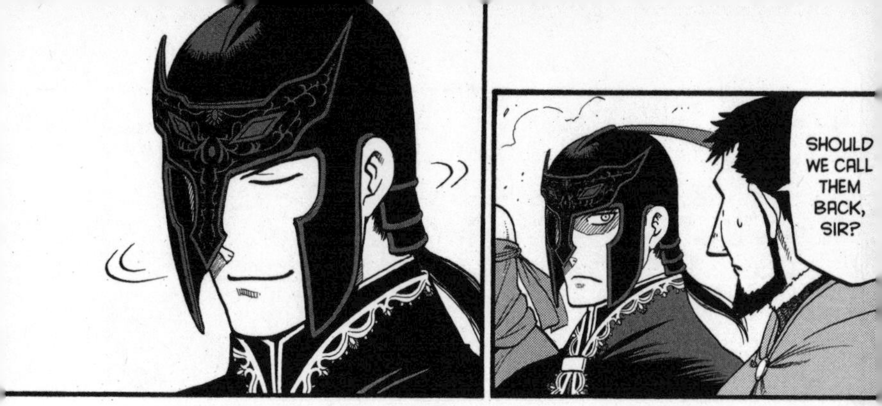
SHOULD WE CALL THEM BACK, SIR?

Chapter 67: Parsian Propriety

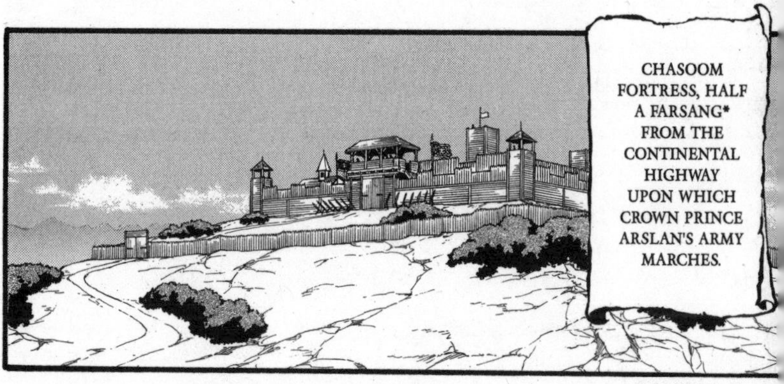
CHASOOM FORTRESS, HALF A FARSANG* FROM THE CONTINENTAL HIGHWAY UPON WHICH CROWN PRINCE ARSLAN'S ARMY MARCHES.

*ABOUT 2.5 KM

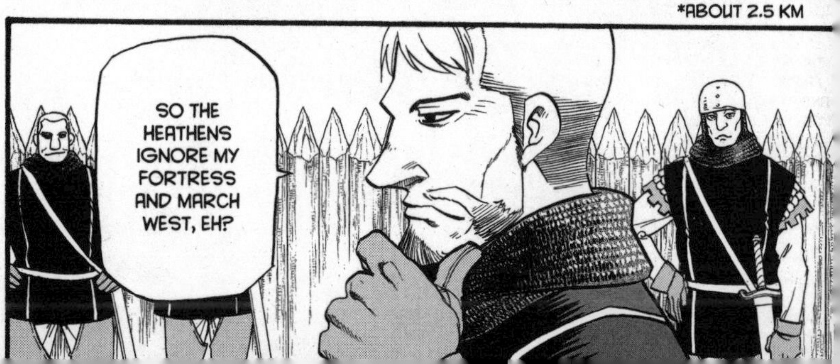
SO THE HEATHENS IGNORE MY FORTRESS AND MARCH WEST, EH?

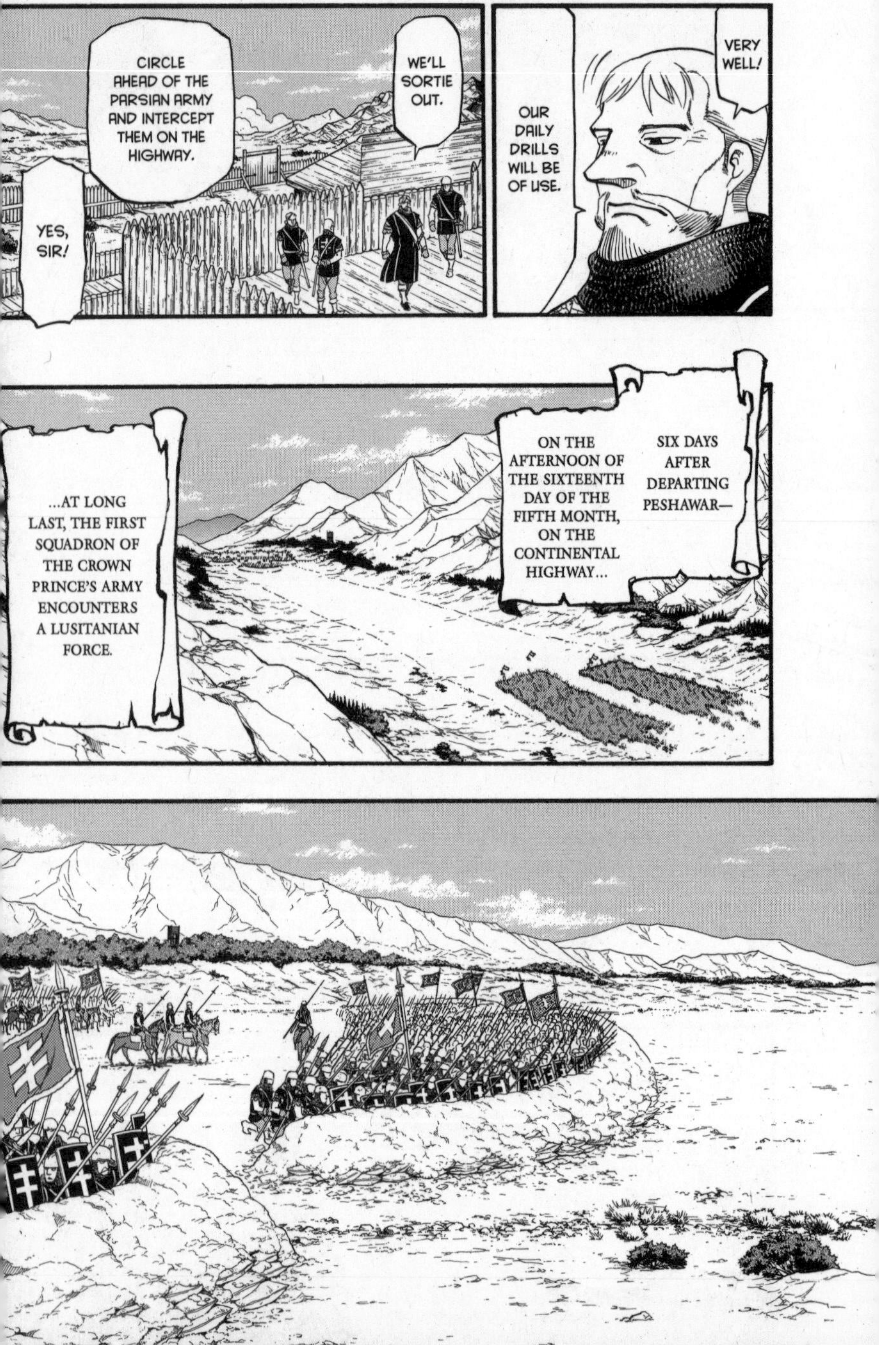
VERY WELL!
OUR DAILY DRILLS WILL BE OF USE.
WE'LL SORTIE OUT.
CIRCLE AHEAD OF THE PARSIAN ARMY AND INTERCEPT THEM ON THE HIGHWAY.
YES, SIR!
SIX DAYS AFTER DEPARTING PESHAWAR—
ON THE AFTERNOON OF THE SIXTEENTH DAY OF THE FIFTH MONTH, ON THE CONTINENTAL HIGHWAY...
...AT LONG LAST, THE FIRST SQUADRON OF THE CROWN PRINCE'S ARMY ENCOUNTERS A LUSITANIAN FORCE.

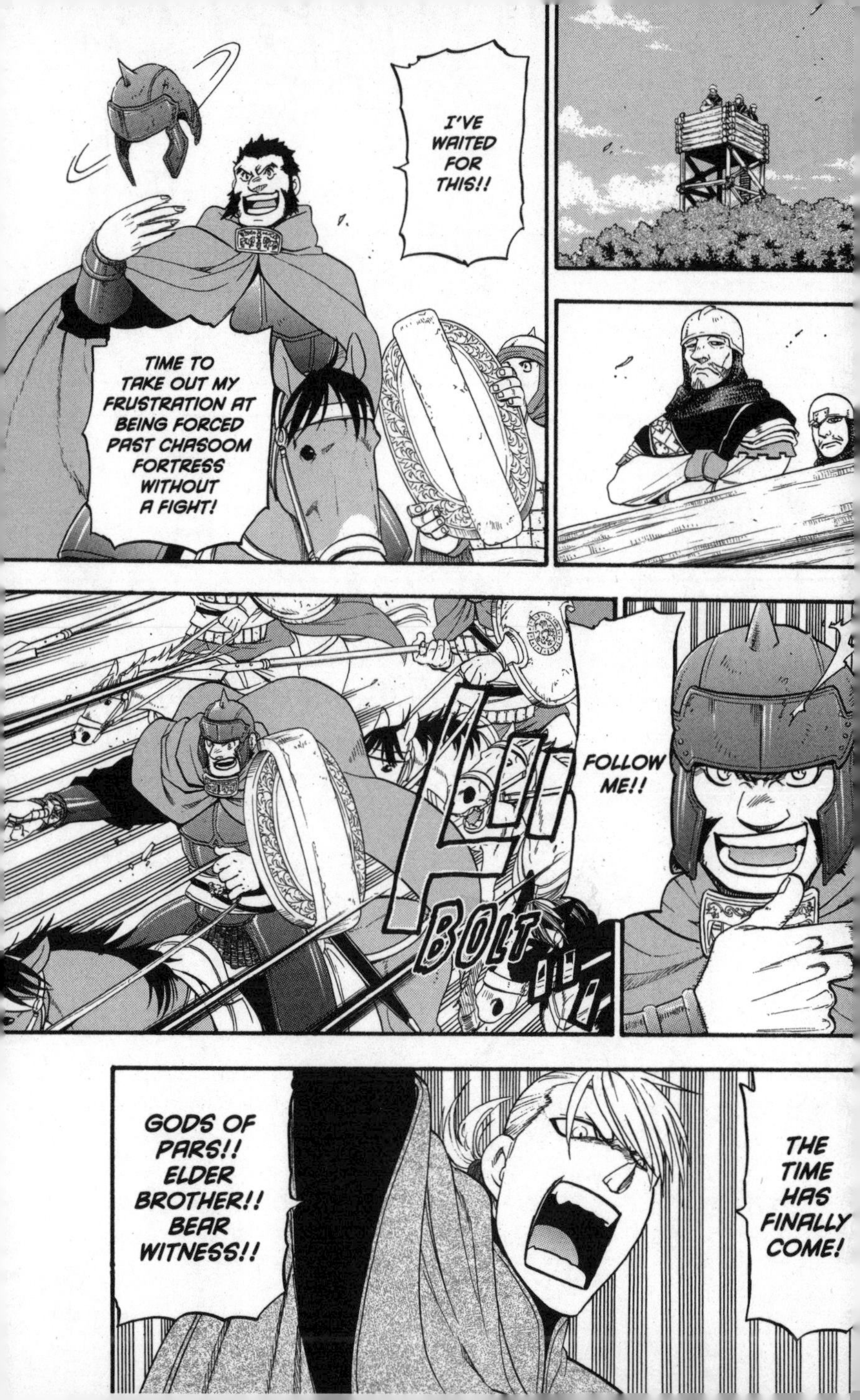
I'VE WAITED FOR THIS!!
TIME TO TAKE OUT MY FRUSTRATION AT BEING FORCED PAST CHASOOM FORTRESS WITHOUT A FIGHT!
FOLLOW ME!!
BOLT!!!
THE TIME HAS FINALLY COME!
GODS OF PARS!! ELDER BROTHER!! BEAR WITNESS!!

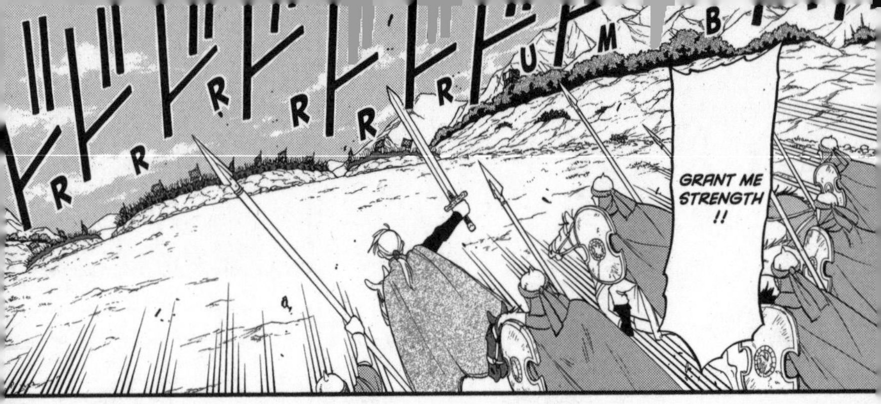
RRRRRRUMB
GRANT ME STRENGTH !!
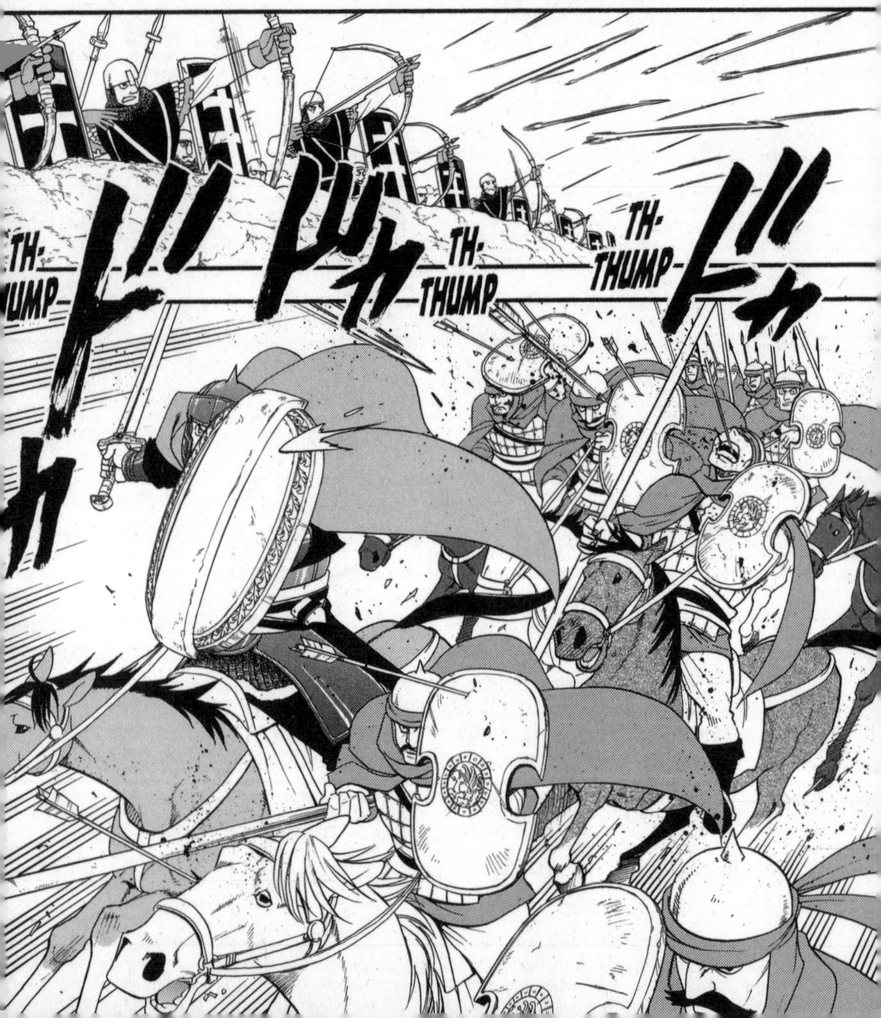
TH-THUMP
TH-THUMP
TH-UMP

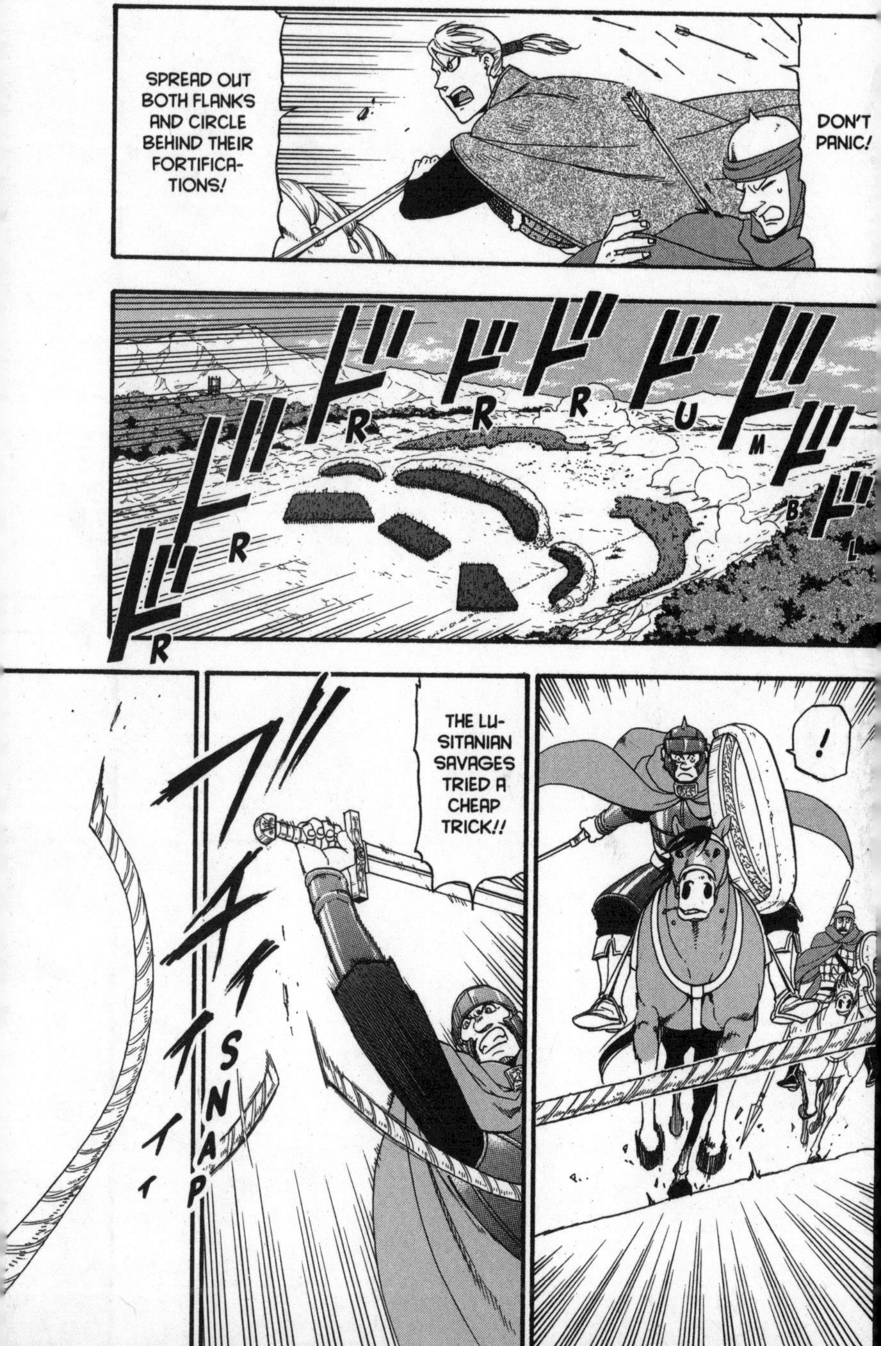
DON'T PANIC!
SPREAD OUT BOTH FLANKS AND CIRCLE BEHIND THEIR FORTIFICA-TIONS!
RRRRRUMBL
!
THE LU-SITANIAN SAVAGES TRIED A CHEAP TRICK!!
SNAP

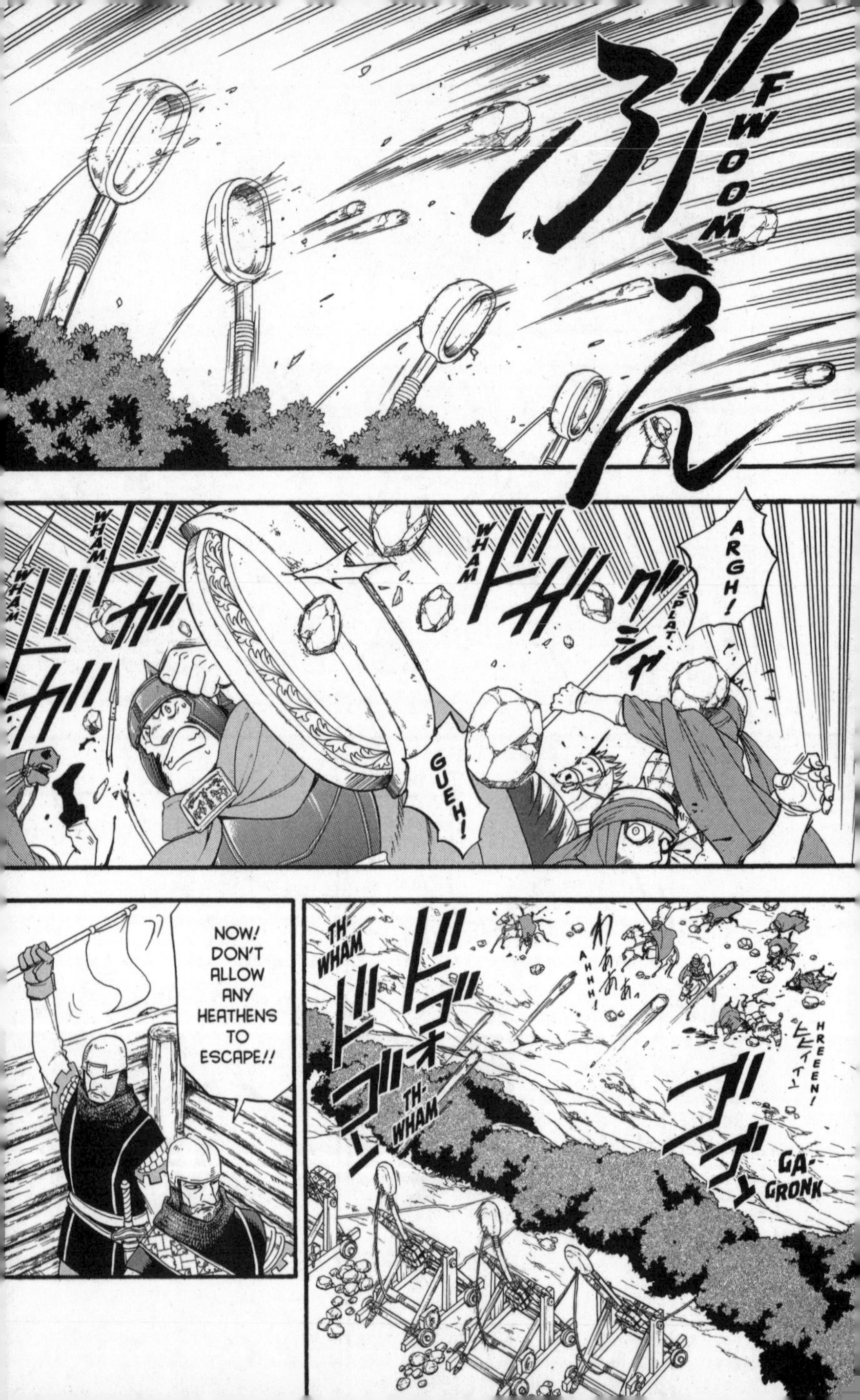

FWOOM
ふぉん
ARGH!
SPLAT
グシャ
WHAM
ドガ
WHAM
ドガ
WHAM
ドガ
GUEH!
TH-WHAM
ドゴォ
TH-WHAM
ドゴォ
わああああ
AHHH!
ヒヒイィン
HREEEN!
ゴゴン
GA-GRONK
NOW! DON'T ALLOW ANY HEATHENS TO ESCAPE!!

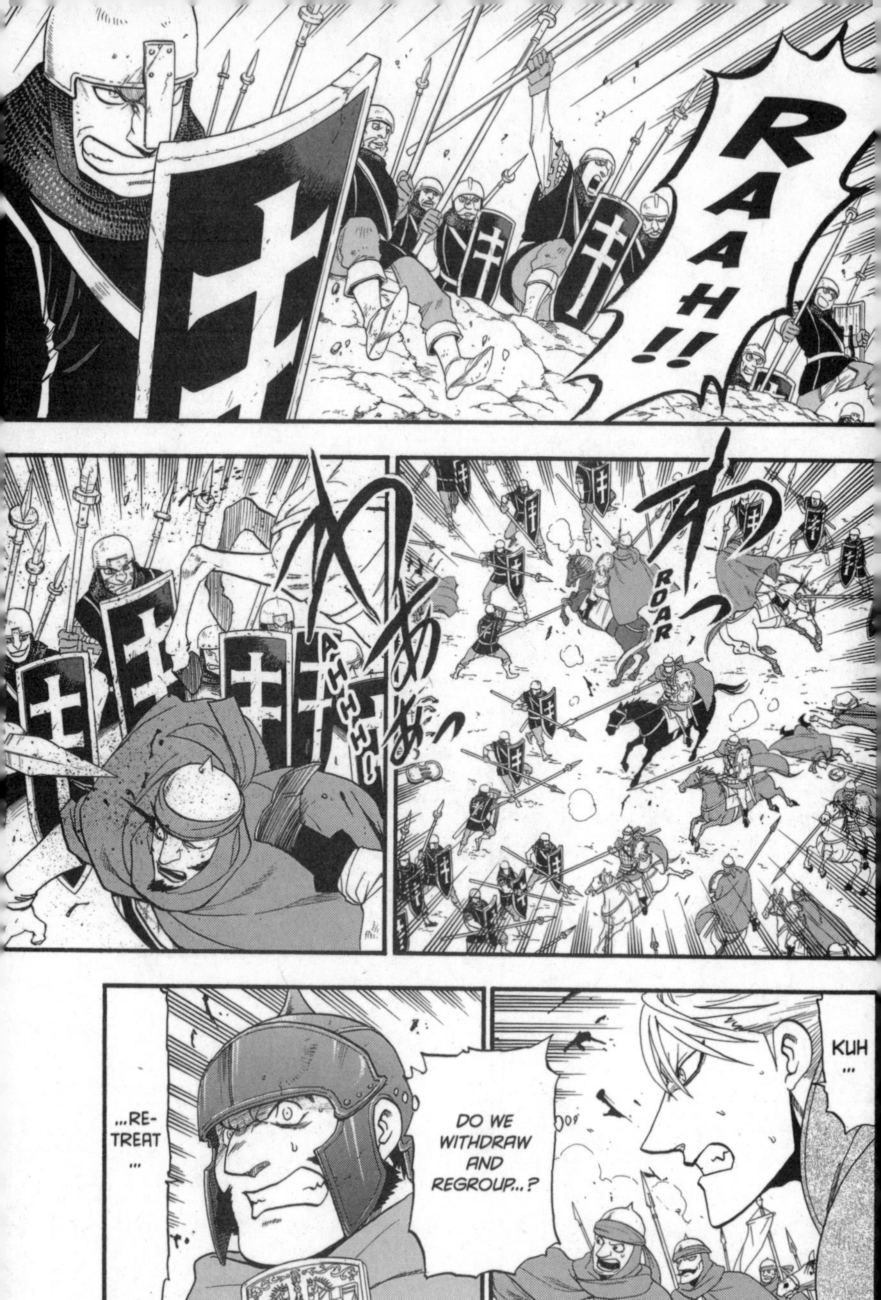
RAAAH!!
ROAR
AHHH!
KUH ...
DO WE WITHDRAW AND REGROUP...?
...RE-TREAT ...

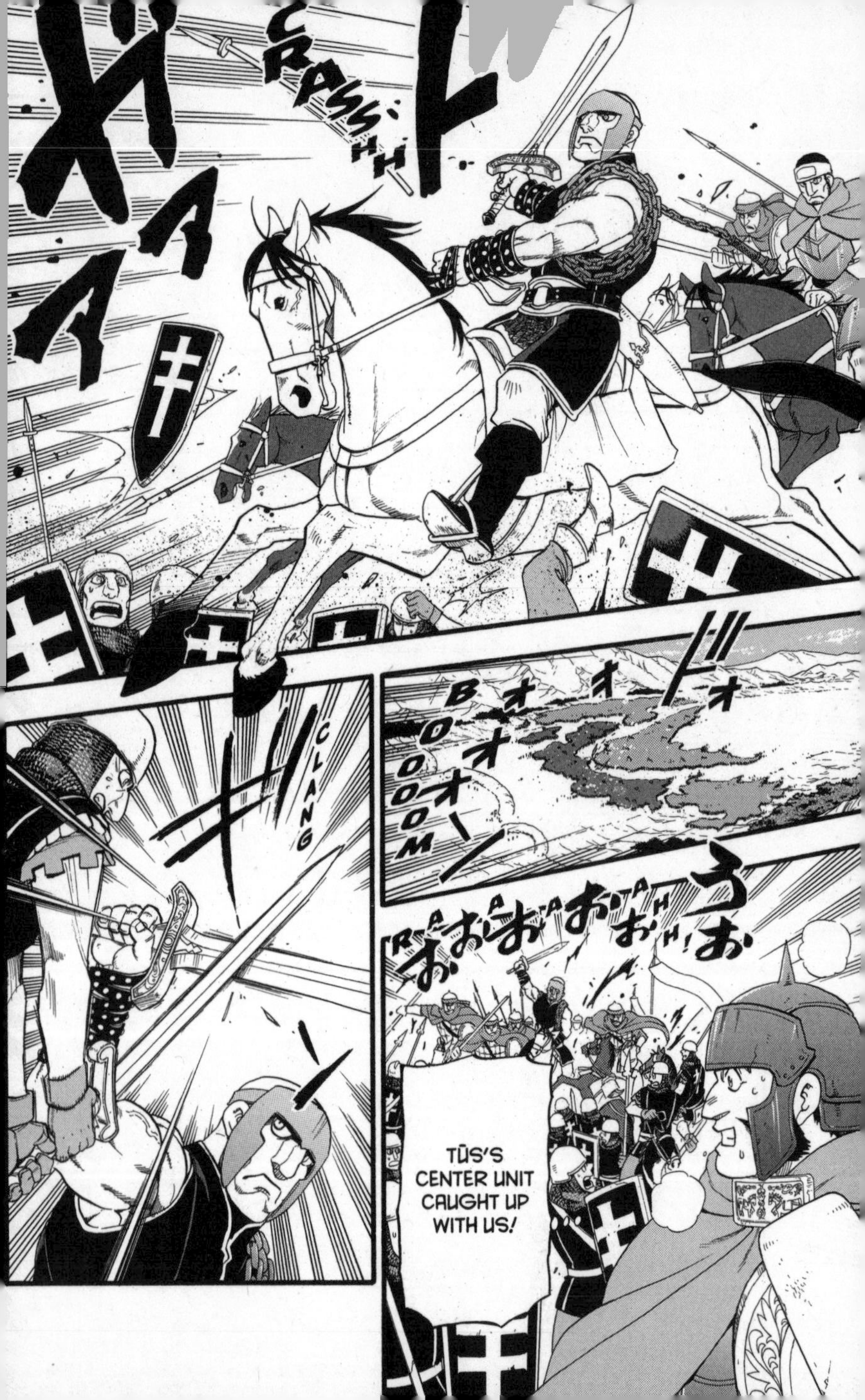
CRASSHH
BOOOOOM
RAAAAHH!
TŪS'S CENTER UNIT CAUGHT UP WITH US!
CLANG

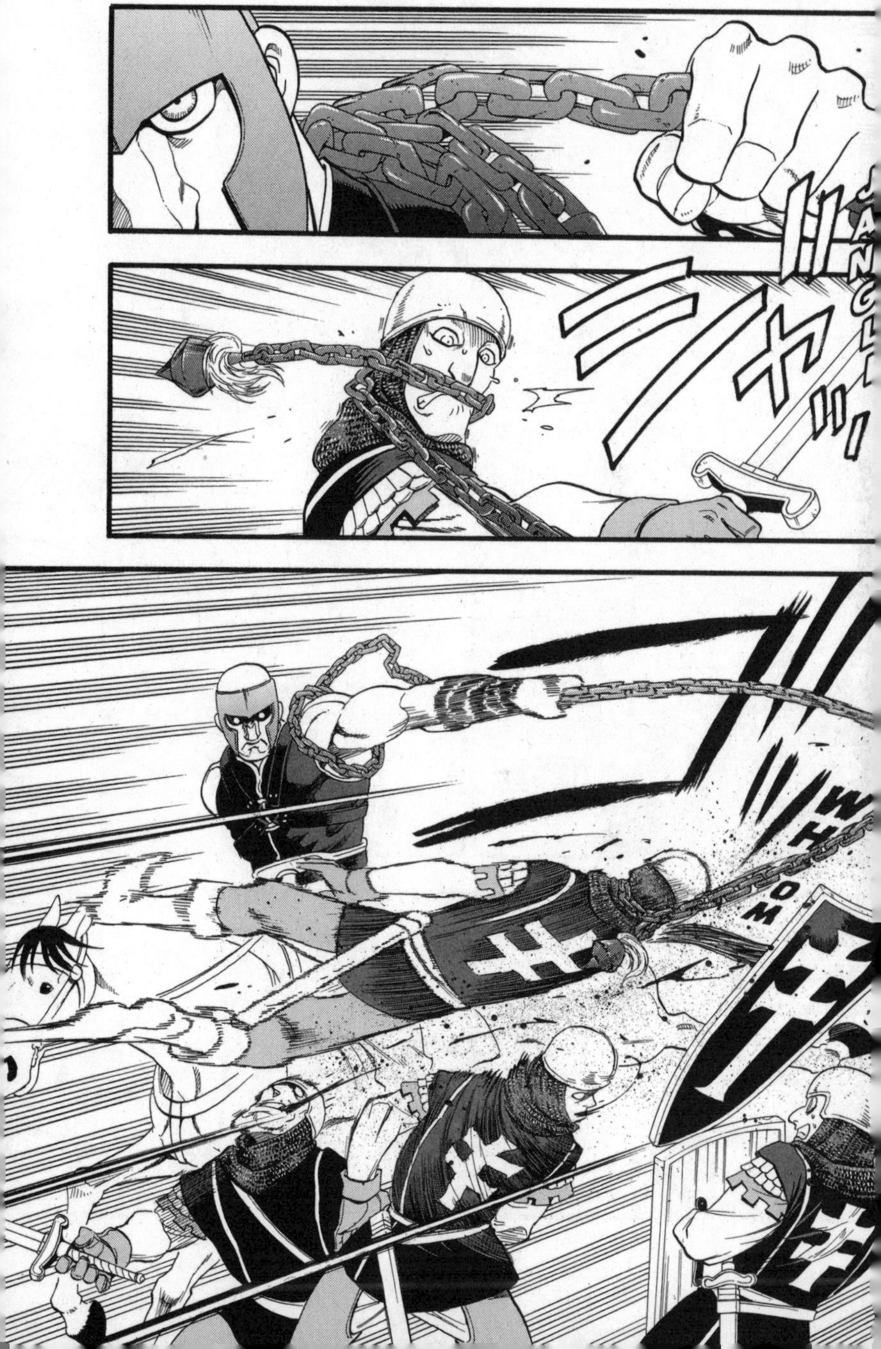
JANGL
WHOOM

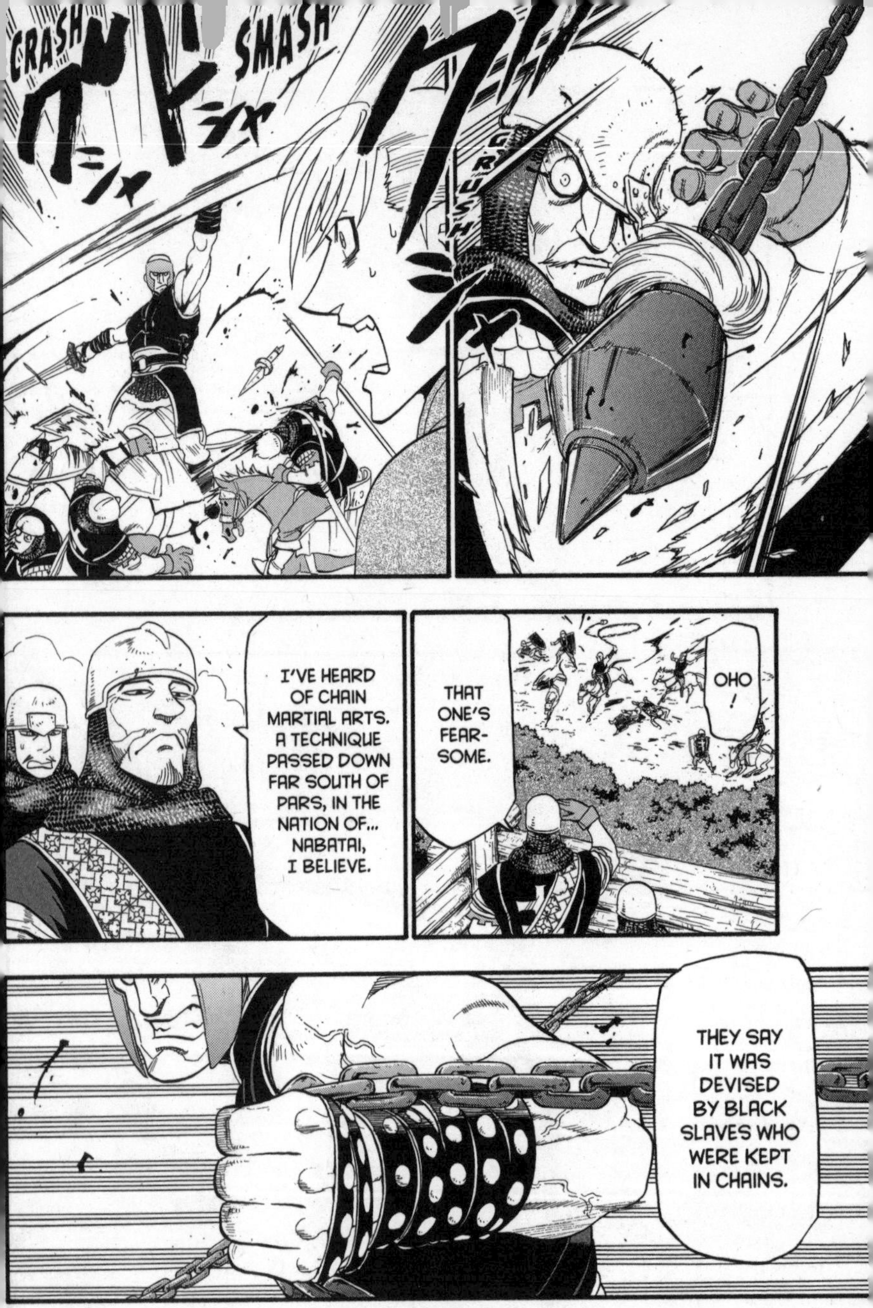
GRUSH
SMASH
CRASH
OHO!
THAT ONE'S FEAR-SOME.
I'VE HEARD OF CHAIN MARTIAL ARTS. A TECHNIQUE PASSED DOWN FAR SOUTH OF PARS, IN THE NATION OF... NABATAI, I BELIEVE.
THEY SAY IT WAS DEVISED BY BLACK SLAVES WHO WERE KEPT IN CHAINS.

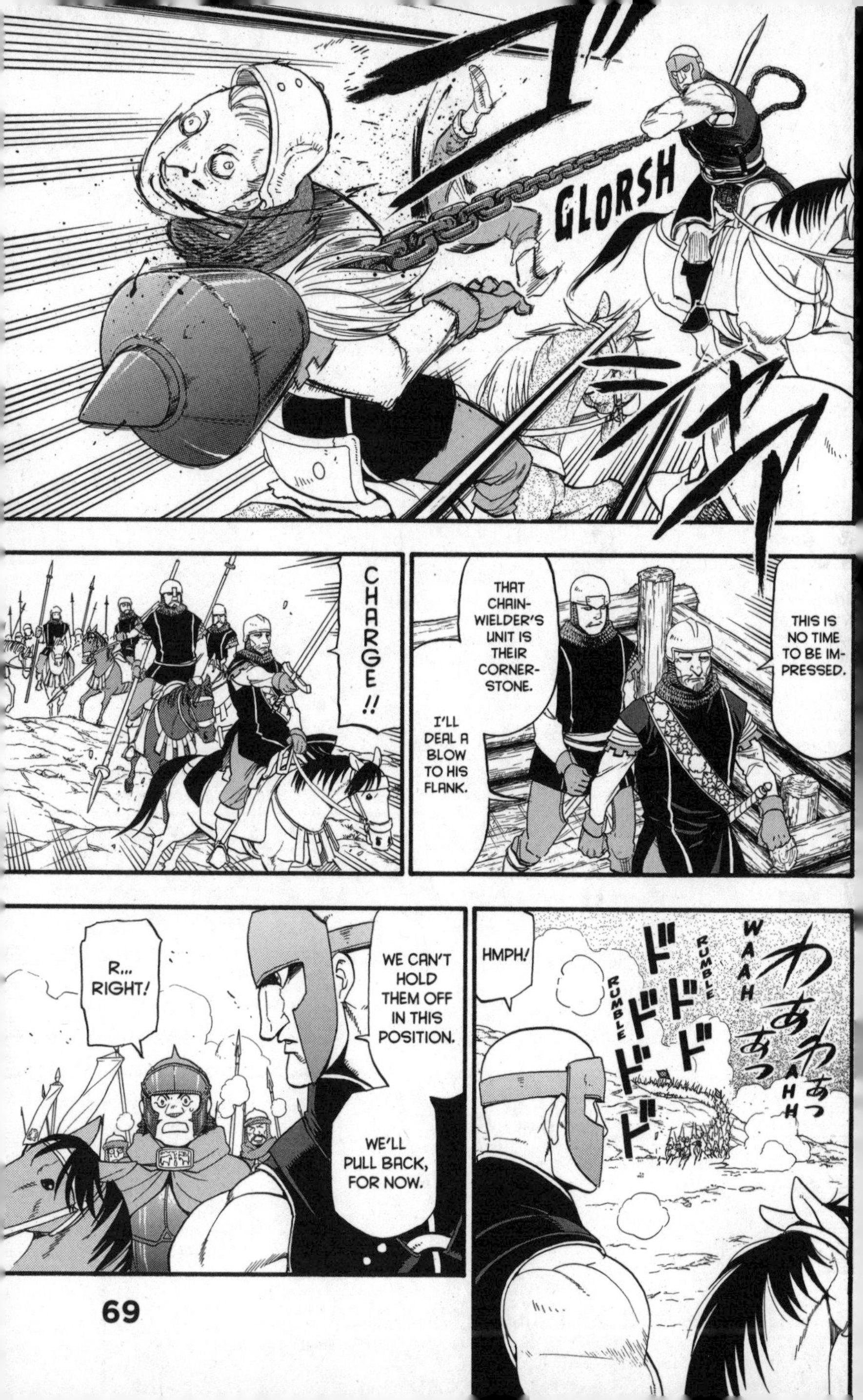
GLORSH
THIS IS NO TIME TO BE IMPRESSED.
THAT CHAIN-WIELDER'S UNIT IS THEIR CORNERSTONE.
I'LL DEAL A BLOW TO HIS FLANK.
CHARGE!!
WAAH
AHH
RUMBLE
RUMBLE
HMPH!
WE CAN'T HOLD THEM OFF IN THIS POSITION.
WE'LL PULL BACK, FOR NOW.
R... RIGHT!

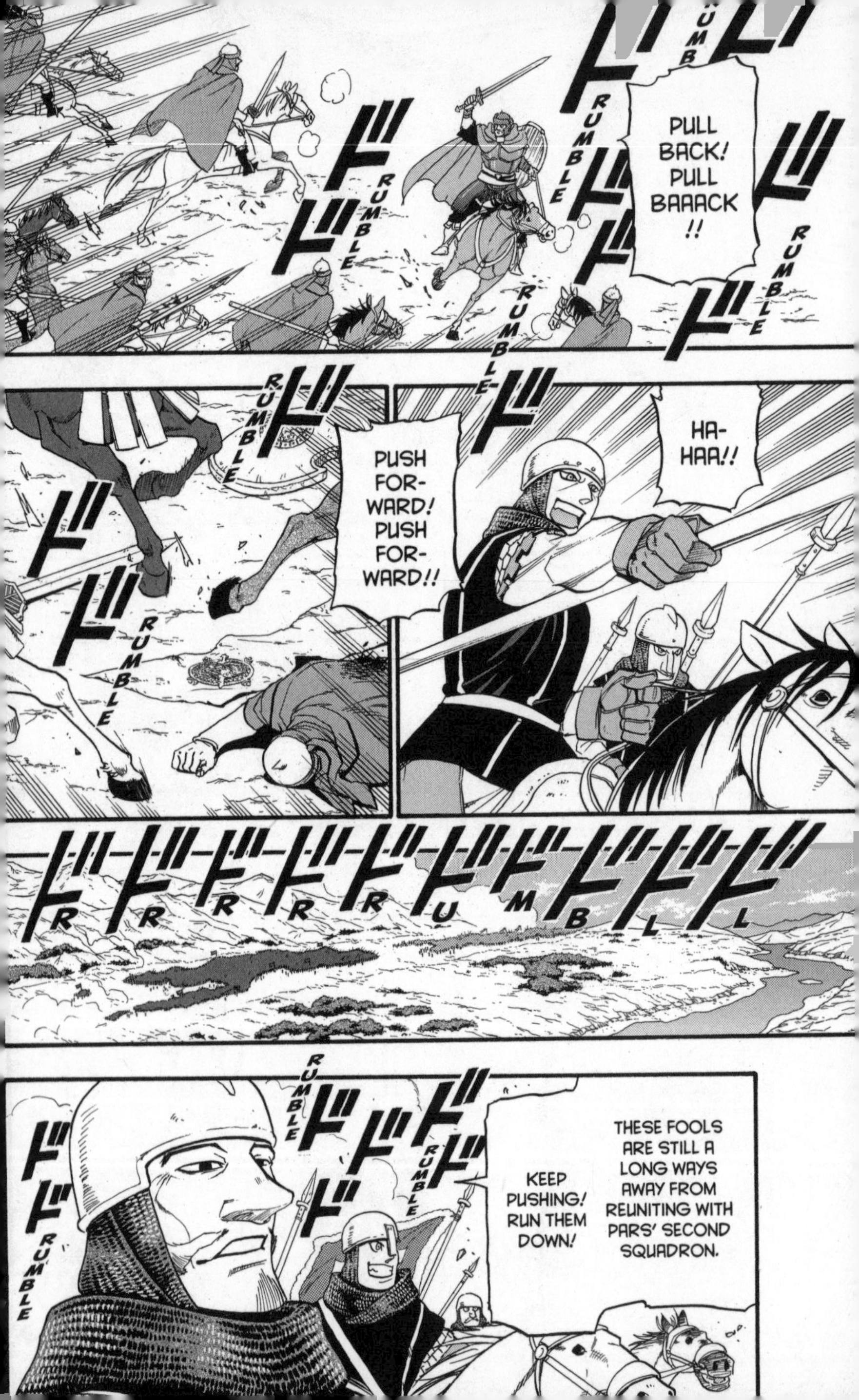
RUMBLE
PULL BACK! PULL BAAACK!!
RUMBLE
RUMBLE
RUMBLE
HA-HAA!!
RUMBLE
PUSH FOR-WARD! PUSH FOR-WARD!!
RUMBLE
RUMBLE
RRRRRUMBLL
THESE FOOLS ARE STILL A LONG WAYS AWAY FROM REUNITING WITH PARS' SECOND SQUADRON.
KEEP PUSHING! RUN THEM DOWN!
RUMBLE
RUMBLE
RUMBLE

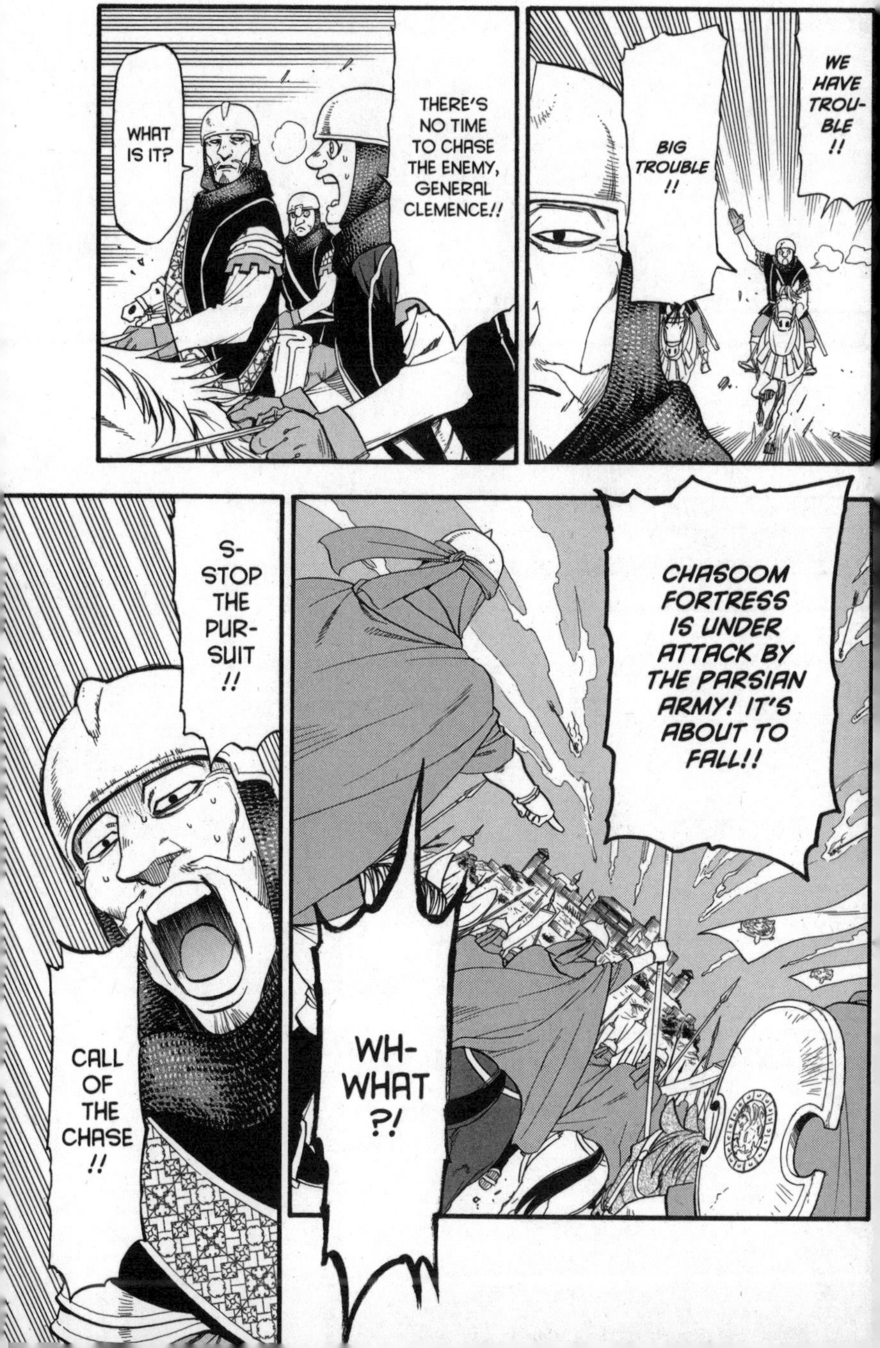
WE HAVE TROUBLE !!
BIG TROUBLE !!
THERE'S NO TIME TO CHASE THE ENEMY, GENERAL CLEMENCE!!
WHAT IS IT?
CHASOOM FORTRESS IS UNDER ATTACK BY THE PARSIAN ARMY! IT'S ABOUT TO FALL!!
WH-WHAT ?!
S-STOP THE PURSUIT !!
CALL OF THE CHASE !!

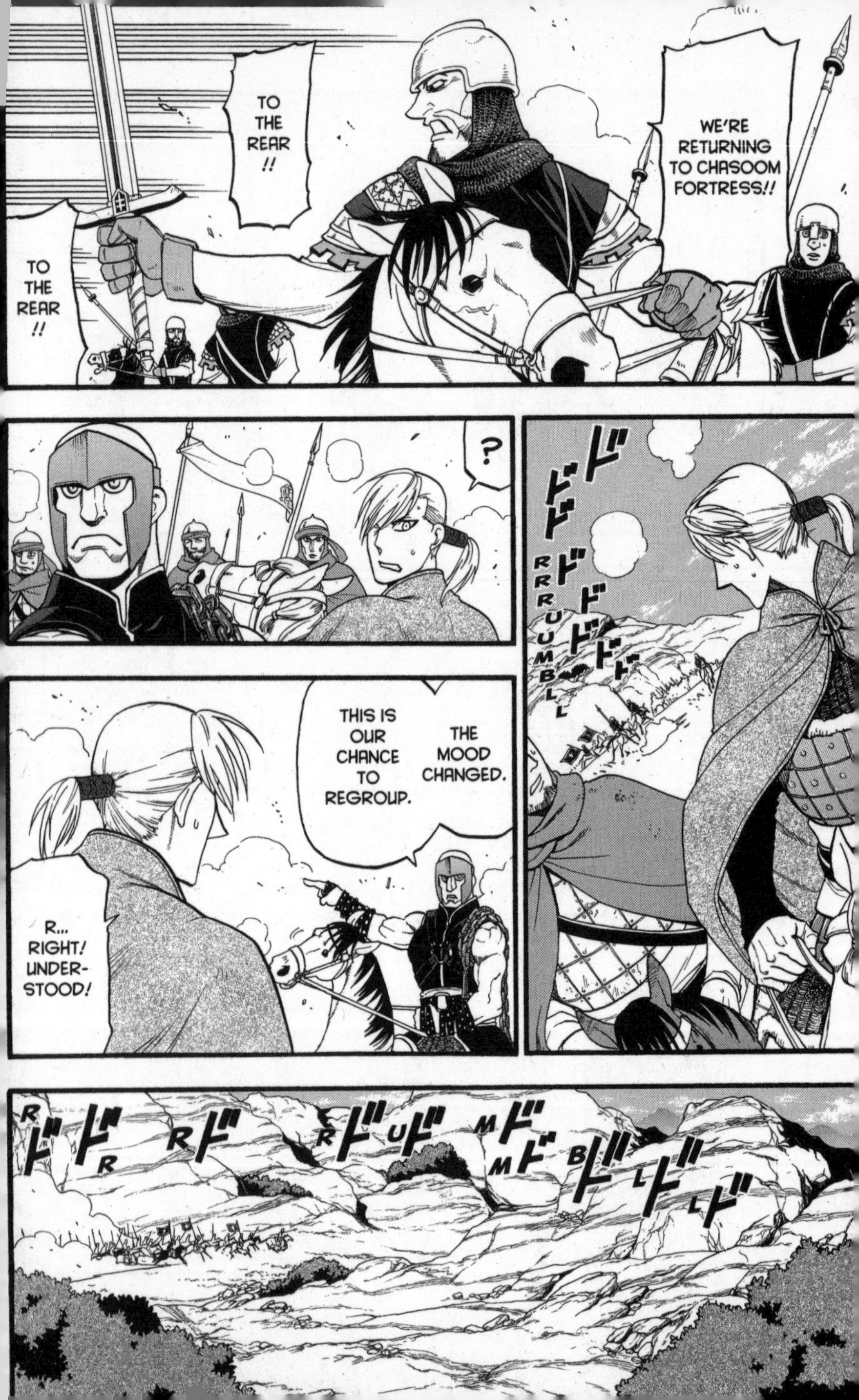

WE'RE RETURNING TO CHASOOM FORTRESS!!
TO THE REAR!!
TO THE REAR!!
ドドドドドドドドド
RRRUMBLL
?
THE MOOD CHANGED.
THIS IS OUR CHANCE TO REGROUP.
R... RIGHT! UNDERSTOOD!
ドドドドドドドドドドド
RRRRUMMBLL

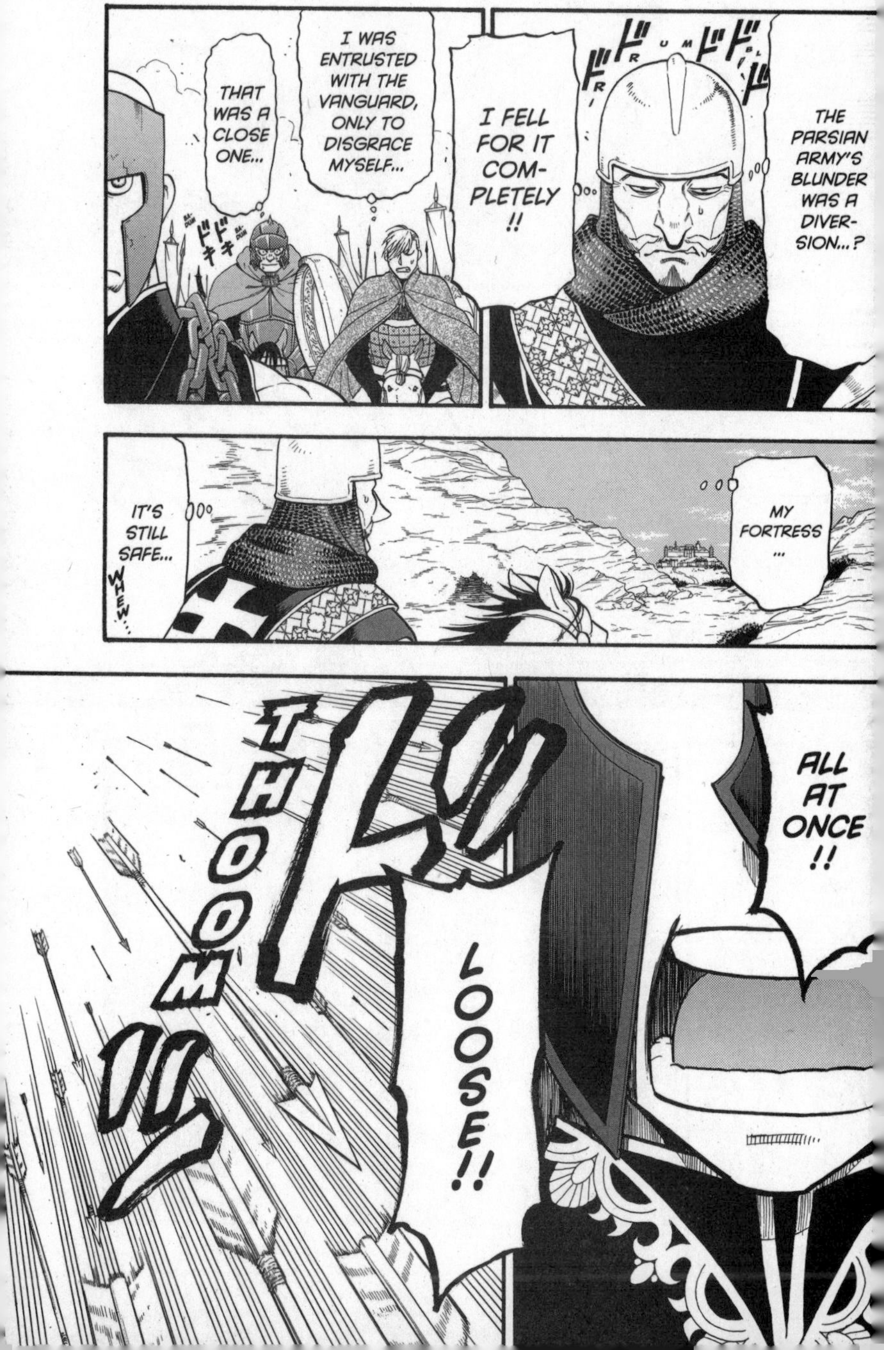
RUMBLE
THE PARSIAN ARMY'S BLUNDER WAS A DIVERSION...?
I FELL FOR IT COMPLETELY!!
I WAS ENTRUSTED WITH THE VANGUARD, ONLY TO DISGRACE MYSELF...
BA-DUM BA-DUM
THAT WAS A CLOSE ONE...
MY FORTRESS...
IT'S STILL SAFE...
WHEW...
ALL AT ONCE!!
LOOSE!!
THOOOM!!

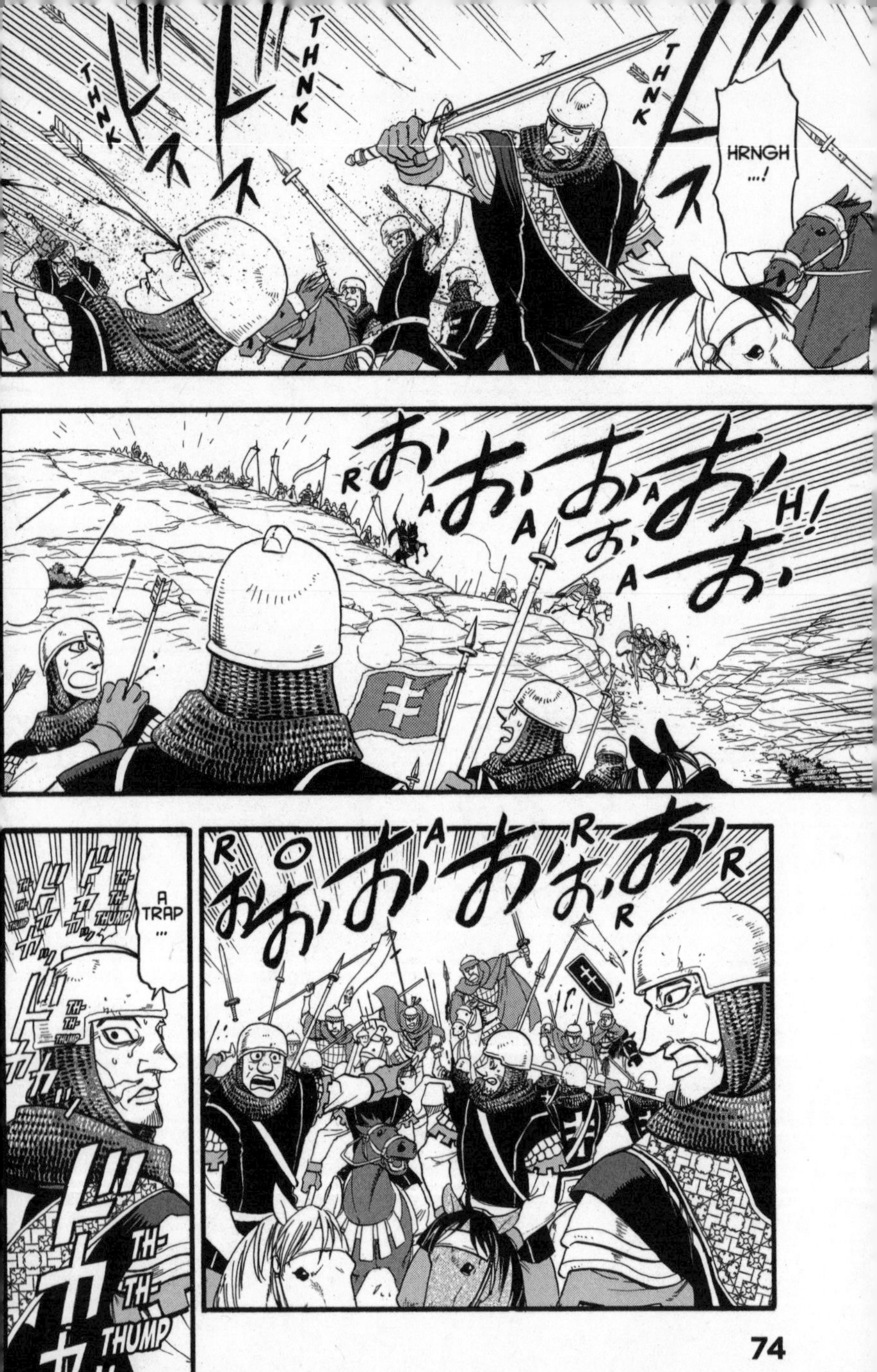
HRNGH ...!
THNK
THNK
THNK
RAAAAAH!
ROARRR
A TRAP ...
TH-TH-THUMP
TH-TH-THUMP
TH-TH-THUMP

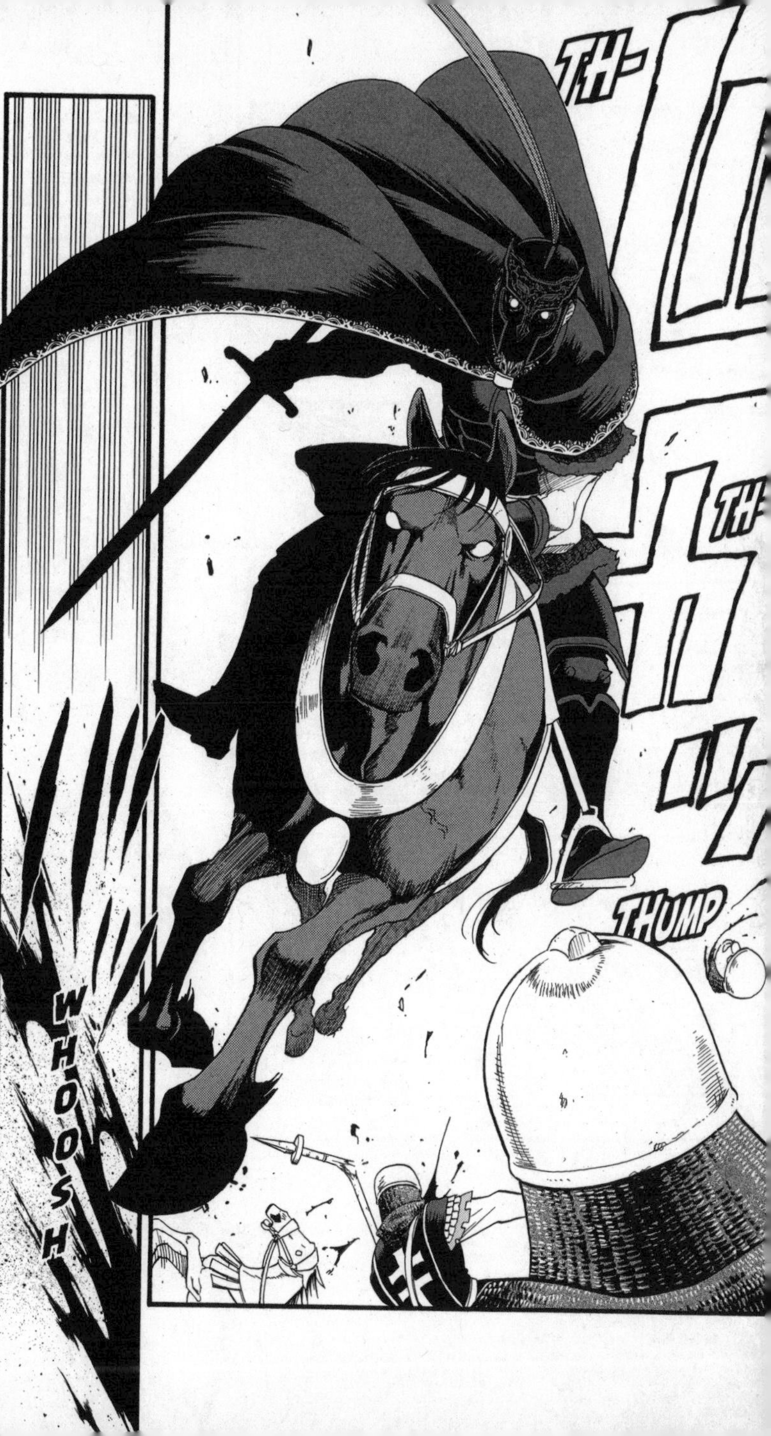
TH-
TH-
THUMP
WHOOSH

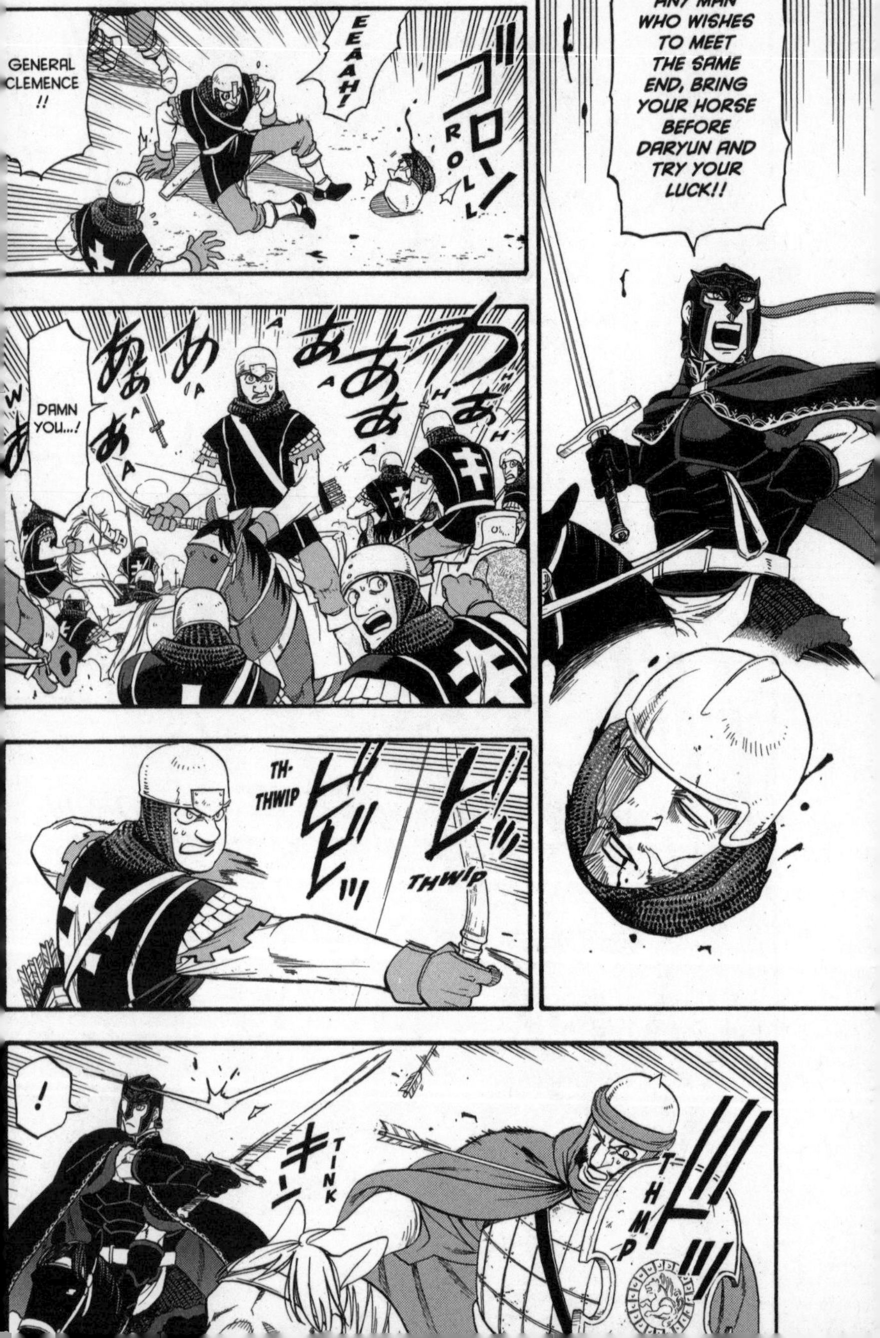
ANY MAN WHO WISHES TO MEET THE SAME END, BRING YOUR HORSE BEFORE DARYUN AND TRY YOUR LUCK!!
EEAAH!
ROLL
GENERAL CLEMENCE !!
WAAAHH
DAMN YOU...!
TH-THWIP
THWIP
THMP
TINK
!

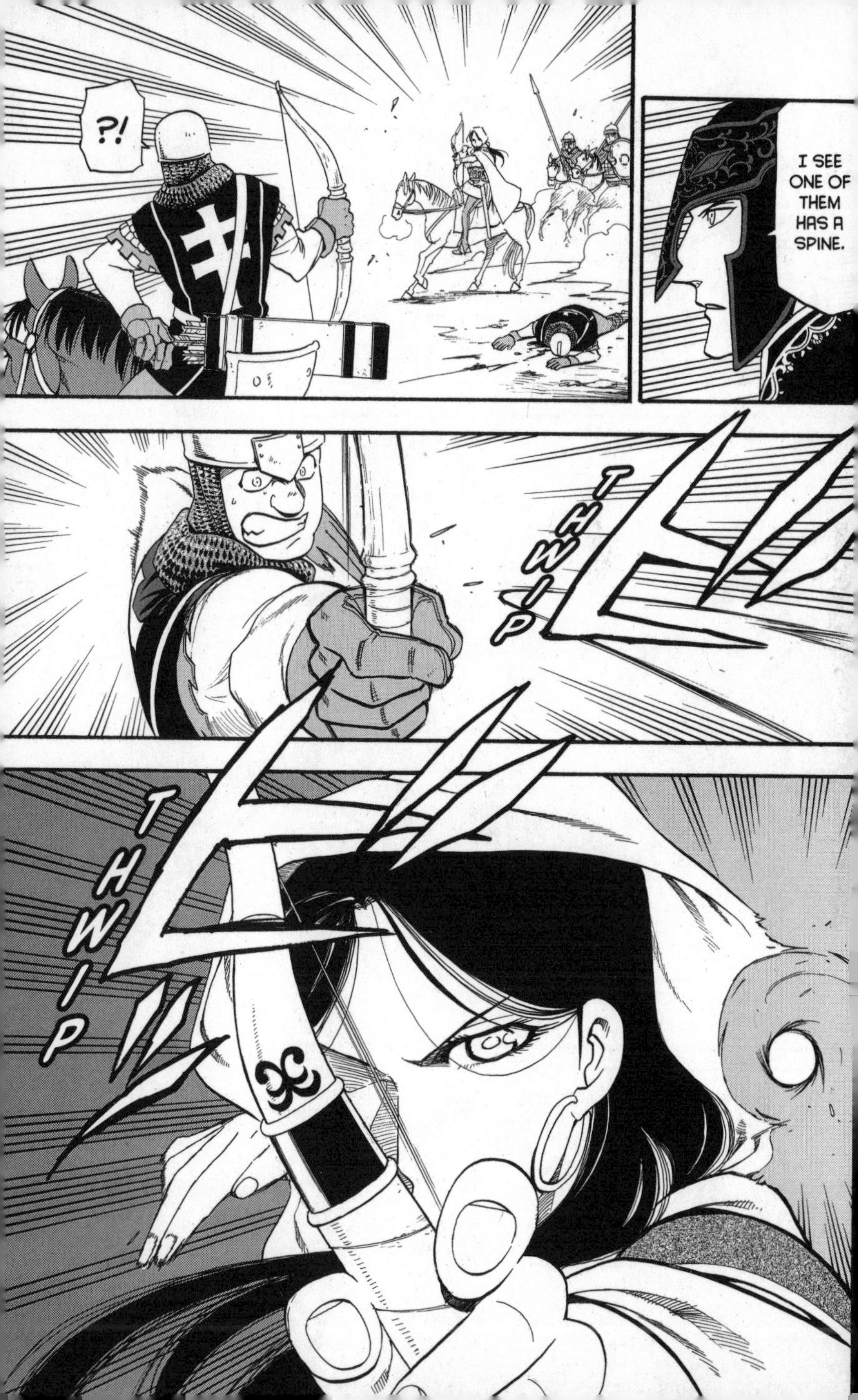
I SEE ONE OF THEM HAS A SPINE.
?!
THWIP
THWIP

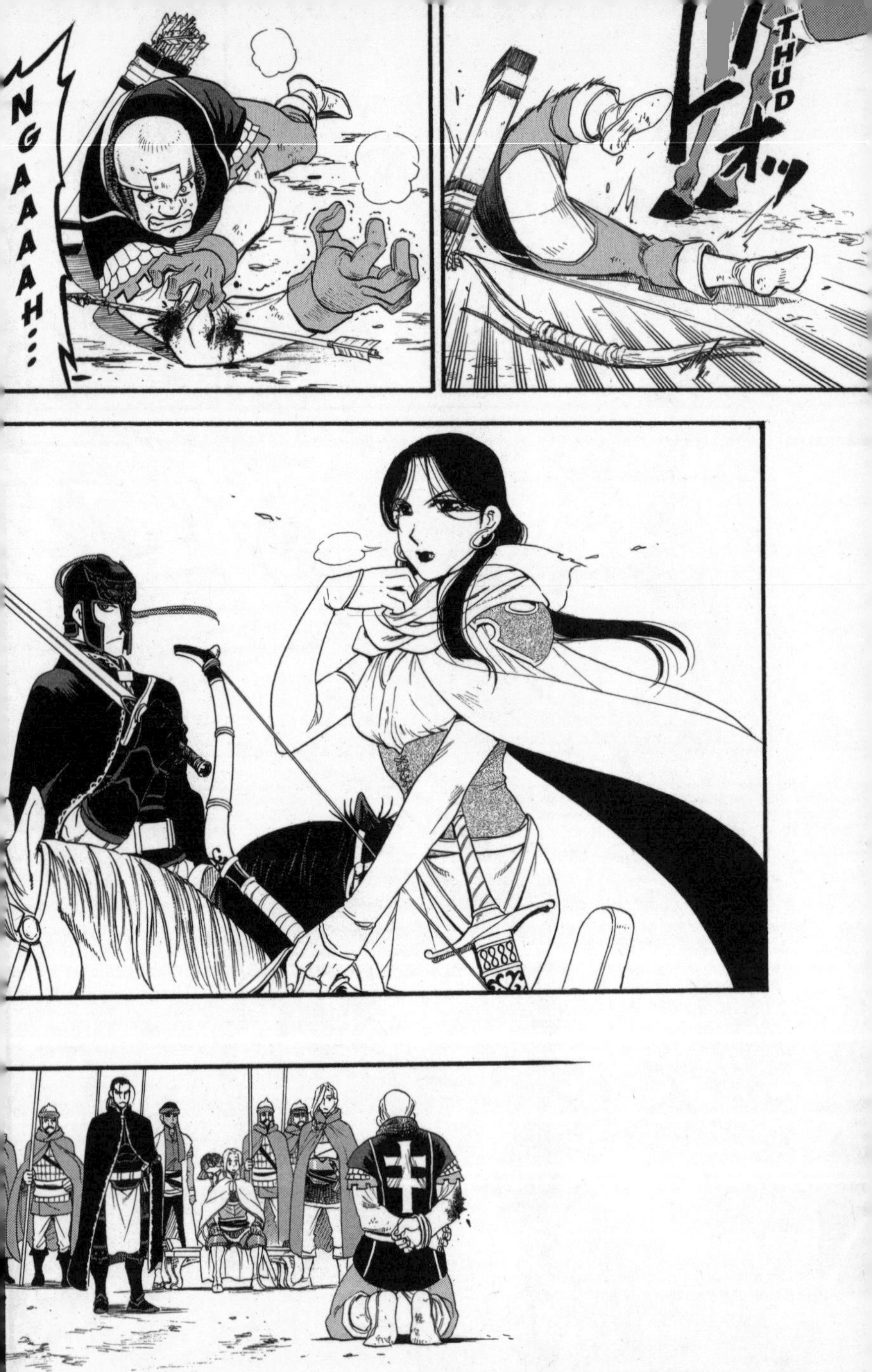
THUD
ドオッ
NGAAAAH...

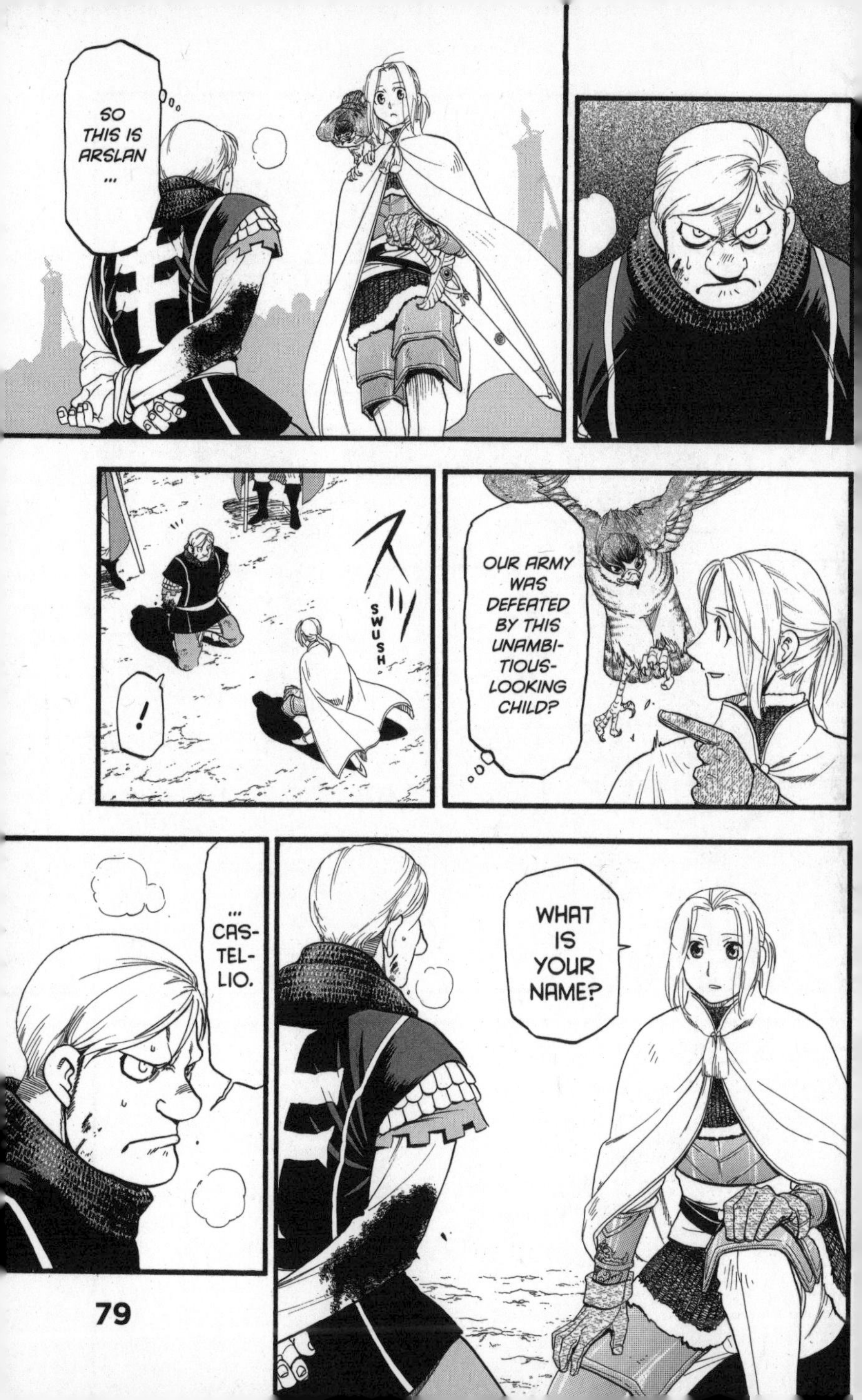
SO THIS IS ARSLAN ...
OUR ARMY WAS DEFEATED BY THIS UNAMBITIOUS-LOOKING CHILD?
SWUSH
!
WHAT IS YOUR NAME?
... CASTELLIO.

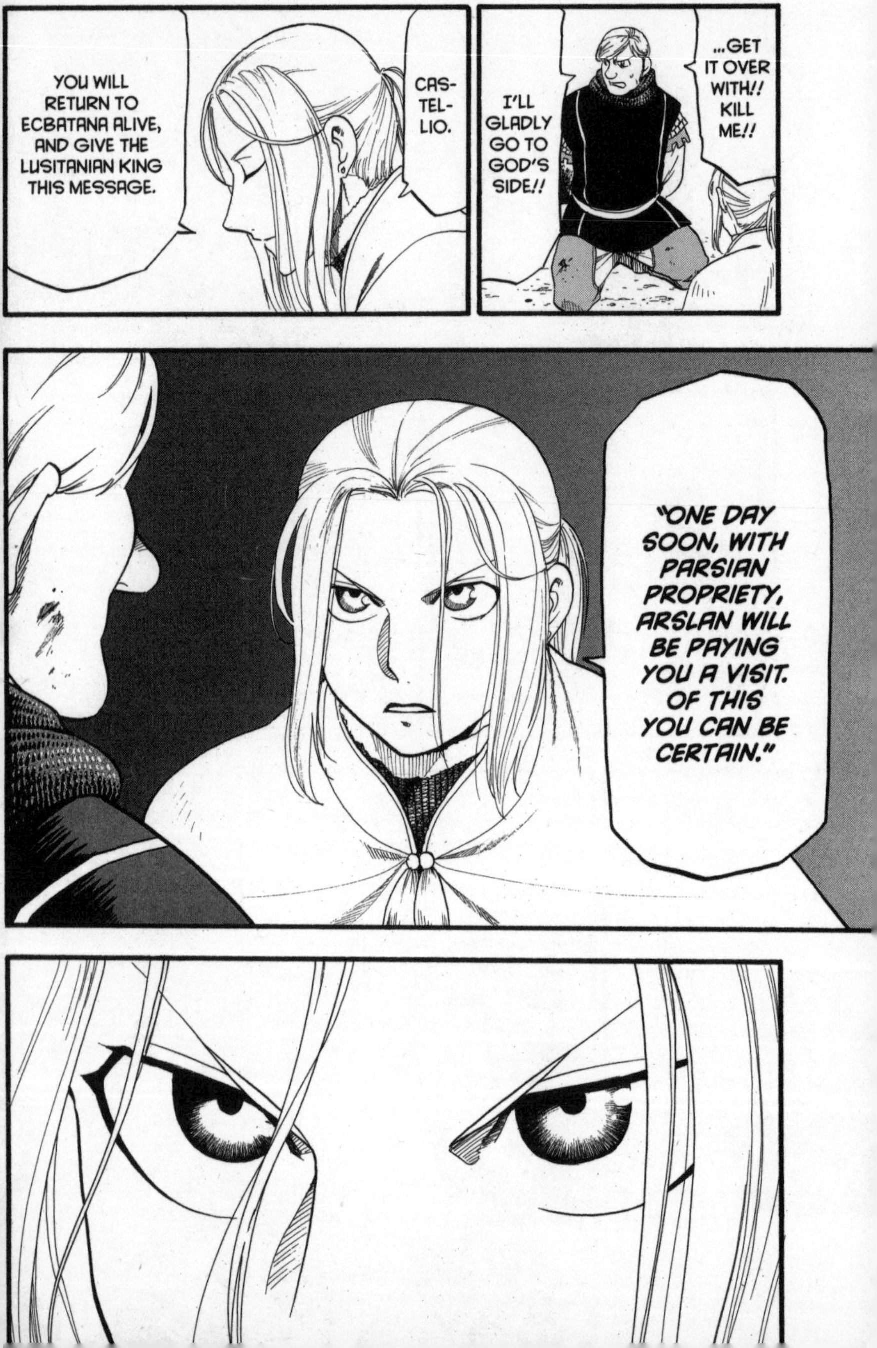
...GET IT OVER WITH!! KILL ME!!
I'LL GLADLY GO TO GOD'S SIDE!!
CAS-TEL-LIO.
YOU WILL RETURN TO ECBATANA ALIVE, AND GIVE THE LUSITANIAN KING THIS MESSAGE.
"ONE DAY SOON, WITH PARSIAN PROPRIETY, ARSLAN WILL BE PAYING YOU A VISIT. OF THIS YOU CAN BE CERTAIN."

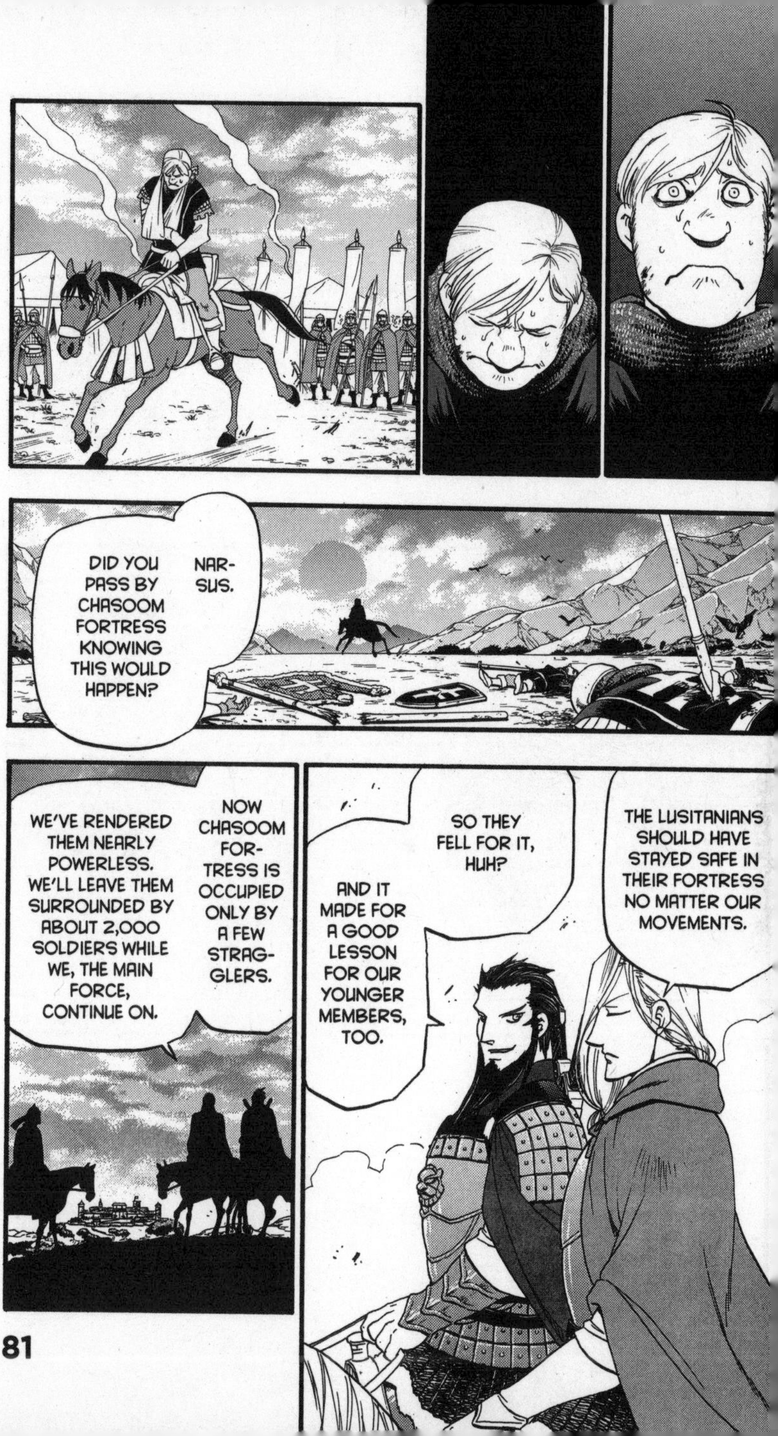

NARSUS.
DID YOU PASS BY CHASOOM FORTRESS KNOWING THIS WOULD HAPPEN?
THE LUSITANIANS SHOULD HAVE STAYED SAFE IN THEIR FORTRESS NO MATTER OUR MOVEMENTS.
SO THEY FELL FOR IT, HUH?
AND IT MADE FOR A GOOD LESSON FOR OUR YOUNGER MEMBERS, TOO.
NOW CHASOOM FORTRESS IS OCCUPIED ONLY BY A FEW STRAGGLERS.
WE'VE RENDERED THEM NEARLY POWERLESS. WE'LL LEAVE THEM SURROUNDED BY ABOUT 2,000 SOLDIERS WHILE WE, THE MAIN FORCE, CONTINUE ON.

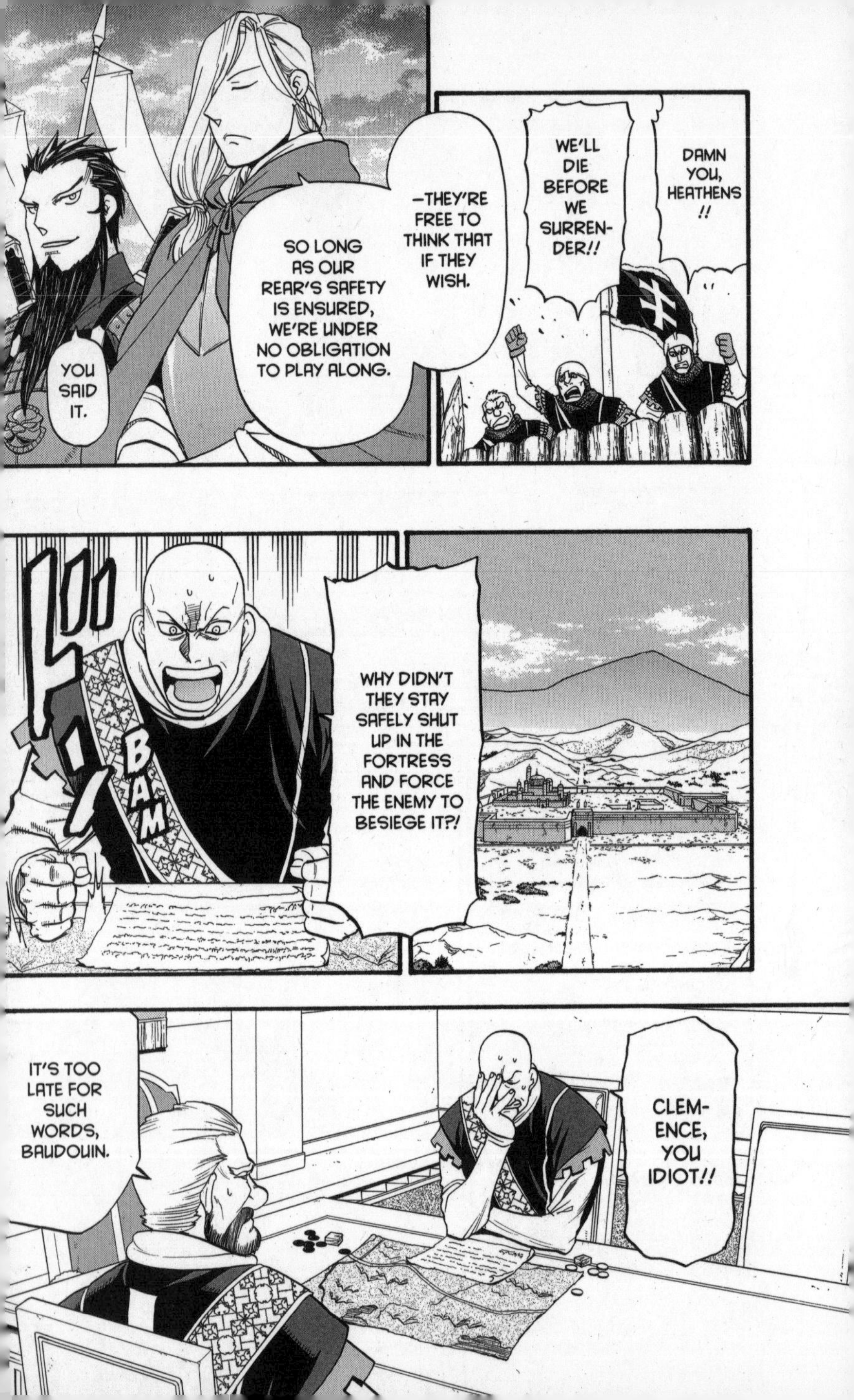
DAMN YOU, HEATHENS!!
WE'LL DIE BEFORE WE SURREN-DER!!
—THEY'RE FREE TO THINK THAT IF THEY WISH.
SO LONG AS OUR REAR'S SAFETY IS ENSURED, WE'RE UNDER NO OBLIGATION TO PLAY ALONG.
YOU SAID IT.
WHY DIDN'T THEY STAY SAFELY SHUT UP IN THE FORTRESS AND FORCE THE ENEMY TO BESIEGE IT?!
BAM
CLEM-ENCE, YOU IDIOT!!
IT'S TOO LATE FOR SUCH WORDS, BAUDOUIN.

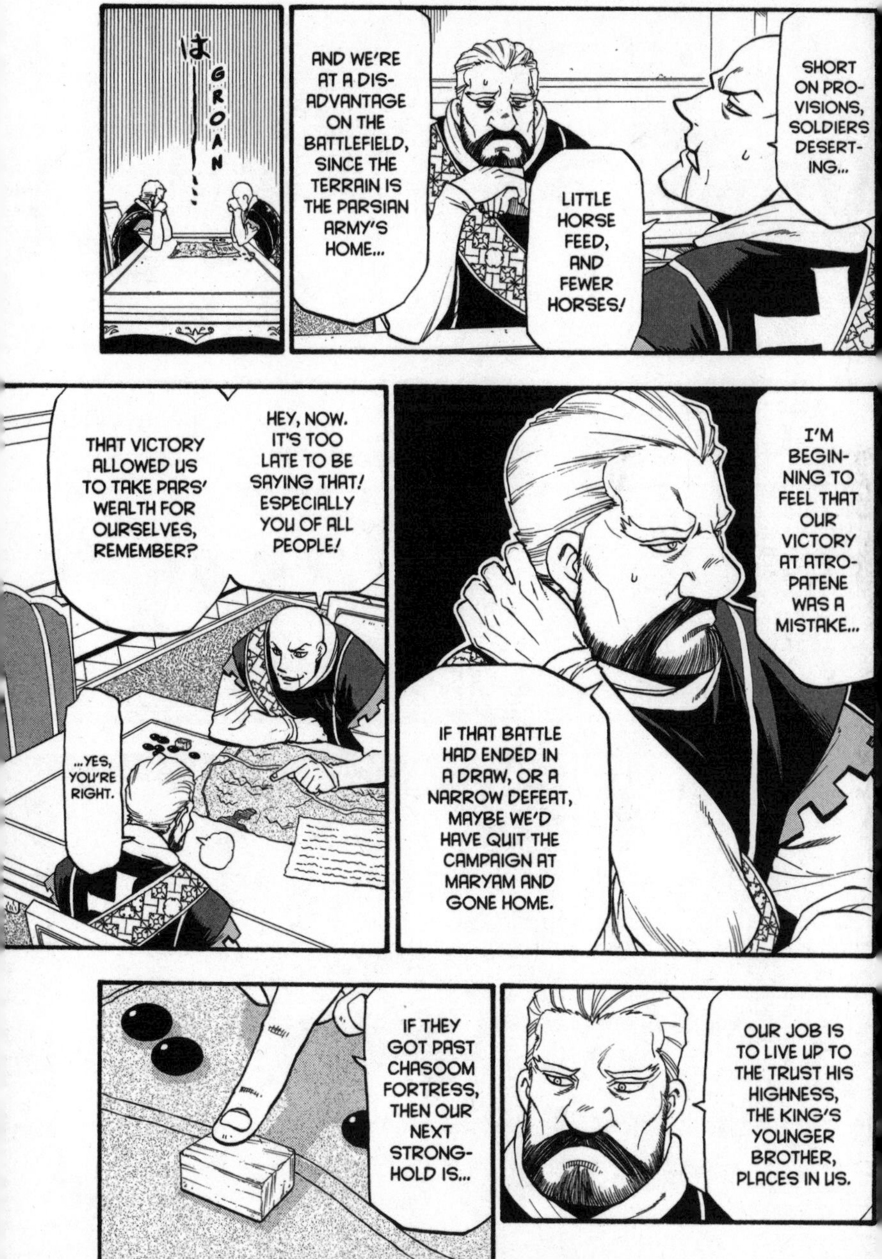
SHORT ON PROVISIONS, SOLDIERS DESERTING...
LITTLE HORSE FEED, AND FEWER HORSES!
AND WE'RE AT A DISADVANTAGE ON THE BATTLEFIELD, SINCE THE TERRAIN IS THE PARSIAN ARMY'S HOME...
は
GROAN
I'M BEGINNING TO FEEL THAT OUR VICTORY AT ATROPATENE WAS A MISTAKE...
IF THAT BATTLE HAD ENDED IN A DRAW, OR A NARROW DEFEAT, MAYBE WE'D HAVE QUIT THE CAMPAIGN AT MARYAM AND GONE HOME.
HEY, NOW. IT'S TOO LATE TO BE SAYING THAT! ESPECIALLY YOU OF ALL PEOPLE!
THAT VICTORY ALLOWED US TO TAKE PARS' WEALTH FOR OURSELVES, REMEMBER?
...YES, YOU'RE RIGHT.
OUR JOB IS TO LIVE UP TO THE TRUST HIS HIGHNESS, THE KING'S YOUNGER BROTHER, PLACES IN US.
IF THEY GOT PAST CHASOOM FORTRESS, THEN OUR NEXT STRONGHOLD IS...

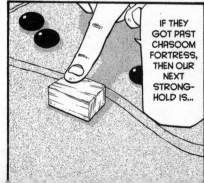

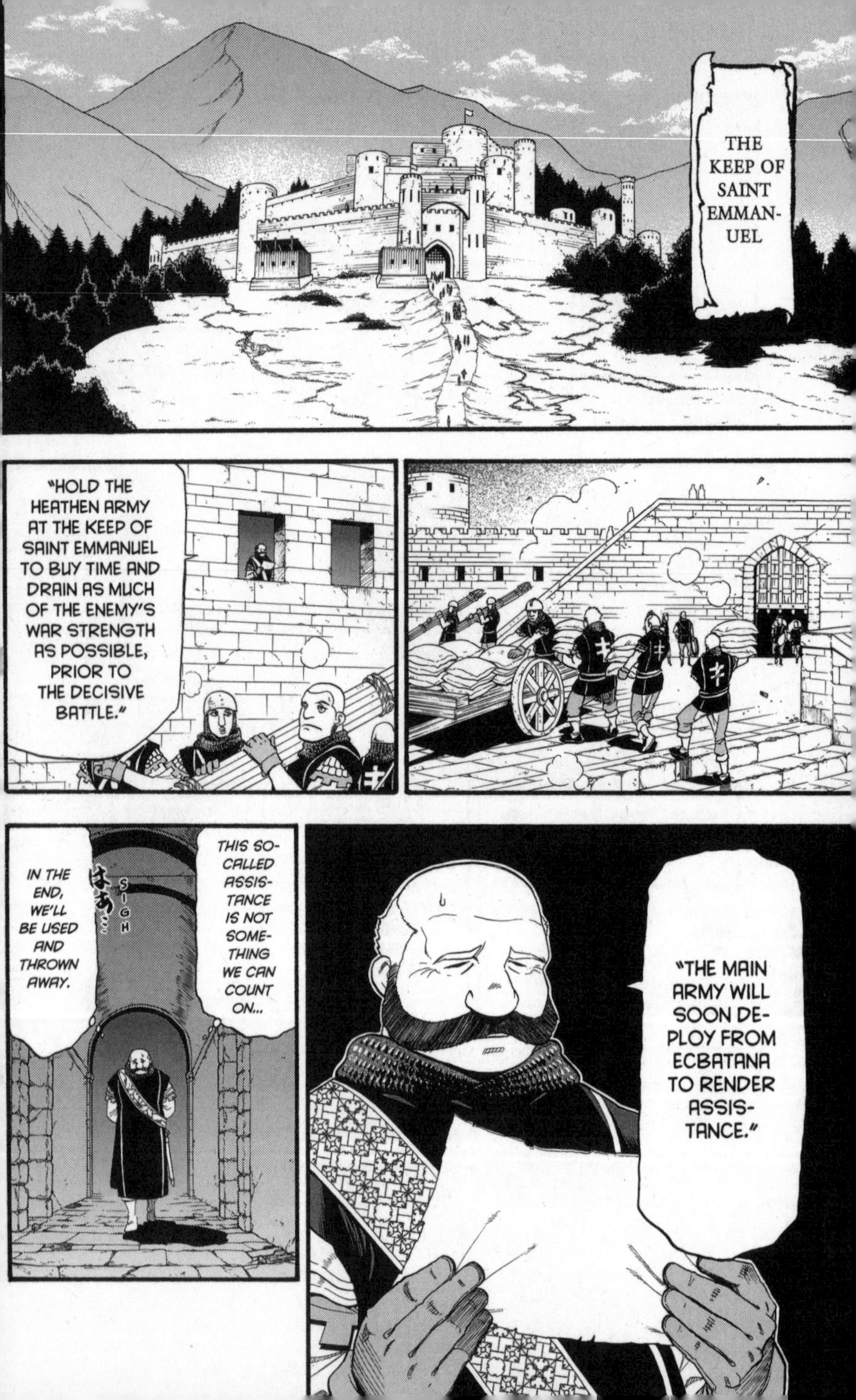
THE KEEP OF SAINT EMMAN-UEL
"HOLD THE HEATHEN ARMY AT THE KEEP OF SAINT EMMANUEL TO BUY TIME AND DRAIN AS MUCH OF THE ENEMY'S WAR STRENGTH AS POSSIBLE, PRIOR TO THE DECISIVE BATTLE."
"THE MAIN ARMY WILL SOON DE-PLOY FROM ECBATANA TO RENDER ASSIS-TANCE."
THIS SO-CALLED ASSIS-TANCE IS NOT SOME-THING WE CAN COUNT ON...
はぁ SIGH
IN THE END, WE'LL BE USED AND THROWN AWAY.

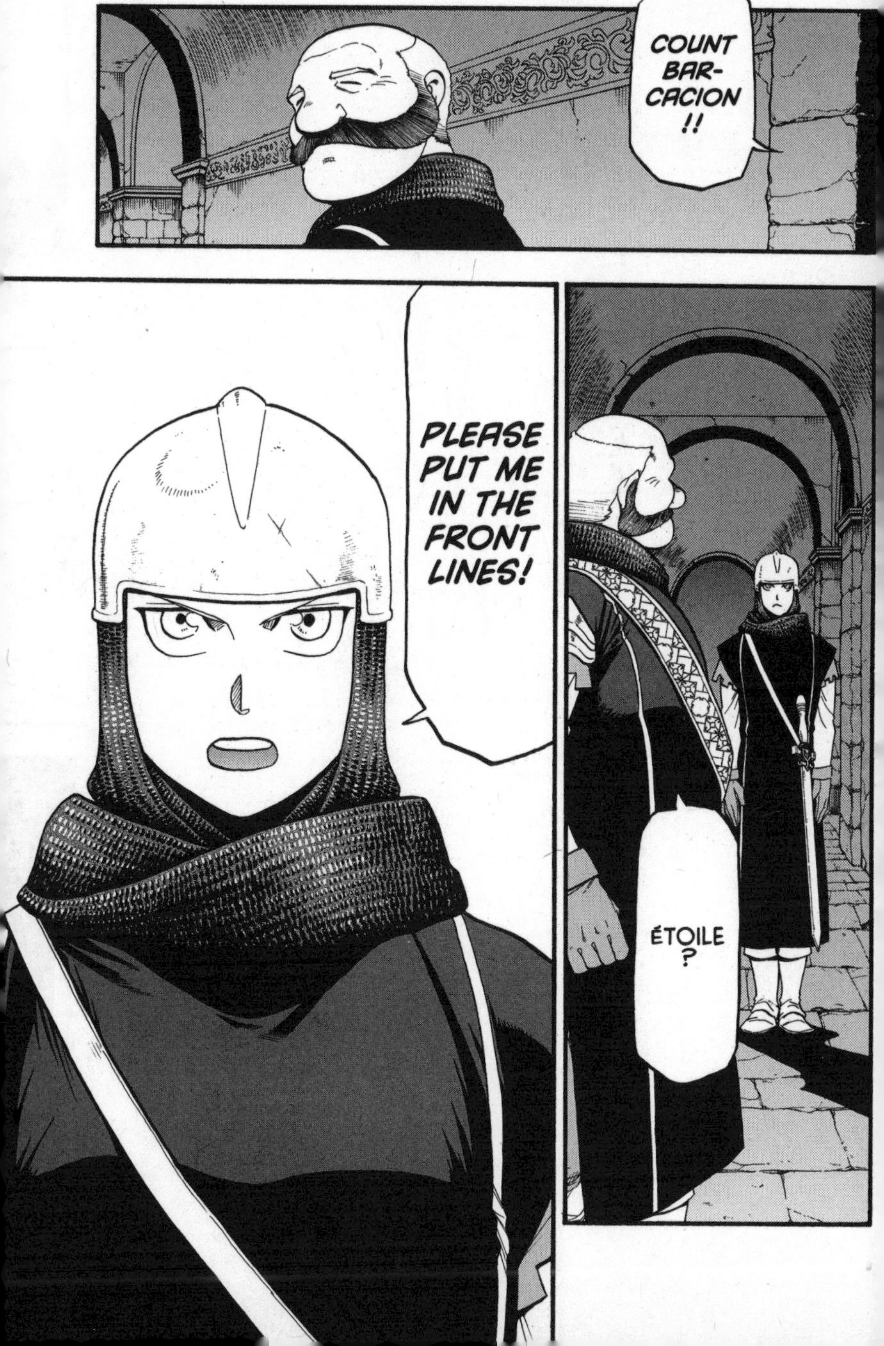
COUNT BAR-CACION !!
ÉTOILE ?
PLEASE PUT ME IN THE FRONT LINES!

THE HEROIC LEGEND OF
ARSLAN

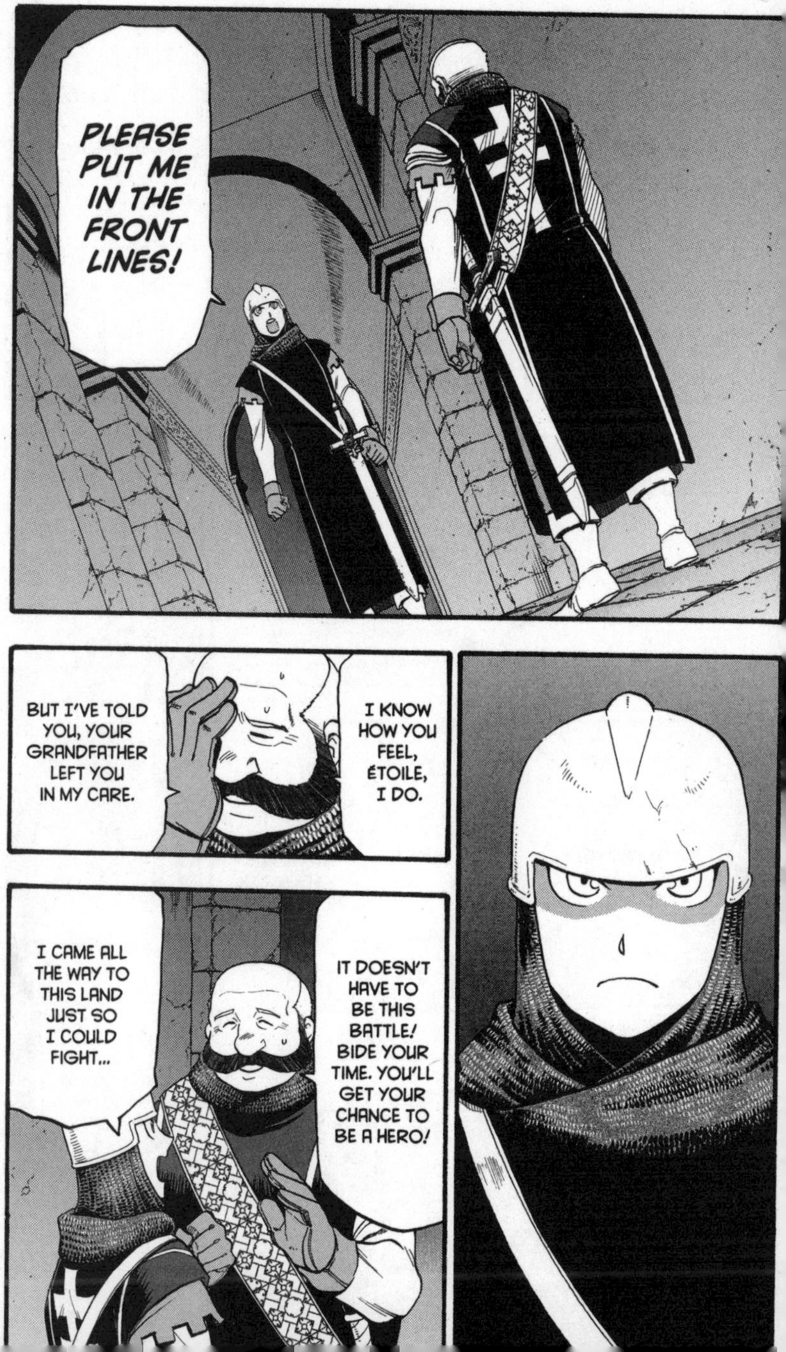
PLEASE PUT ME IN THE FRONT LINES!
I KNOW HOW YOU FEEL, ÉTOILE, I DO.
BUT I'VE TOLD YOU, YOUR GRANDFATHER LEFT YOU IN MY CARE.
I CAME ALL THE WAY TO THIS LAND JUST SO I COULD FIGHT...
IT DOESN'T HAVE TO BE THIS BATTLE! BIDE YOUR TIME. YOU'LL GET YOUR CHANCE TO BE A HERO!

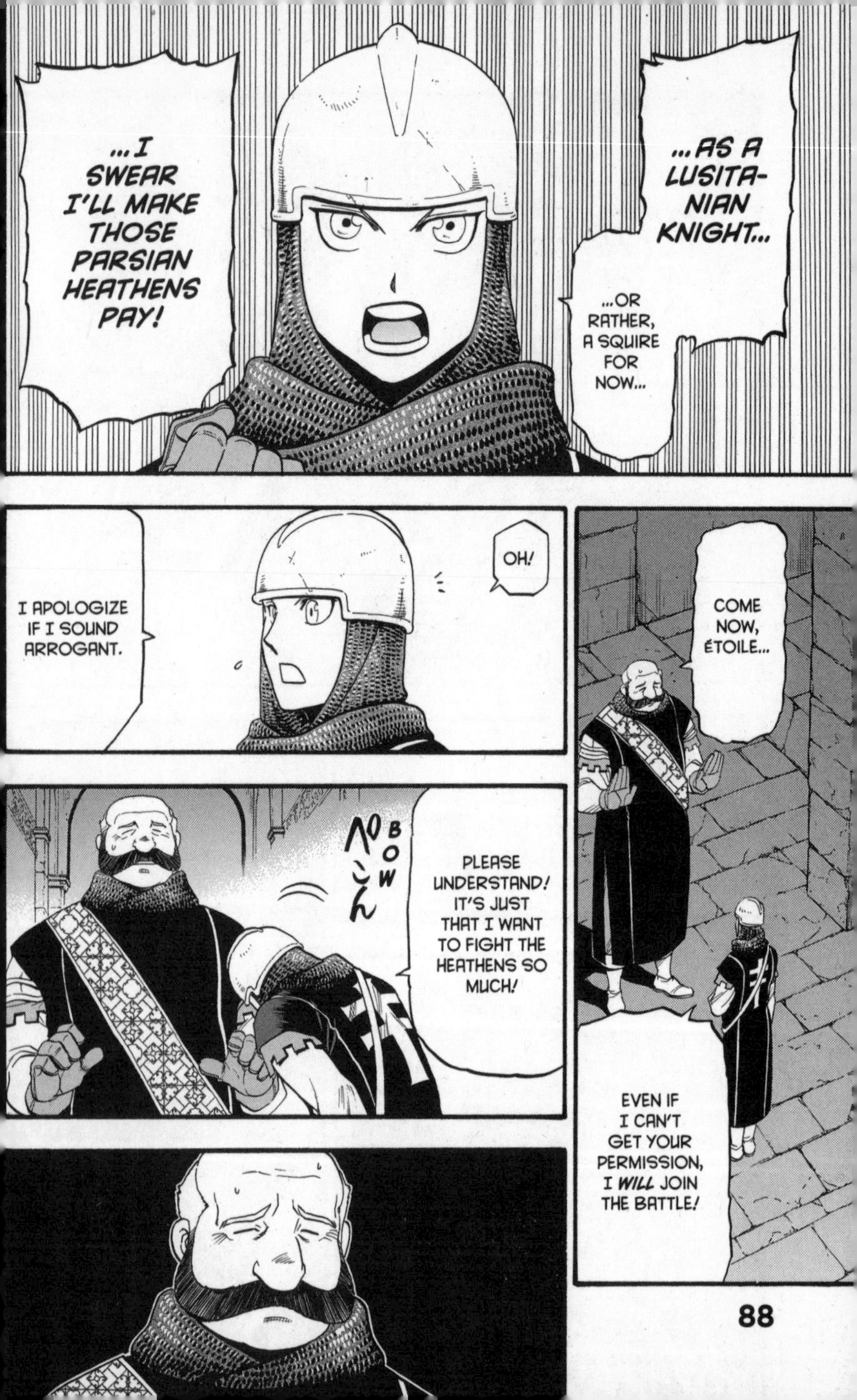
...AS A LUSITANIAN KNIGHT...
...OR RATHER, A SQUIRE FOR NOW...
...I SWEAR I'LL MAKE THOSE PARSIAN HEATHENS PAY!
COME NOW, ÉTOILE...
EVEN IF I CAN'T GET YOUR PERMISSION, I *WILL* JOIN THE BATTLE!
OH!
I APOLOGIZE IF I SOUND ARROGANT.
PLEASE UNDERSTAND! IT'S JUST THAT I WANT TO FIGHT THE HEATHENS SO MUCH!
BOW
ぺこん

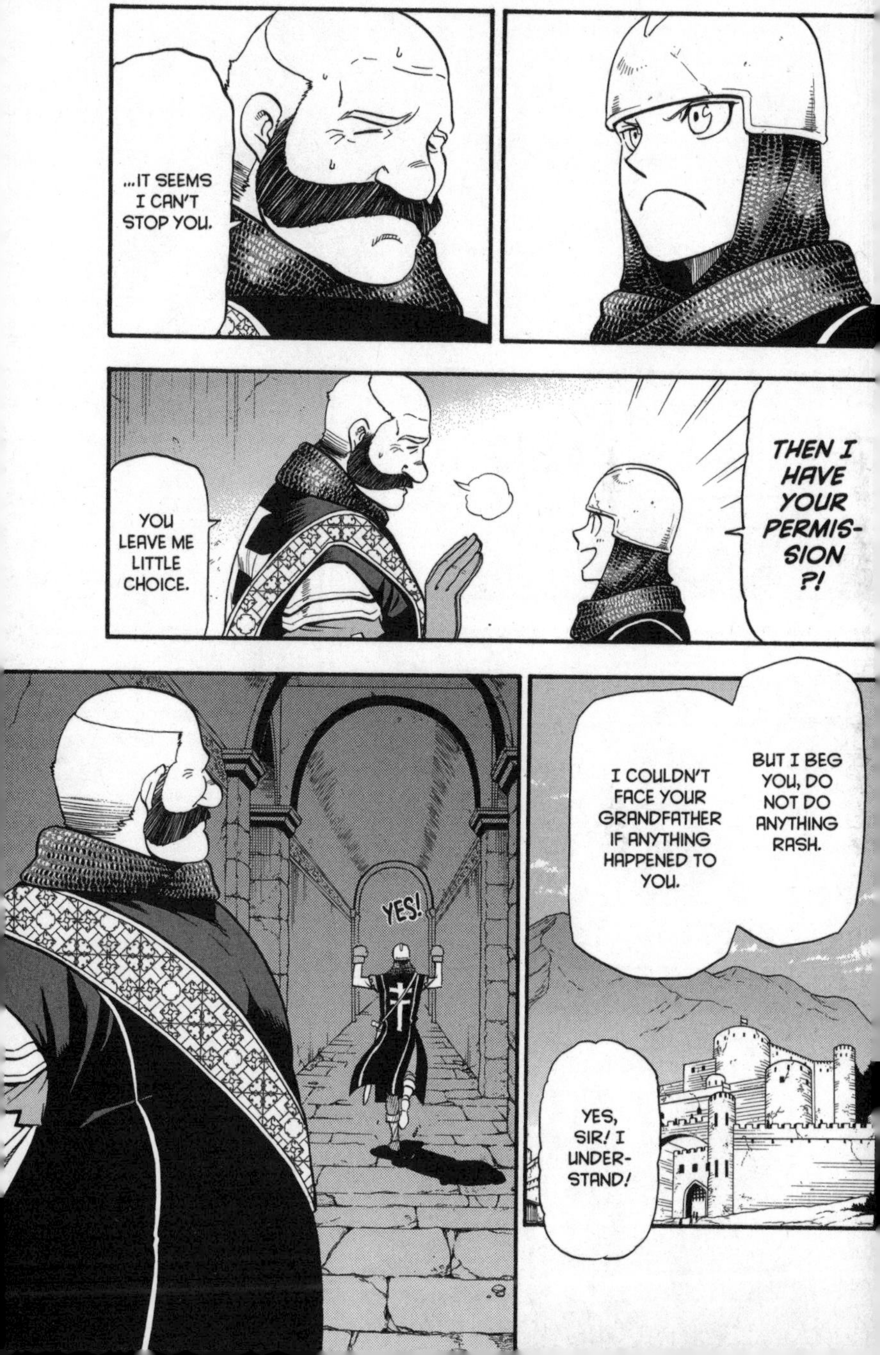
...IT SEEMS I CAN'T STOP YOU.
THEN I HAVE YOUR PERMISSION?!
YOU LEAVE ME LITTLE CHOICE.
BUT I BEG YOU, DO NOT DO ANYTHING RASH.
I COULDN'T FACE YOUR GRANDFATHER IF ANYTHING HAPPENED TO YOU.
YES, SIR! I UNDERSTAND!
YES!

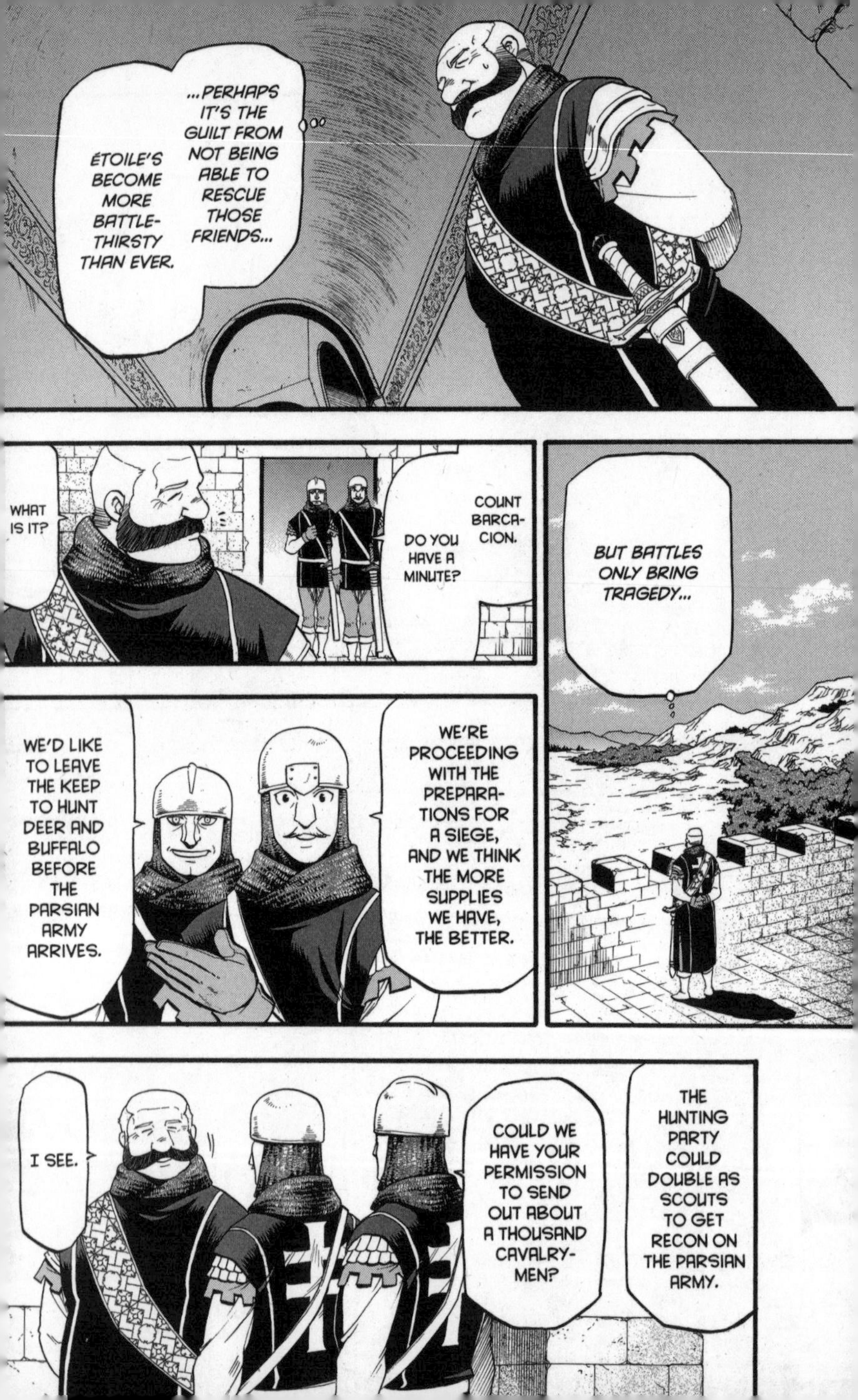
ÉTOILE'S BECOME MORE BATTLE-THIRSTY THAN EVER. ...PERHAPS IT'S THE GUILT FROM NOT BEING ABLE TO RESCUE THOSE FRIENDS...
BUT BATTLES ONLY BRING TRAGEDY...
COUNT BARCA-CION. DO YOU HAVE A MINUTE?
WHAT IS IT?
WE'RE PROCEEDING WITH THE PREPARA-TIONS FOR A SIEGE, AND WE THINK THE MORE SUPPLIES WE HAVE, THE BETTER.
WE'D LIKE TO LEAVE THE KEEP TO HUNT DEER AND BUFFALO BEFORE THE PARSIAN ARMY ARRIVES.
THE HUNTING PARTY COULD DOUBLE AS SCOUTS TO GET RECON ON THE PARSIAN ARMY.
COULD WE HAVE YOUR PERMISSION TO SEND OUT ABOUT A THOUSAND CAVALRY-MEN?
I SEE.

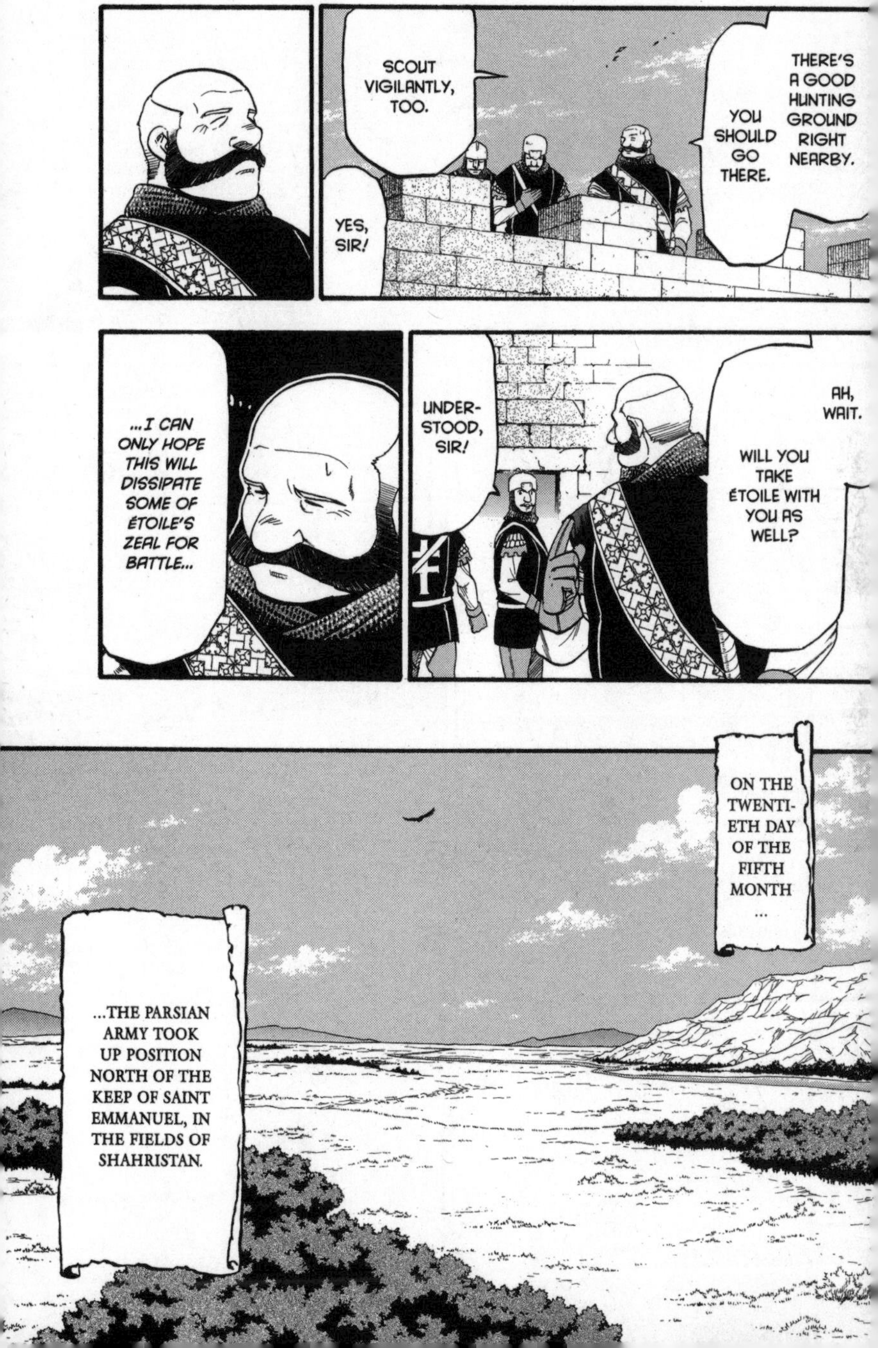
THERE'S A GOOD HUNTING GROUND RIGHT NEARBY.
YOU SHOULD GO THERE.
SCOUT VIGILANTLY, TOO.
YES, SIR!
AH, WAIT.
WILL YOU TAKE ÉTOILE WITH YOU AS WELL?
UNDER-STOOD, SIR!
...I CAN ONLY HOPE THIS WILL DISSIPATE SOME OF ÉTOILE'S ZEAL FOR BATTLE...
ON THE TWENTI-ETH DAY OF THE FIFTH MONTH ...
...THE PARSIAN ARMY TOOK UP POSITION NORTH OF THE KEEP OF SAINT EMMANUEL, IN THE FIELDS OF SHAHRISTAN.

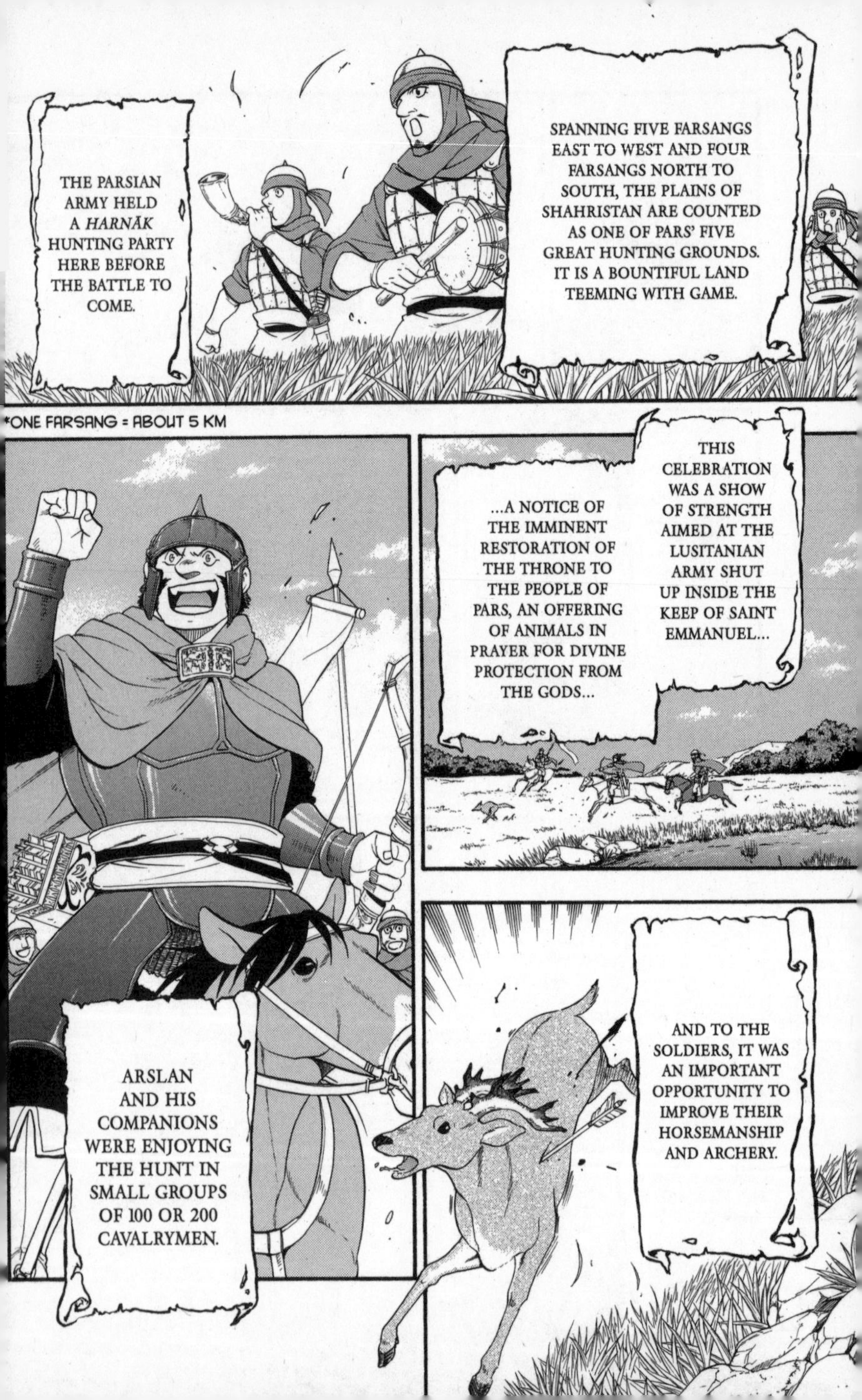
SPANNING FIVE FARSANGS EAST TO WEST AND FOUR FARSANGS NORTH TO SOUTH, THE PLAINS OF SHAHRISTAN ARE COUNTED AS ONE OF PARS' FIVE GREAT HUNTING GROUNDS. IT IS A BOUNTIFUL LAND TEEMING WITH GAME.
THE PARSIAN ARMY HELD A *HARNĀK* HUNTING PARTY HERE BEFORE THE BATTLE TO COME.
*ONE FARSANG = ABOUT 5 KM
THIS CELEBRATION WAS A SHOW OF STRENGTH AIMED AT THE LUSITANIAN ARMY SHUT UP INSIDE THE KEEP OF SAINT EMMANUEL...
...A NOTICE OF THE IMMINENT RESTORATION OF THE THRONE TO THE PEOPLE OF PARS, AN OFFERING OF ANIMALS IN PRAYER FOR DIVINE PROTECTION FROM THE GODS...
AND TO THE SOLDIERS, IT WAS AN IMPORTANT OPPORTUNITY TO IMPROVE THEIR HORSEMANSHIP AND ARCHERY.
ARSLAN AND HIS COMPANIONS WERE ENJOYING THE HUNT IN SMALL GROUPS OF 100 OR 200 CAVALRYMEN.

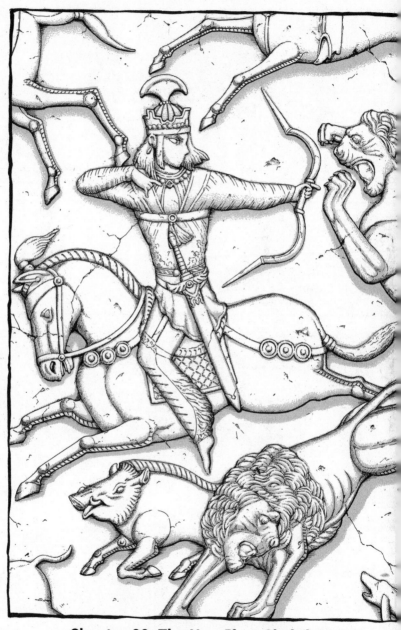

Chapter 68: The Harnāk at Shahristan

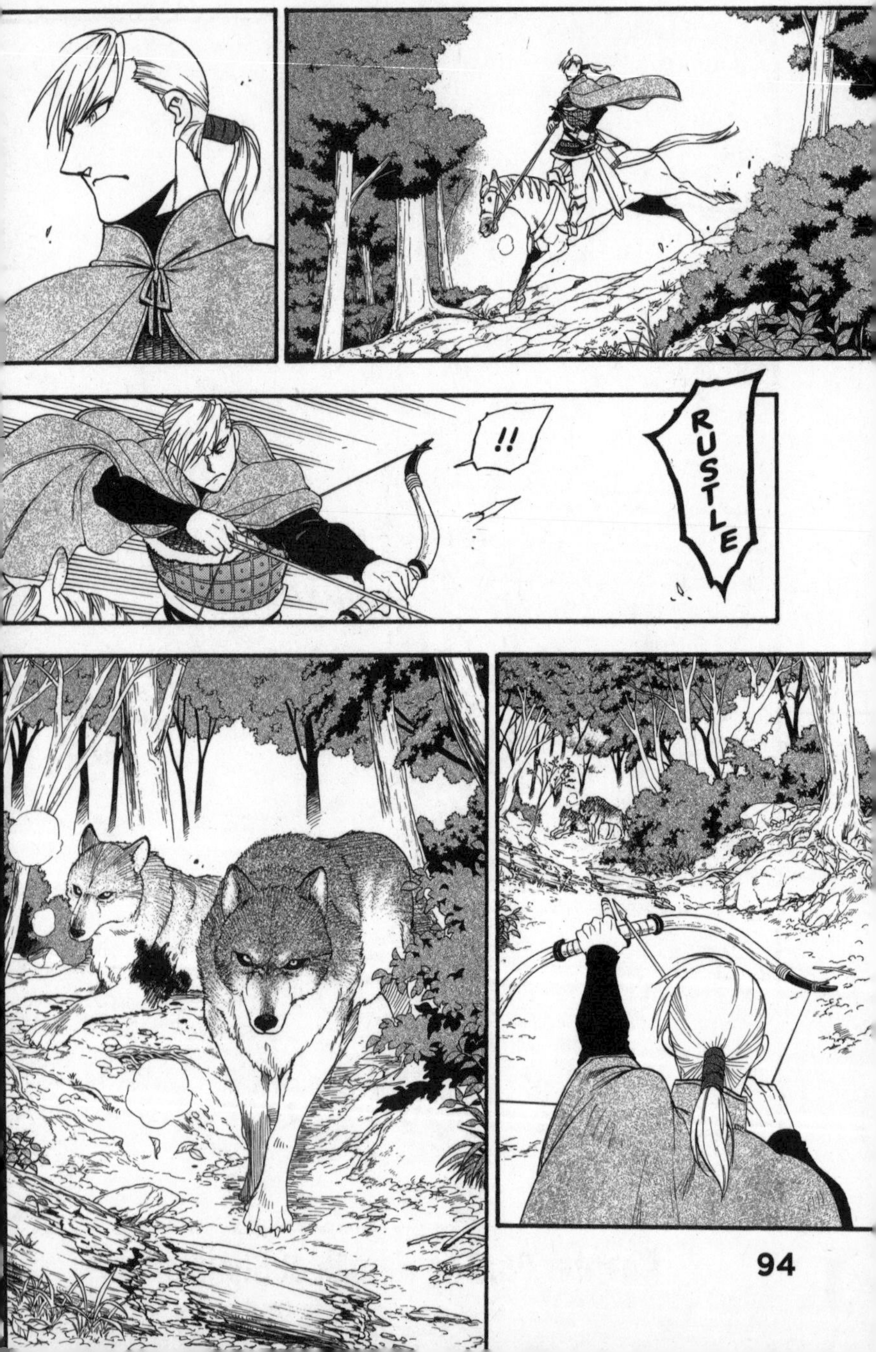
RUSTLE
!!

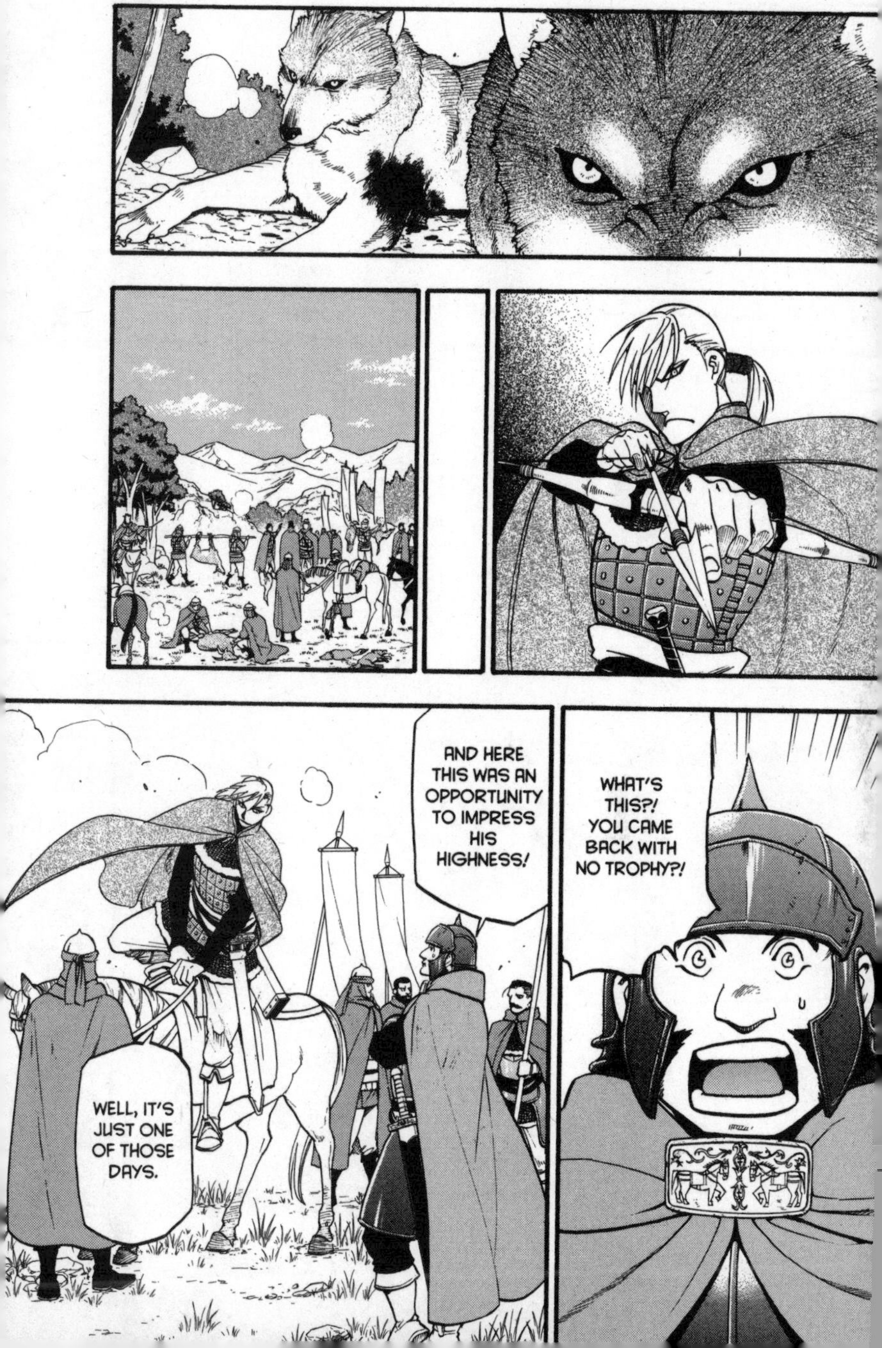
WHAT'S THIS?! YOU CAME BACK WITH NO TROPHY?!
AND HERE THIS WAS AN OPPORTUNITY TO IMPRESS HIS HIGHNESS!
WELL, IT'S JUST ONE OF THOSE DAYS.

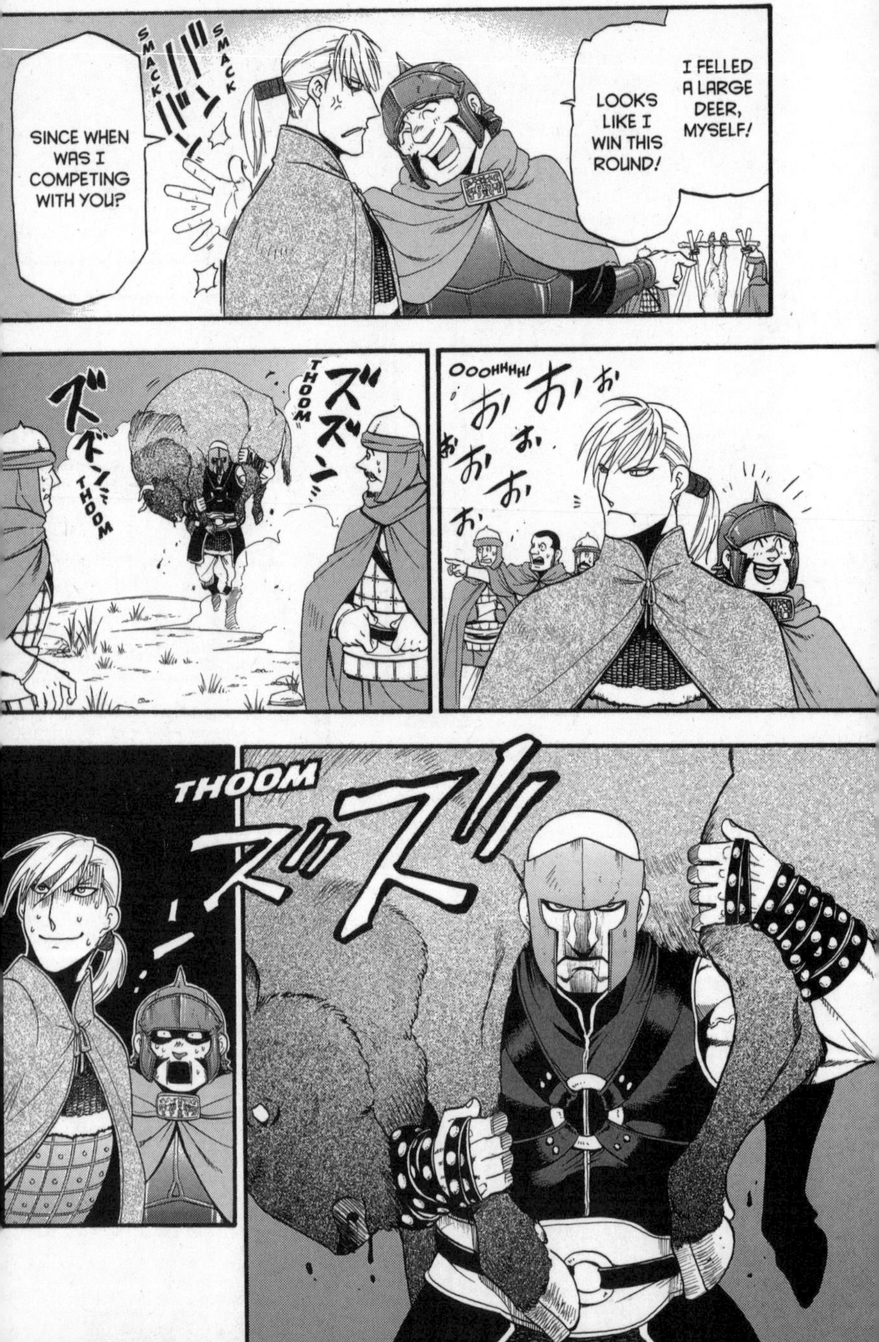
I FELLED A LARGE DEER, MYSELF!
LOOKS LIKE I WIN THIS ROUND!
SMACK SMACK
SINCE WHEN WAS I COMPETING WITH YOU?
OOOHHHH!
おおおおおおお
ズズン
THOOM
ズズン
THOOM
THOOM
ズズ

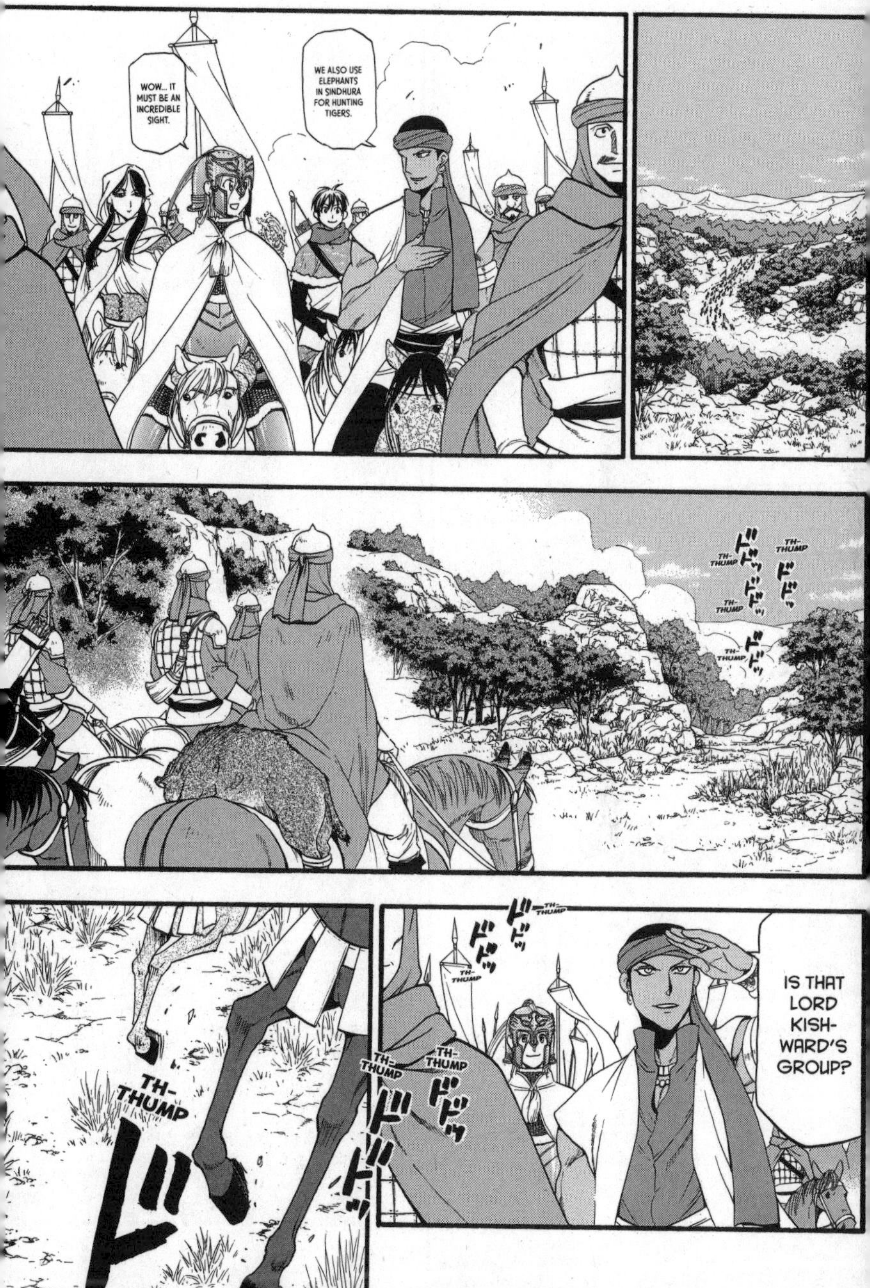
WE ALSO USE ELEPHANTS IN SINDHURA FOR HUNTING TIGERS.
WOW... IT MUST BE AN INCREDIBLE SIGHT.
TH-THUMP
TH-THUMP
TH-THUMP
TH-THUMP
TH-THUMP
IS THAT LORD KISHWARD'S GROUP?
TH-THUMP
TH-THUMP
TH-THUMP
TH-THUMP

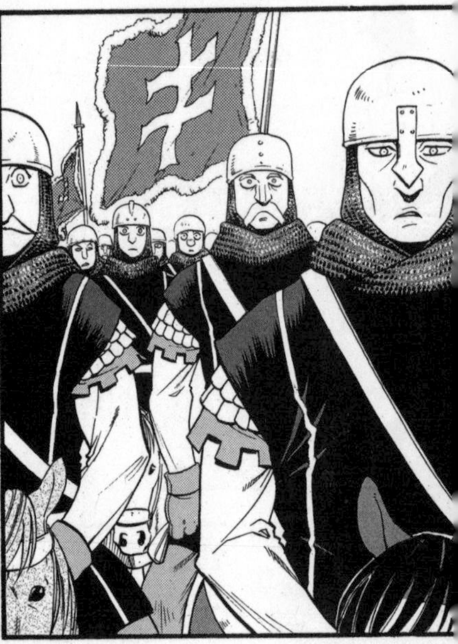
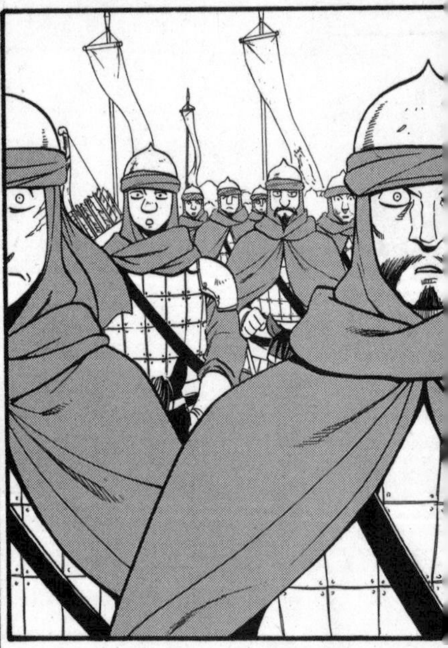
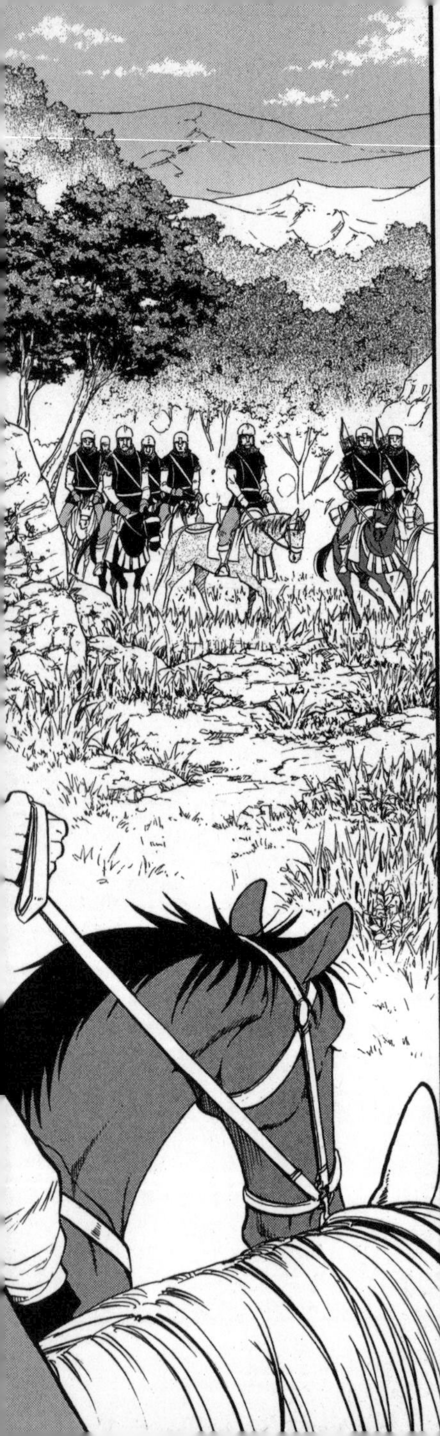

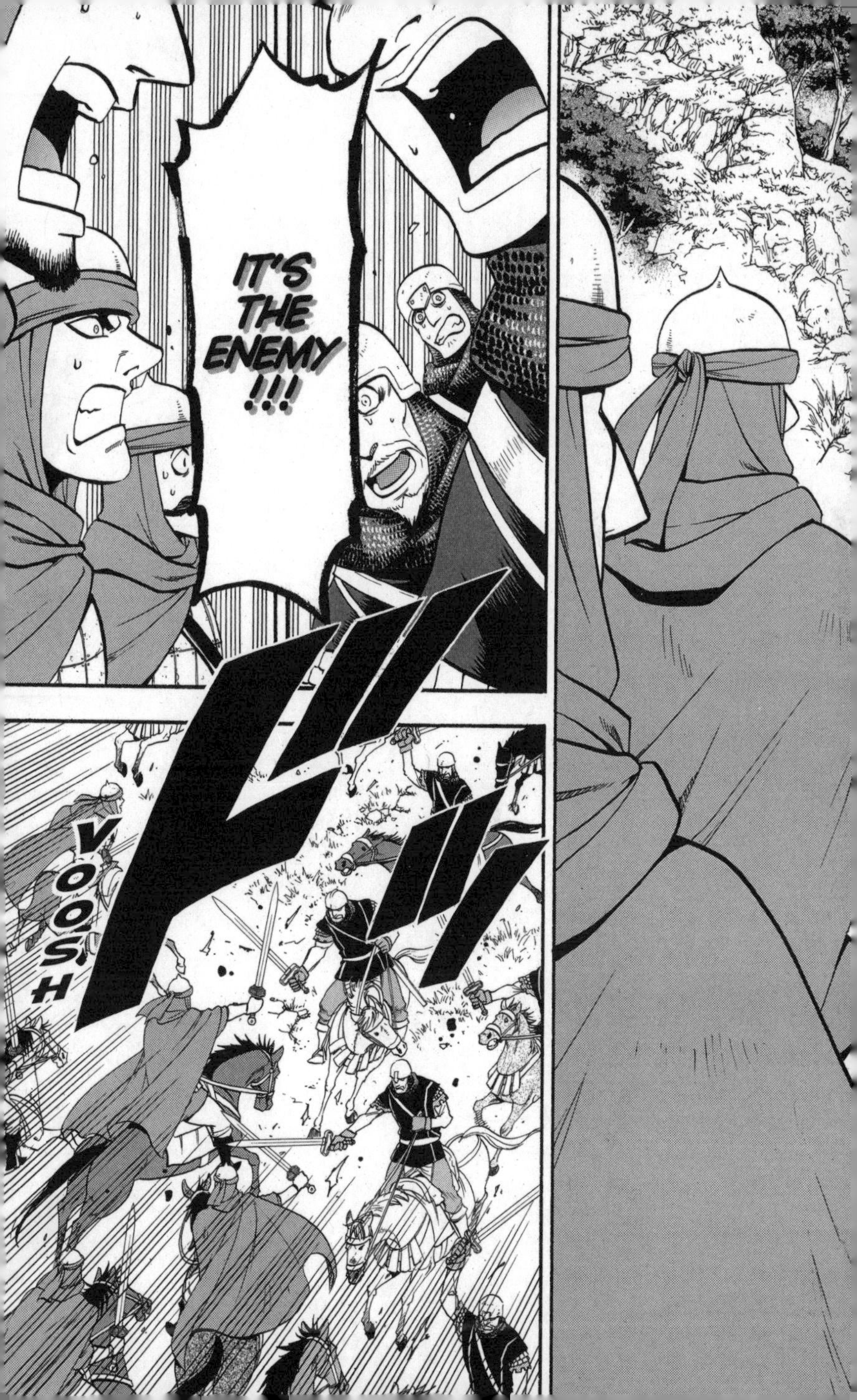
IT'S THE ENEMY!!!
VOOSH

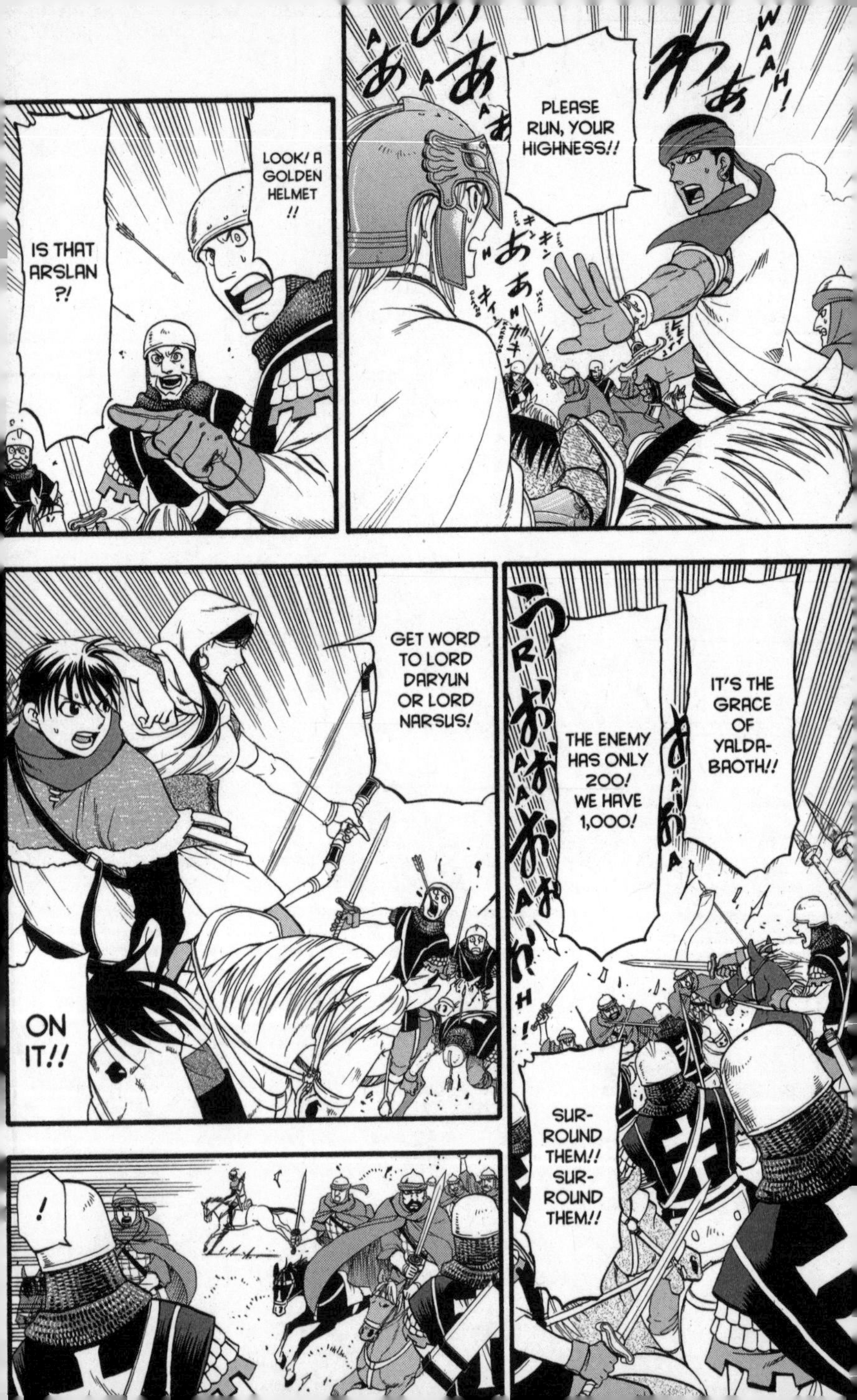
WAAH!
PLEASE RUN, YOUR HIGHNESS!!
LOOK! A GOLDEN HELMET!!
IS THAT ARSLAN?!
IT'S THE GRACE OF YALDABAOTH!!
THE ENEMY HAS ONLY 200! WE HAVE 1,000!
RAAAAAH!
SUR-ROUND THEM!! SUR-ROUND THEM!!
GET WORD TO LORD DARYUN OR LORD NARSUS!
ON IT!!
!

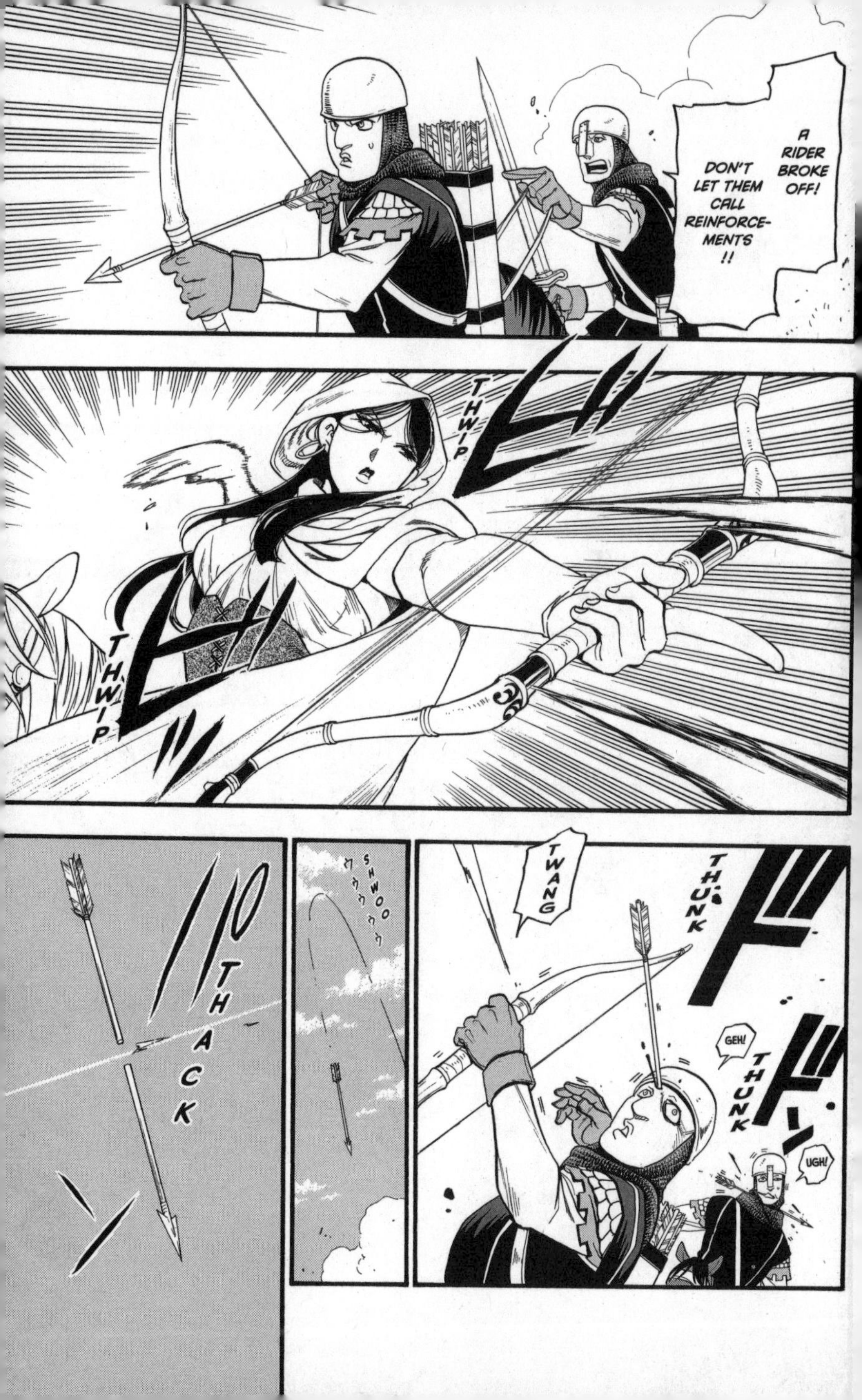
A RIDER BROKE OFF!
DON'T LET THEM CALL REINFORCEMENTS!!
THWIP
THWIP
TWANG
THUNK
GEH!
THUNK
UGH!
SHWOO
THACK

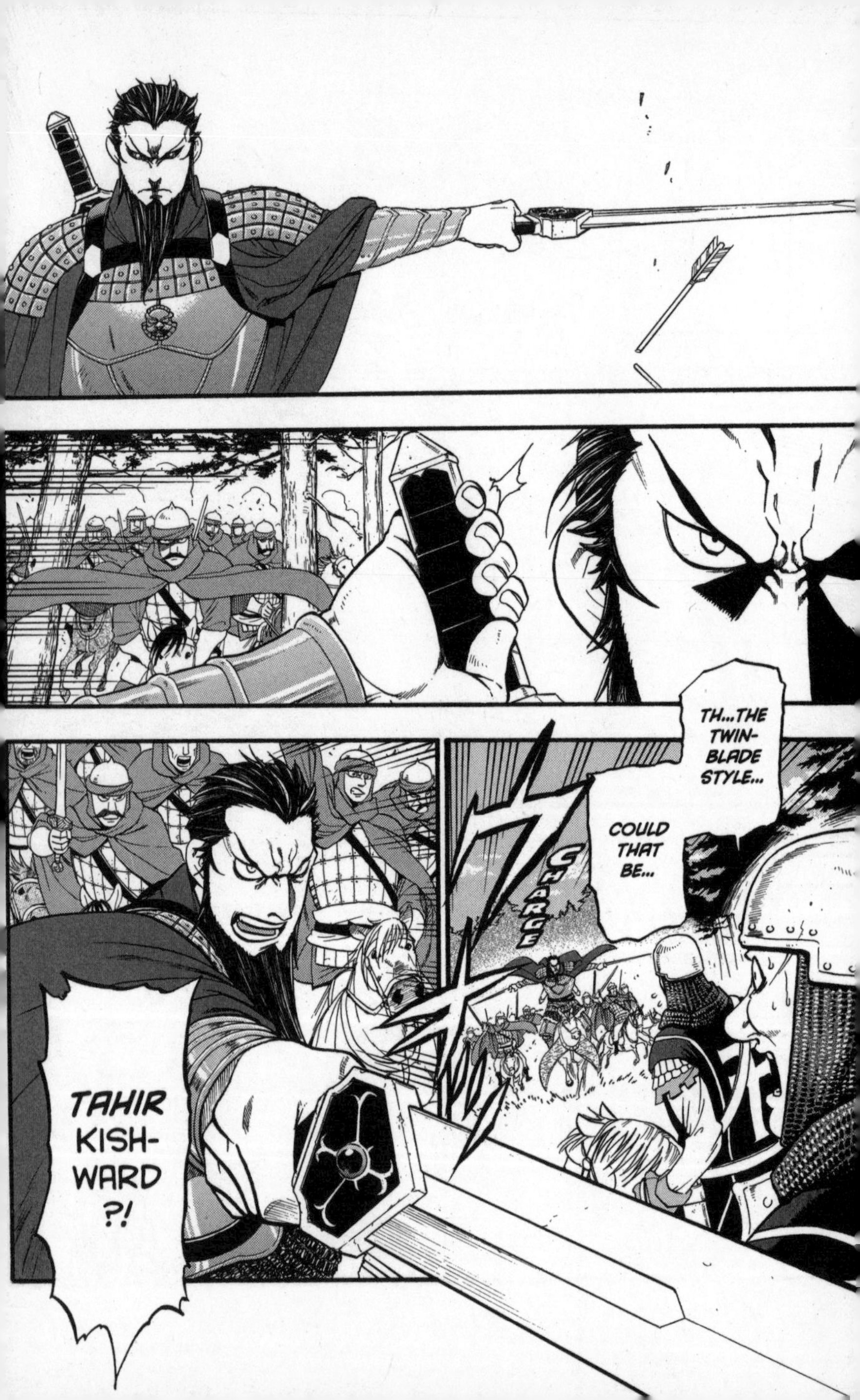
TH...THE TWIN-BLADE STYLE...
COULD THAT BE...
CHARGE
TAHIR KISH-WARD ?!

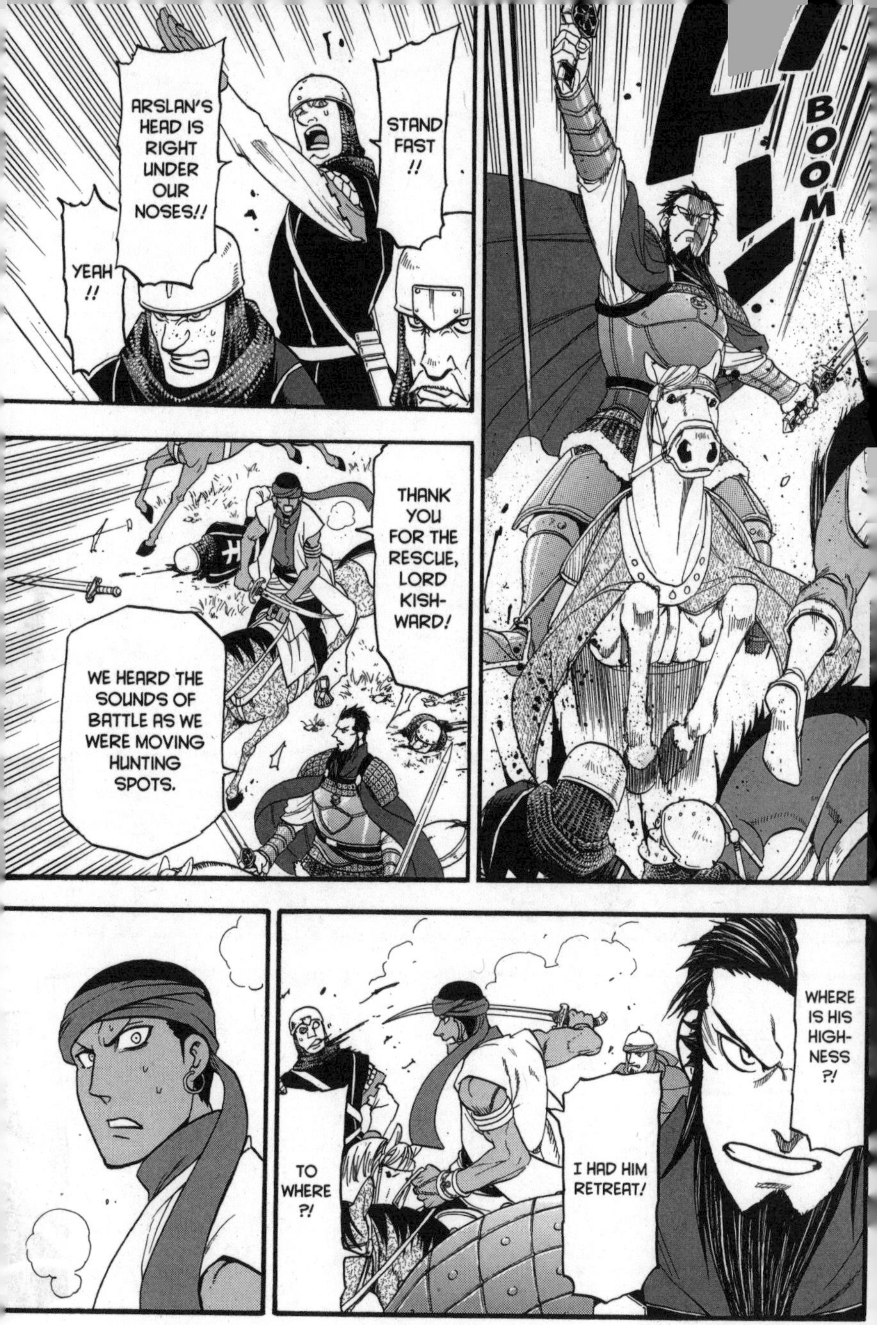
BOOM
STAND FAST!!
ARSLAN'S HEAD IS RIGHT UNDER OUR NOSES!!
YEAH!!
THANK YOU FOR THE RESCUE, LORD KISHWARD!
WE HEARD THE SOUNDS OF BATTLE AS WE WERE MOVING HUNTING SPOTS.
WHERE IS HIS HIGHNESS?!
I HAD HIM RETREAT!
TO WHERE?!

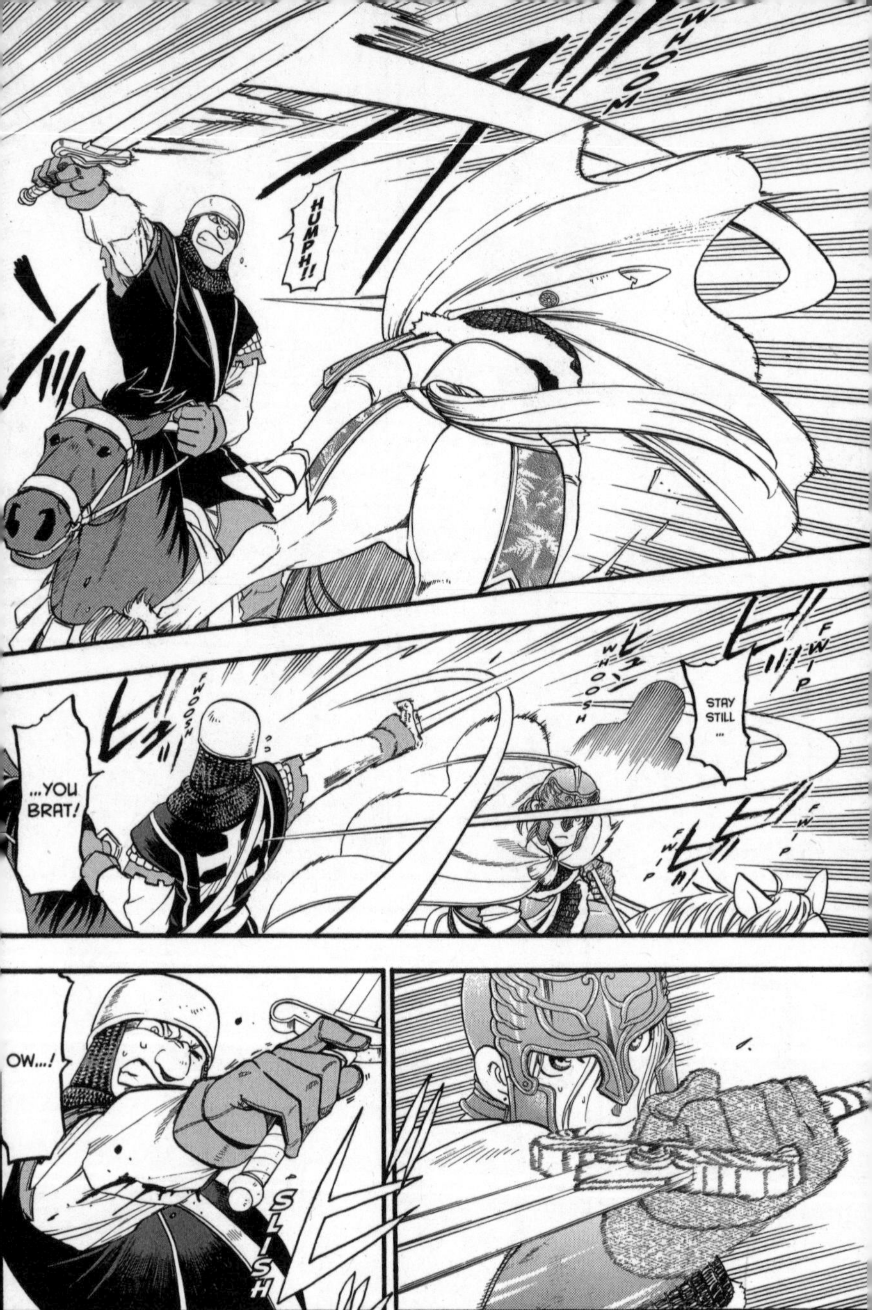
WHOOM
HUMPH!!
FWIP
WHOOSH
STAY STILL...
FWIP
FWIP
FWOOSH
...YOU BRAT!
SLISH
OW...!

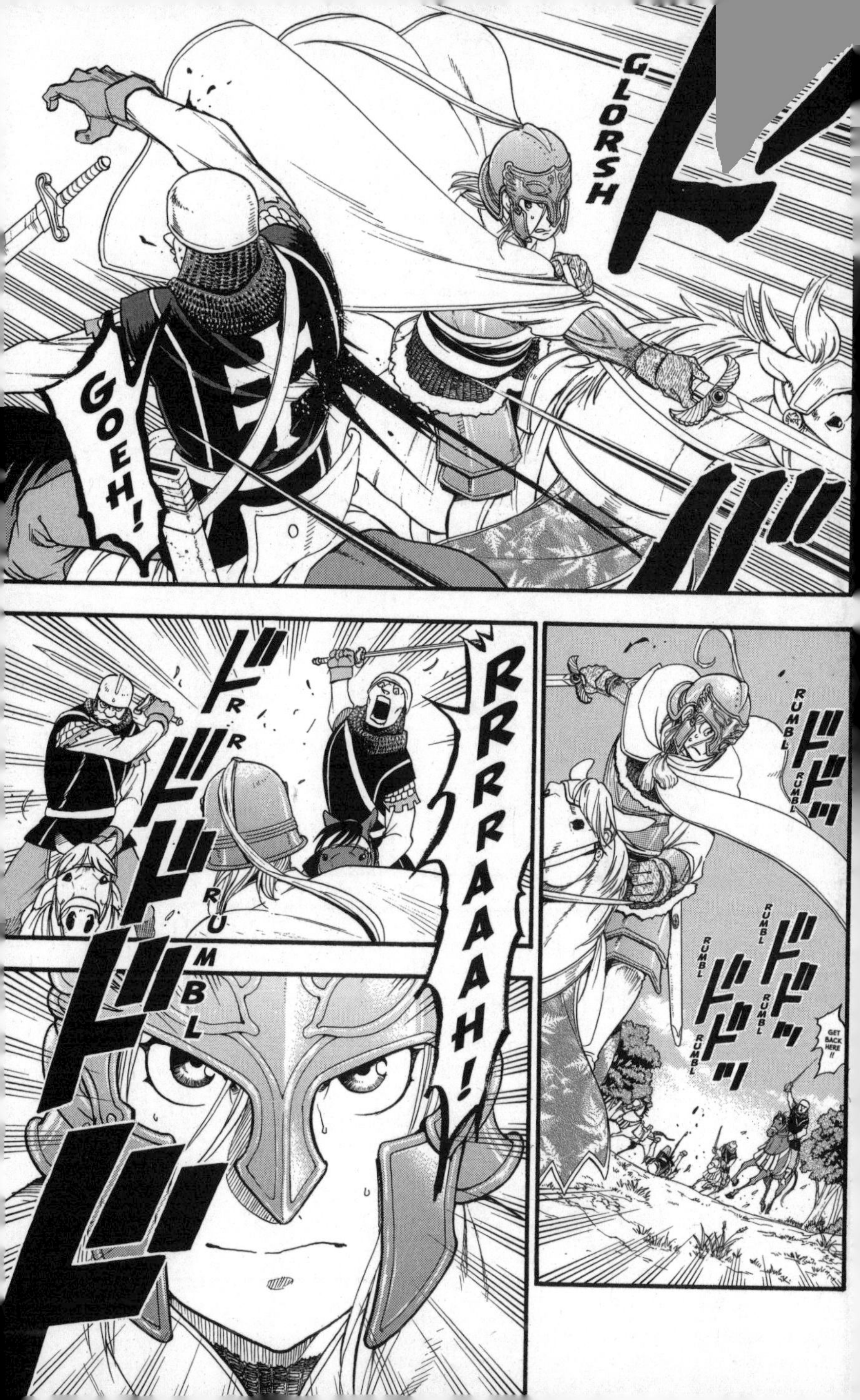
GLORSH
GOEH!
RUMBL
RUMBL
RUMBL
RUMBL
RUMBL
RUMBL
GET BACK HERE!!
RRRRAAAAH!
RRR
RUMBL

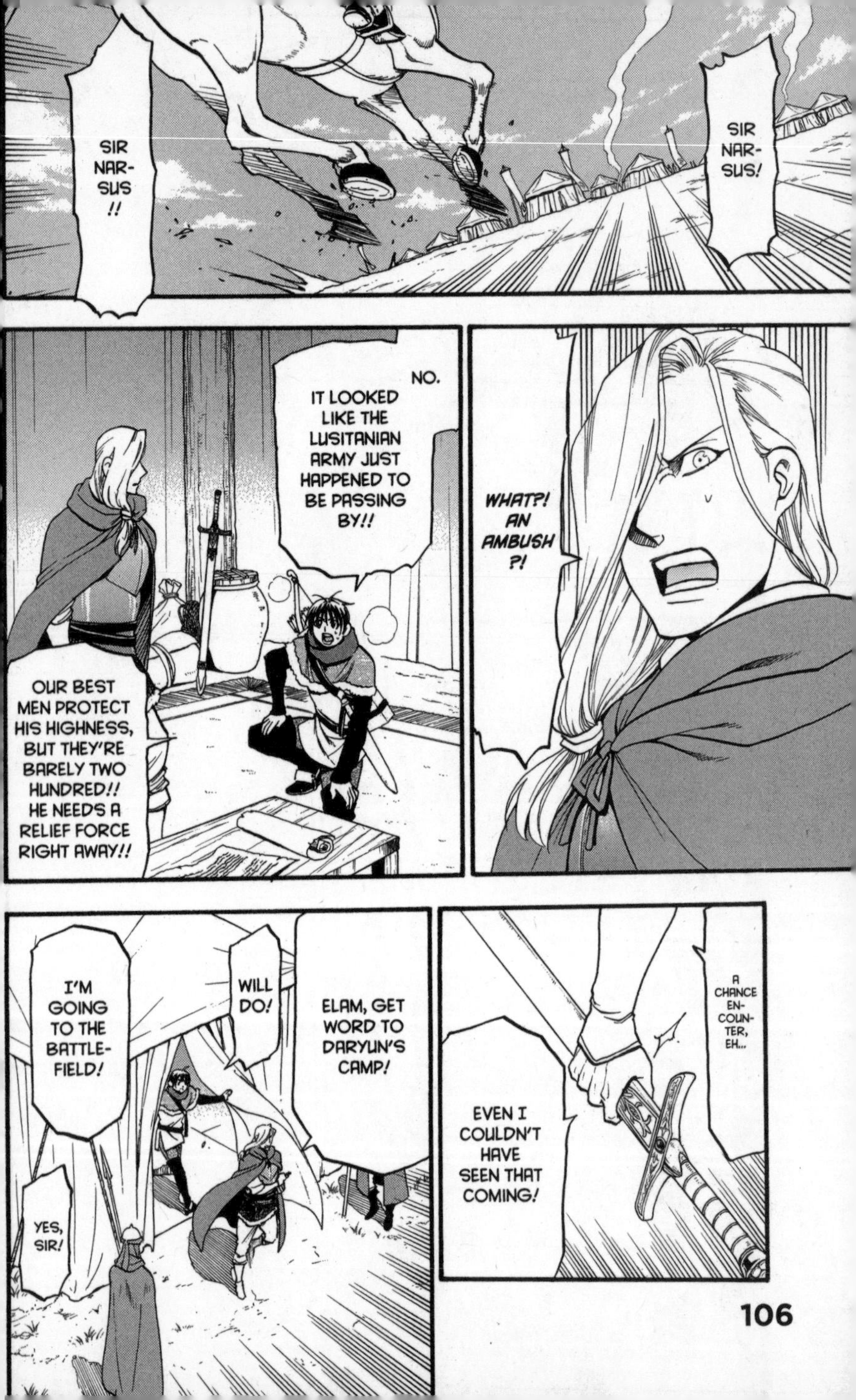
SIR NARSUS!
SIR NARSUS!!
WHAT?! AN AMBUSH?!
NO. IT LOOKED LIKE THE LUSITANIAN ARMY JUST HAPPENED TO BE PASSING BY!!
OUR BEST MEN PROTECT HIS HIGHNESS, BUT THEY'RE BARELY TWO HUNDRED!! HE NEEDS A RELIEF FORCE RIGHT AWAY!!
A CHANCE ENCOUNTER, EH...
EVEN I COULDN'T HAVE SEEN THAT COMING!
ELAM, GET WORD TO DARYUN'S CAMP!
WILL DO!
I'M GOING TO THE BATTLEFIELD!
YES, SIR!

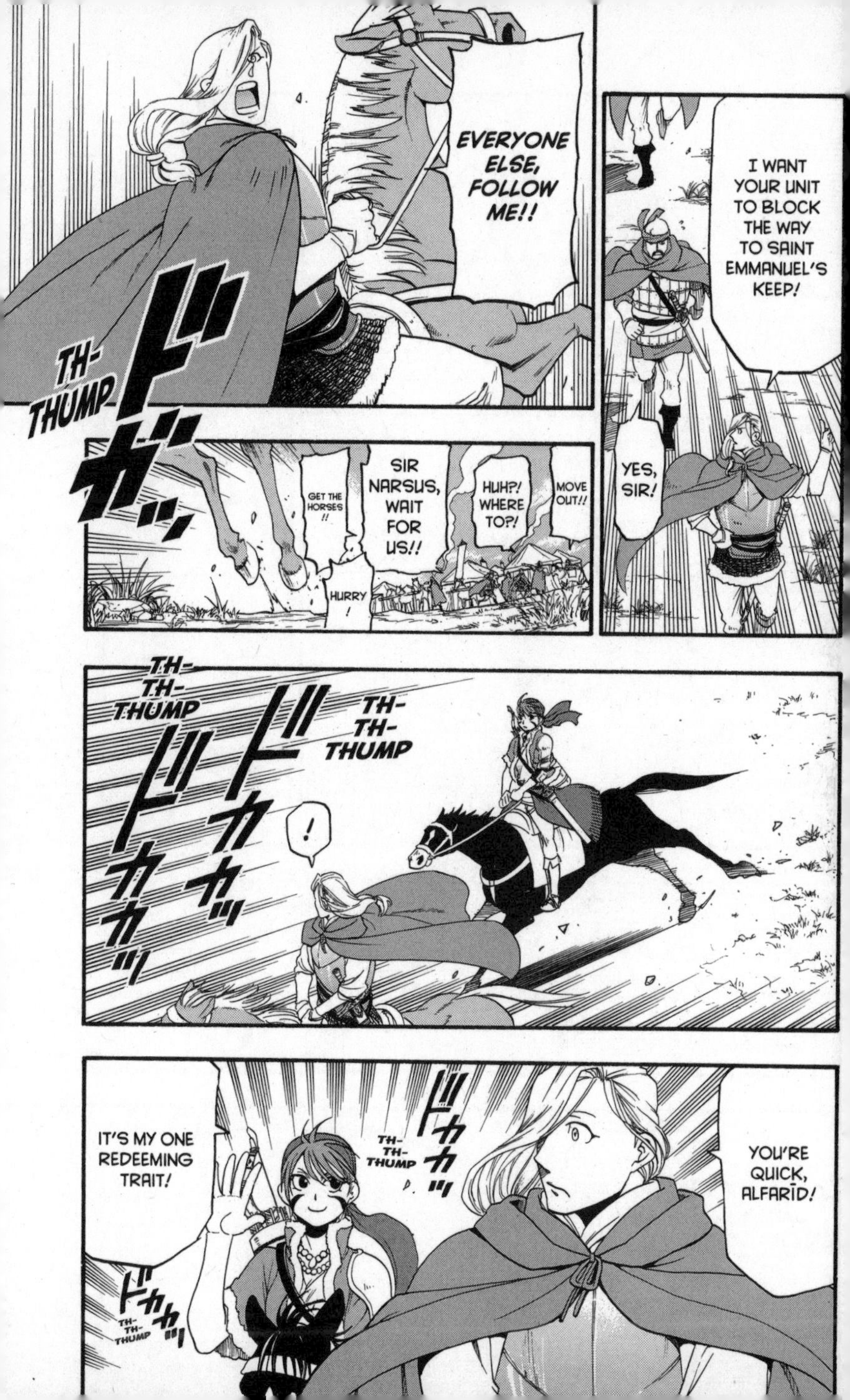
I WANT YOUR UNIT TO BLOCK THE WAY TO SAINT EMMANUEL'S KEEP!
YES, SIR!
EVERYONE ELSE, FOLLOW ME!!
TH-THUMP
MOVE OUT!!
HUH?! WHERE TO?!
SIR NARSUS, WAIT FOR US!!
GET THE HORSES!!
HURRY!
TH-TH-THUMP
!
TH-TH-THUMP
YOU'RE QUICK, ALFARĪD!
TH-TH-THUMP
IT'S MY ONE REDEEMING TRAIT!
TH-TH-THUMP

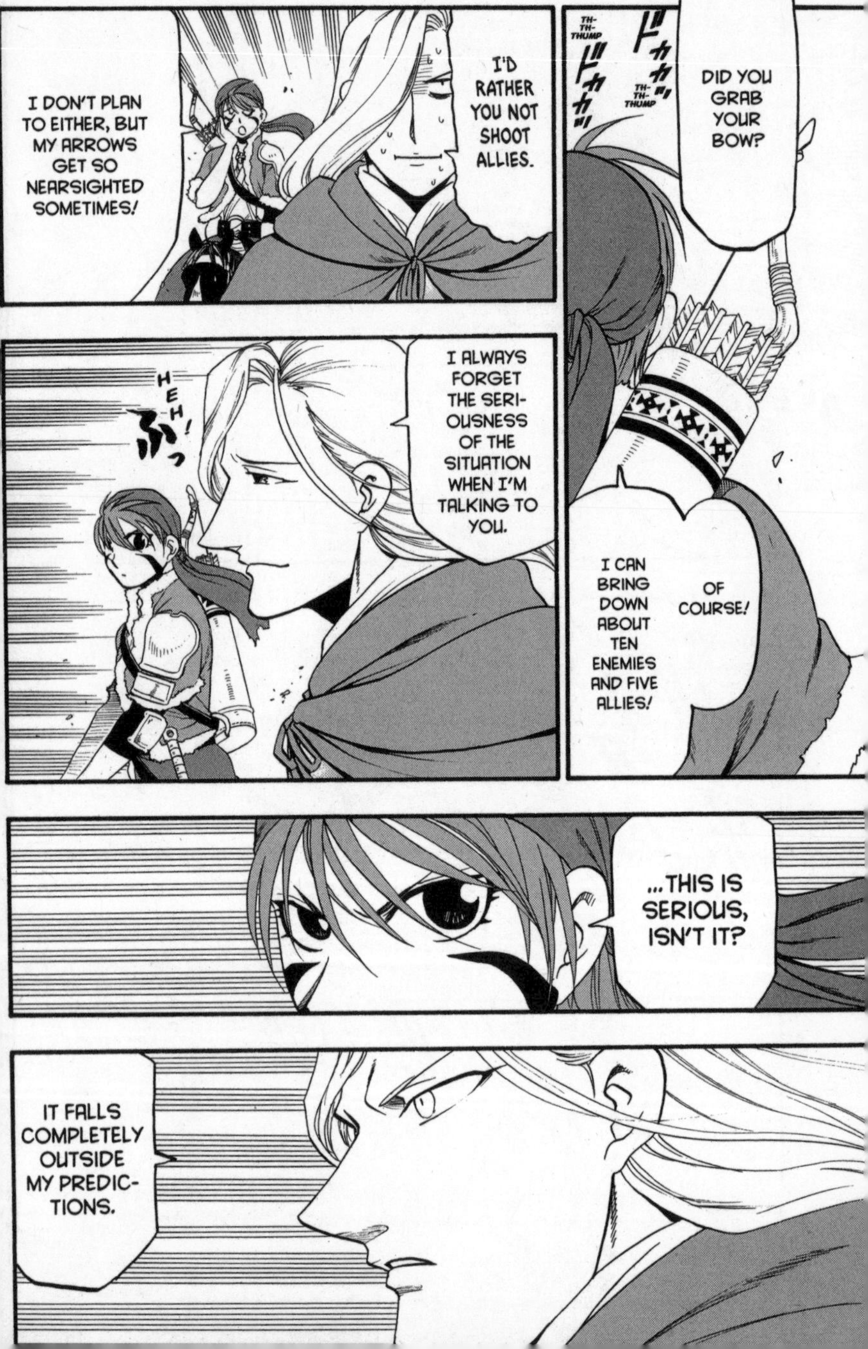
TH-TH-THUMP
TH-TH-THUMP
DID YOU GRAB YOUR BOW?
OF COURSE!
I CAN BRING DOWN ABOUT TEN ENEMIES AND FIVE ALLIES!
I'D RATHER YOU NOT SHOOT ALLIES.
I DON'T PLAN TO EITHER, BUT MY ARROWS GET SO NEARSIGHTED SOMETIMES!
HEH!
I ALWAYS FORGET THE SERI-OUSNESS OF THE SITUATION WHEN I'M TALKING TO YOU.
...THIS IS SERIOUS, ISN'T IT?
IT FALLS COMPLETELY OUTSIDE MY PREDIC-TIONS.

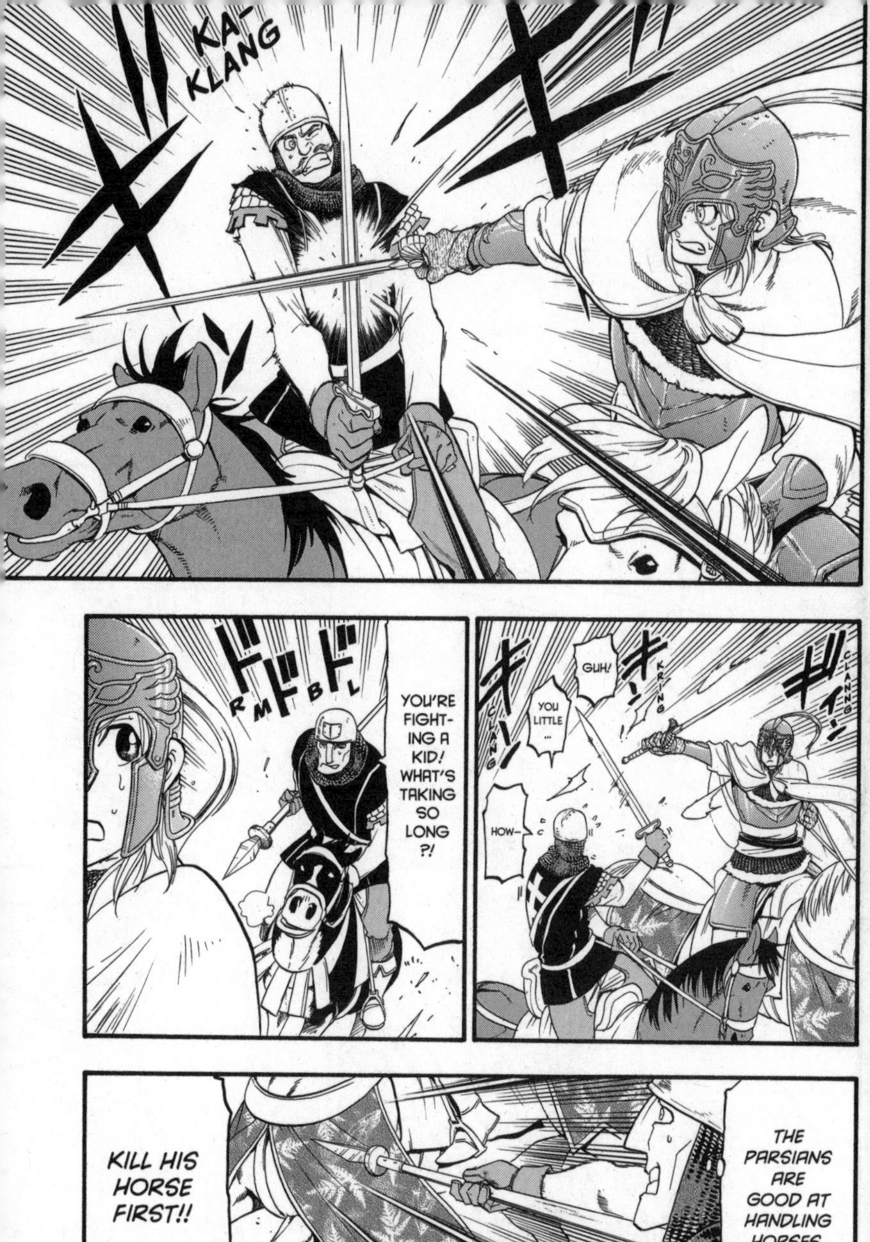
KA-KLANG
CLANNG
KRING
GUH!
YOU LITTLE ...
HOW-
CLANG
RMBL
YOU'RE FIGHTING A KID! WHAT'S TAKING SO LONG ?!
THE PARSIANS ARE GOOD AT HANDLING HORSES.
KILL HIS HORSE FIRST!!

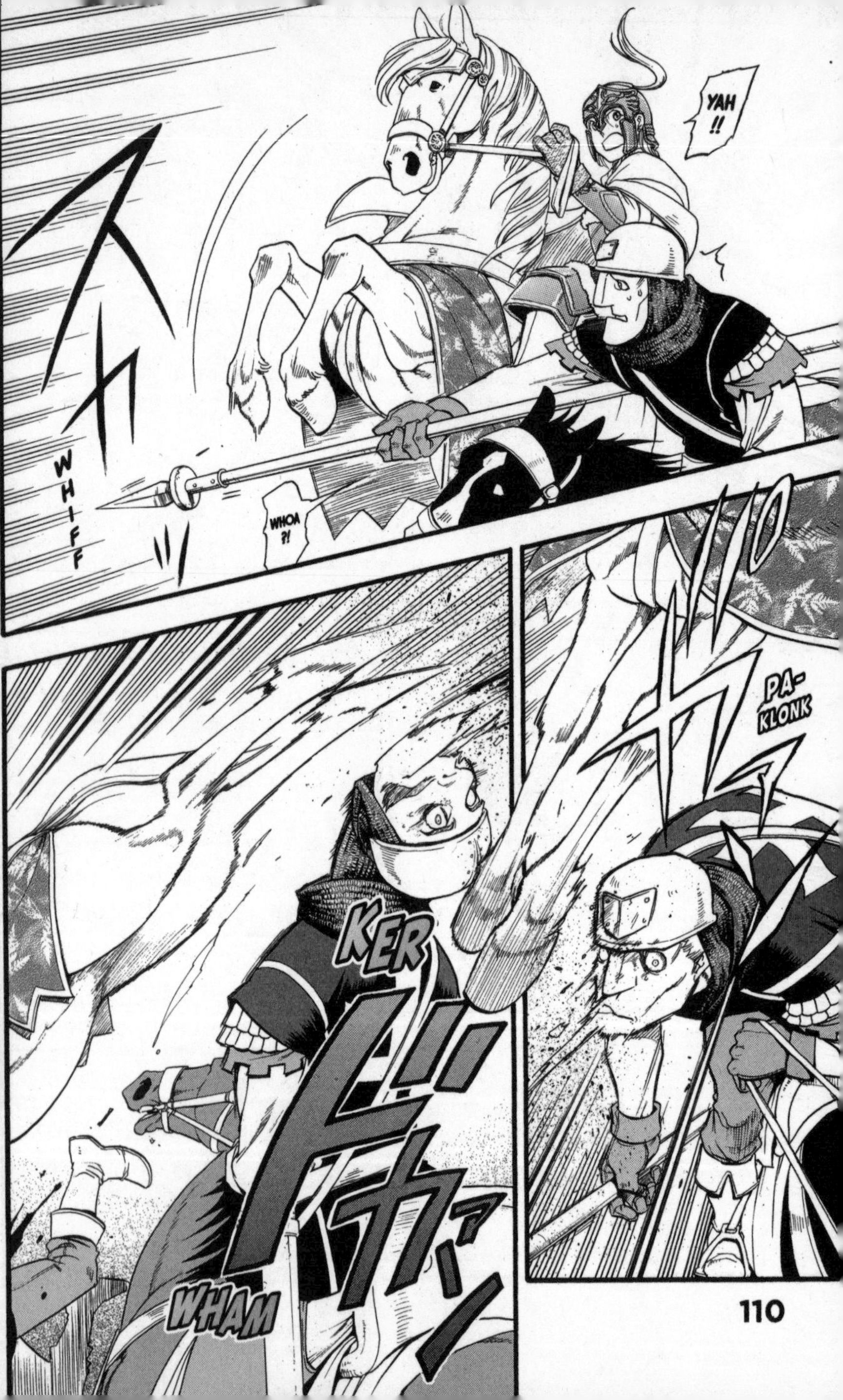

YAH !!
WHIFF
WHOA ?!
PA-KLONK
KER
WHAM

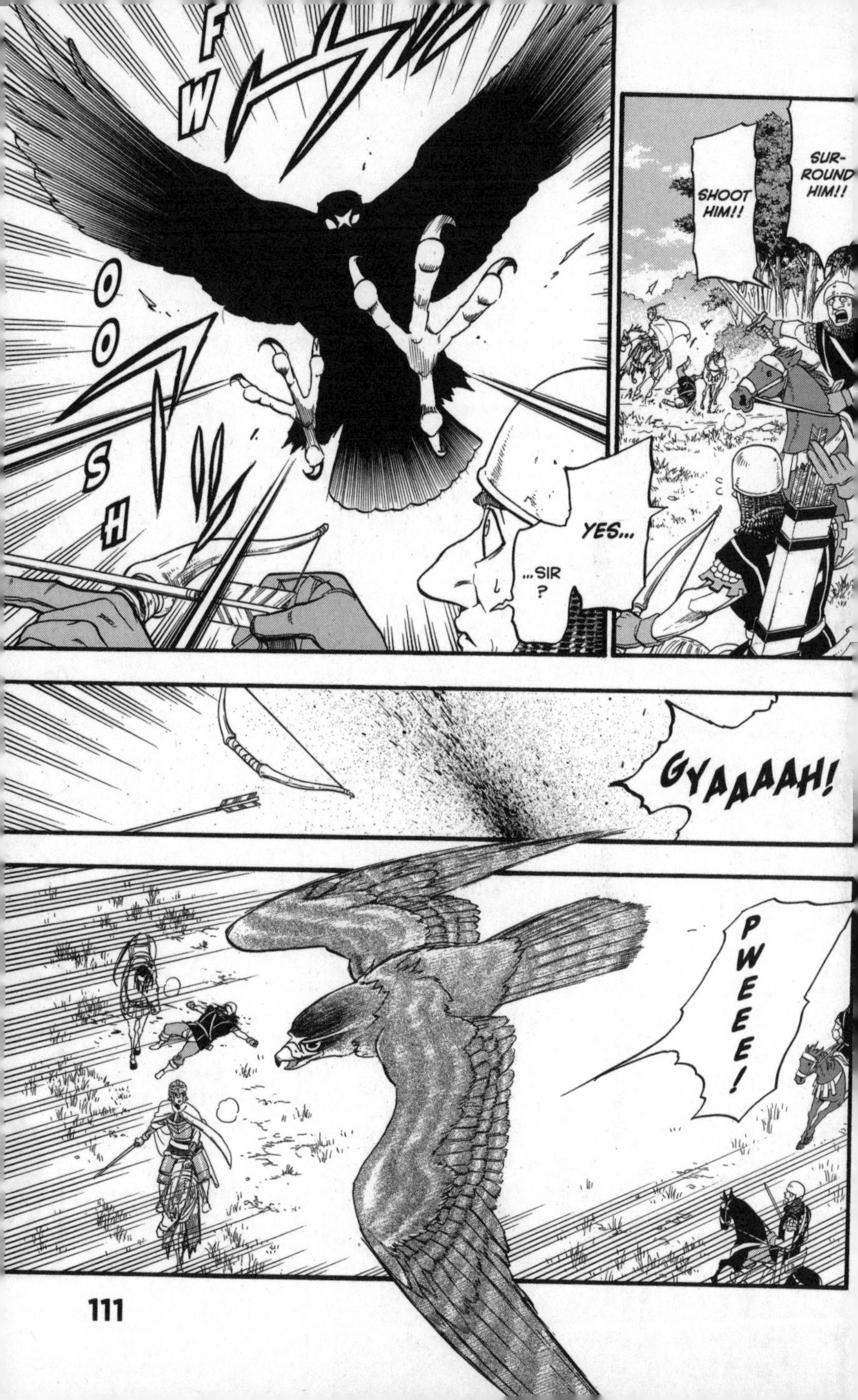
SUR-ROUND HIM!!
SHOOT HIM!!
YES...
...SIR?
FW
OOSH
GYAAAAH!
PWEEE!

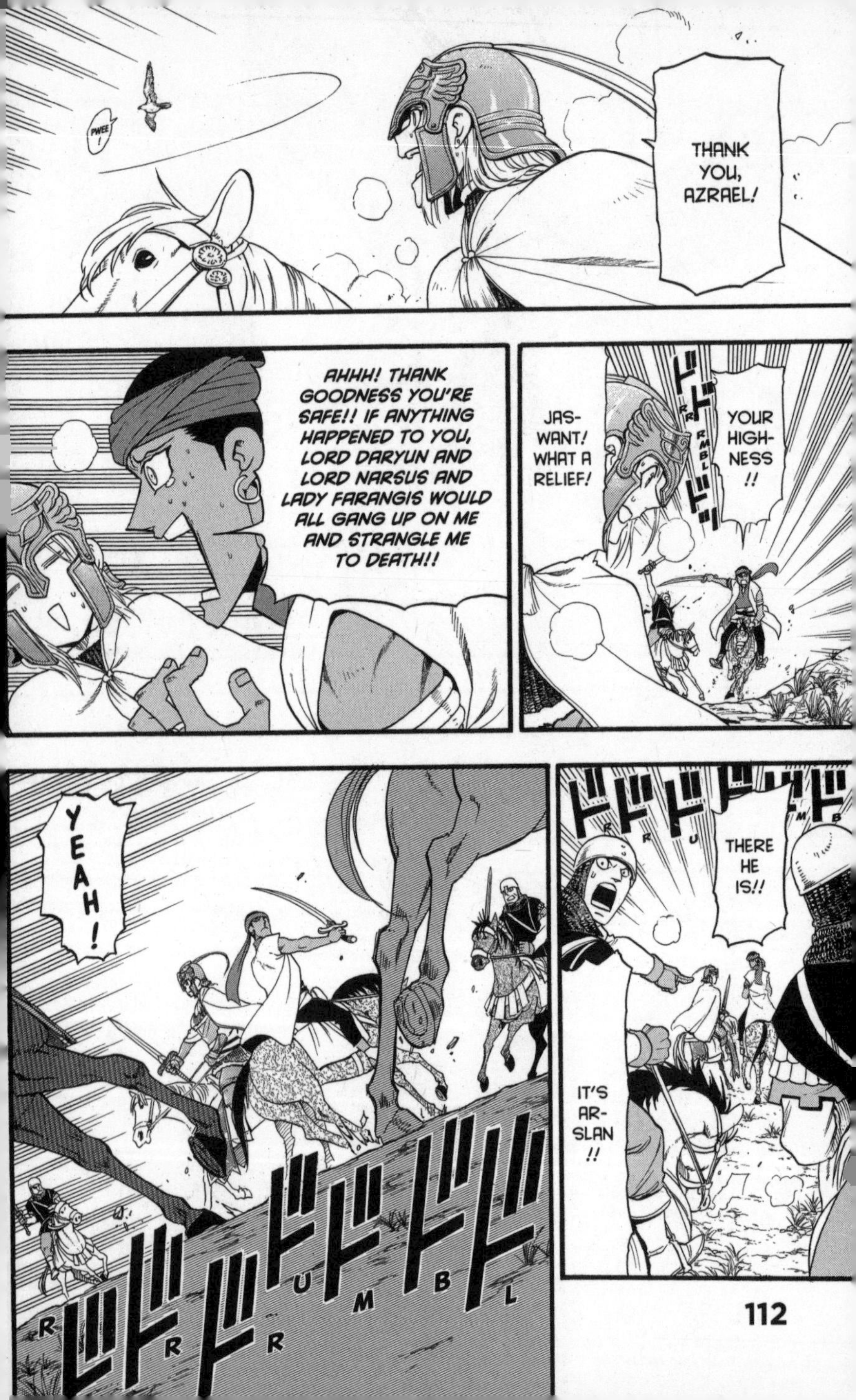
PWEE!
THANK YOU, AZRAEL!
RRMBL
YOUR HIGHNESS!!
JASWANT! WHAT A RELIEF!
AHHH! THANK GOODNESS YOU'RE SAFE!! IF ANYTHING HAPPENED TO YOU, LORD DARYUN AND LORD NARSUS AND LADY FARANGIS WOULD ALL GANG UP ON ME AND STRANGLE ME TO DEATH!!
RRUMB
THERE HE IS!!
IT'S ARSLAN!!
YEAH!
RRRUMBL

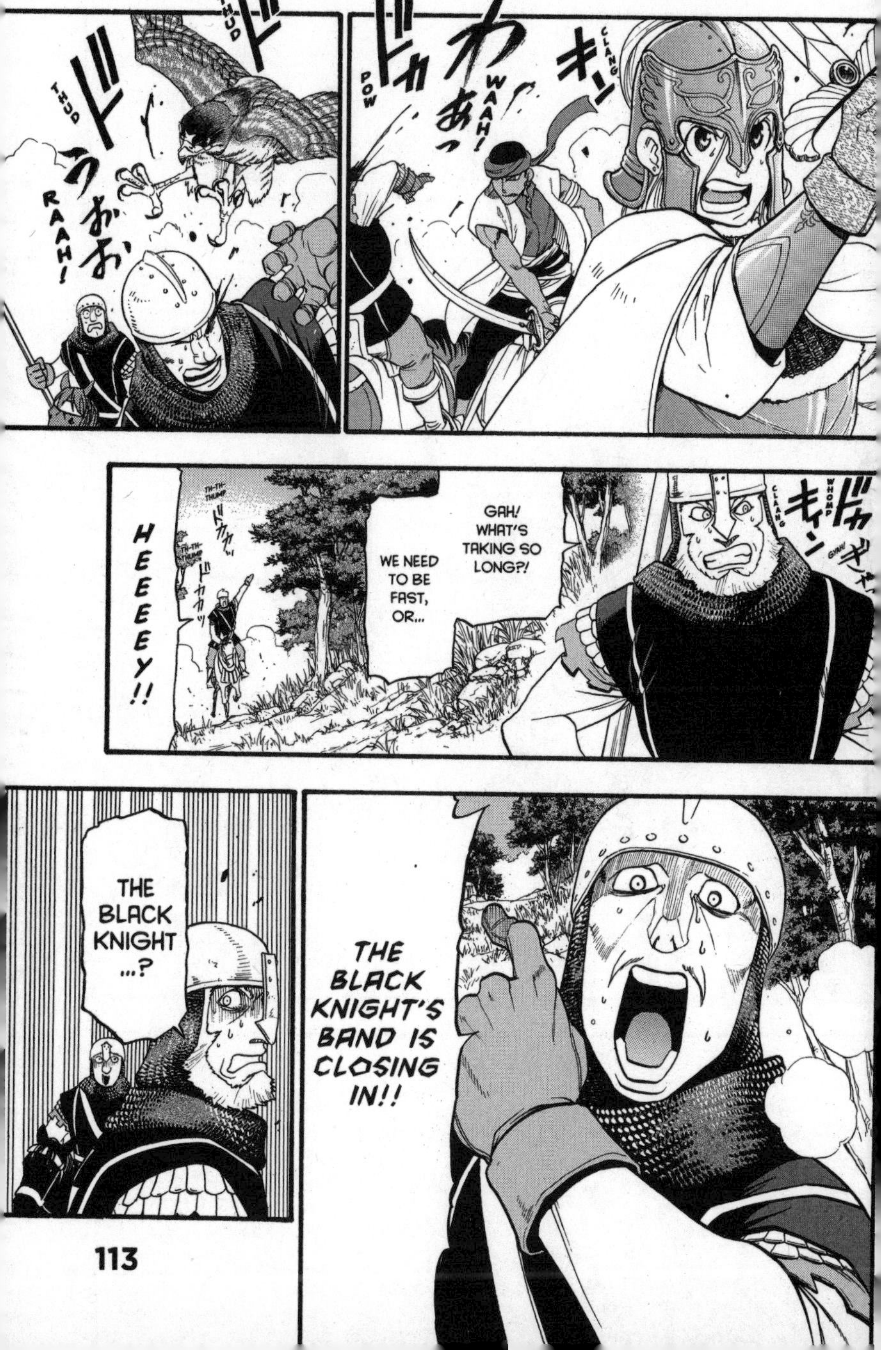
キン
CLANG
わあっ
WAAAH!
ドカ
POW
ドド
THUD THUD
うおお
RAAAH!
キィン
CLANG
ドカ
WHOMP
ぎゃっ
GYAH!
GAH! WHAT'S TAKING SO LONG?!
WE NEED TO BE FAST, OR...
ドカカッ
TH-TH-THUMP
ドカカッ
TH-TH-THUMP
HEEEEEY!!
THE BLACK KNIGHT'S BAND IS CLOSING IN!!
THE BLACK KNIGHT ...?

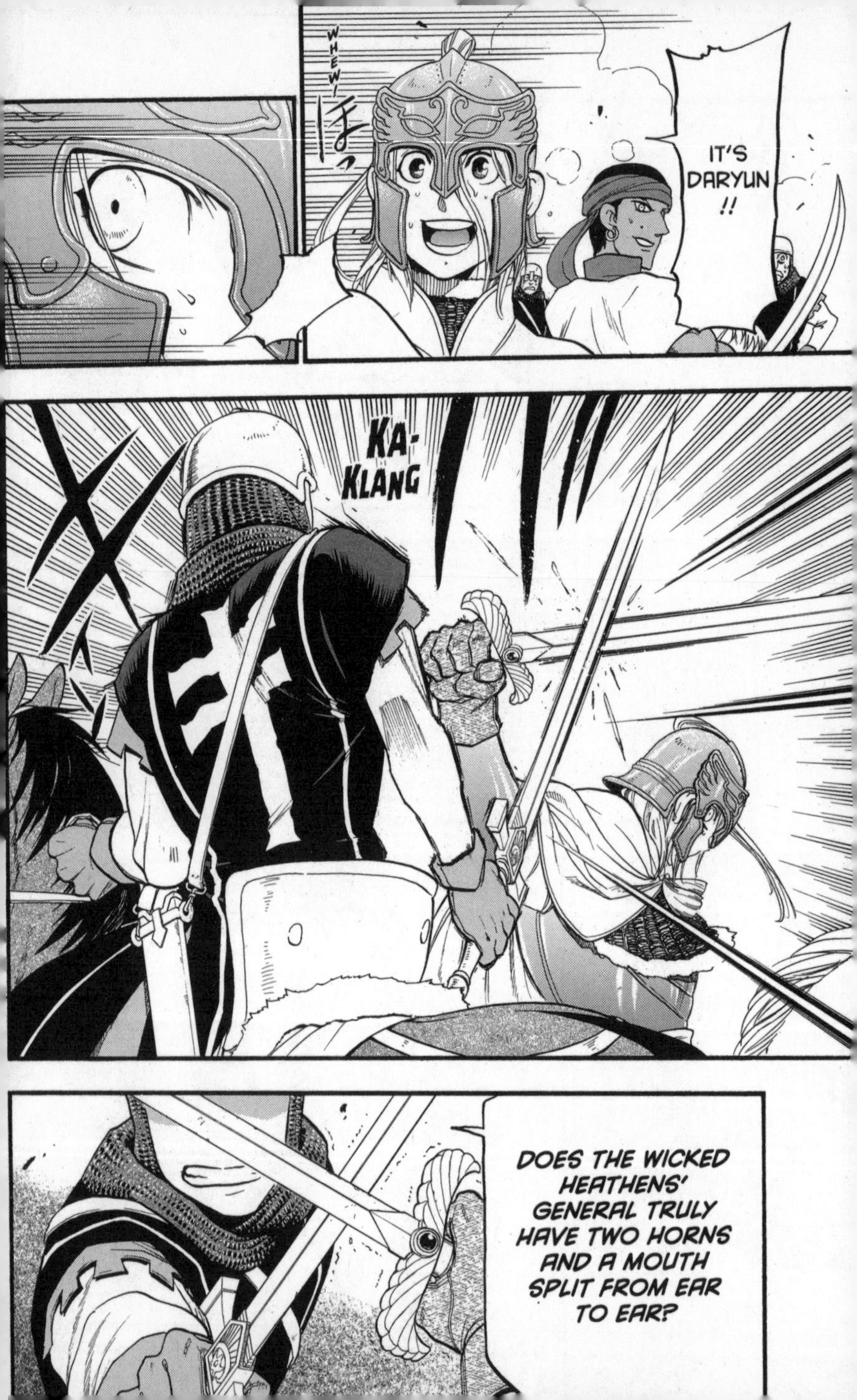

IT'S DARYUN !!
WHEW!
ほっ
KA-KLANG
DOES THE WICKED HEATHENS' GENERAL TRULY HAVE TWO HORNS AND A MOUTH SPLIT FROM EAR TO EAR?

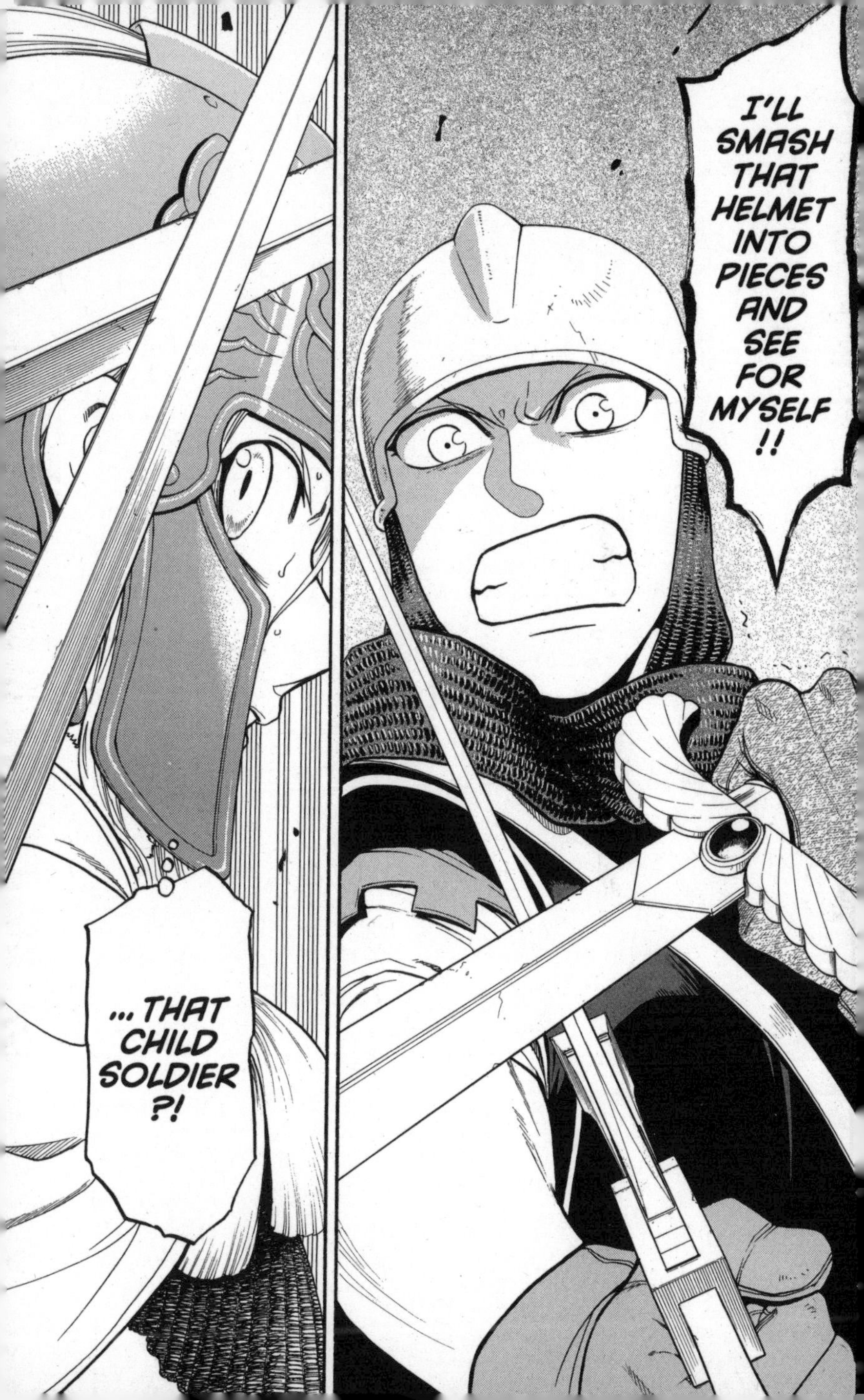
I'LL SMASH THAT HELMET INTO PIECES AND SEE FOR MYSELF!!
...THAT CHILD SOLDIER?!

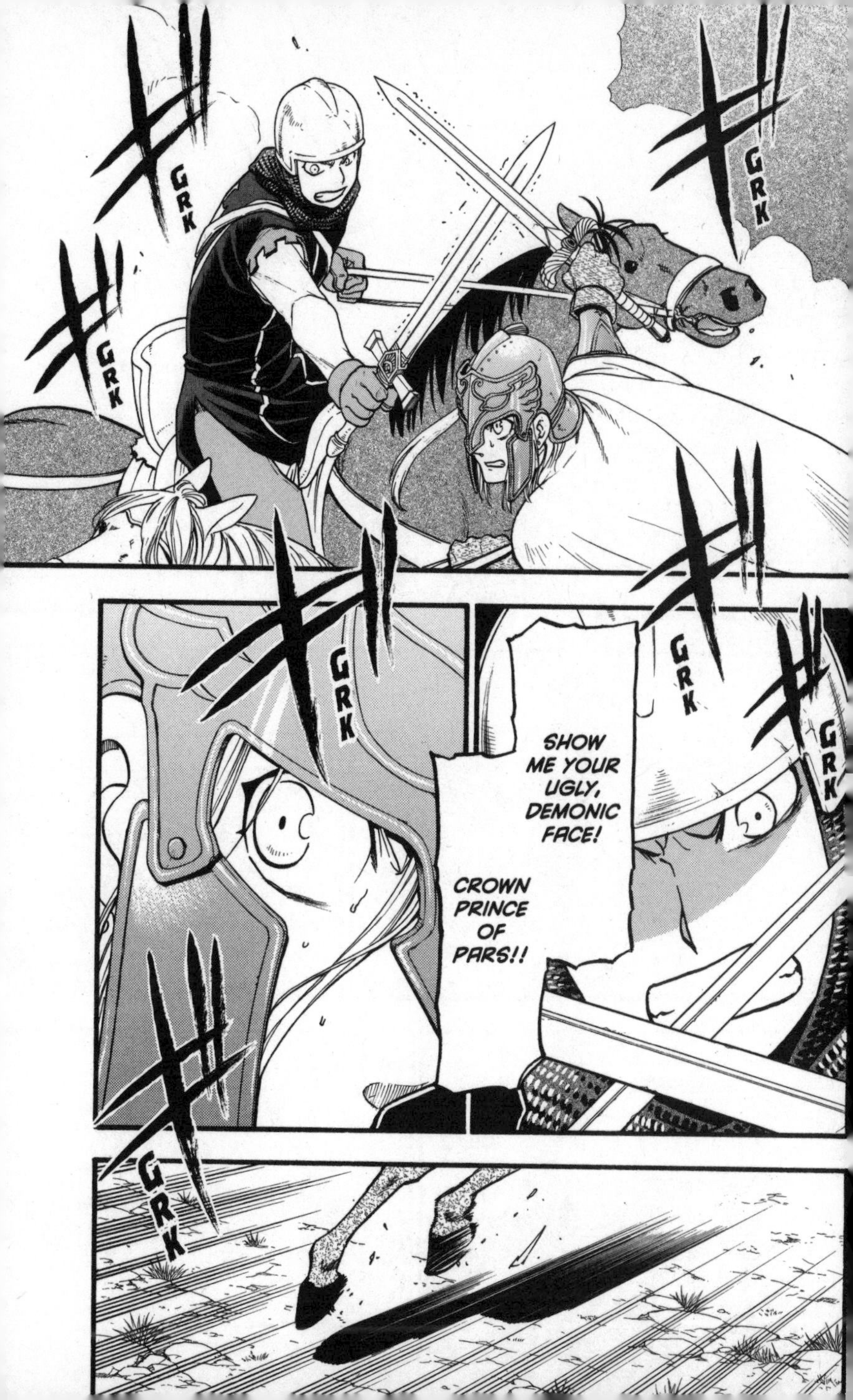
GRK
GRK
GRK
GRK
GRK
SHOW ME YOUR UGLY, DEMONIC FACE!
CROWN PRINCE OF PARS!!
GRK
GRK

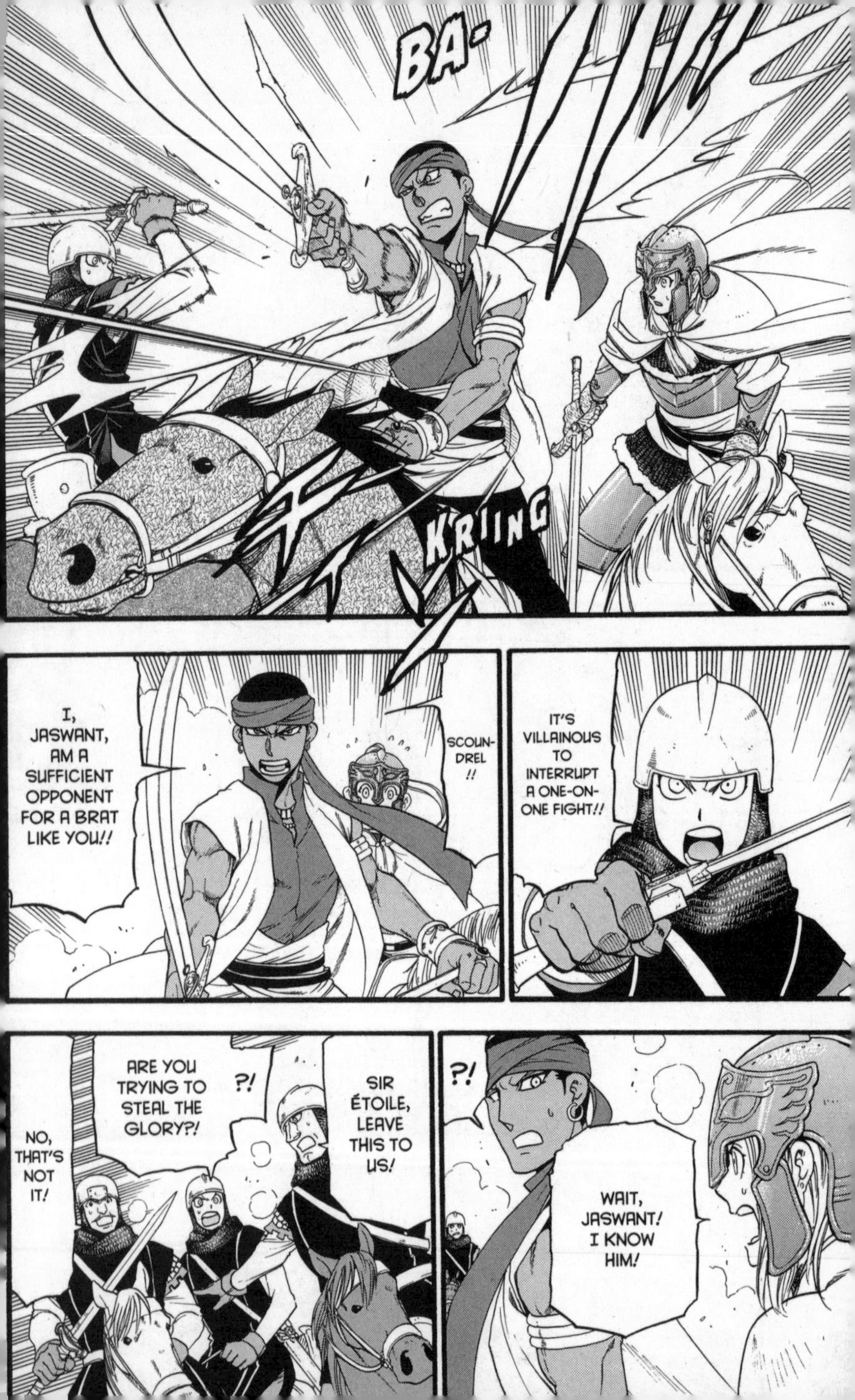
BA-
K'RIING
IT'S VILLAINOUS TO INTERRUPT A ONE-ON-ONE FIGHT!!
SCOUN-DREL!!
I, JASWANT, AM A SUFFICIENT OPPONENT FOR A BRAT LIKE YOU!!
?!
WAIT, JASWANT! I KNOW HIM!
SIR ÉTOILE, LEAVE THIS TO US!
?!
ARE YOU TRYING TO STEAL THE GLORY?!
NO, THAT'S NOT IT!

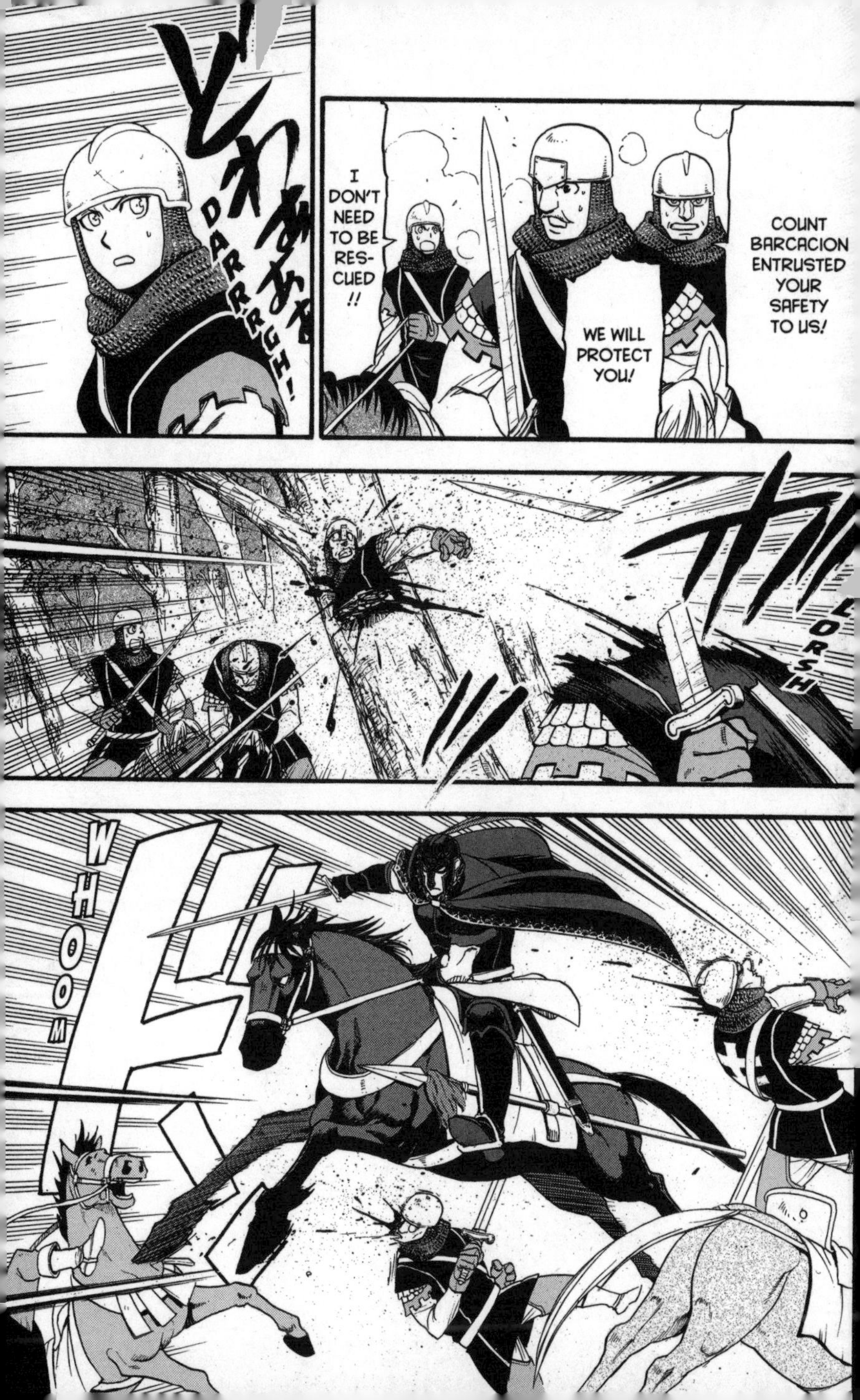
COUNT BARCACION ENTRUSTED YOUR SAFETY TO US!
WE WILL PROTECT YOU!
I DON'T NEED TO BE RES-CUED !!
DARRRGH!
LORSH
WHOOOM

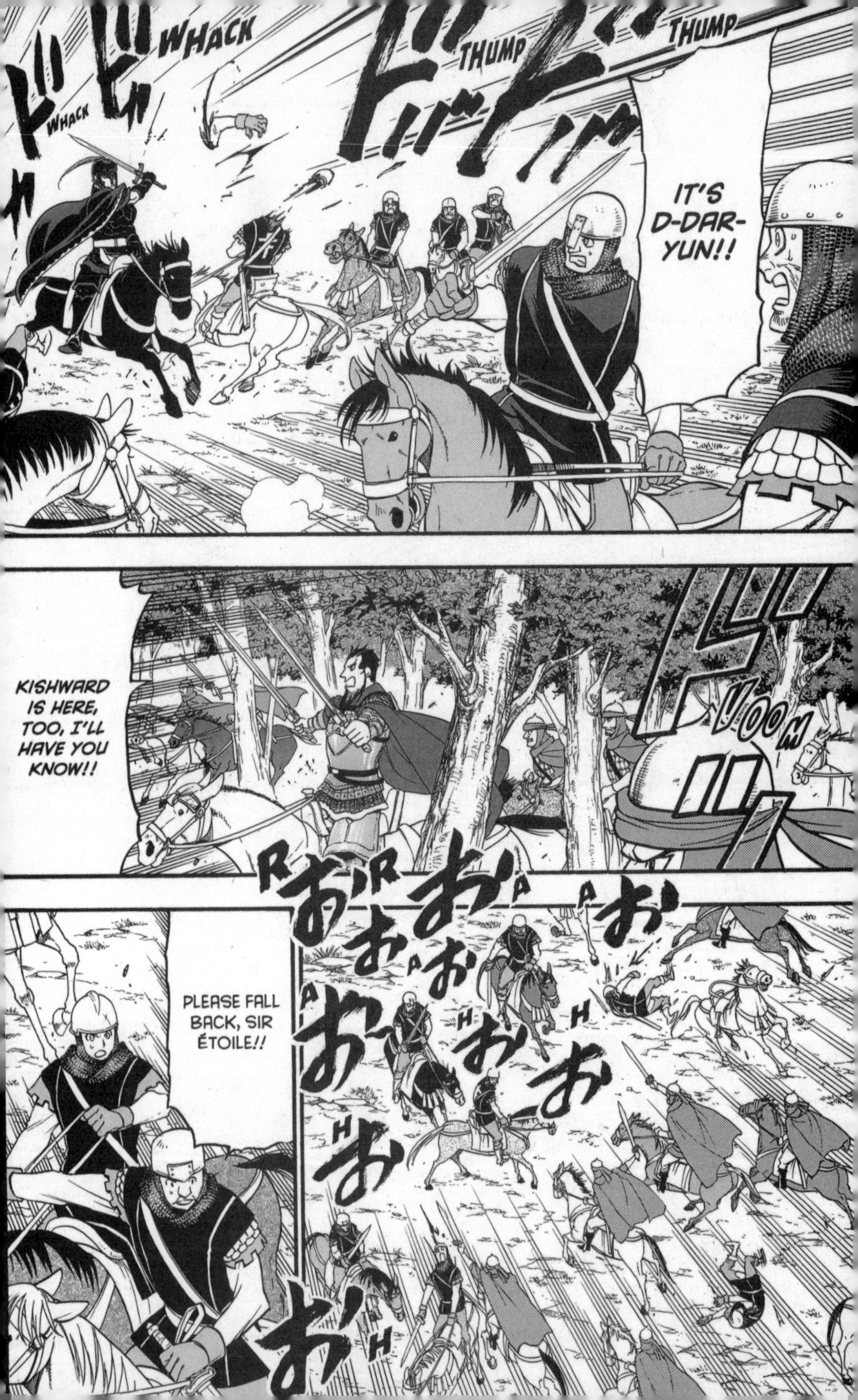
THUMP
THUMP
WHACK
WHACK
IT'S D-DAR-YUN!!
VOOM
KISHWARD IS HERE, TOO, I'LL HAVE YOU KNOW!!
PLEASE FALL BACK, SIR ÉTOILE!!

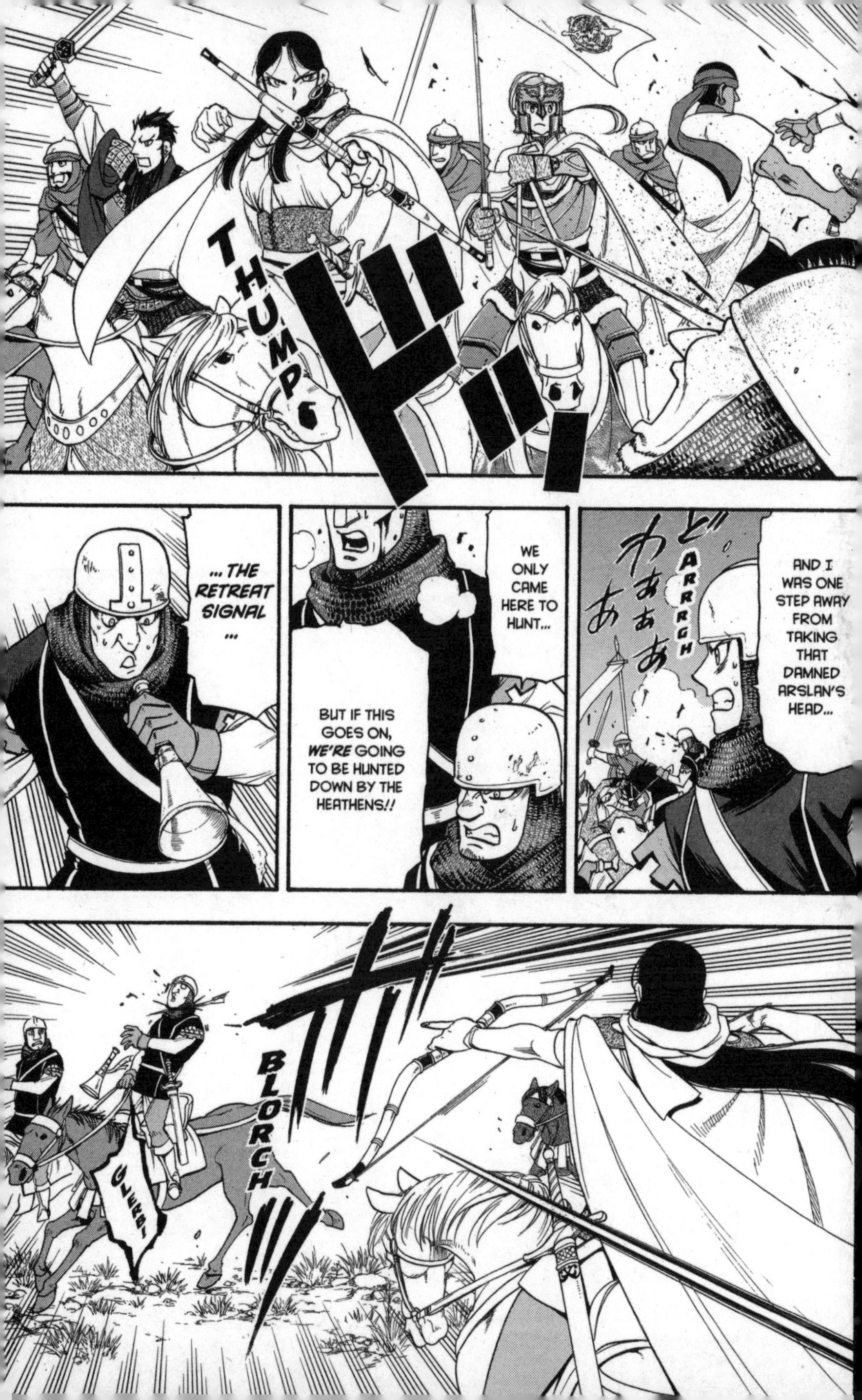
THUMP
AND I WAS ONE STEP AWAY FROM TAKING THAT DAMNED ARSLAN'S HEAD...
ARRRGH
わあああ
WE ONLY CAME HERE TO HUNT...
BUT IF THIS GOES ON, WE'RE GOING TO BE HUNTED DOWN BY THE HEATHENS!!
...THE RETREAT SIGNAL ...
BLORCH
GLERB!

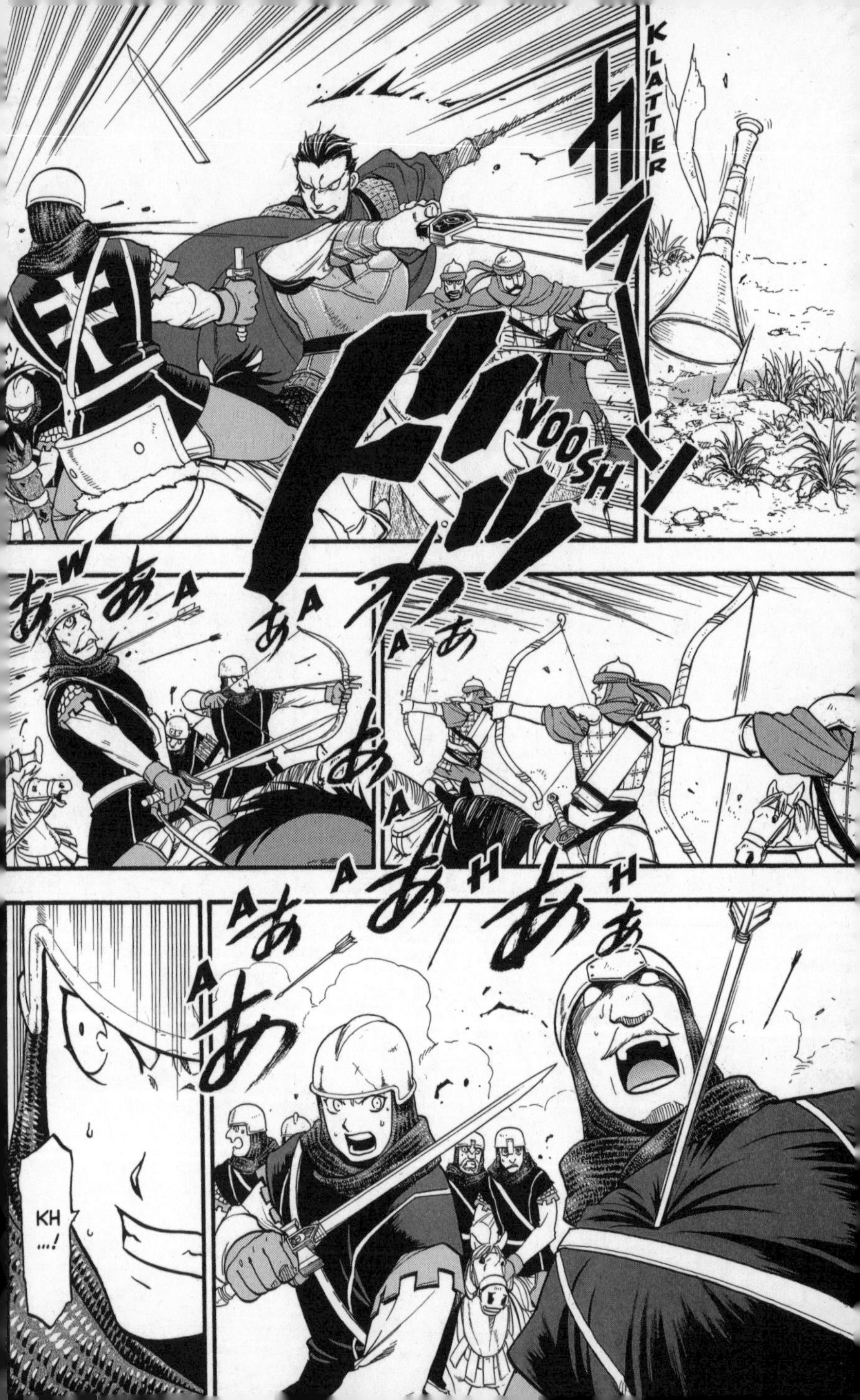
KLLATTER
VOOSH
WAAAAAAAHH
KH ...!

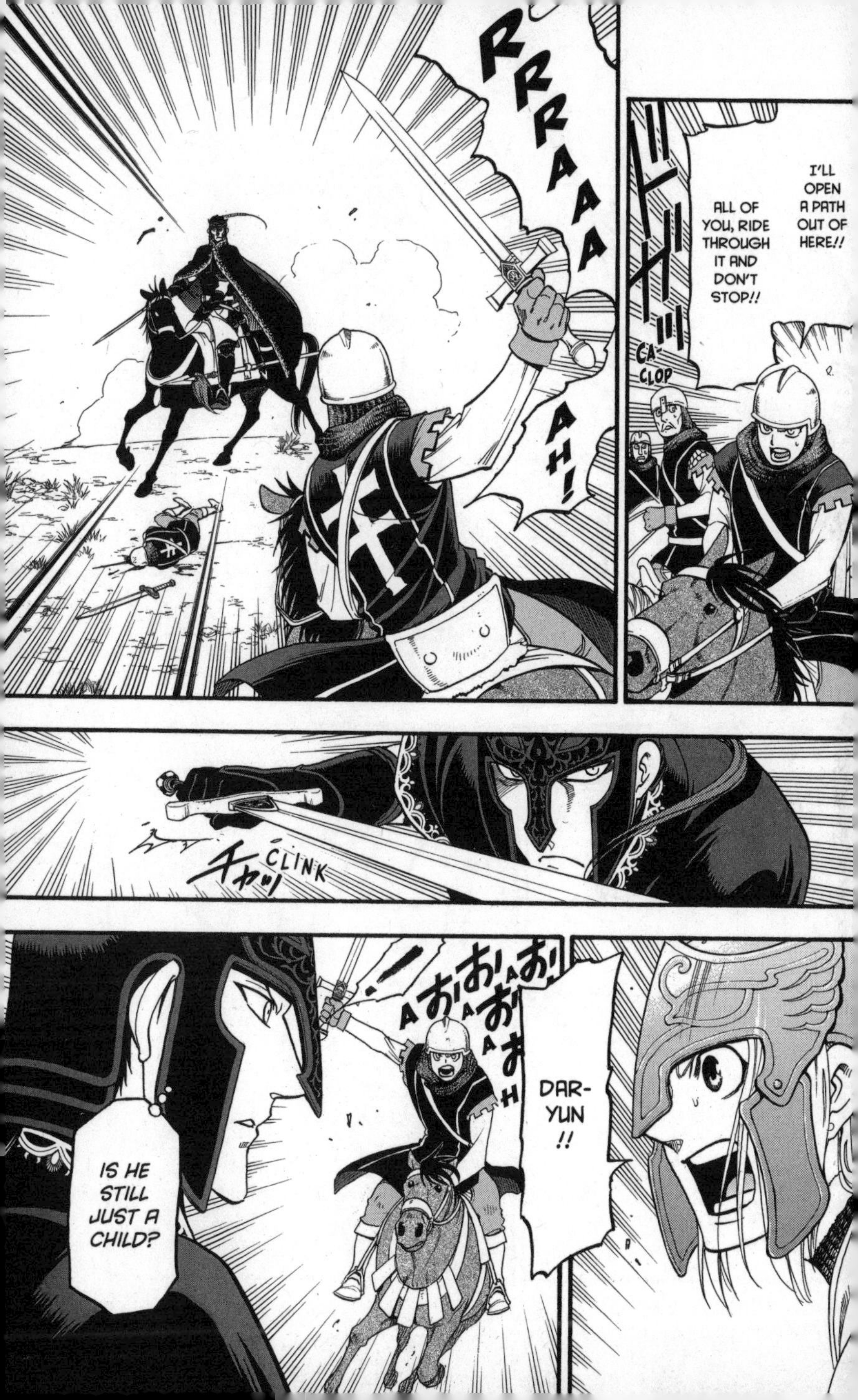
I'LL OPEN A PATH OUT OF HERE!!
ALL OF YOU, RIDE THROUGH IT AND DON'T STOP!!
CA-CLOP
RRRAAAAH!
CLINK
チャリ
DAR-YUN!!
AAAAH
IS HE STILL JUST A CHILD?

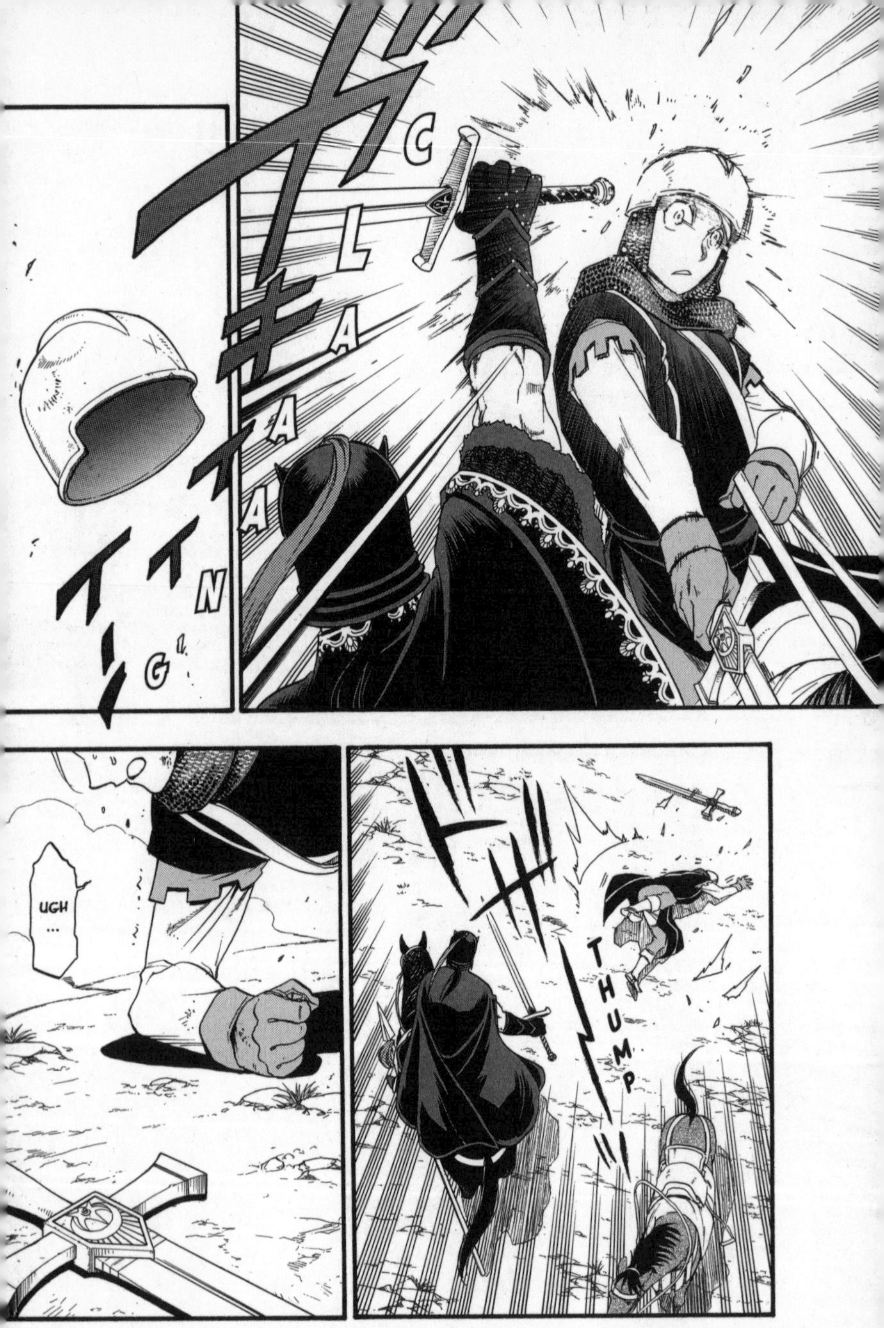
CLAAANG
THUMP!!!
UGH ...

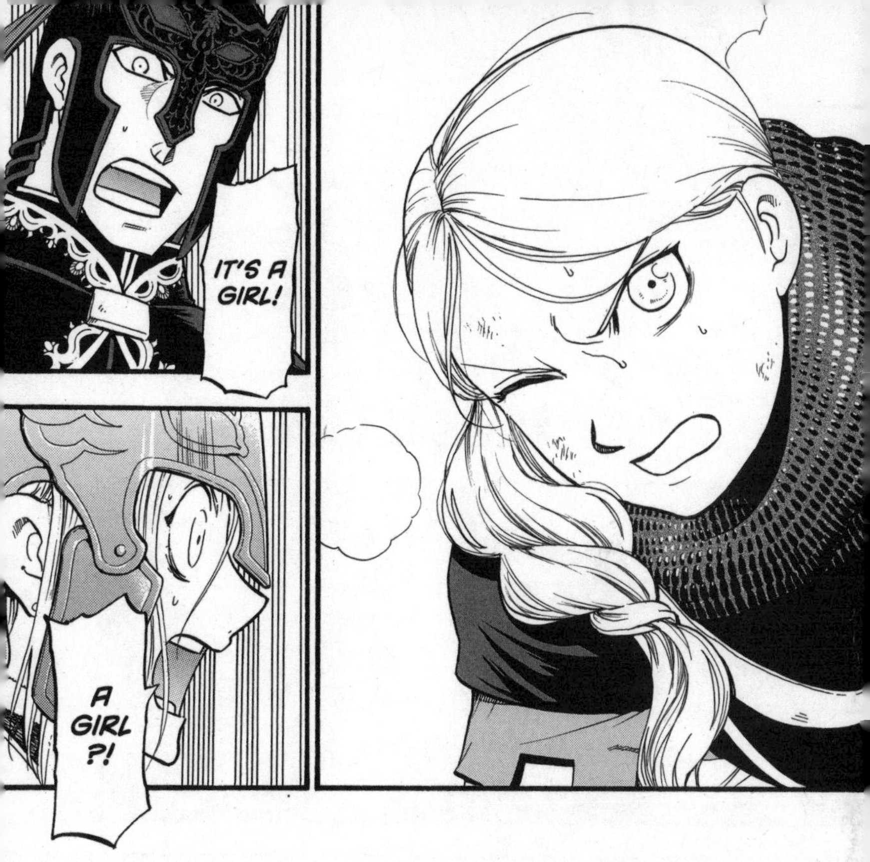
IT'S A GIRL!
A GIRL ?!

Chapter 69: The Girl of the Keep of Saint Emmanuel

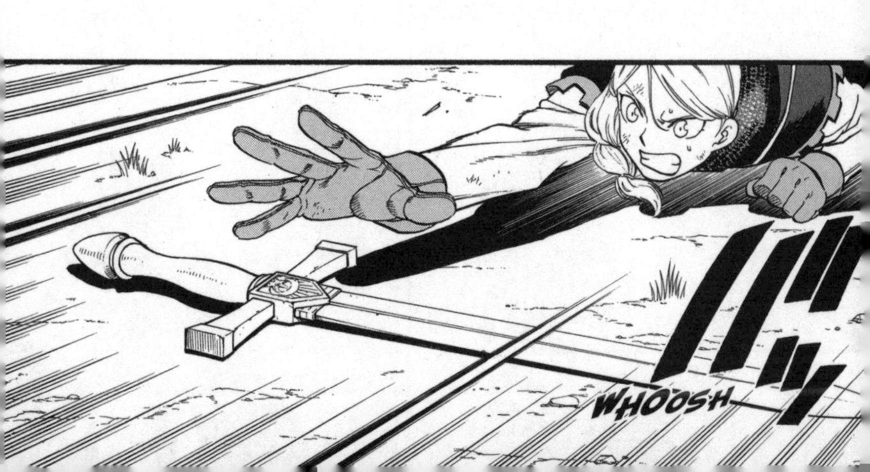
WHOOSH

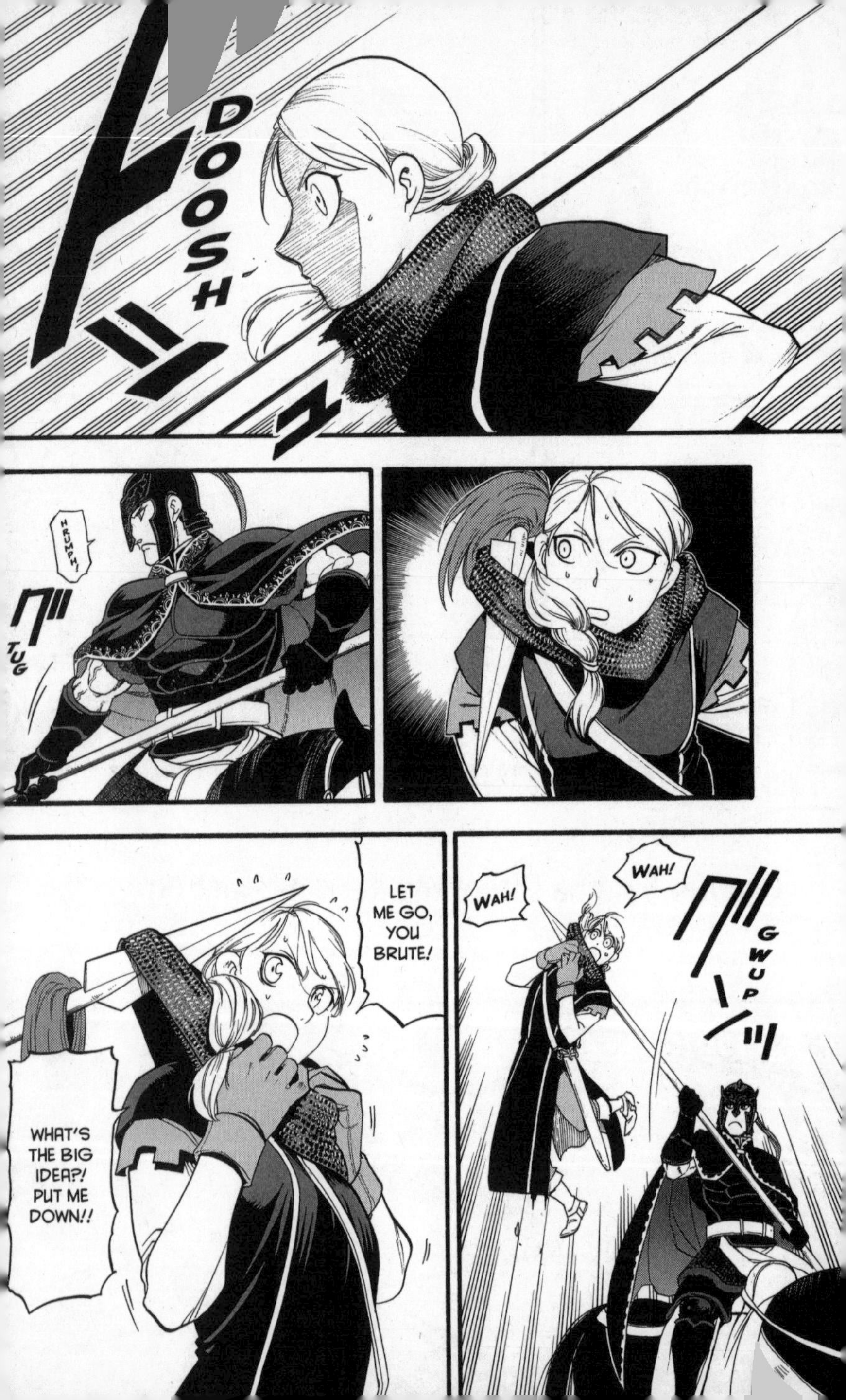
DOOSH
HRUMPH!
TUG
WAH!
WAH!
GWUP
LET ME GO, YOU BRUTE!
WHAT'S THE BIG IDEA?! PUT ME DOWN!!

IF WE LEAVE YOU HERE, YOU'LL LIKELY LOSE YOUR LIFE ON THIS BATTLEFIELD.

A CHILD'S DEATH IS A CRUEL THING, AND I CAN'T TURN MY BACK.

FLAIL FLAIL FLAIL FLAIL FLAIL

LET ME GOOOOO!

WH...!

TIE HER UP FOR NOW.

DON'T BE TOO ROUGH WITH HER.

AS YOU SAY, SIR!

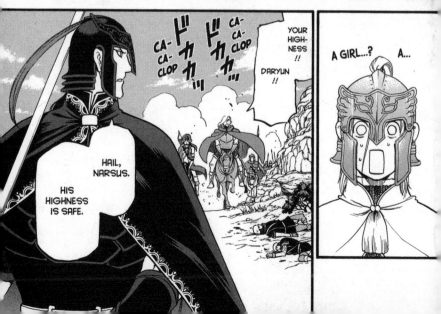

CA-CA-CLOP CA-CA-CLOP CA-CA-CLOP

YOUR HIGH-NESS!!

DARYUN!!

HAIL, NARSUS.

HIS HIGHNESS IS SAFE.

A GIRL...? A...

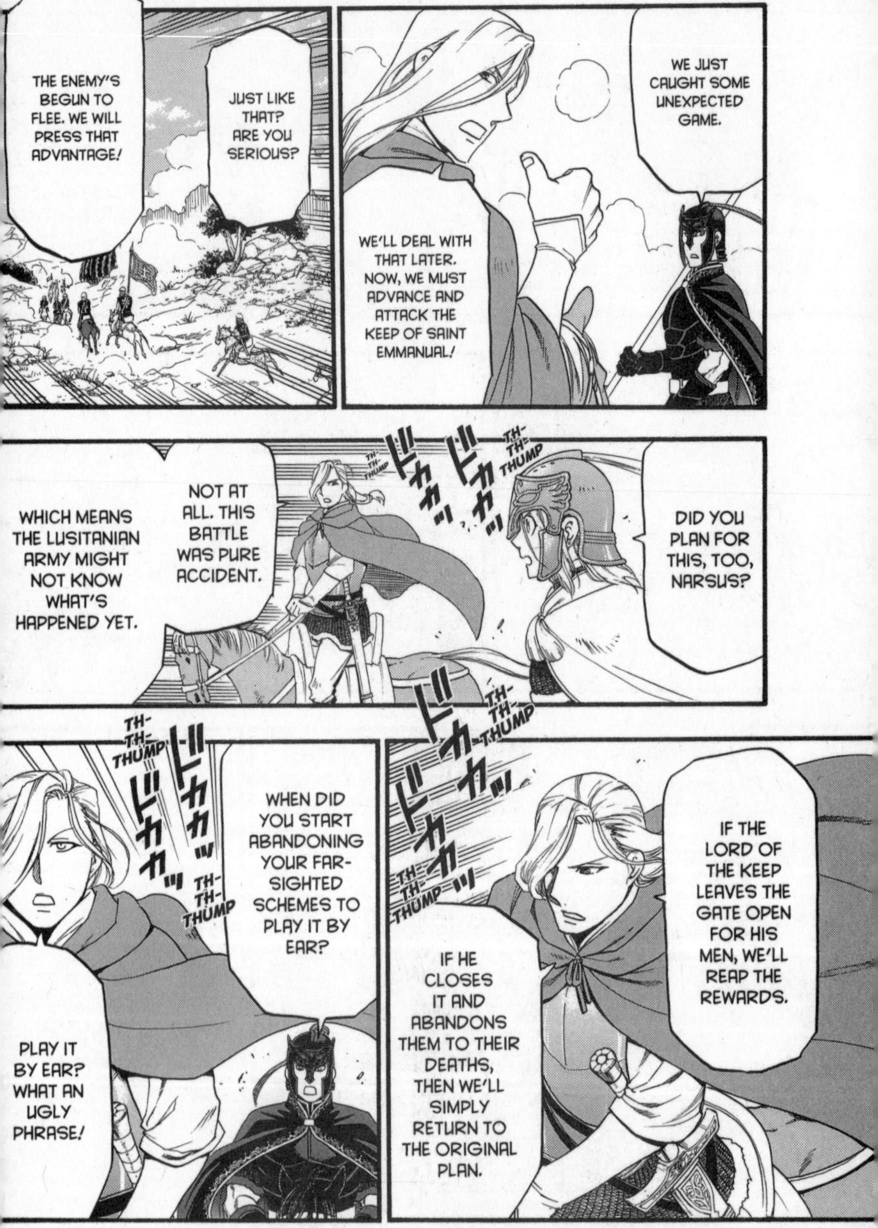

WE JUST CAUGHT SOME UNEXPECTED GAME.
WE'LL DEAL WITH THAT LATER. NOW, WE MUST ADVANCE AND ATTACK THE KEEP OF SAINT EMMANUAL!
THE ENEMY'S BEGUN TO FLEE. WE WILL PRESS THAT ADVANTAGE!
JUST LIKE THAT? ARE YOU SERIOUS?
TH-TH-THUMP
TH-TH-THUMP
DID YOU PLAN FOR THIS, TOO, NARSUS?
NOT AT ALL. THIS BATTLE WAS PURE ACCIDENT.
WHICH MEANS THE LUSITANIAN ARMY MIGHT NOT KNOW WHAT'S HAPPENED YET.
TH-TH-THUMP
TH-TH-THUMP
IF THE LORD OF THE KEEP LEAVES THE GATE OPEN FOR HIS MEN, WE'LL REAP THE REWARDS.
IF HE CLOSES IT AND ABANDONS THEM TO THEIR DEATHS, THEN WE'LL SIMPLY RETURN TO THE ORIGINAL PLAN.
TH-TH-THUMP
TH-TH-THUMP
WHEN DID YOU START ABANDONING YOUR FAR-SIGHTED SCHEMES TO PLAY IT BY EAR?
PLAY IT BY EAR? WHAT AN UGLY PHRASE!

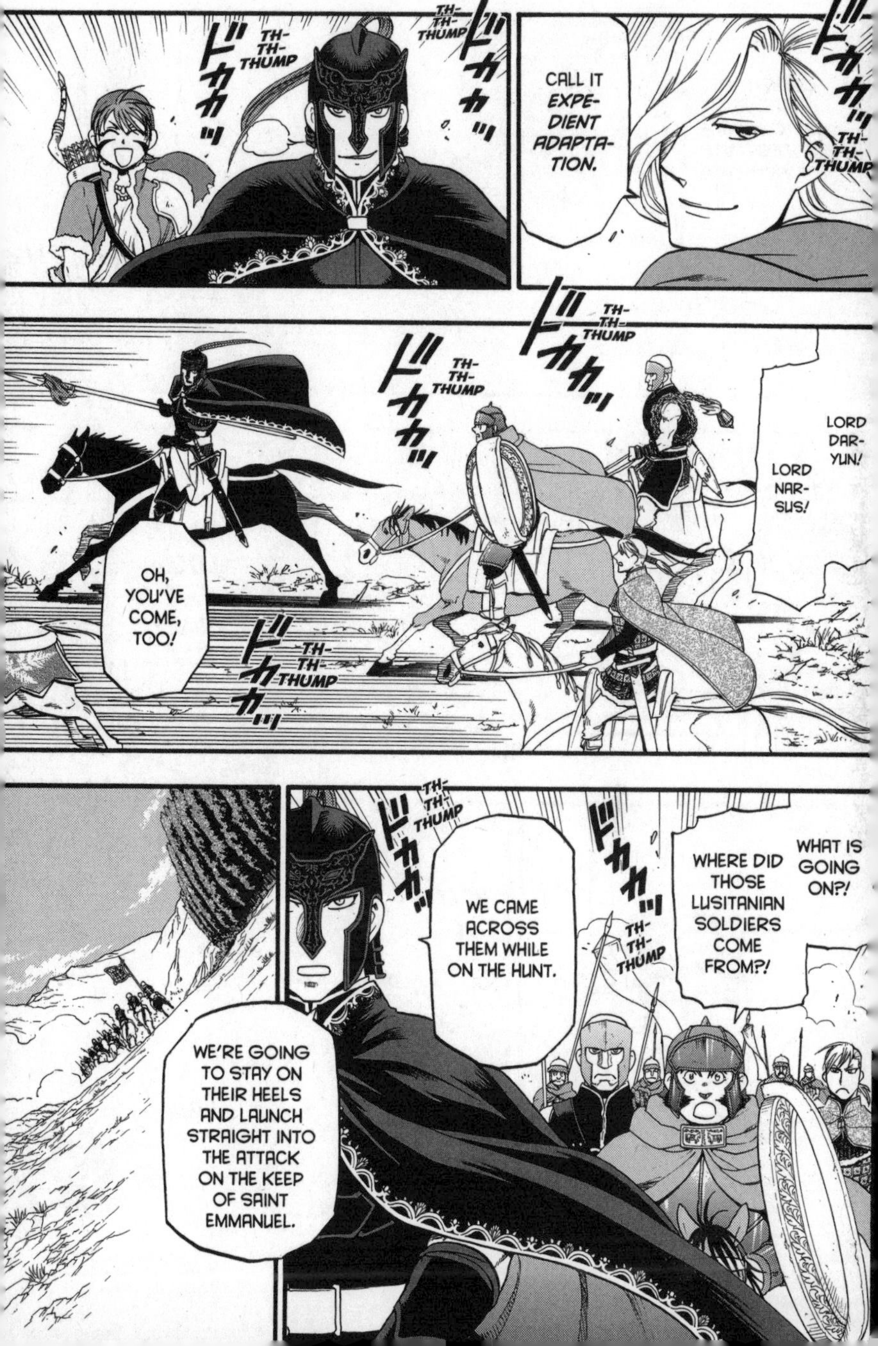
ドカカッ
TH-TH-THUMP
CALL IT EXPEDIENT ADAPTATION.
ドカカッ
TH-TH-THUMP
ドカカッ
TH-TH-THUMP
ドカカッ
TH-TH-THUMP
LORD DARYUN!
LORD NARSUS!
ドカカッ
TH-TH-THUMP
OH, YOU'VE COME, TOO!
ドカカッ
TH-TH-THUMP
WHAT IS GOING ON?!
WHERE DID THOSE LUSITANIAN SOLDIERS COME FROM?!
ドカカッ
TH-TH-THUMP
WE CAME ACROSS THEM WHILE ON THE HUNT.
ドカカッ
TH-TH-THUMP
WE'RE GOING TO STAY ON THEIR HEELS AND LAUNCH STRAIGHT INTO THE ATTACK ON THE KEEP OF SAINT EMMANUEL.

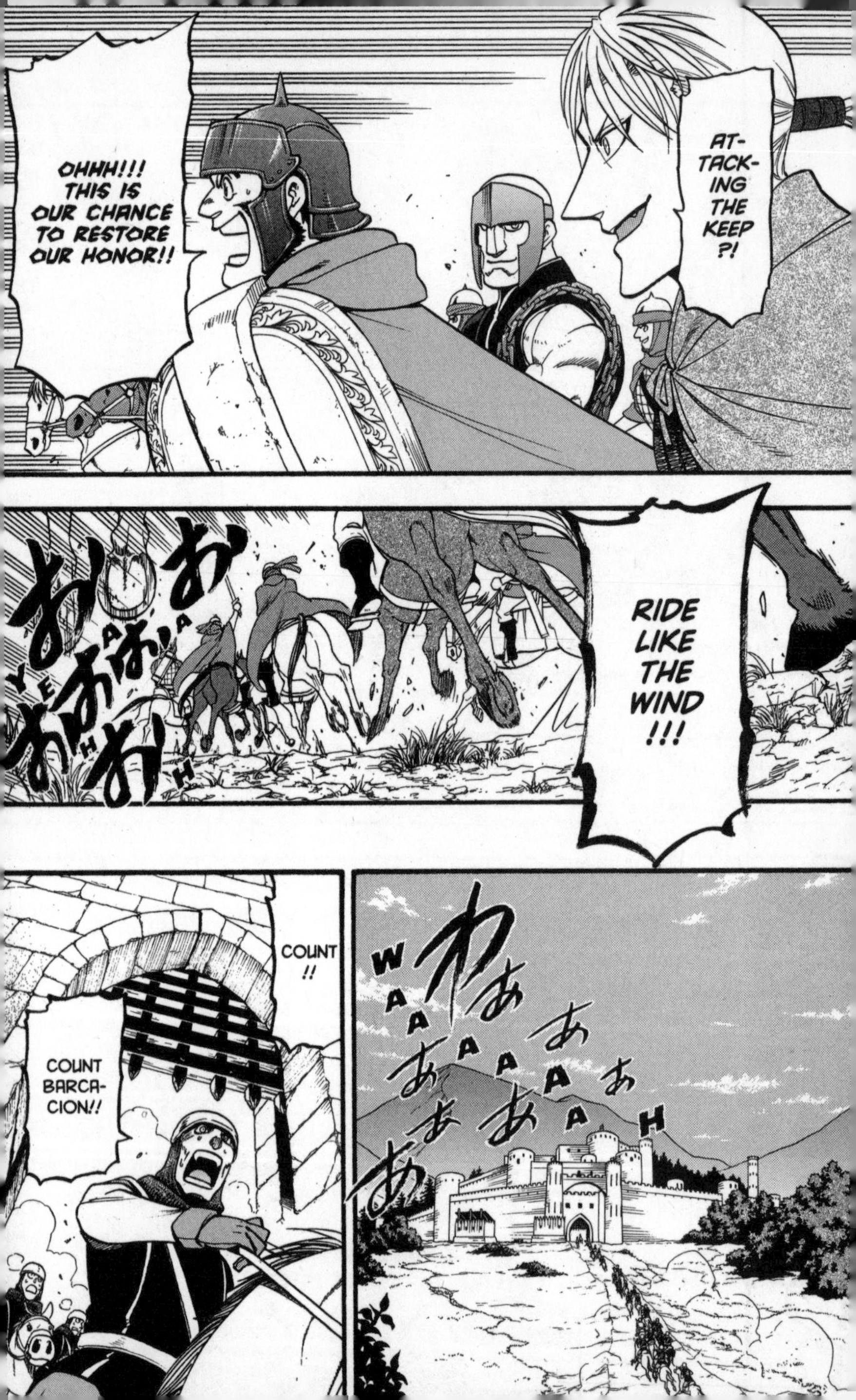
AT-TACKING THE KEEP?!
OHHH!!! THIS IS OUR CHANCE TO RESTORE OUR HONOR!!
RIDE LIKE THE WIND!!!
COUNT!!
COUNT BARCACION!!

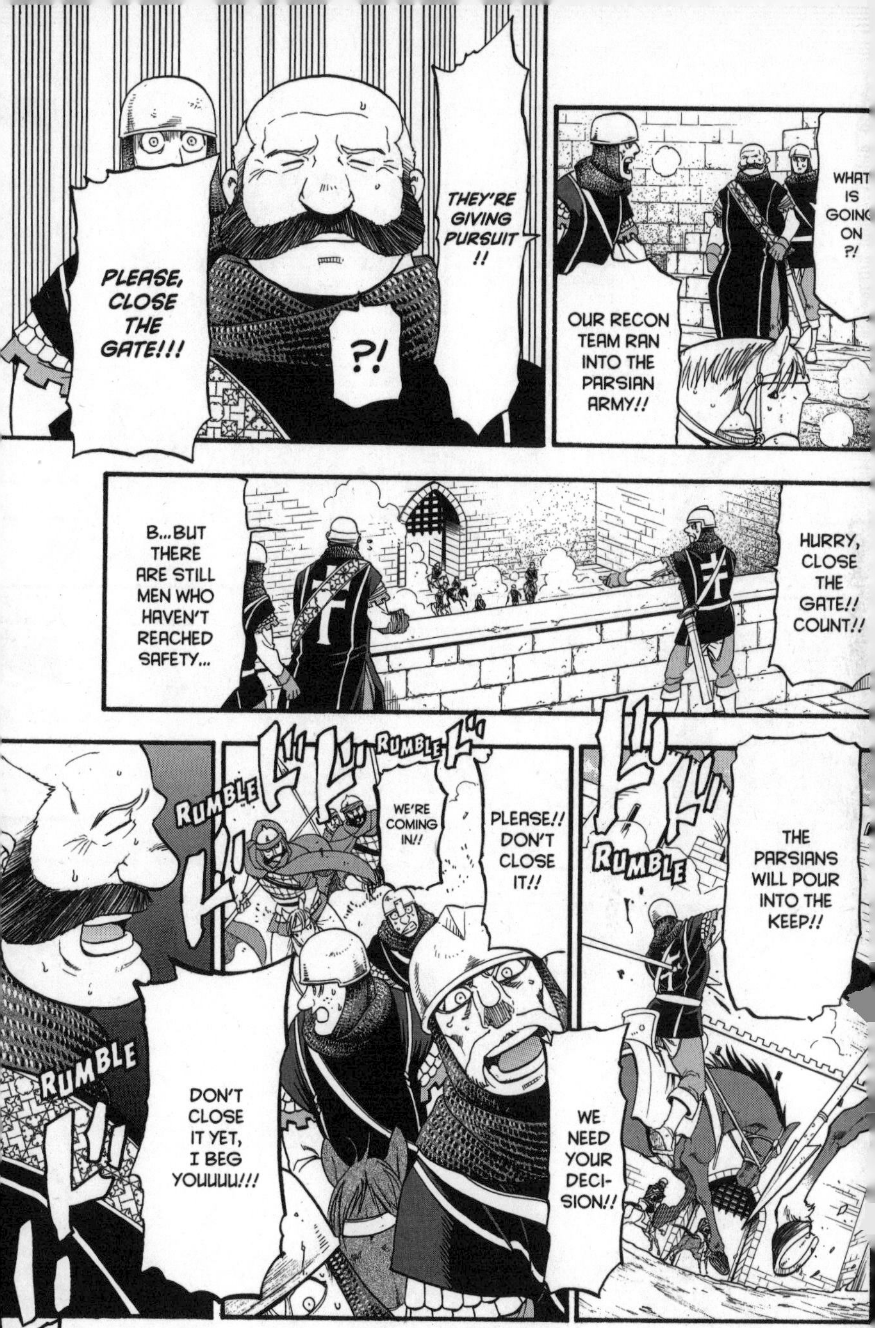
WHAT IS GOING ON ?!
OUR RECON TEAM RAN INTO THE PARSIAN ARMY!!
THEY'RE GIVING PURSUIT !!
?!
PLEASE, CLOSE THE GATE!!!
HURRY, CLOSE THE GATE!! COUNT!!
B...BUT THERE ARE STILL MEN WHO HAVEN'T REACHED SAFETY...
RUMBLE
THE PARSIANS WILL POUR INTO THE KEEP!!
RUMBLE
PLEASE!! DON'T CLOSE IT!!
WE'RE COMING IN!!
RUMBLE
WE NEED YOUR DECISION!!
DON'T CLOSE IT YET, I BEG YOUUUU!!!
RUMBLE

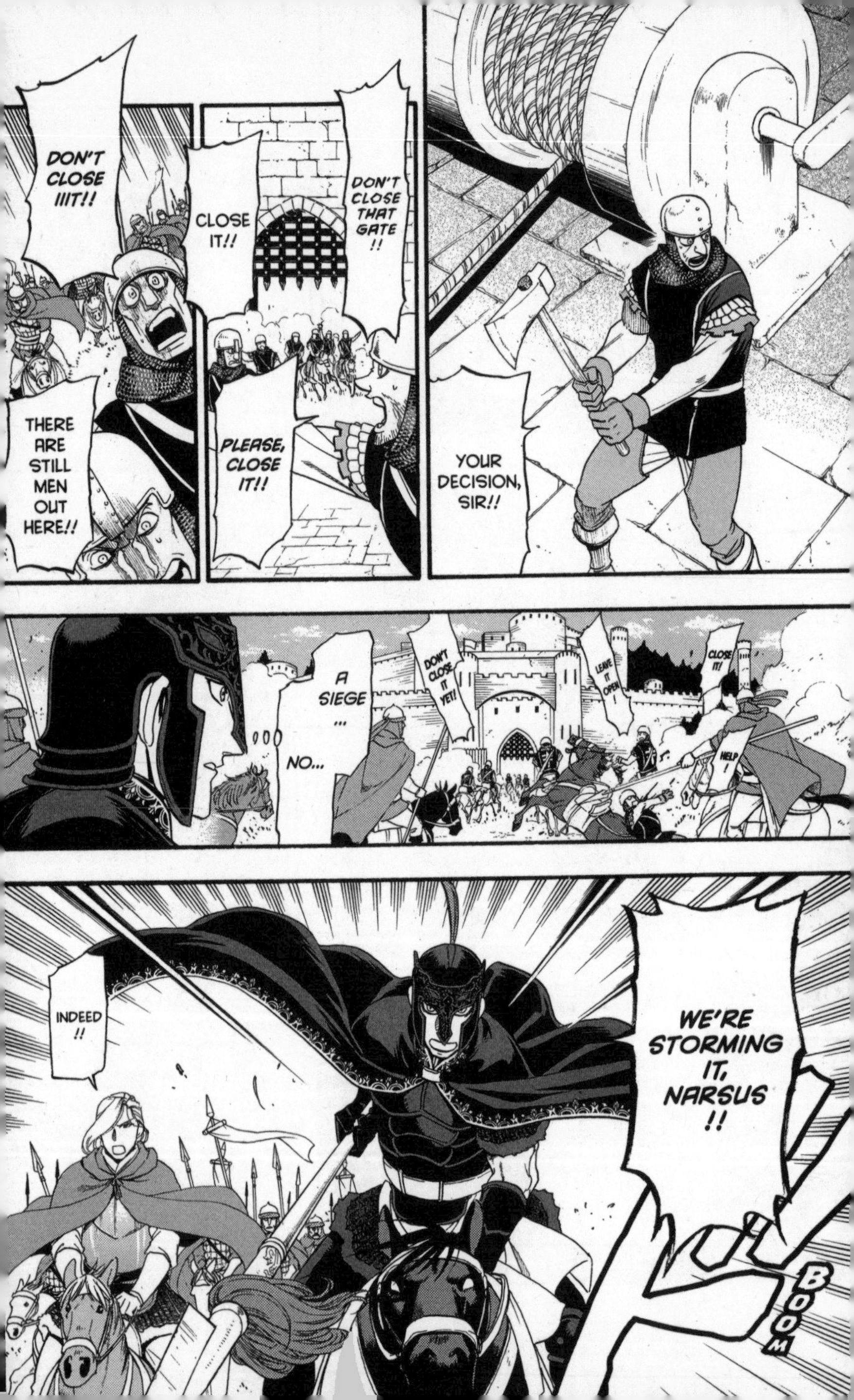
YOUR DECISION, SIR!!
DON'T CLOSE THAT GATE !!
CLOSE IT!!
PLEASE, CLOSE IT!!
DON'T CLOSE IIIT!!
THERE ARE STILL MEN OUT HERE!!
CLOSE IT!
LEAVE IT OPEN!
HELP!
DON'T CLOSE IT YET!
A SIEGE ...
NO...
...
WE'RE STORMING IT, NARSUS!!
BOOM
INDEED!!

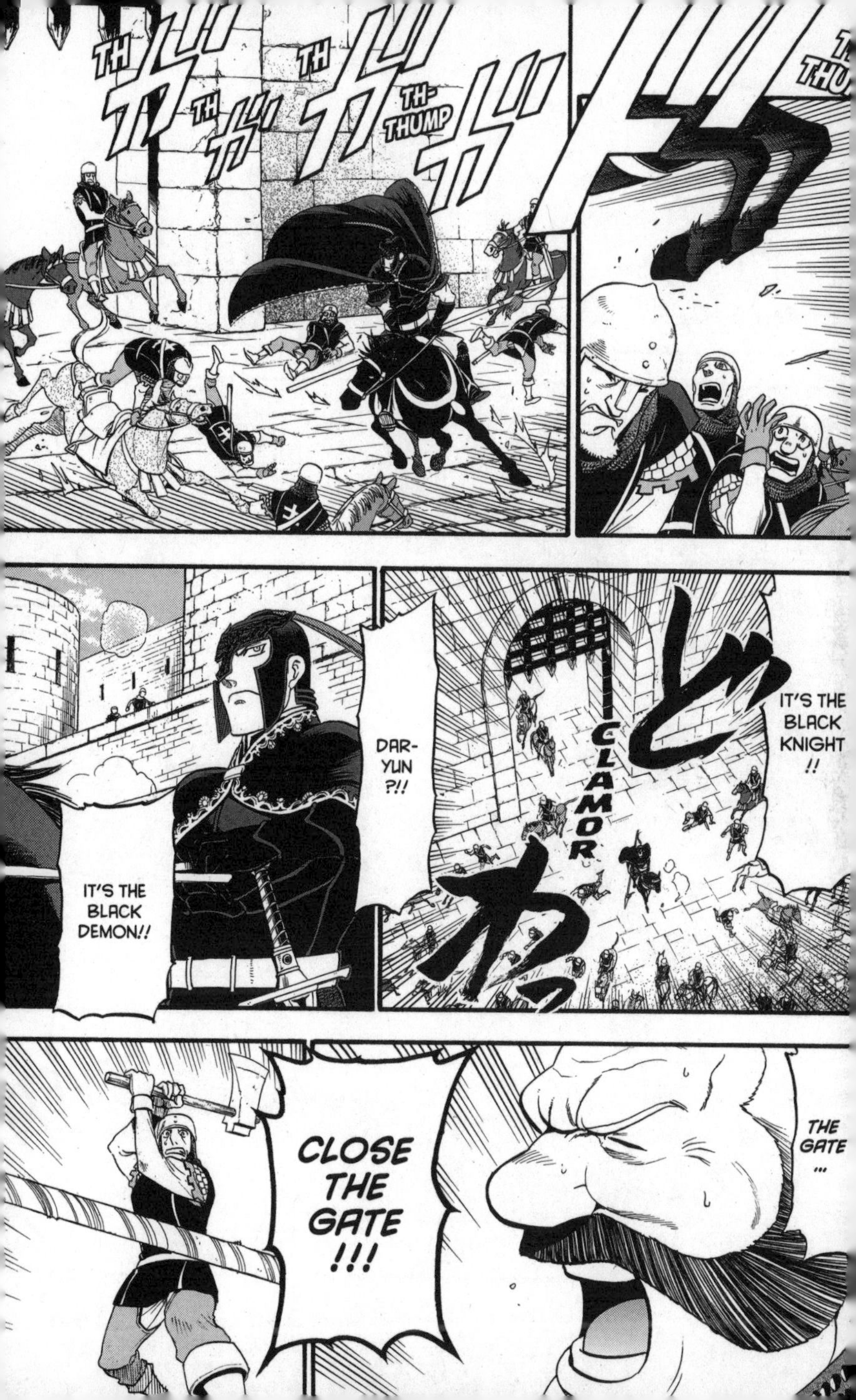
THUMP
TH
TH
TH
TH-THUMP
IT'S THE BLACK KNIGHT !!
CLAMOR
DAR-YUN ?!!
IT'S THE BLACK DEMON!!
THE GATE ...
CLOSE THE GATE !!!

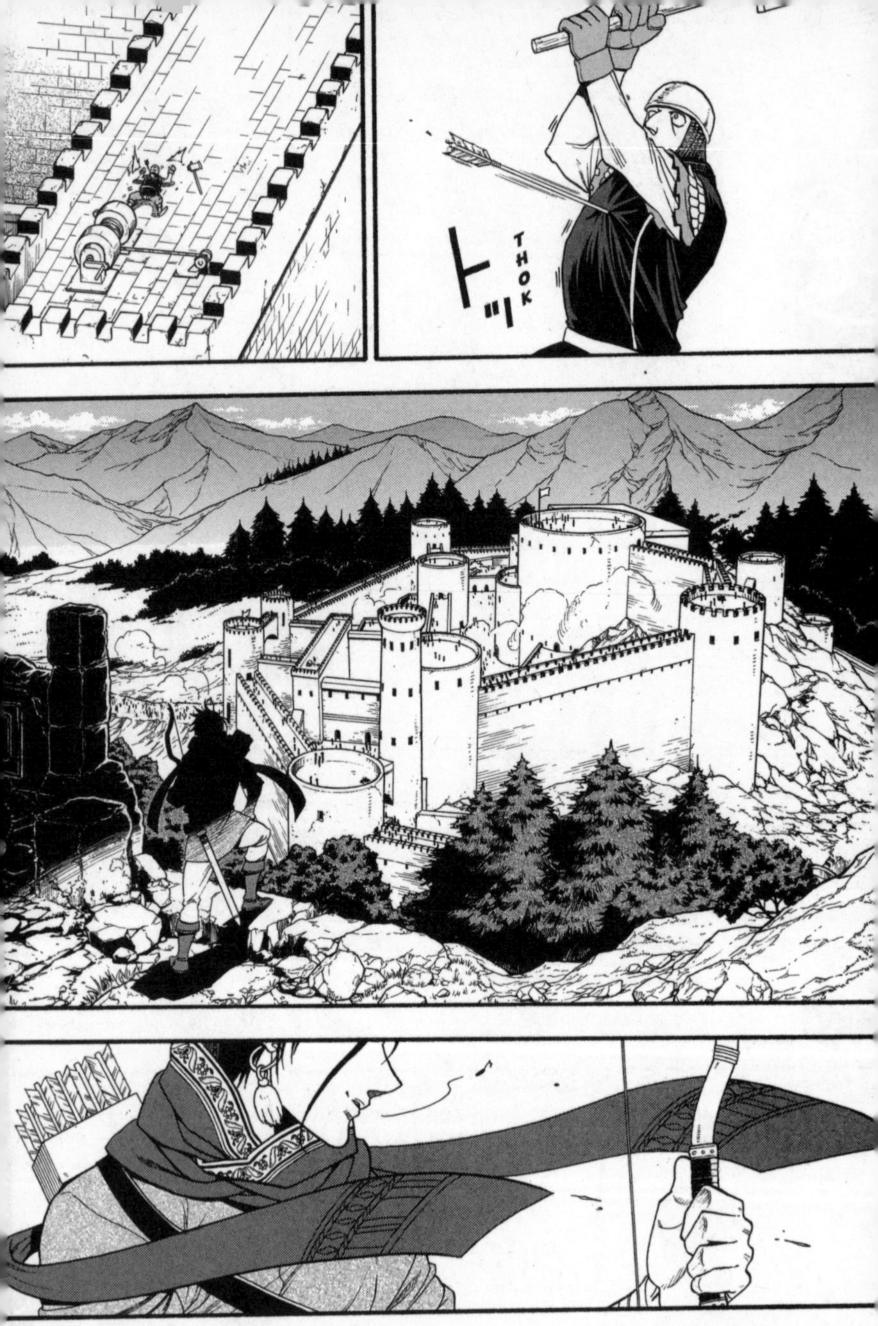
トッ
THOK

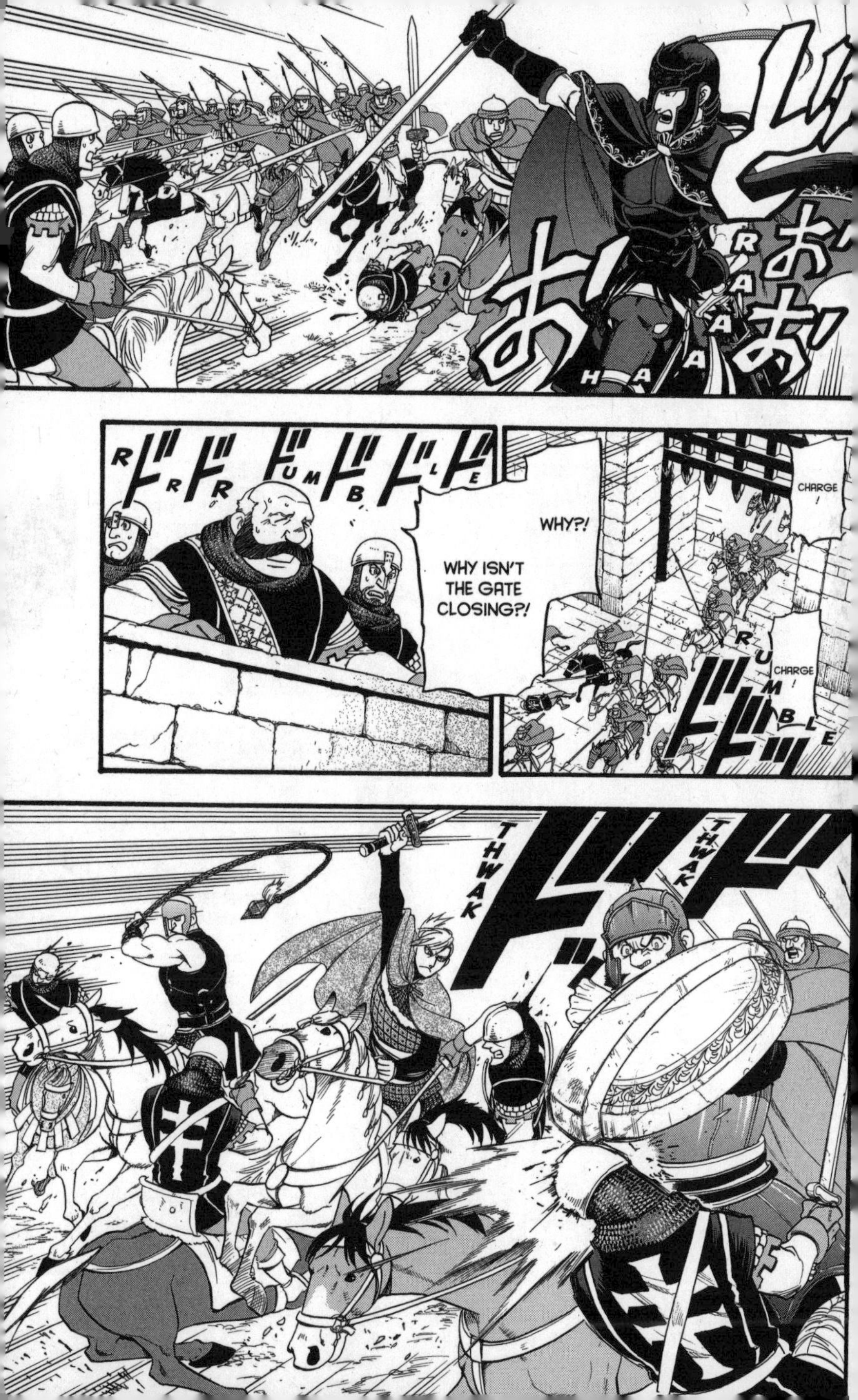
CHARGE!
CHARGE!
RUMBLE
WHY?!
WHY ISN'T THE GATE CLOSING?!
RRRUMBLE
THWAK
THWAK

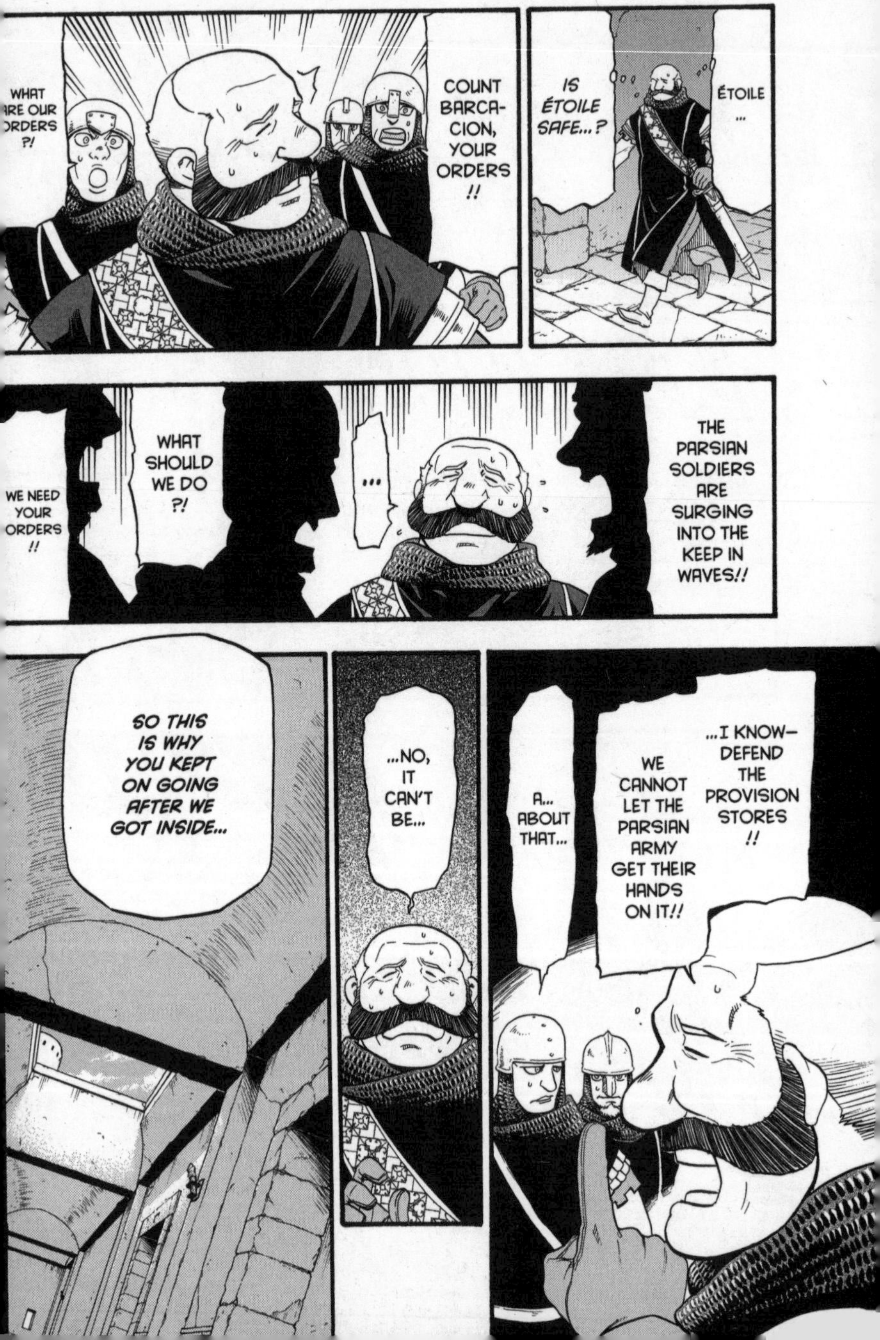
ÉTOILE ...
IS ÉTOILE SAFE...?
COUNT BARCACION, YOUR ORDERS!!
WHAT ARE OUR ORDERS?!
THE PARSIAN SOLDIERS ARE SURGING INTO THE KEEP IN WAVES!!
...
WHAT SHOULD WE DO?!
WE NEED YOUR ORDERS!!
...I KNOW—DEFEND THE PROVISION STORES!!
WE CANNOT LET THE PARSIAN ARMY GET THEIR HANDS ON IT!!
A... ABOUT THAT...
...NO, IT CAN'T BE...
SO THIS IS WHY YOU KEPT ON GOING AFTER WE GOT INSIDE...

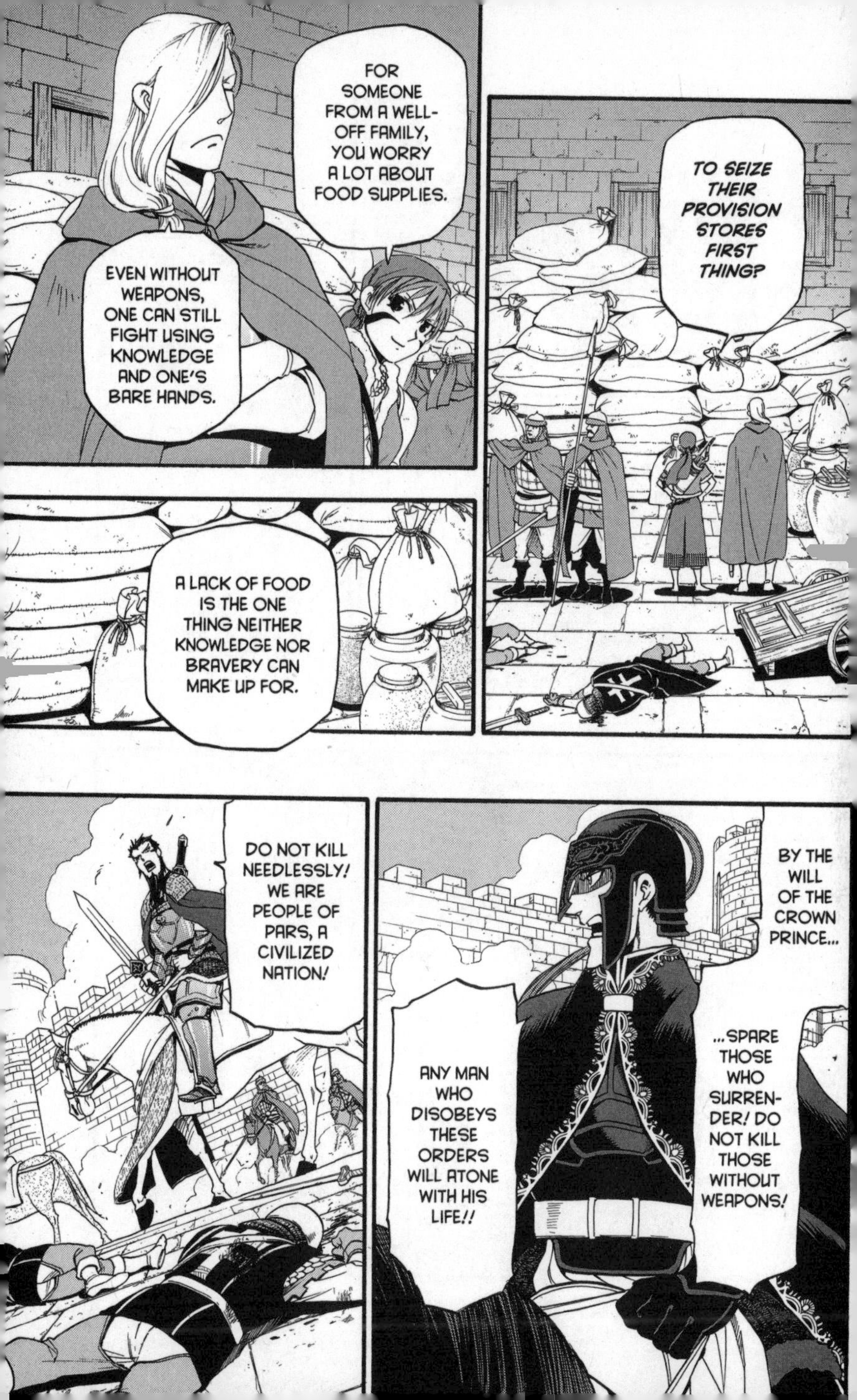
TO SEIZE THEIR PROVISION STORES FIRST THING?
FOR SOMEONE FROM A WELL-OFF FAMILY, YOU WORRY A LOT ABOUT FOOD SUPPLIES.
EVEN WITHOUT WEAPONS, ONE CAN STILL FIGHT USING KNOWLEDGE AND ONE'S BARE HANDS.
A LACK OF FOOD IS THE ONE THING NEITHER KNOWLEDGE NOR BRAVERY CAN MAKE UP FOR.
BY THE WILL OF THE CROWN PRINCE...
...SPARE THOSE WHO SURREN-DER! DO NOT KILL THOSE WITHOUT WEAPONS!
ANY MAN WHO DISOBEYS THESE ORDERS WILL ATONE WITH HIS LIFE!!
DO NOT KILL NEEDLESSLY! WE ARE PEOPLE OF PARS, A CIVILIZED NATION!

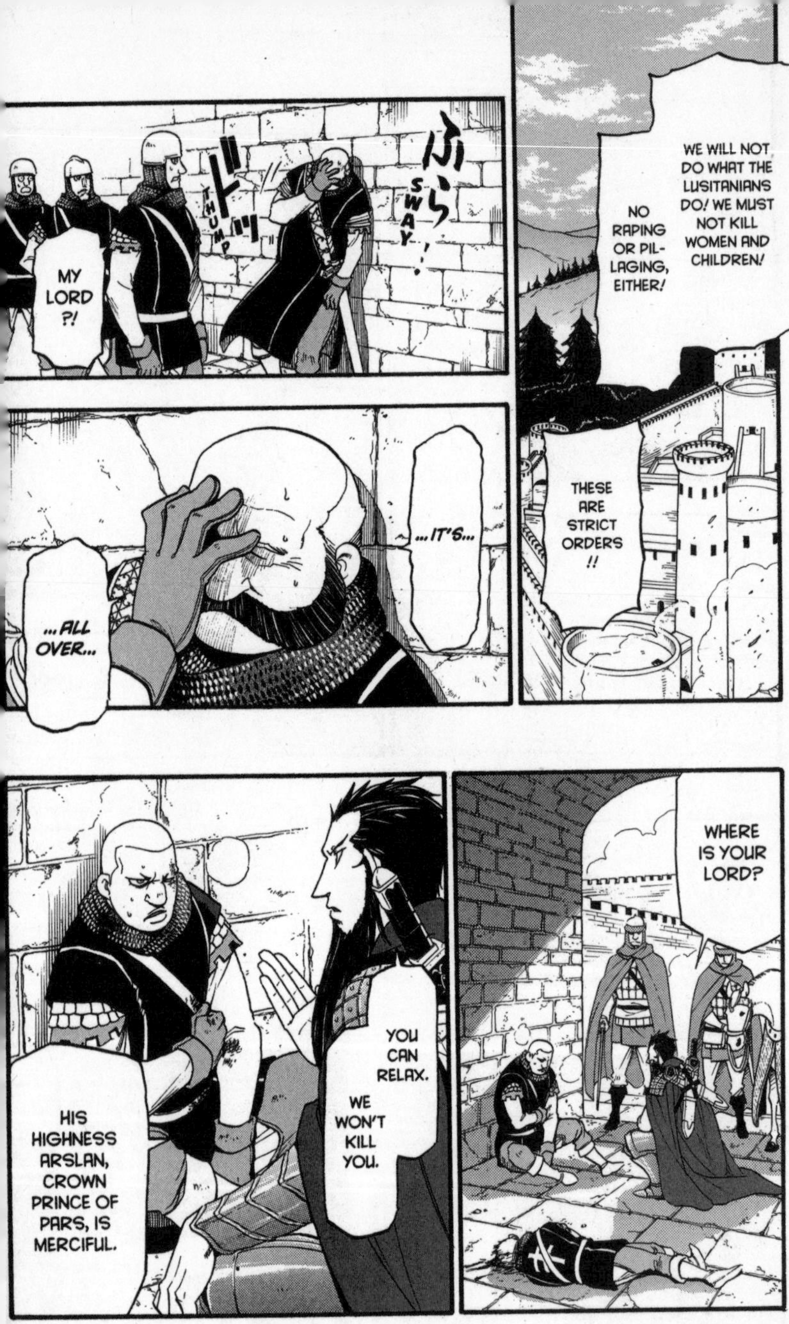
WE WILL NOT DO WHAT THE LUSITANIANS DO! WE MUST NOT KILL WOMEN AND CHILDREN!
NO RAPING OR PIL-LAGING, EITHER!
THESE ARE STRICT ORDERS!!
ふら SWAY!!
ド THUMP
MY LORD?!
...IT'S...
...ALL OVER...
WHERE IS YOUR LORD?
YOU CAN RELAX.
WE WON'T KILL YOU.
HIS HIGHNESS ARSLAN, CROWN PRINCE OF PARS, IS MERCIFUL.

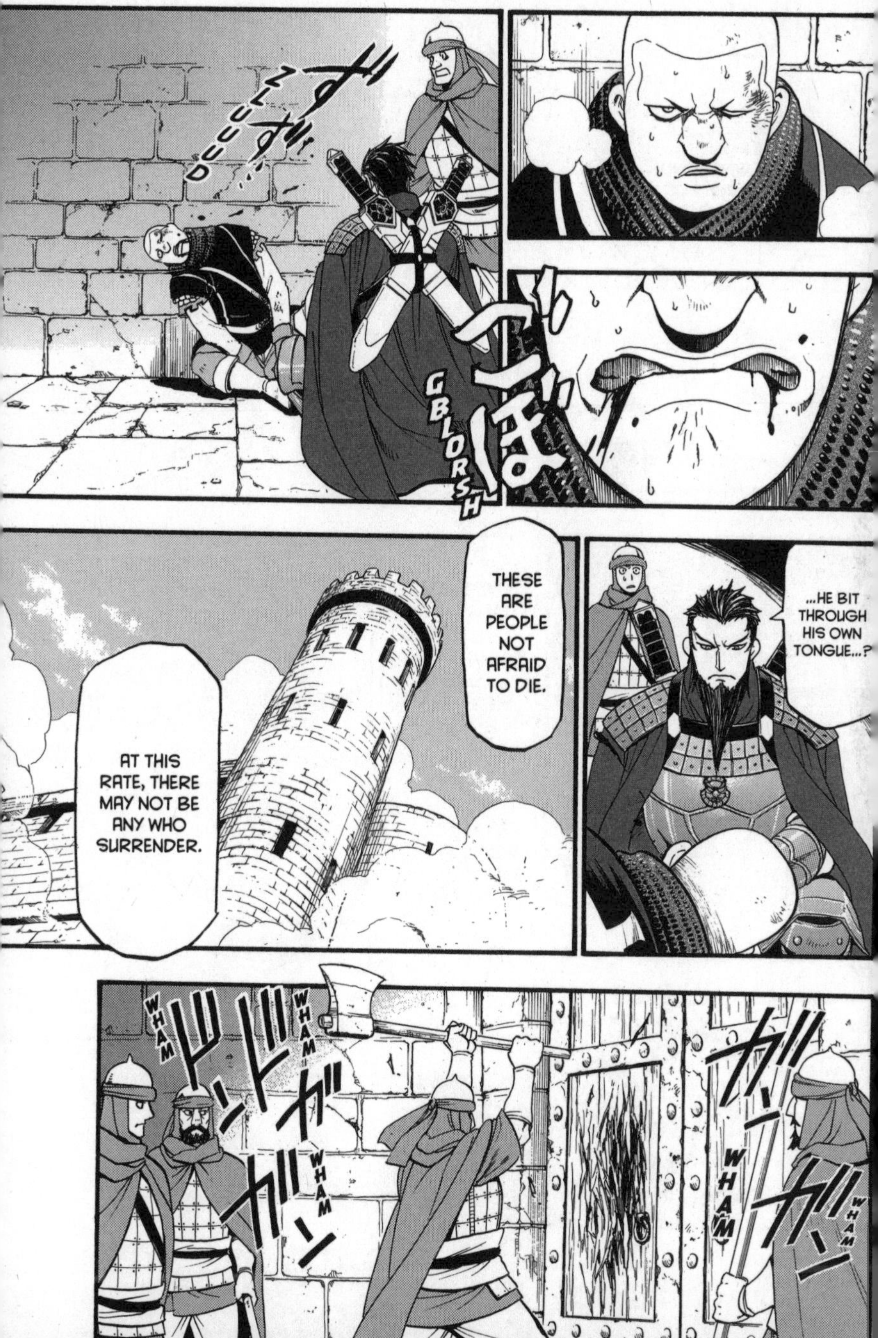

ZUUUD
GBLORSH
...HE BIT THROUGH HIS OWN TONGUE...?
THESE ARE PEOPLE NOT AFRAID TO DIE.
AT THIS RATE, THERE MAY NOT BE ANY WHO SURRENDER.
WHAM
WHAM
WHAM
WHAM
WHAM

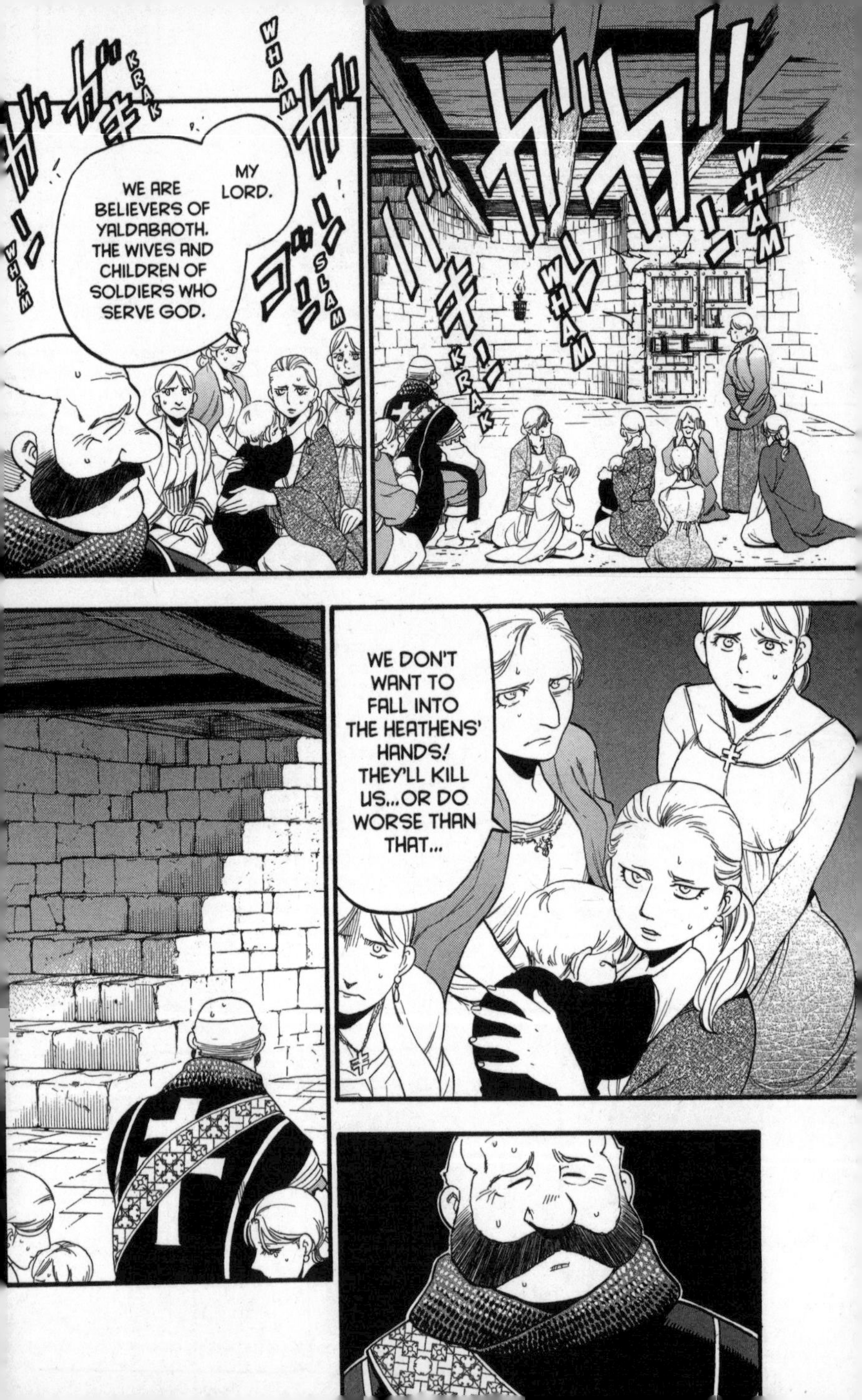
WHAM
WHAM
KRAK
WHAM
KRAK
MY LORD.
WE ARE BELIEVERS OF YALDABAOTH. THE WIVES AND CHILDREN OF SOLDIERS WHO SERVE GOD.
SLAM
WHAM
WE DON'T WANT TO FALL INTO THE HEATHENS' HANDS! THEY'LL KILL US...OR DO WORSE THAN THAT...

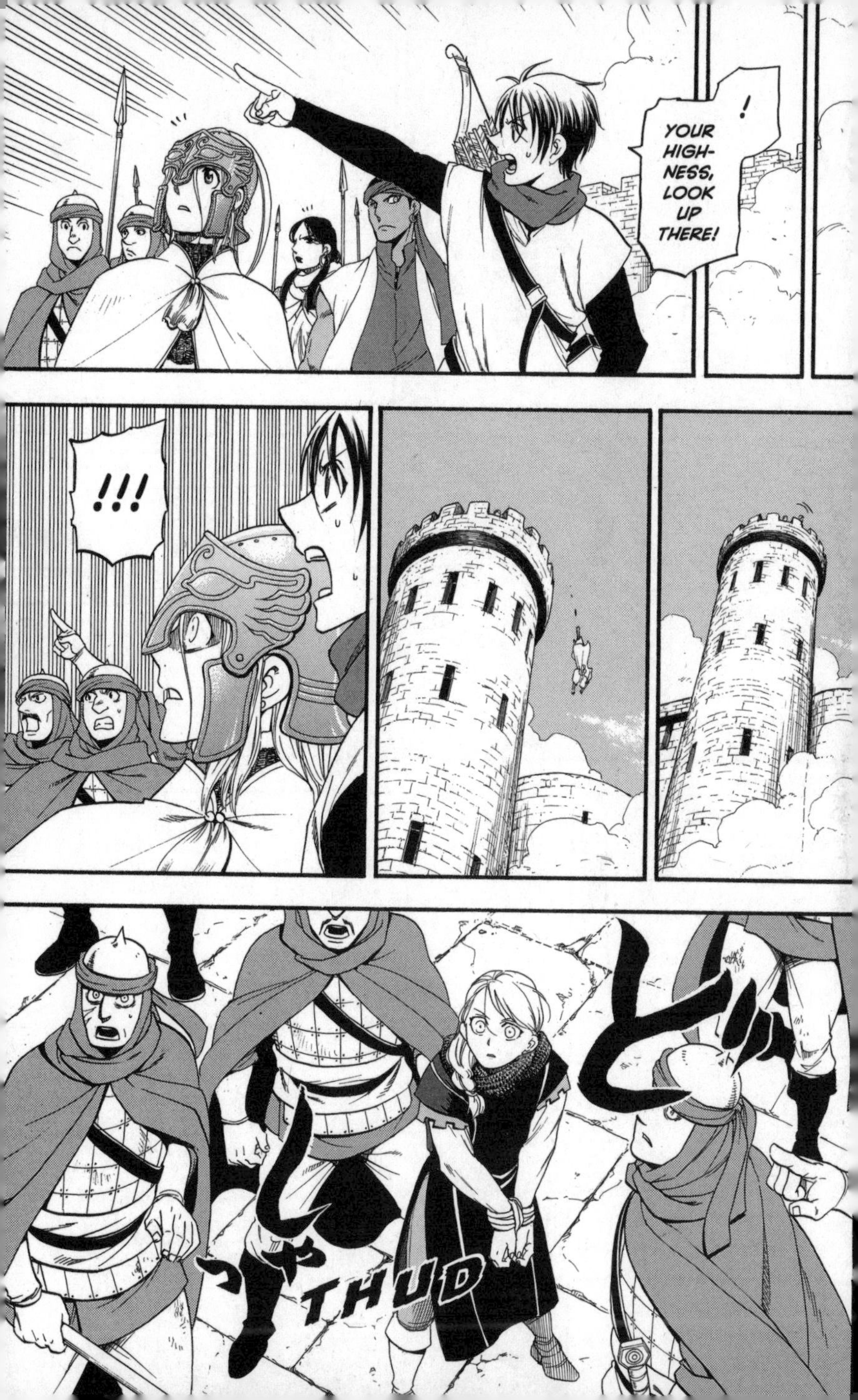
!
YOUR HIGH-NESS, LOOK UP THERE!
!!!
THUD

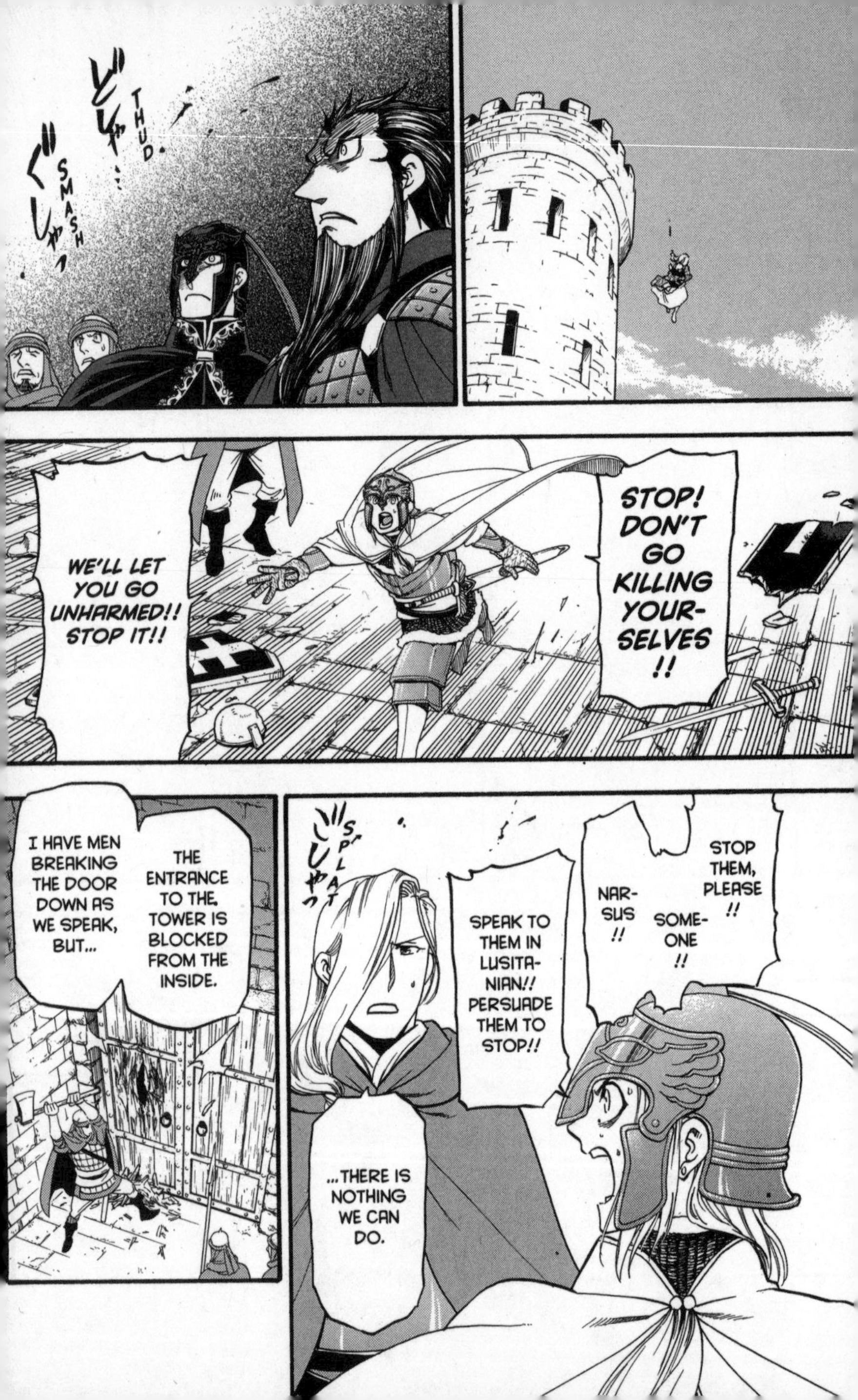
THUD
SMASH
STOP! DON'T GO KILLING YOURSELVES!!
WE'LL LET YOU GO UNHARMED!! STOP IT!!
STOP THEM, PLEASE!!
SOMEONE!!
NARSUS!!
SPEAK TO THEM IN LUSITANIAN!! PERSUADE THEM TO STOP!!
SPLAT
...THERE IS NOTHING WE CAN DO.
THE ENTRANCE TO THE TOWER IS BLOCKED FROM THE INSIDE.
I HAVE MEN BREAKING THE DOOR DOWN AS WE SPEAK, BUT...

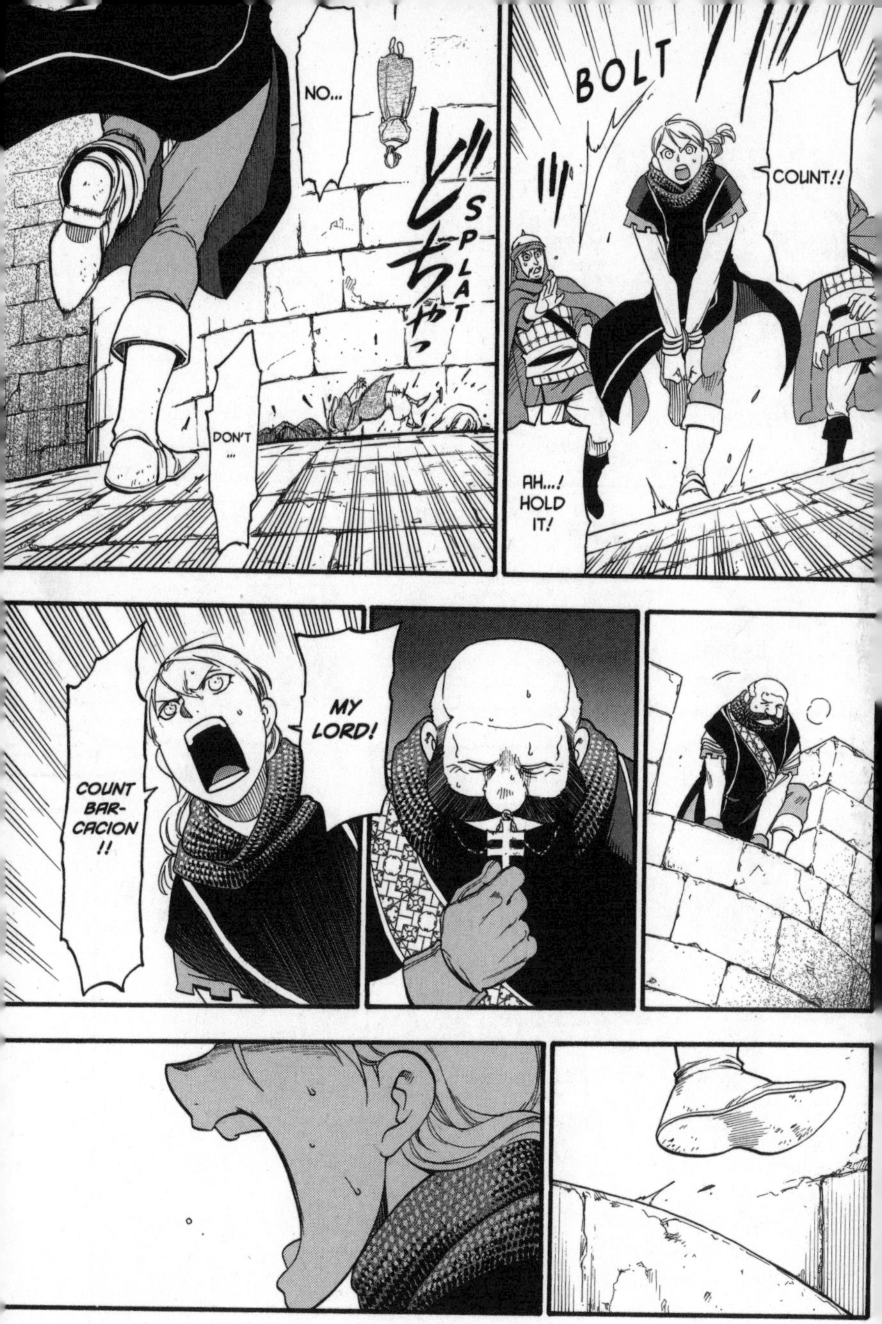

BOLT
COUNT!!
AH...! HOLD IT!
NO...
SPLAT
DON'T ...
MY LORD!
COUNT BAR-CACION !!

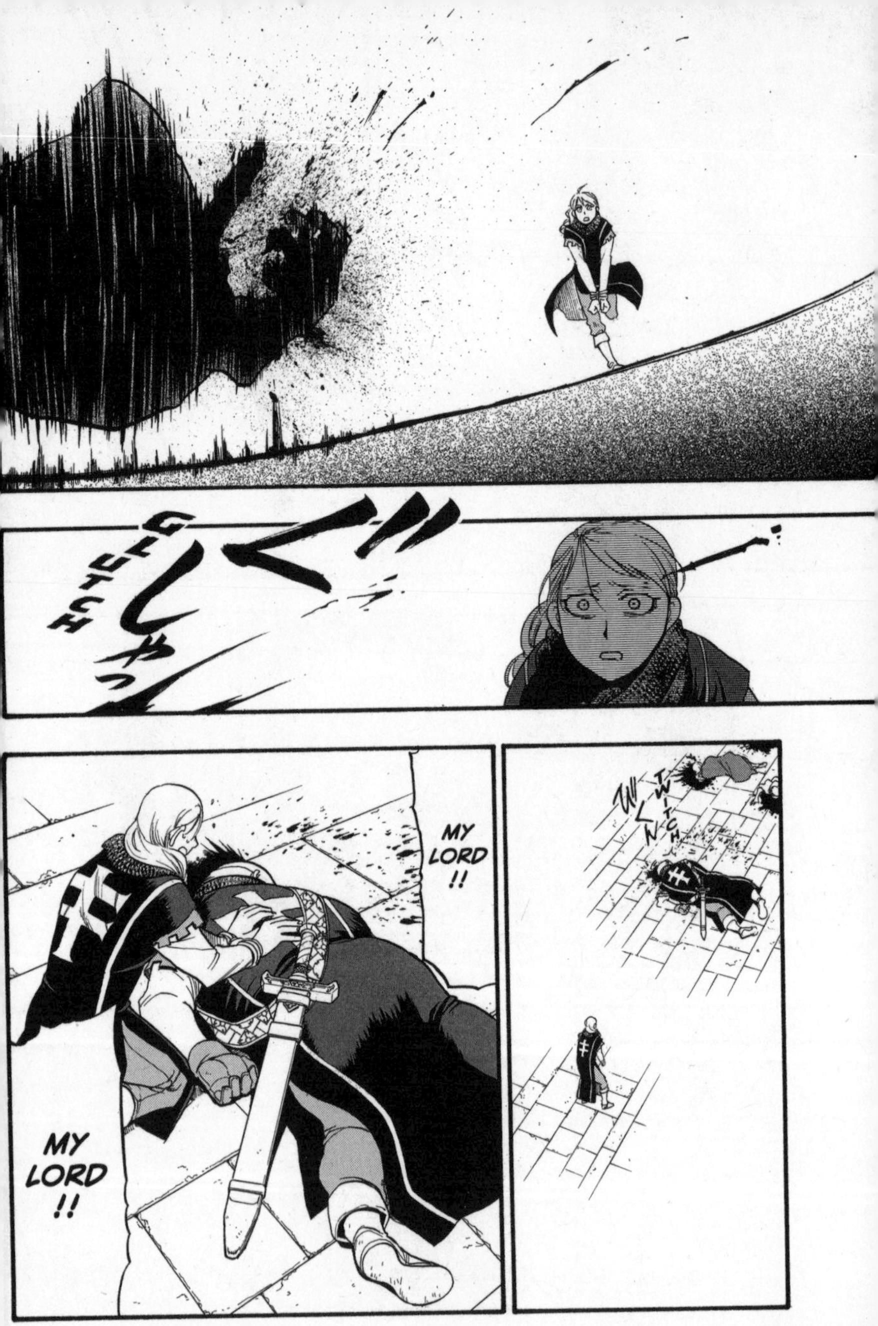
ぐしゃっ
GLUTCH
TWITCH
MY LORD !!
MY LORD !!

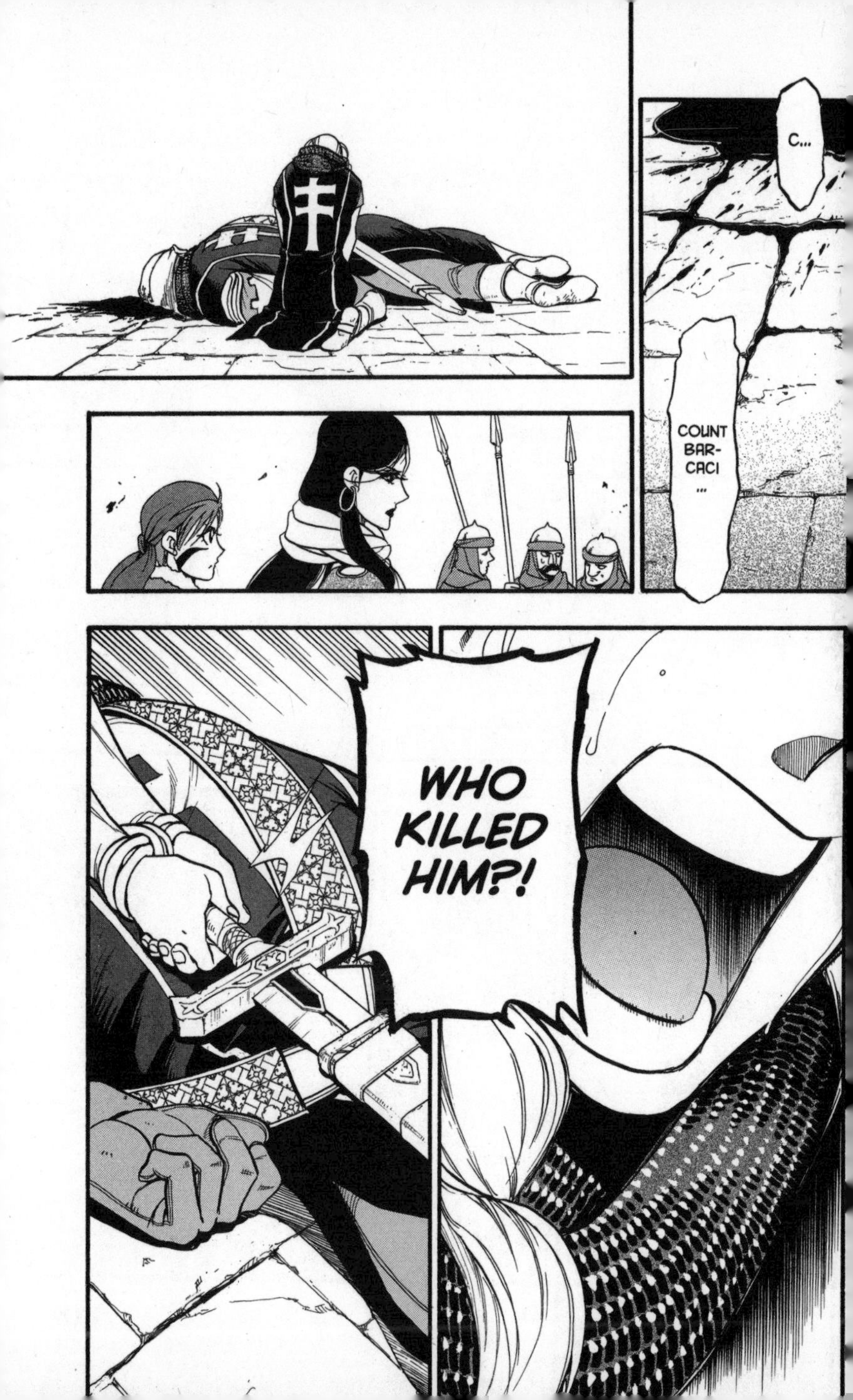
C...
COUNT BAR-CACI ...
WHO KILLED HIM?!

I WILL AVENGE HIM! SO, ENEMY OF MY LORD, NAME YOURSELF!!!

NAME YOUR-SELF!!

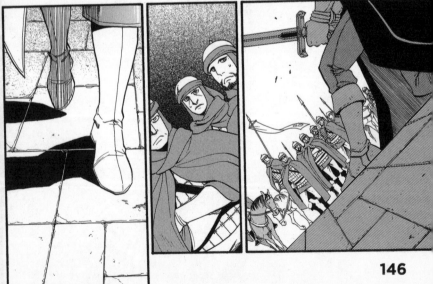

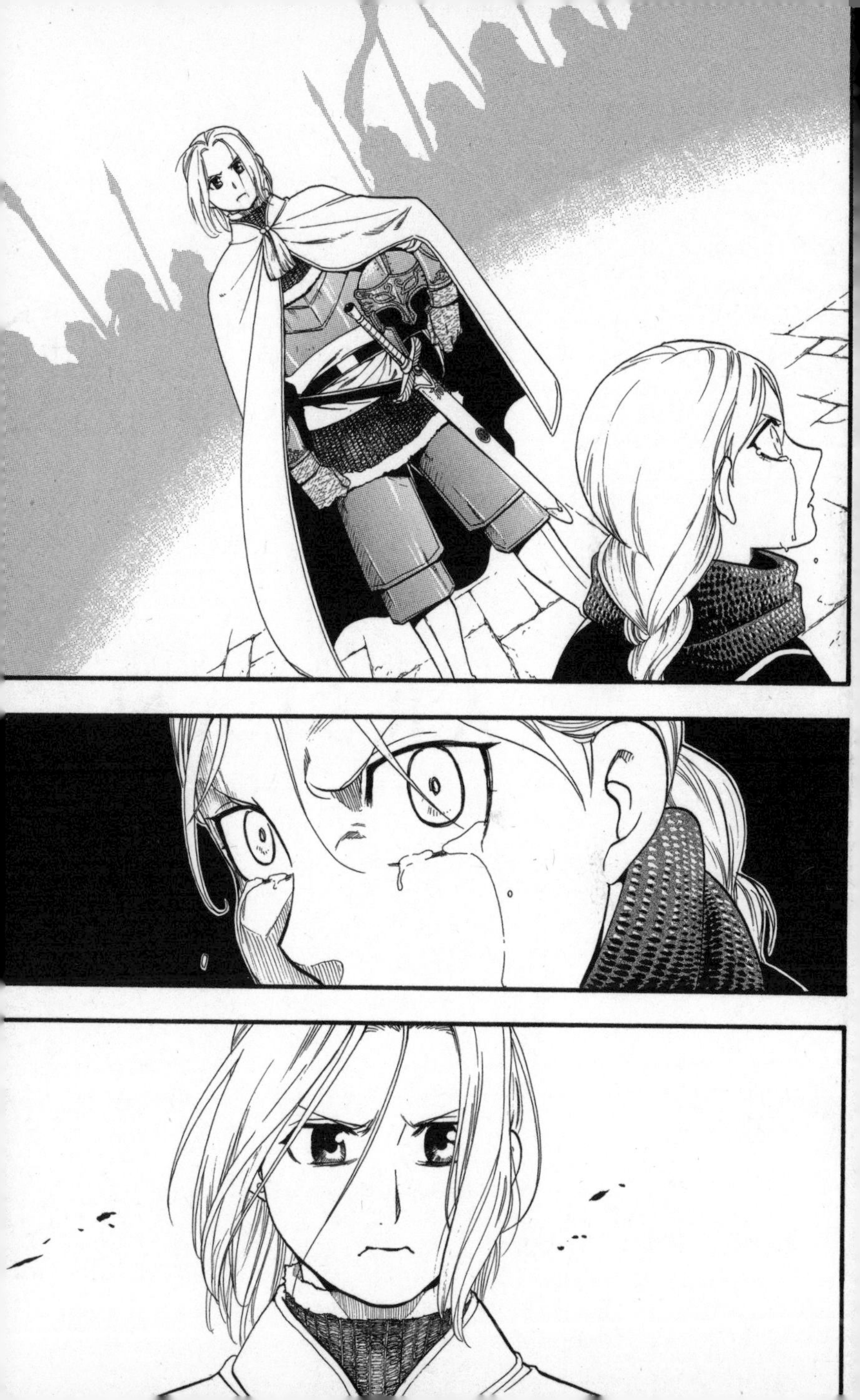

THE HEROIC LEGEND OF
ARSLAN

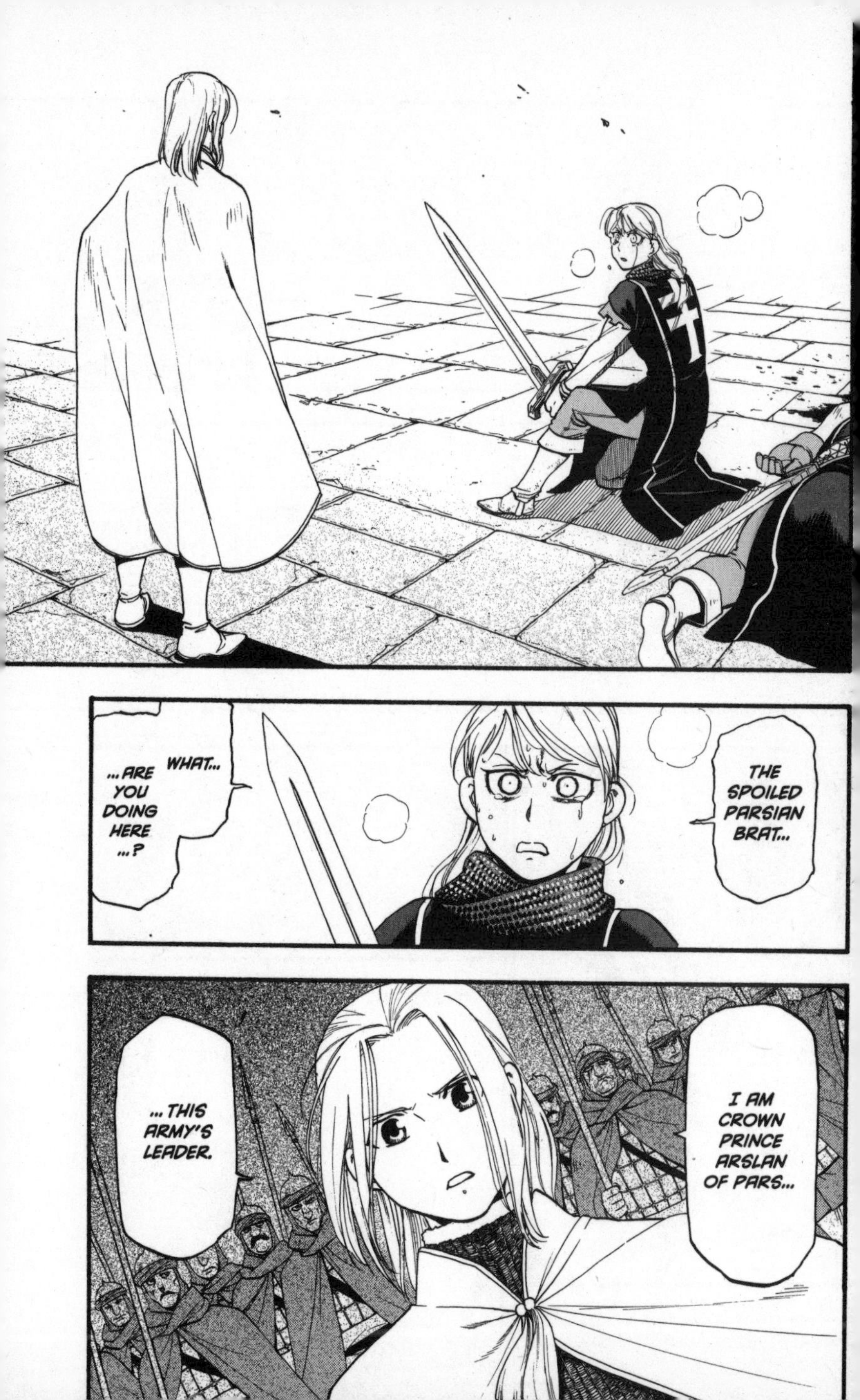
THE SPOILED PARSIAN BRAT...
WHAT... ...ARE YOU DOING HERE ...?
I AM CROWN PRINCE ARSLAN OF PARS...
...THIS ARMY'S LEADER.

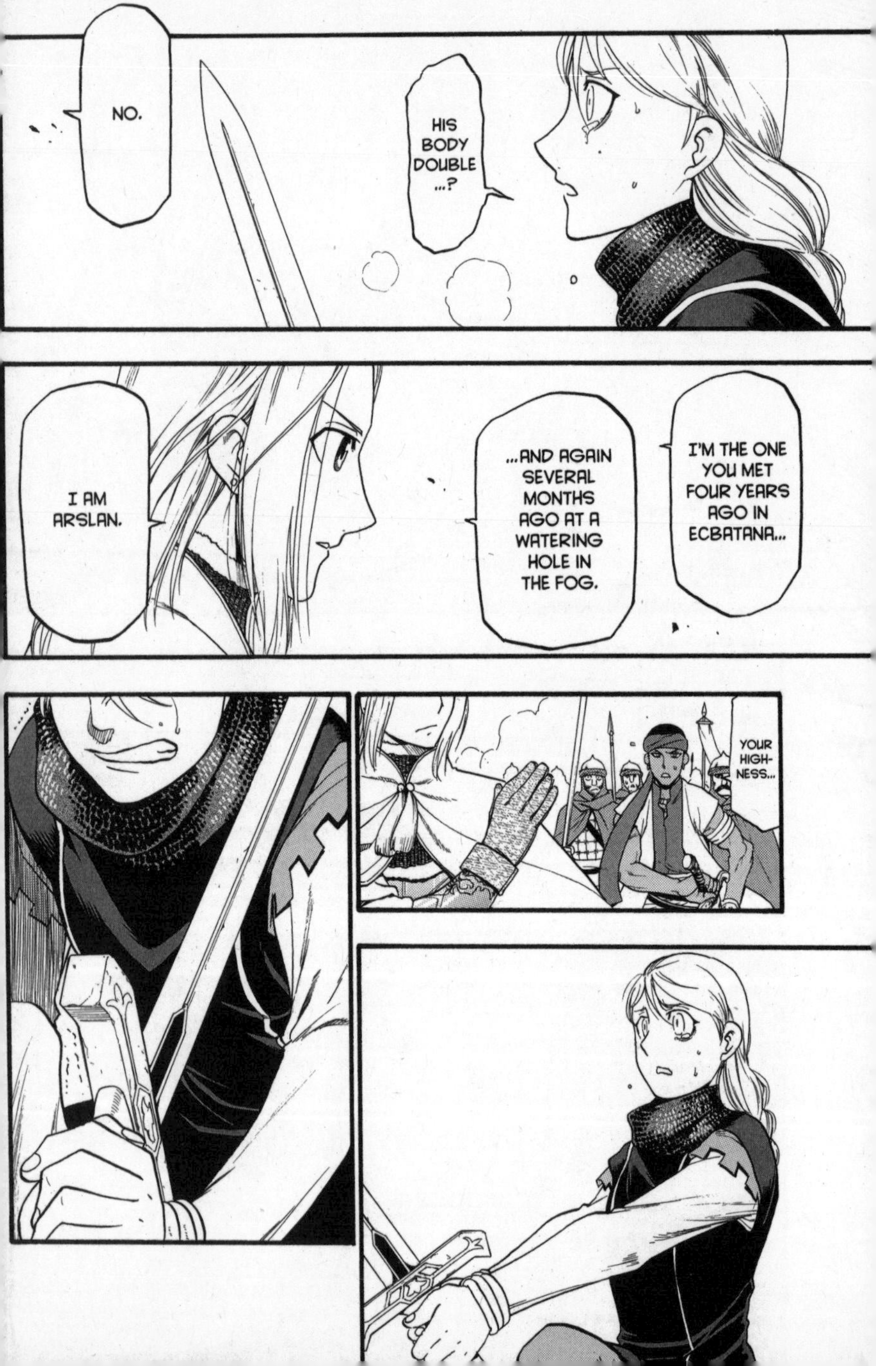
HIS BODY DOUBLE ...?
NO.
I'M THE ONE YOU MET FOUR YEARS AGO IN ECBATANA...
...AND AGAIN SEVERAL MONTHS AGO AT A WATERING HOLE IN THE FOG.
I AM ARSLAN.
YOUR HIGHNESS...

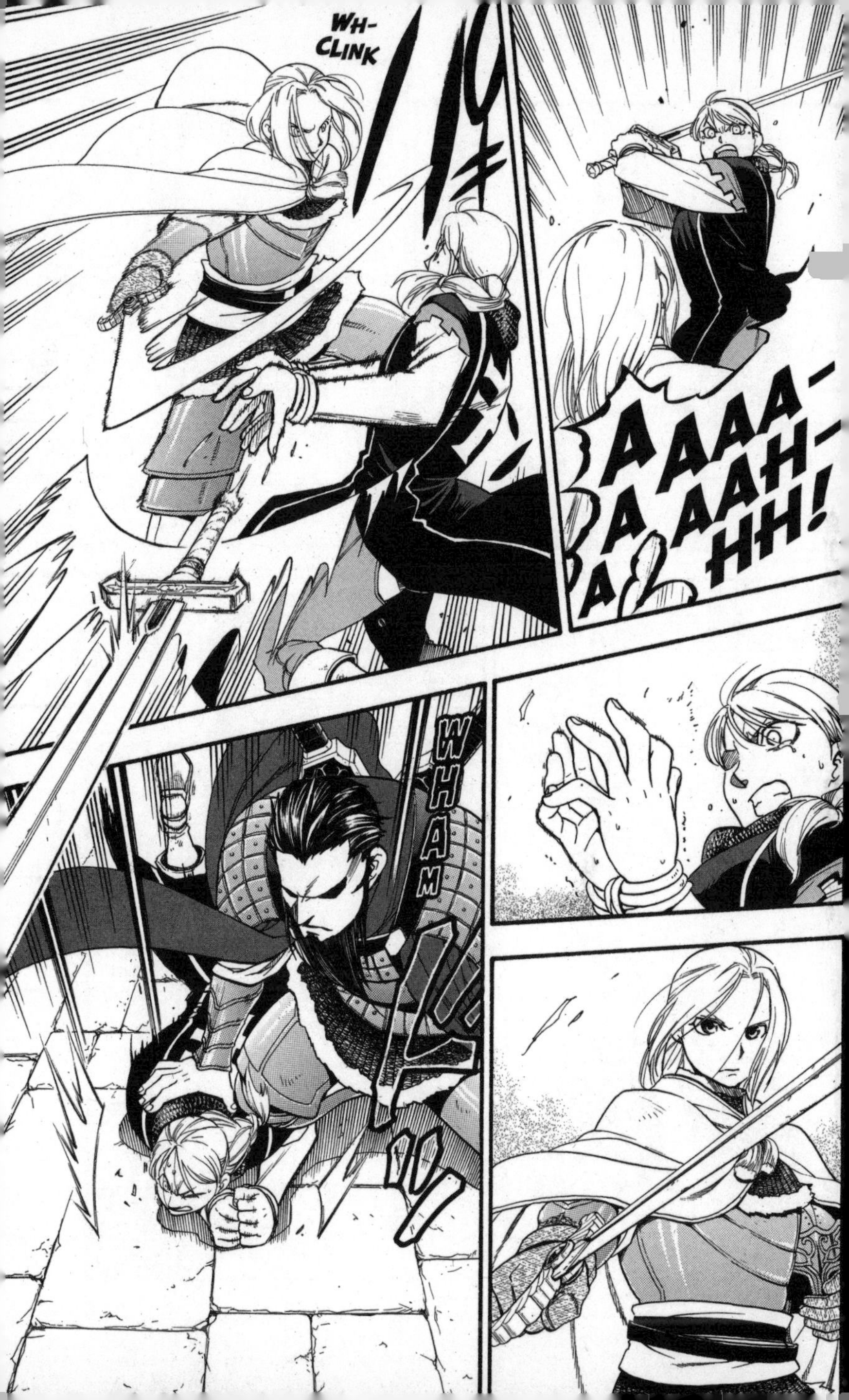

AAAA-AAAAH-HH!
WH-CLINK
WHAM

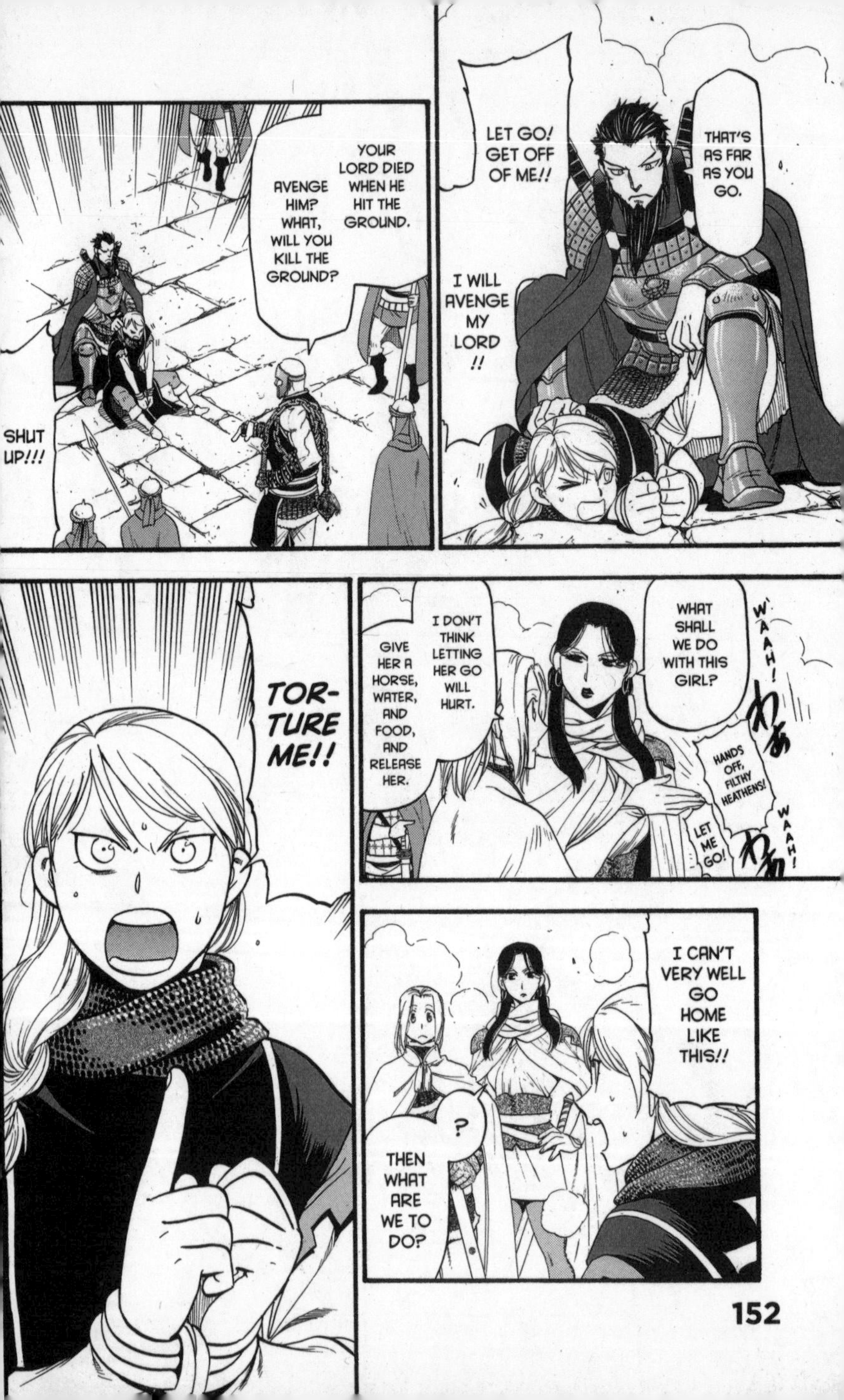
THAT'S AS FAR AS YOU GO.
LET GO! GET OFF OF ME!!
I WILL AVENGE MY LORD!!
YOUR LORD DIED WHEN HE HIT THE GROUND.
AVENGE HIM? WHAT, WILL YOU KILL THE GROUND?
SHUT UP!!!
WHAT SHALL WE DO WITH THIS GIRL?
WAAH!
HANDS OFF, FILTHY HEATHENS!
LET ME GO!
WAAH!
I DON'T THINK LETTING HER GO WILL HURT.
GIVE HER A HORSE, WATER, AND FOOD, AND RELEASE HER.
I CAN'T VERY WELL GO HOME LIKE THIS!!
?
THEN WHAT ARE WE TO DO?
TOR-TURE ME!!

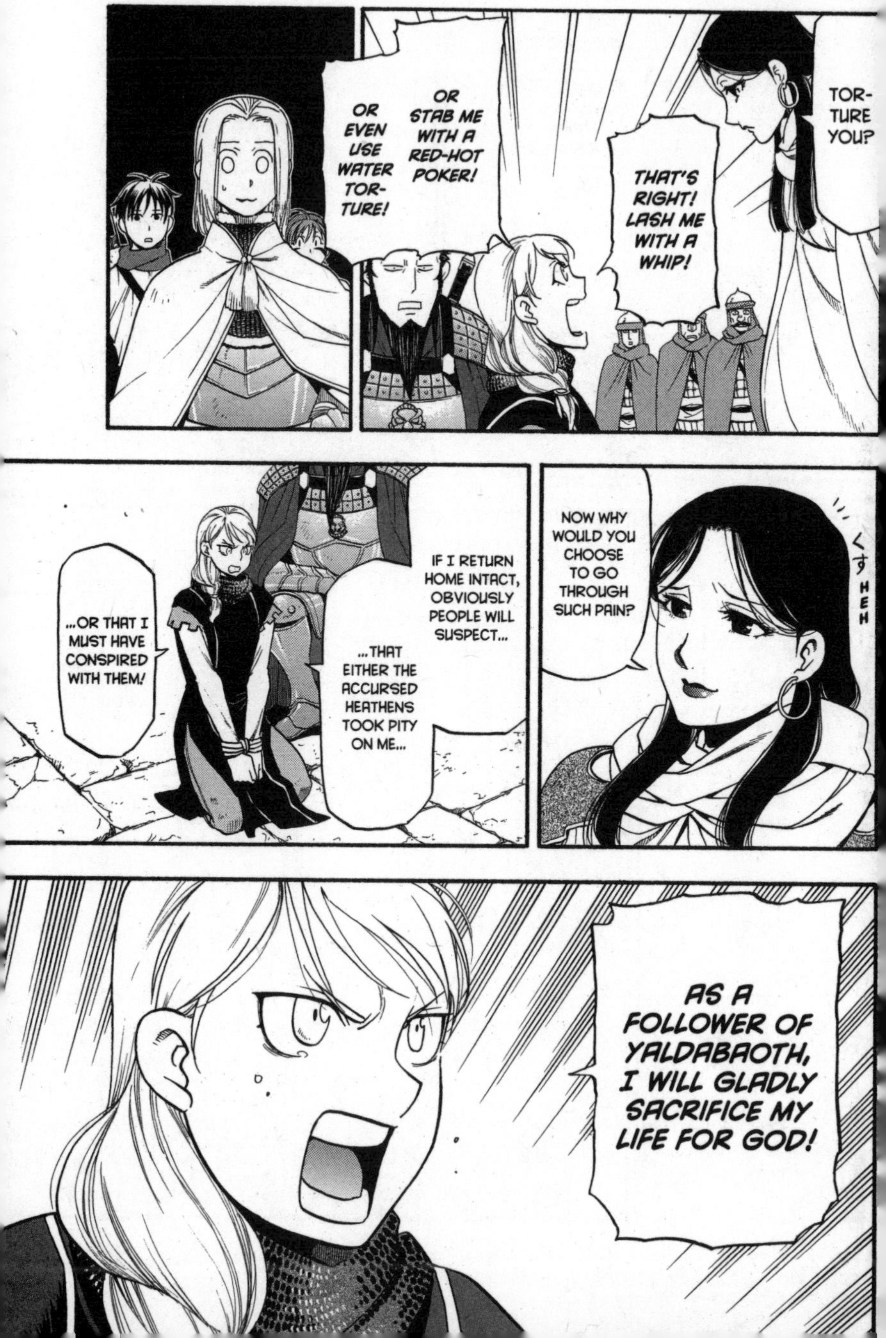
TOR-TURE YOU?
THAT'S RIGHT! LASH ME WITH A WHIP!
OR STAB ME WITH A RED-HOT POKER!
OR EVEN USE WATER TOR-TURE!
くす HEH
NOW WHY WOULD YOU CHOOSE TO GO THROUGH SUCH PAIN?
IF I RETURN HOME INTACT, OBVIOUSLY PEOPLE WILL SUSPECT...
...THAT EITHER THE ACCURSED HEATHENS TOOK PITY ON ME...
...OR THAT I MUST HAVE CONSPIRED WITH THEM!
AS A FOLLOWER OF YALDABAOTH, I WILL GLADLY SACRIFICE MY LIFE FOR GOD!

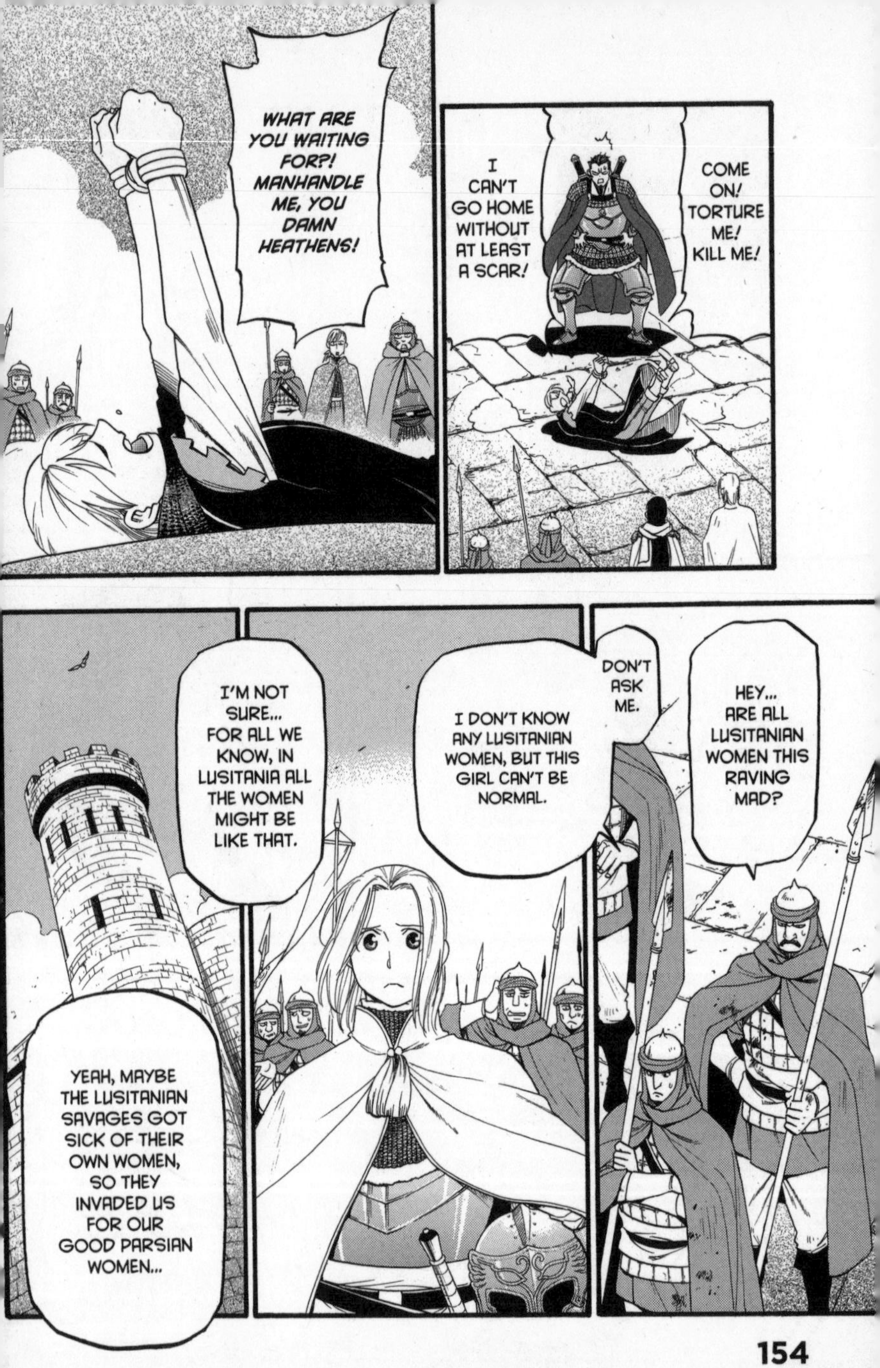
COME ON! TORTURE ME! KILL ME!
I CAN'T GO HOME WITHOUT AT LEAST A SCAR!
WHAT ARE YOU WAITING FOR?! MANHANDLE ME, YOU DAMN HEATHENS!
HEY... ARE ALL LUSITANIAN WOMEN THIS RAVING MAD?
DON'T ASK ME.
I DON'T KNOW ANY LUSITANIAN WOMEN, BUT THIS GIRL CAN'T BE NORMAL.
I'M NOT SURE... FOR ALL WE KNOW, IN LUSITANIA ALL THE WOMEN MIGHT BE LIKE THAT.
YEAH, MAYBE THE LUSITANIAN SAVAGES GOT SICK OF THEIR OWN WOMEN, SO THEY INVADED US FOR OUR GOOD PARSIAN WOMEN...

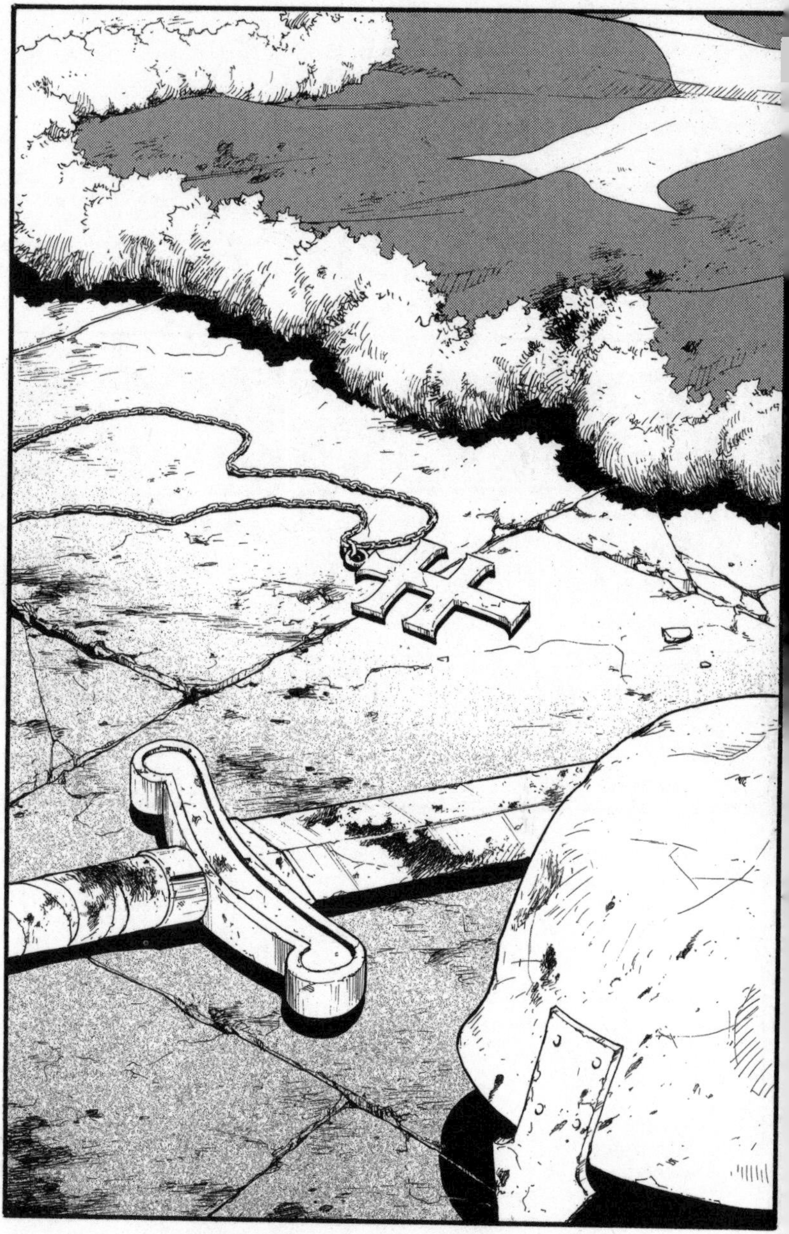

Chapter 70: Moment of Life or Death

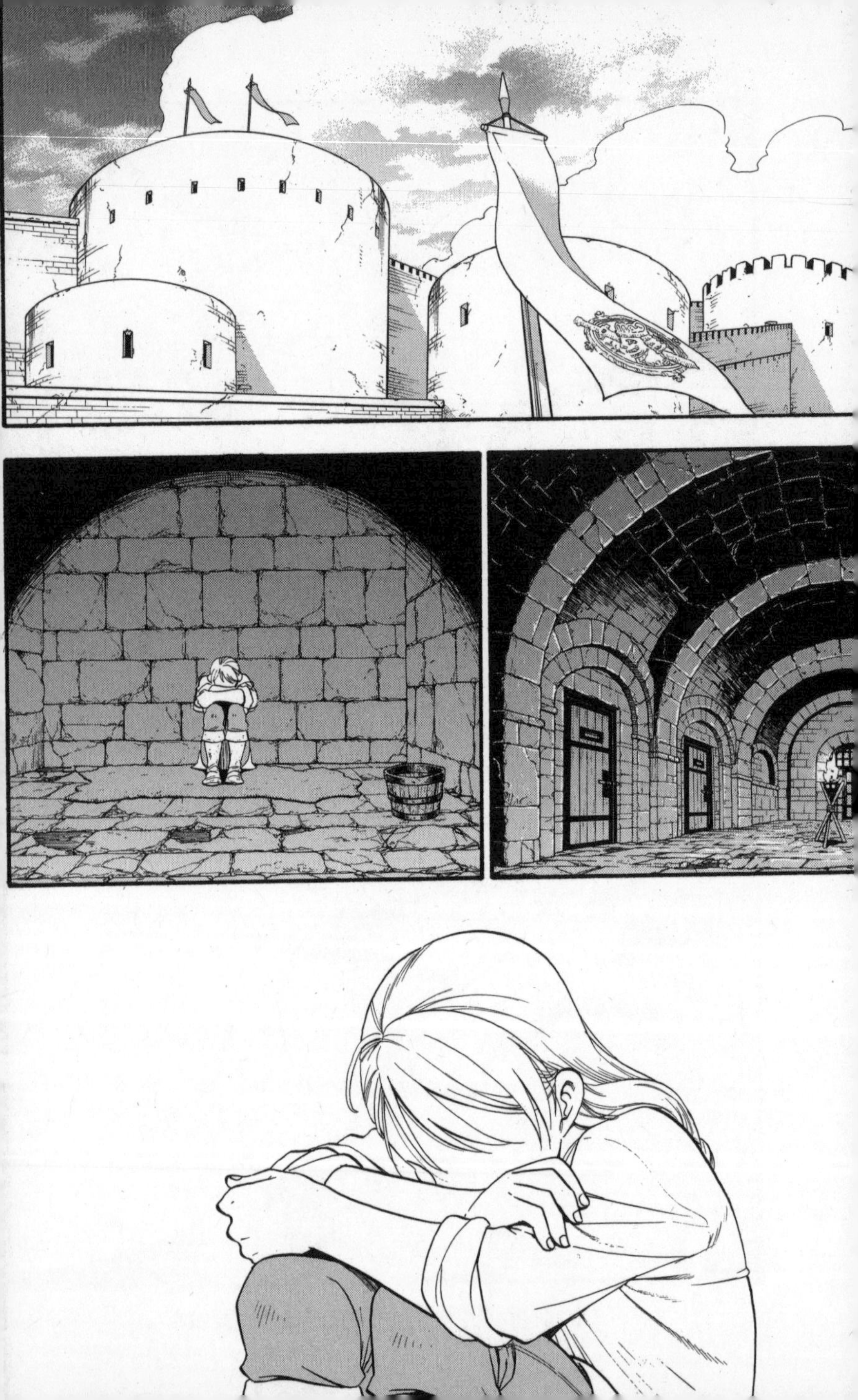

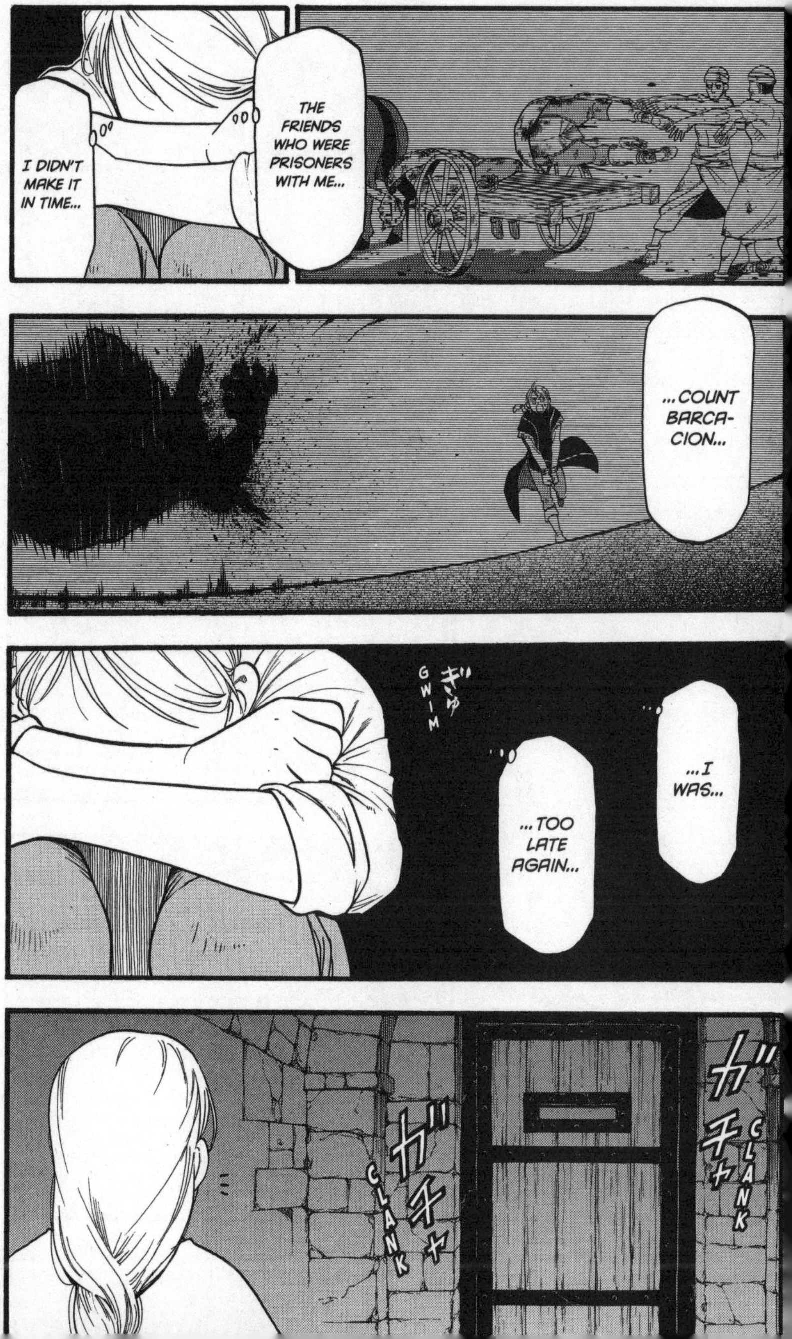
THE FRIENDS WHO WERE PRISONERS WITH ME...
I DIDN'T MAKE IT IN TIME...
...COUNT BARCA-CION...
...I WAS...
...TOO LATE AGAIN...
GWIM
CLANK
CLANK

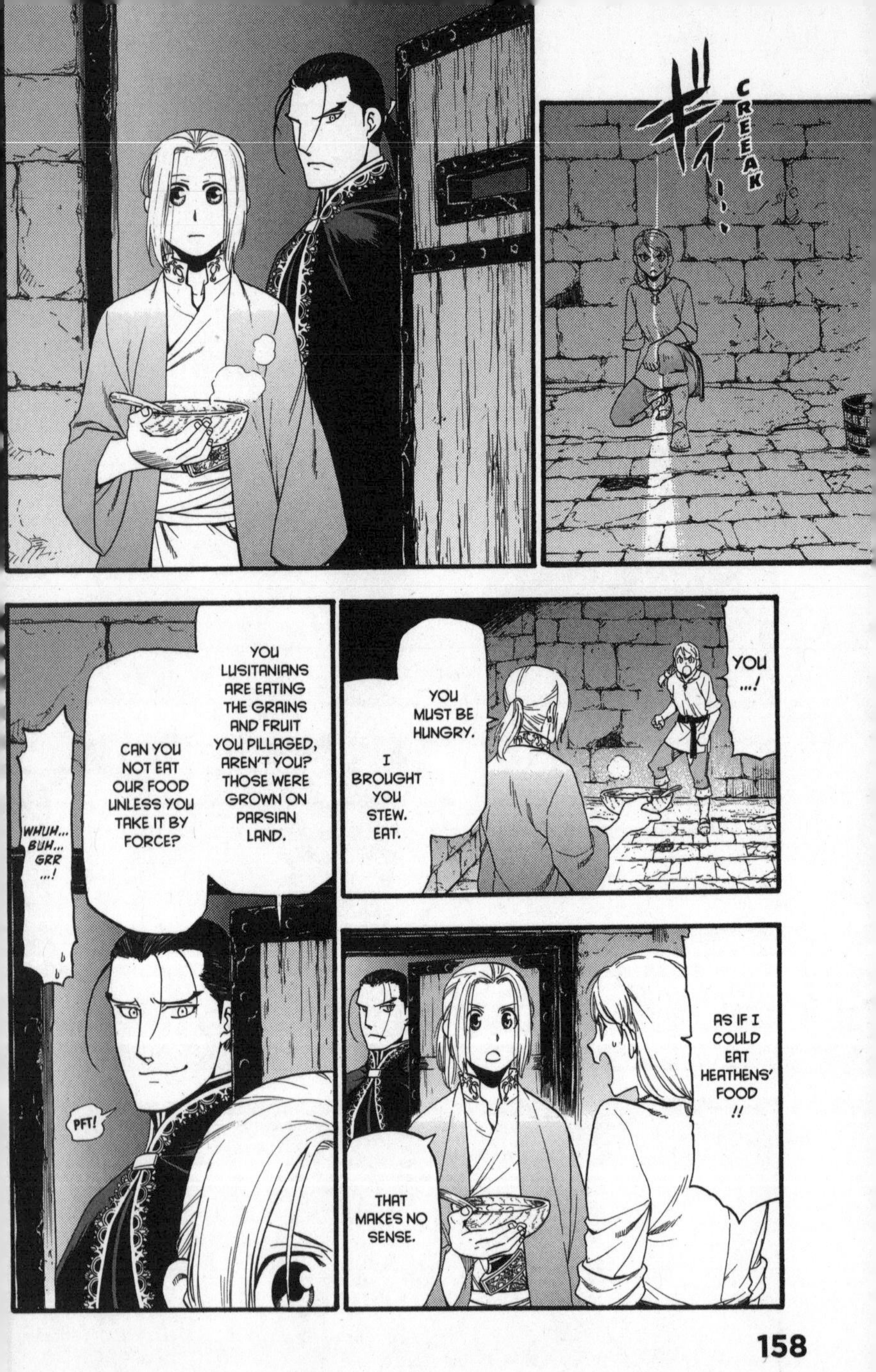
ギィ…
CREEAK
YOU ...!
YOU MUST BE HUNGRY.
I BROUGHT YOU STEW. EAT.
AS IF I COULD EAT HEATHENS' FOOD !!
THAT MAKES NO SENSE.
YOU LUSITANIANS ARE EATING THE GRAINS AND FRUIT YOU PILLAGED, AREN'T YOU? THOSE WERE GROWN ON PARSIAN LAND.
CAN YOU NOT EAT OUR FOOD UNLESS YOU TAKE IT BY FORCE?
WHUH... BUH... GRR ...!
PFT!

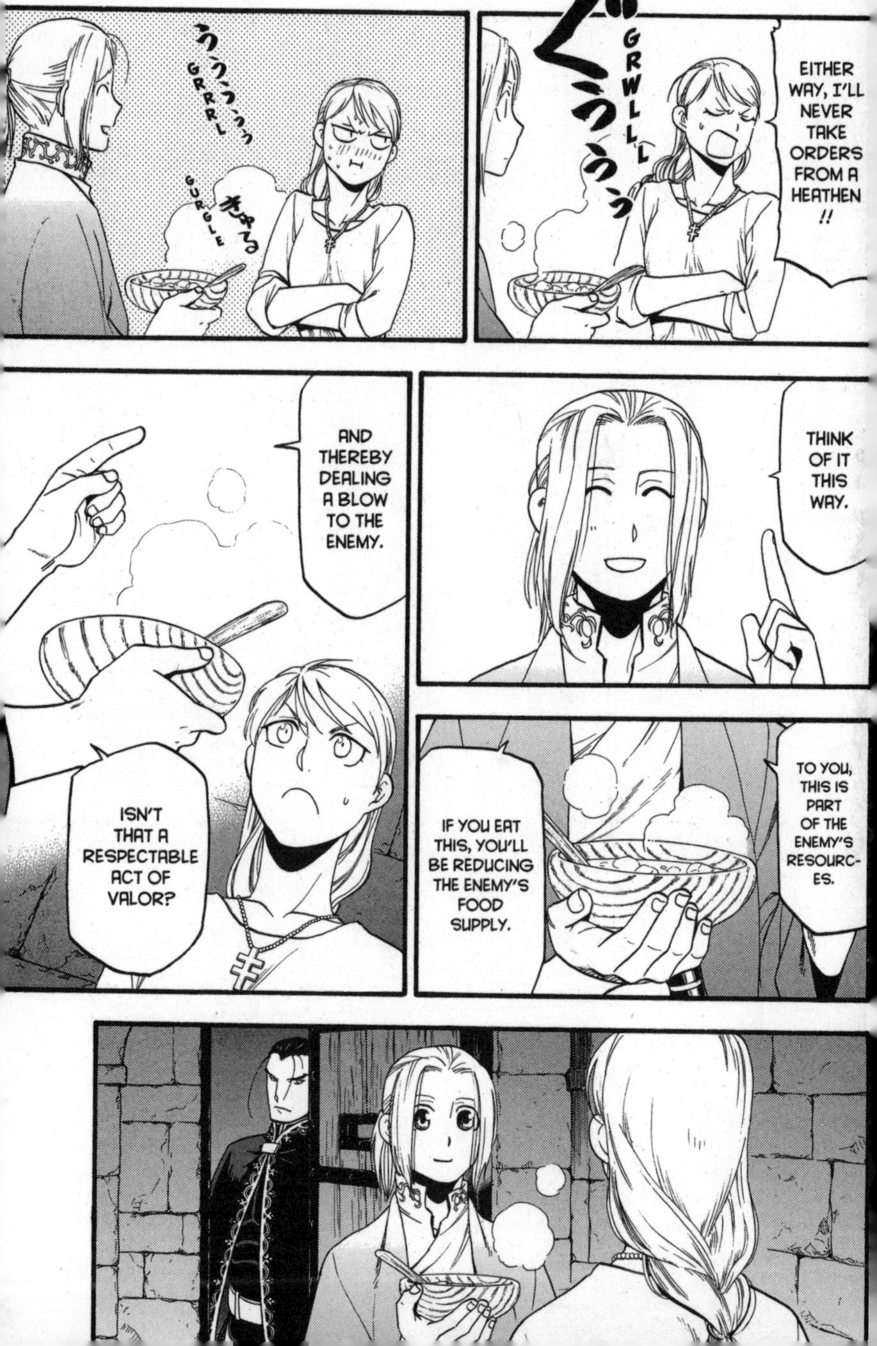
ぐうううう
GRWLLL
EITHER WAY, I'LL NEVER TAKE ORDERS FROM A HEATHEN!!
うううううう
GRRRL
きゅる
GURGLE
THINK OF IT THIS WAY.
TO YOU, THIS IS PART OF THE ENEMY'S RESOURC-ES.
IF YOU EAT THIS, YOU'LL BE REDUCING THE ENEMY'S FOOD SUPPLY.
AND THEREBY DEALING A BLOW TO THE ENEMY.
ISN'T THAT A RESPECTABLE ACT OF VALOR?

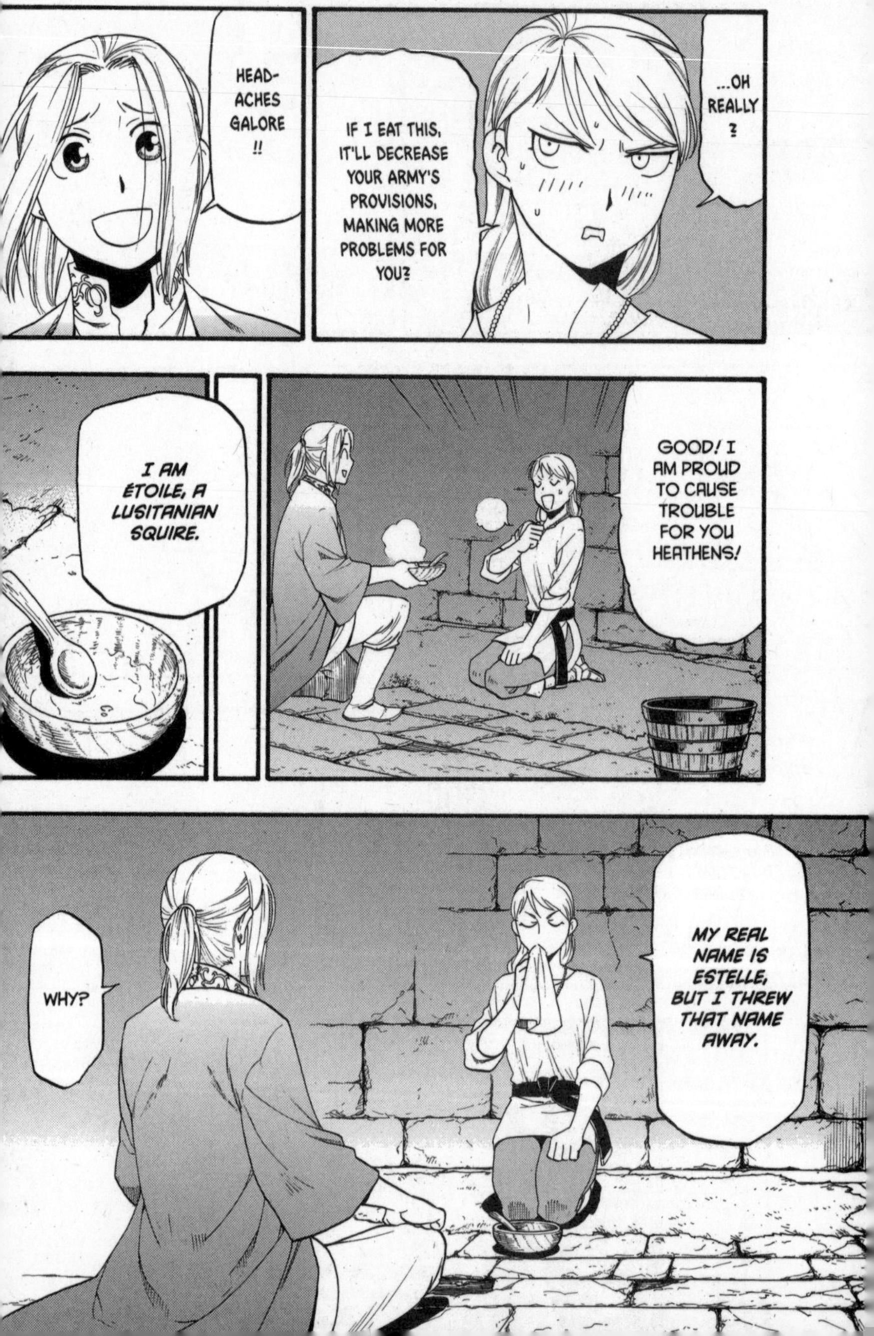
...OH REALLY?
IF I EAT THIS, IT'LL DECREASE YOUR ARMY'S PROVISIONS, MAKING MORE PROBLEMS FOR YOU?
HEAD-ACHES GALORE!!
GOOD! I AM PROUD TO CAUSE TROUBLE FOR YOU HEATHENS!
I AM ÉTOILE, A LUSITANIAN SQUIRE.
MY REAL NAME IS ESTELLE, BUT I THREW THAT NAME AWAY.
WHY?

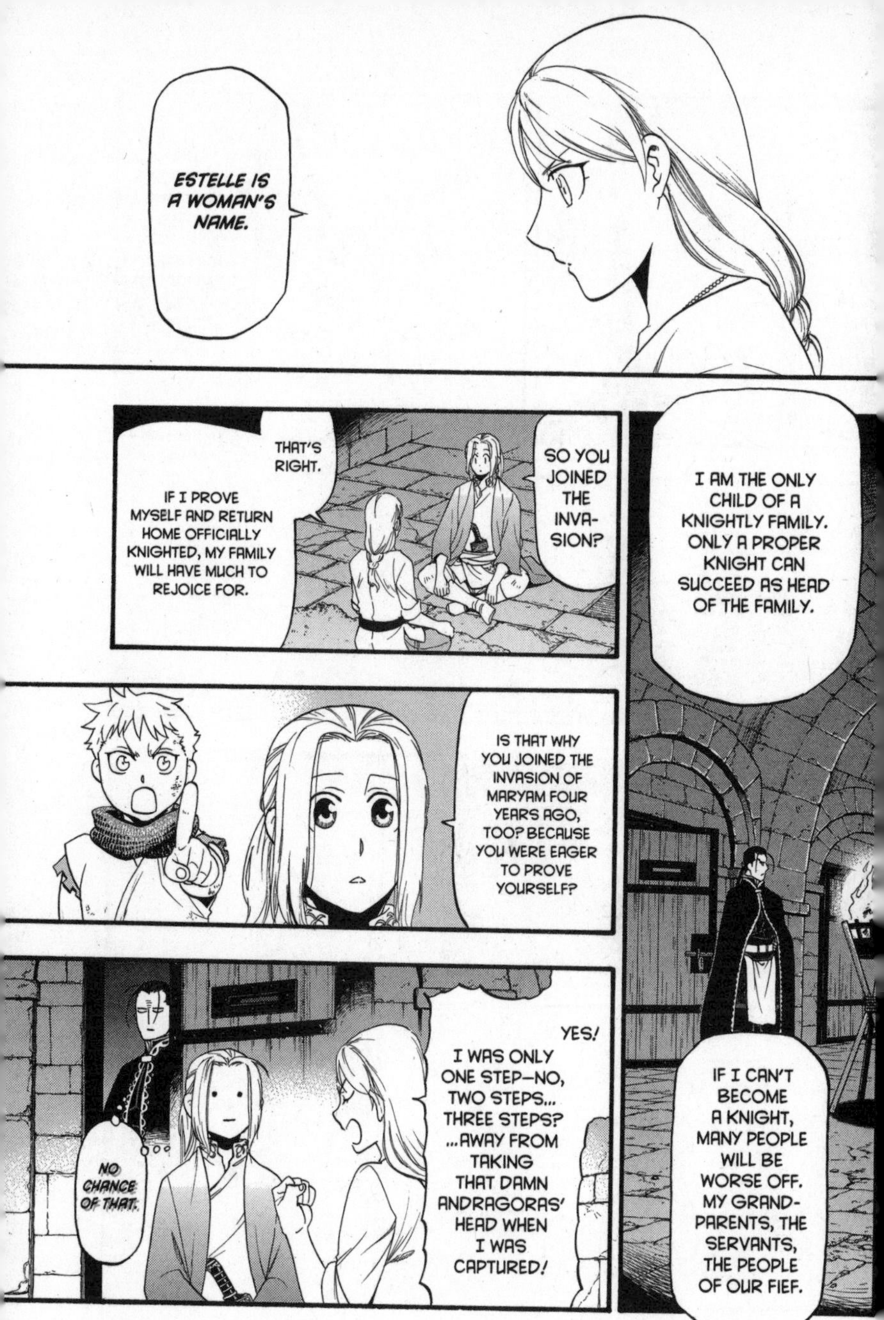
ESTELLE IS A WOMAN'S NAME.
I AM THE ONLY CHILD OF A KNIGHTLY FAMILY. ONLY A PROPER KNIGHT CAN SUCCEED AS HEAD OF THE FAMILY.
IF I CAN'T BECOME A KNIGHT, MANY PEOPLE WILL BE WORSE OFF. MY GRAND-PARENTS, THE SERVANTS, THE PEOPLE OF OUR FIEF.
SO YOU JOINED THE INVA-SION?
THAT'S RIGHT.
IF I PROVE MYSELF AND RETURN HOME OFFICIALLY KNIGHTED, MY FAMILY WILL HAVE MUCH TO REJOICE FOR.
IS THAT WHY YOU JOINED THE INVASION OF MARYAM FOUR YEARS AGO, TOO? BECAUSE YOU WERE EAGER TO PROVE YOURSELF?
YES!
I WAS ONLY ONE STEP—NO, TWO STEPS... THREE STEPS? ...AWAY FROM TAKING THAT DAMN ANDRAGORAS' HEAD WHEN I WAS CAPTURED!
NO CHANCE OF THAT.

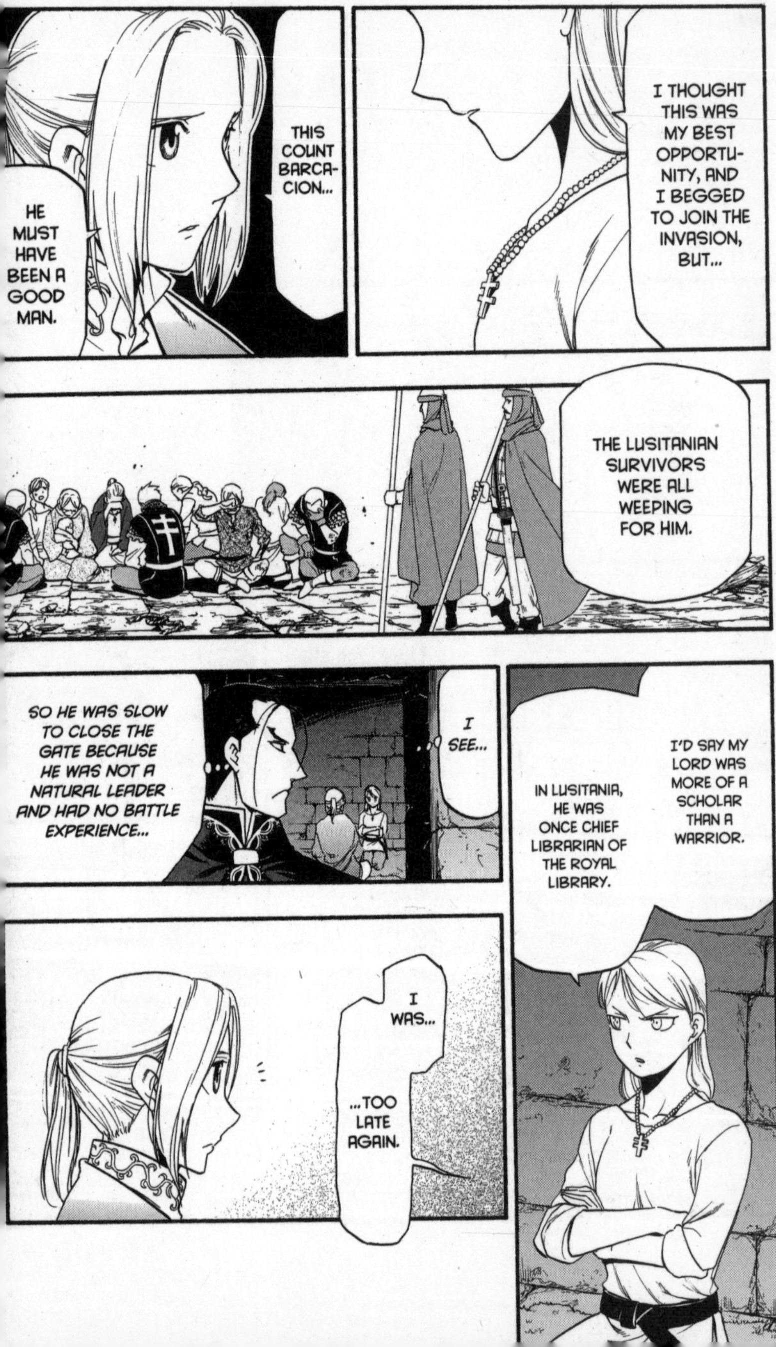
I THOUGHT THIS WAS MY BEST OPPORTU-NITY, AND I BEGGED TO JOIN THE INVASION, BUT...
THIS COUNT BARCA-CION...
HE MUST HAVE BEEN A GOOD MAN.
THE LUSITANIAN SURVIVORS WERE ALL WEEPING FOR HIM.
I'D SAY MY LORD WAS MORE OF A SCHOLAR THAN A WARRIOR.
IN LUSITANIA, HE WAS ONCE CHIEF LIBRARIAN OF THE ROYAL LIBRARY.
I SEE...
SO HE WAS SLOW TO CLOSE THE GATE BECAUSE HE WAS NOT A NATURAL LEADER AND HAD NO BATTLE EXPERIENCE...
I WAS...
...TOO LATE AGAIN.

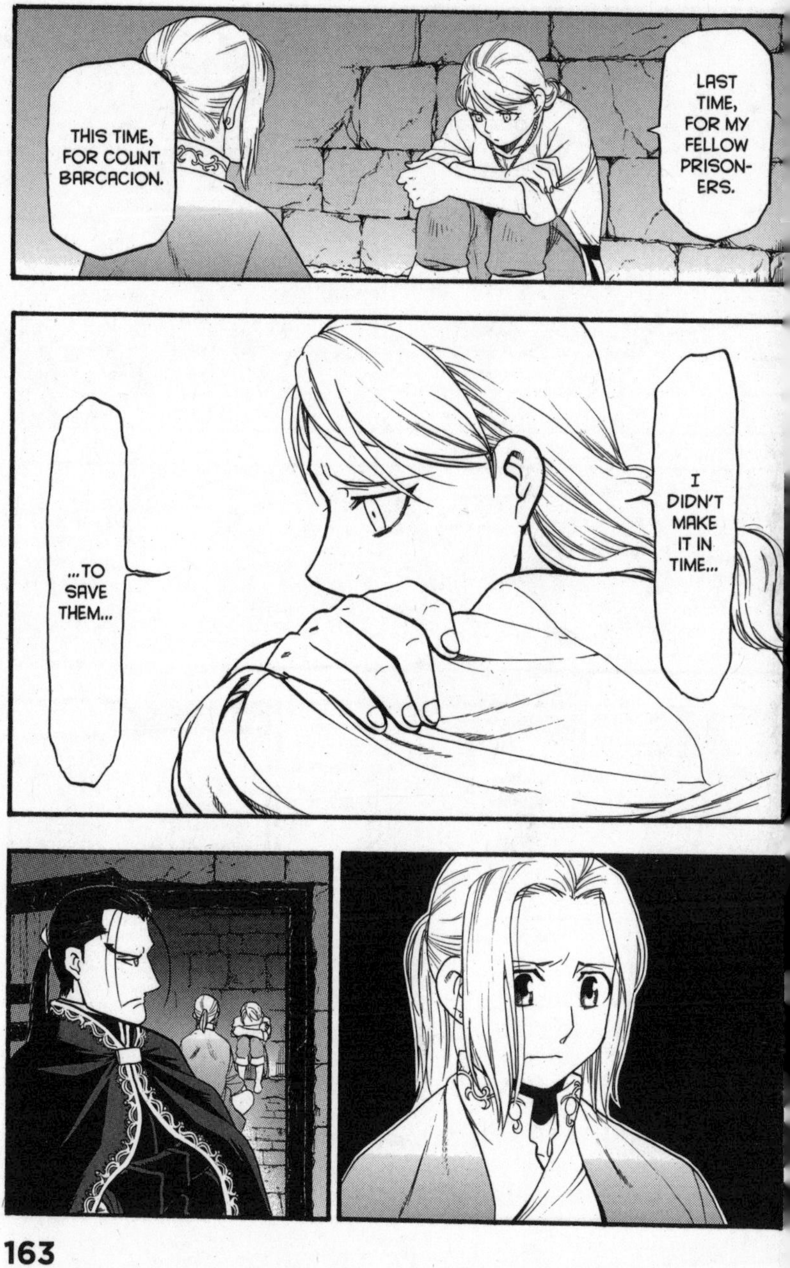
LAST TIME, FOR MY FELLOW PRISONERS.
THIS TIME, FOR COUNT BARCACION.
I DIDN'T MAKE IT IN TIME...
...TO SAVE THEM...

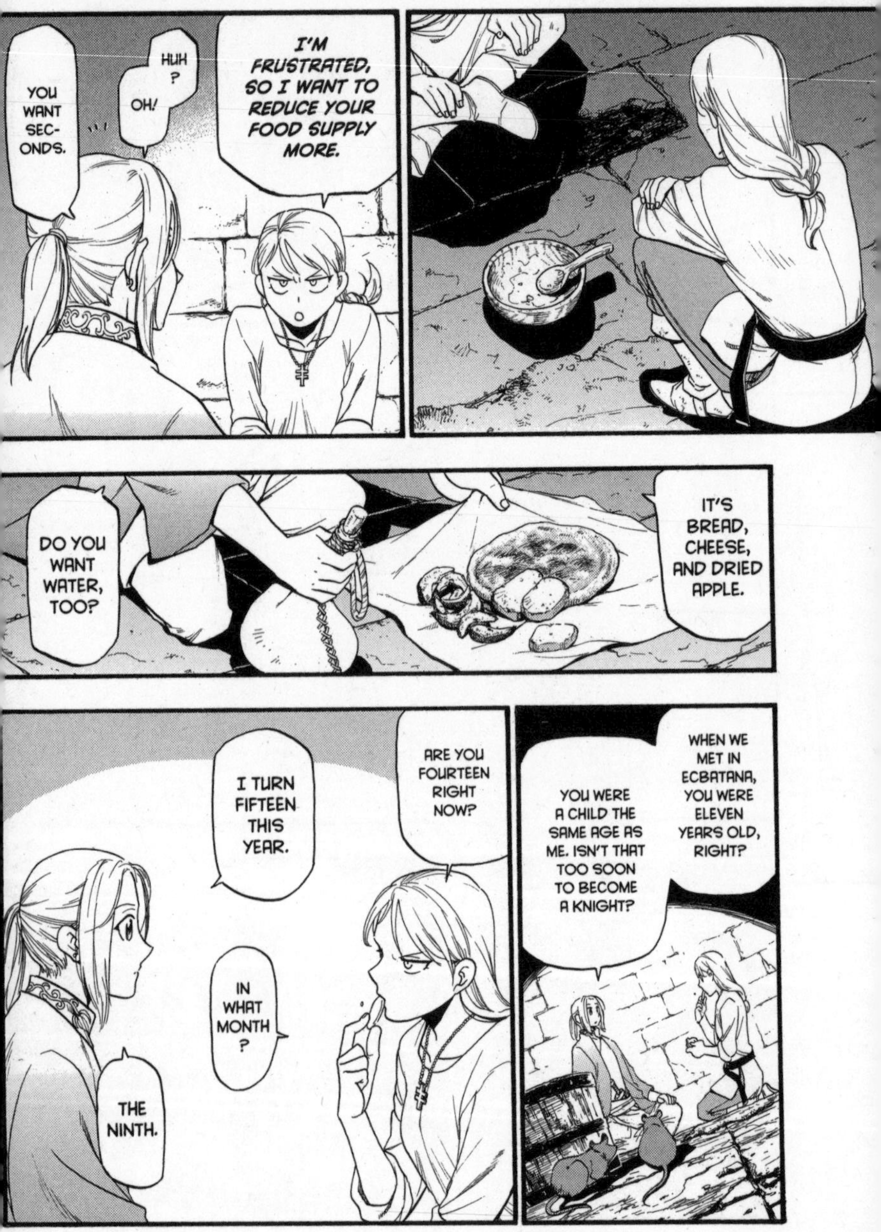
I'M FRUSTRATED, SO I WANT TO REDUCE YOUR FOOD SUPPLY MORE.
HUH? OH!
...
YOU WANT SEC-ONDS.
IT'S BREAD, CHEESE, AND DRIED APPLE.
DO YOU WANT WATER, TOO?
WHEN WE MET IN ECBATANA, YOU WERE ELEVEN YEARS OLD, RIGHT?
YOU WERE A CHILD THE SAME AGE AS ME. ISN'T THAT TOO SOON TO BECOME A KNIGHT?
ARE YOU FOURTEEN RIGHT NOW?
I TURN FIFTEEN THIS YEAR.
IN WHAT MONTH?
THE NINTH.

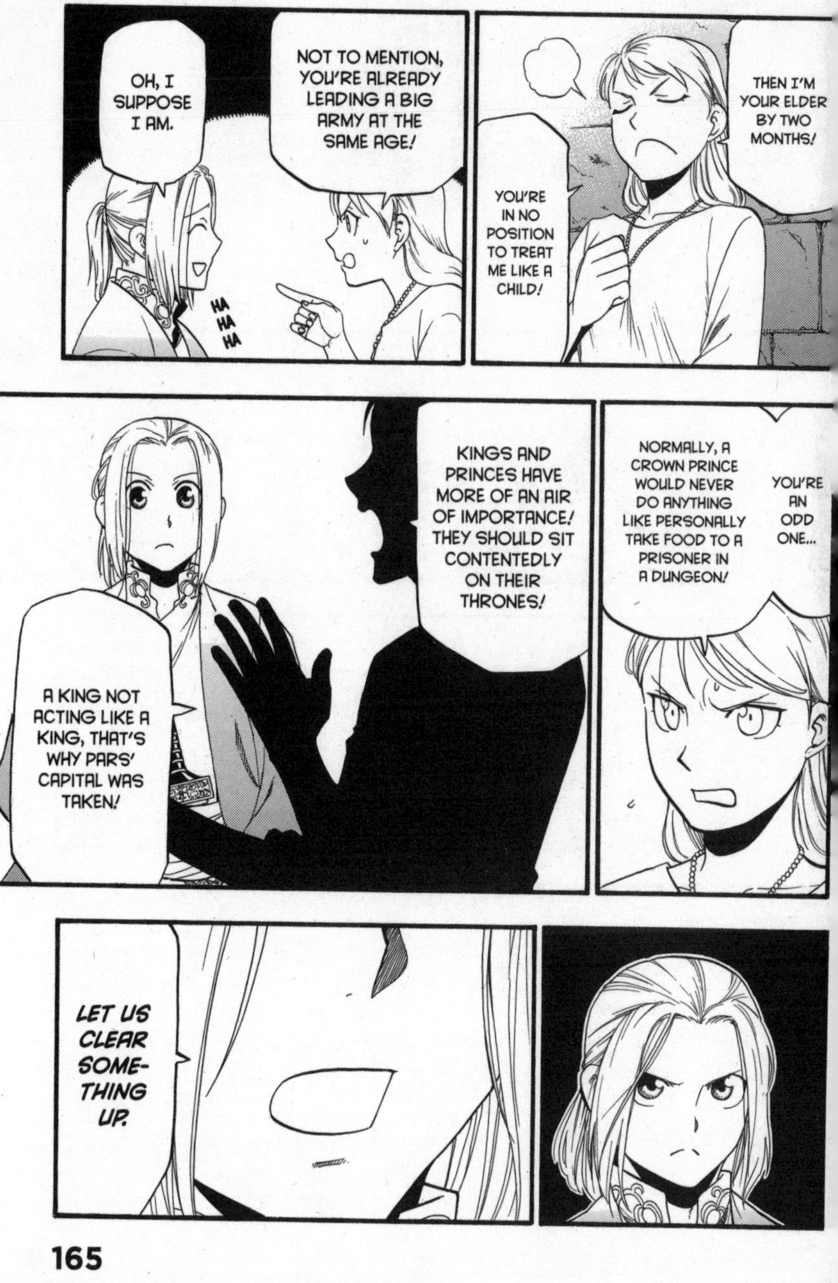
THEN I'M YOUR ELDER BY TWO MONTHS!
YOU'RE IN NO POSITION TO TREAT ME LIKE A CHILD!
NOT TO MENTION, YOU'RE ALREADY LEADING A BIG ARMY AT THE SAME AGE!
OH, I SUPPOSE I AM.
HA HA HA
YOU'RE AN ODD ONE...
NORMALLY, A CROWN PRINCE WOULD NEVER DO ANYTHING LIKE PERSONALLY TAKE FOOD TO A PRISONER IN A DUNGEON!
KINGS AND PRINCES HAVE MORE OF AN AIR OF IMPORTANCE! THEY SHOULD SIT CONTENTEDLY ON THEIR THRONES!
A KING NOT ACTING LIKE A KING, THAT'S WHY PARS' CAPITAL WAS TAKEN!
LET US CLEAR SOME-THING UP.

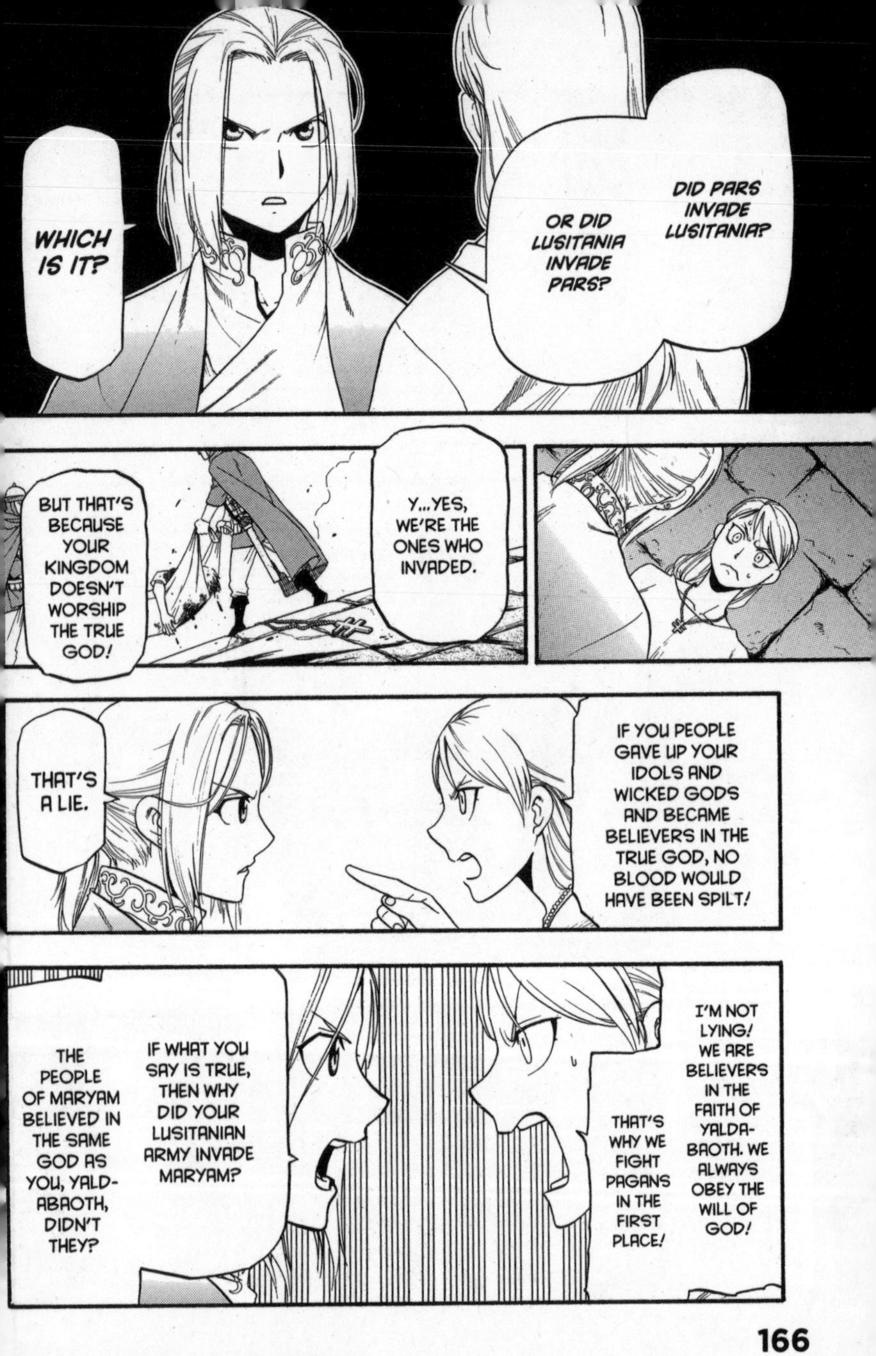
DID PARS INVADE LUSITANIA?
OR DID LUSITANIA INVADE PARS?
WHICH IS IT?
Y...YES, WE'RE THE ONES WHO INVADED.
BUT THAT'S BECAUSE YOUR KINGDOM DOESN'T WORSHIP THE TRUE GOD!
IF YOU PEOPLE GAVE UP YOUR IDOLS AND WICKED GODS AND BECAME BELIEVERS IN THE TRUE GOD, NO BLOOD WOULD HAVE BEEN SPILT!
THAT'S A LIE.
I'M NOT LYING! WE ARE BELIEVERS IN THE FAITH OF YALDA-BAOTH. WE ALWAYS OBEY THE WILL OF GOD!
THAT'S WHY WE FIGHT PAGANS IN THE FIRST PLACE!
IF WHAT YOU SAY IS TRUE, THEN WHY DID YOUR LUSITANIAN ARMY INVADE MARYAM?
THE PEOPLE OF MARYAM BELIEVED IN THE SAME GOD AS YOU, YALD-ABAOTH, DIDN'T THEY?

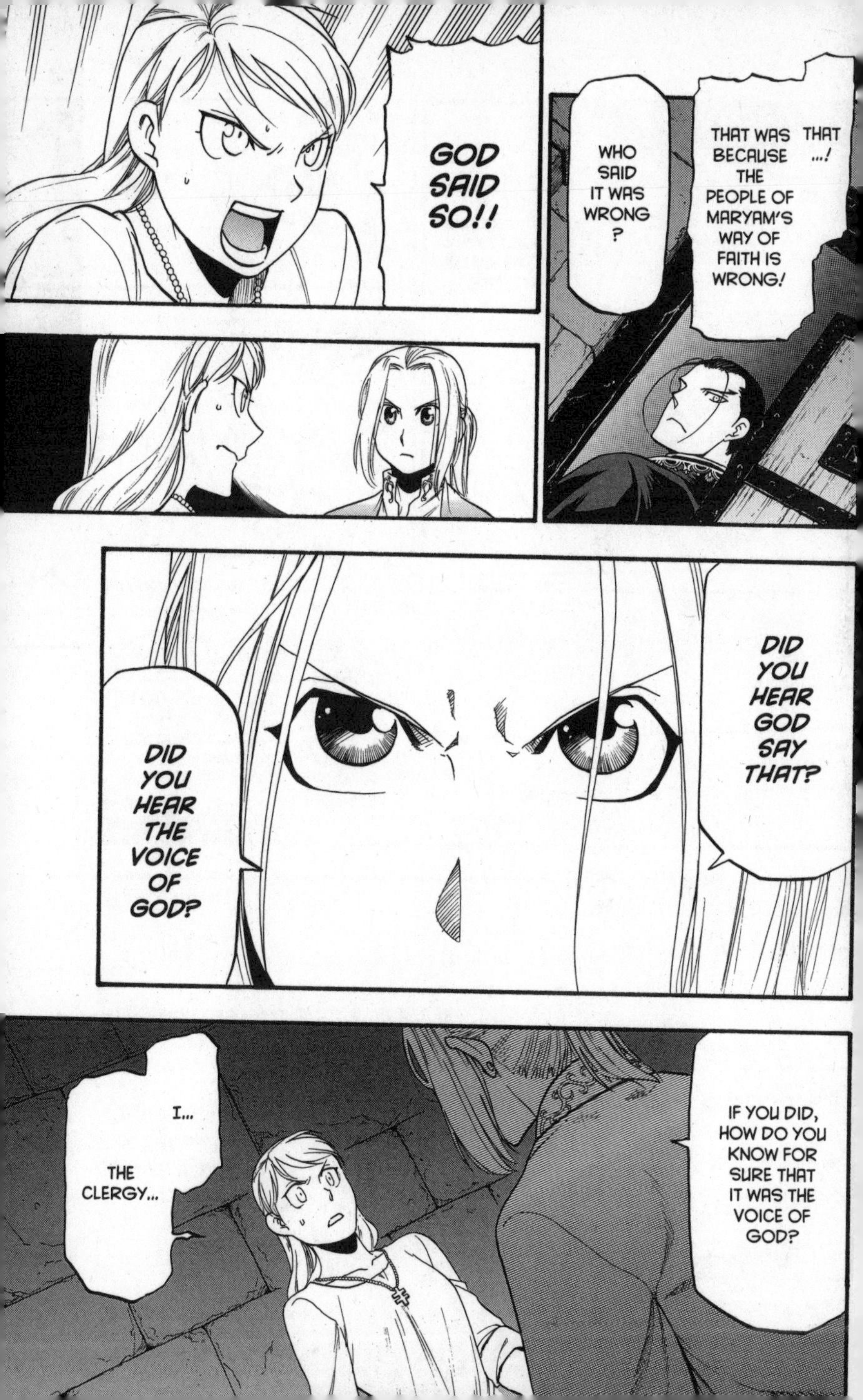
THAT ...!
THAT WAS BECAUSE THE PEOPLE OF MARYAM'S WAY OF FAITH IS WRONG!
WHO SAID IT WAS WRONG ?
GOD SAID SO!!
DID YOU HEAR GOD SAY THAT?
DID YOU HEAR THE VOICE OF GOD?
IF YOU DID, HOW DO YOU KNOW FOR SURE THAT IT WAS THE VOICE OF GOD?
I...
THE CLERGY...

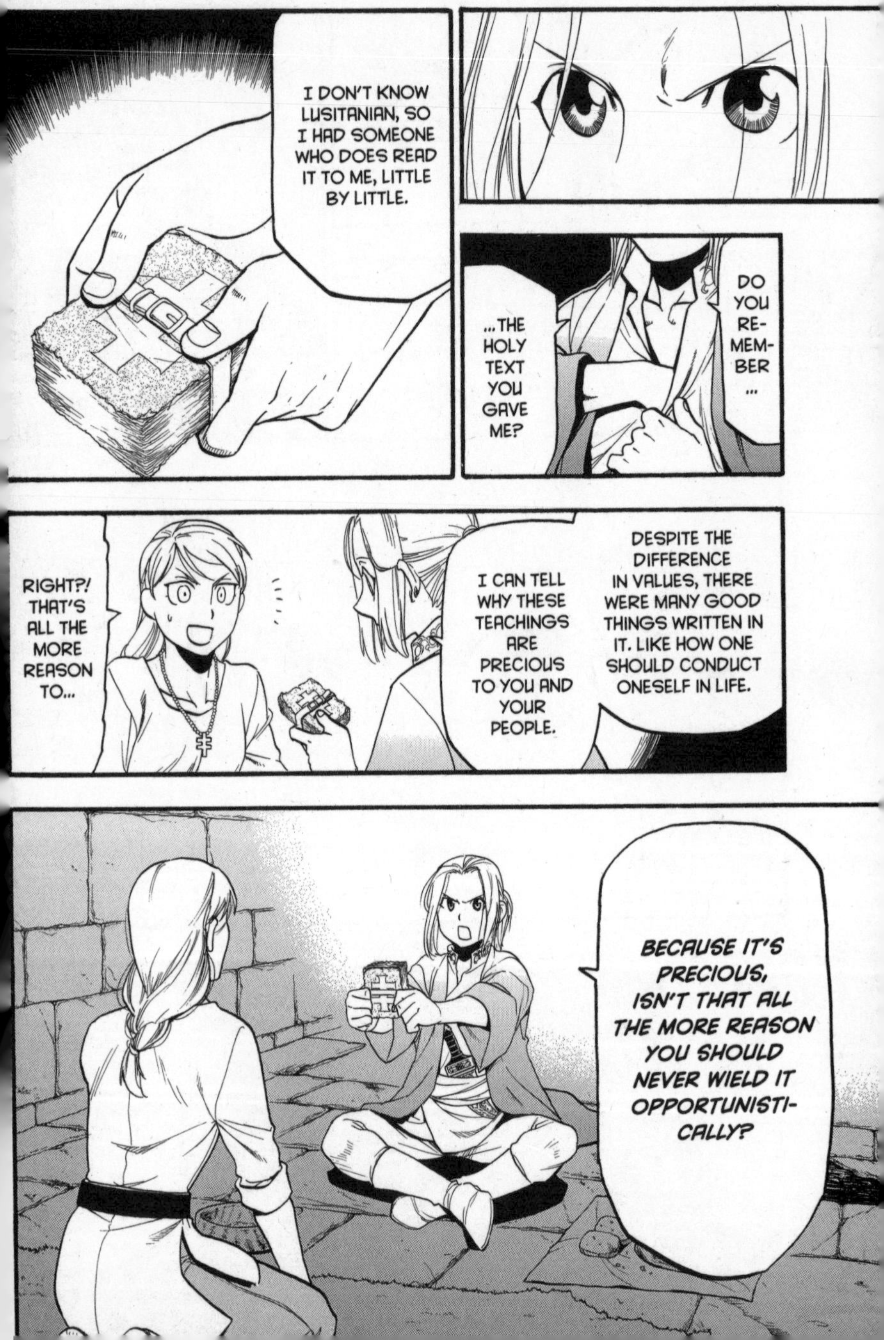
DO YOU REMEMBER...
...THE HOLY TEXT YOU GAVE ME?
I DON'T KNOW LUSITANIAN, SO I HAD SOMEONE WHO DOES READ IT TO ME, LITTLE BY LITTLE.
DESPITE THE DIFFERENCE IN VALUES, THERE WERE MANY GOOD THINGS WRITTEN IN IT. LIKE HOW ONE SHOULD CONDUCT ONESELF IN LIFE.
I CAN TELL WHY THESE TEACHINGS ARE PRECIOUS TO YOU AND YOUR PEOPLE.
RIGHT?! THAT'S ALL THE MORE REASON TO...
BECAUSE IT'S PRECIOUS, ISN'T THAT ALL THE MORE REASON YOU SHOULD NEVER WIELD IT OPPORTUNISTICALLY?

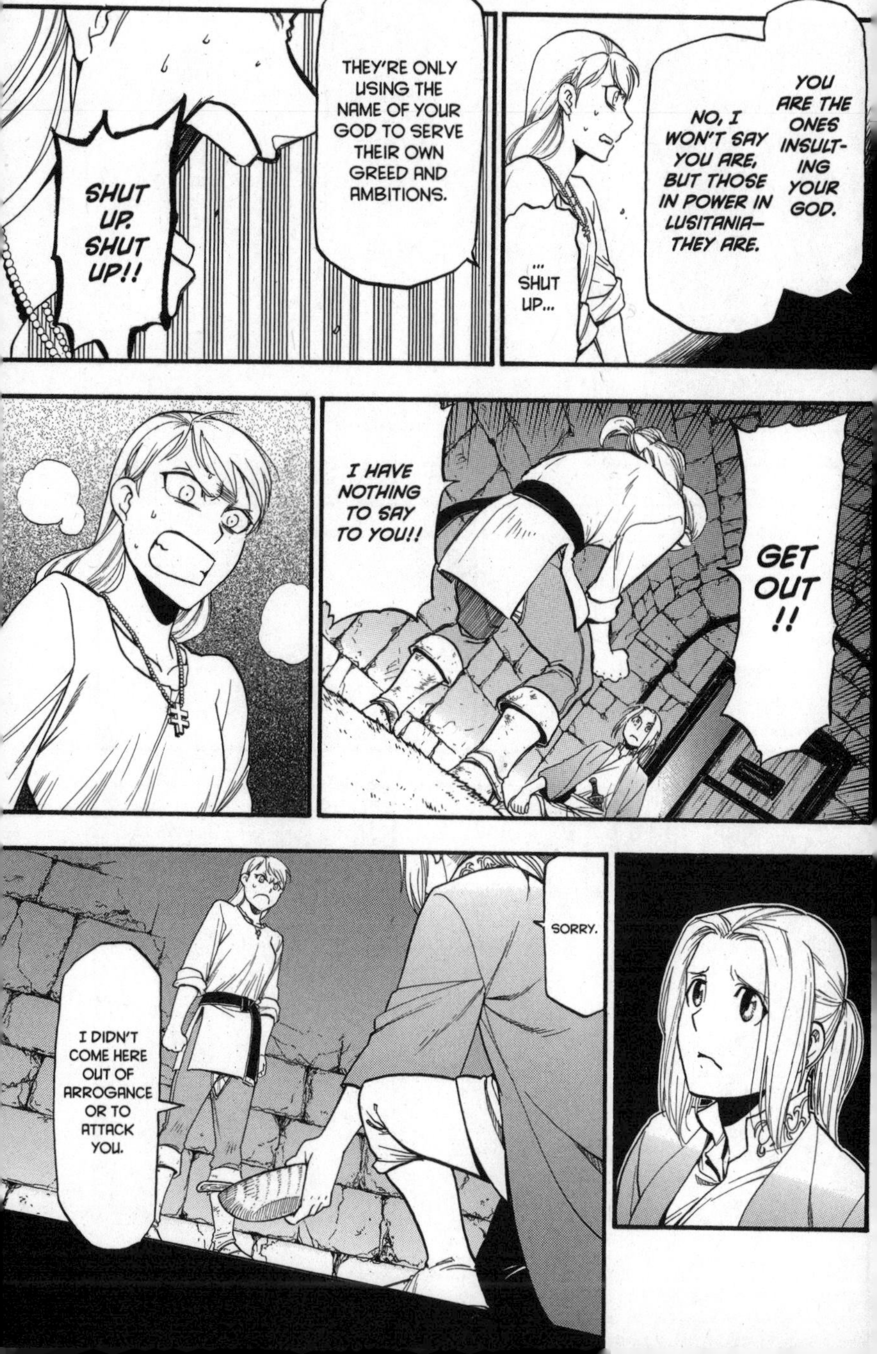
YOU ARE THE ONES INSULTING YOUR GOD.
NO, I WON'T SAY YOU ARE, BUT THOSE IN POWER IN LUSITANIA—THEY ARE.
... SHUT UP...
THEY'RE ONLY USING THE NAME OF YOUR GOD TO SERVE THEIR OWN GREED AND AMBITIONS.
SHUT UP. SHUT UP!!
GET OUT!!
I HAVE NOTHING TO SAY TO YOU!!
SORRY.
I DIDN'T COME HERE OUT OF ARROGANCE OR TO ATTACK YOU.

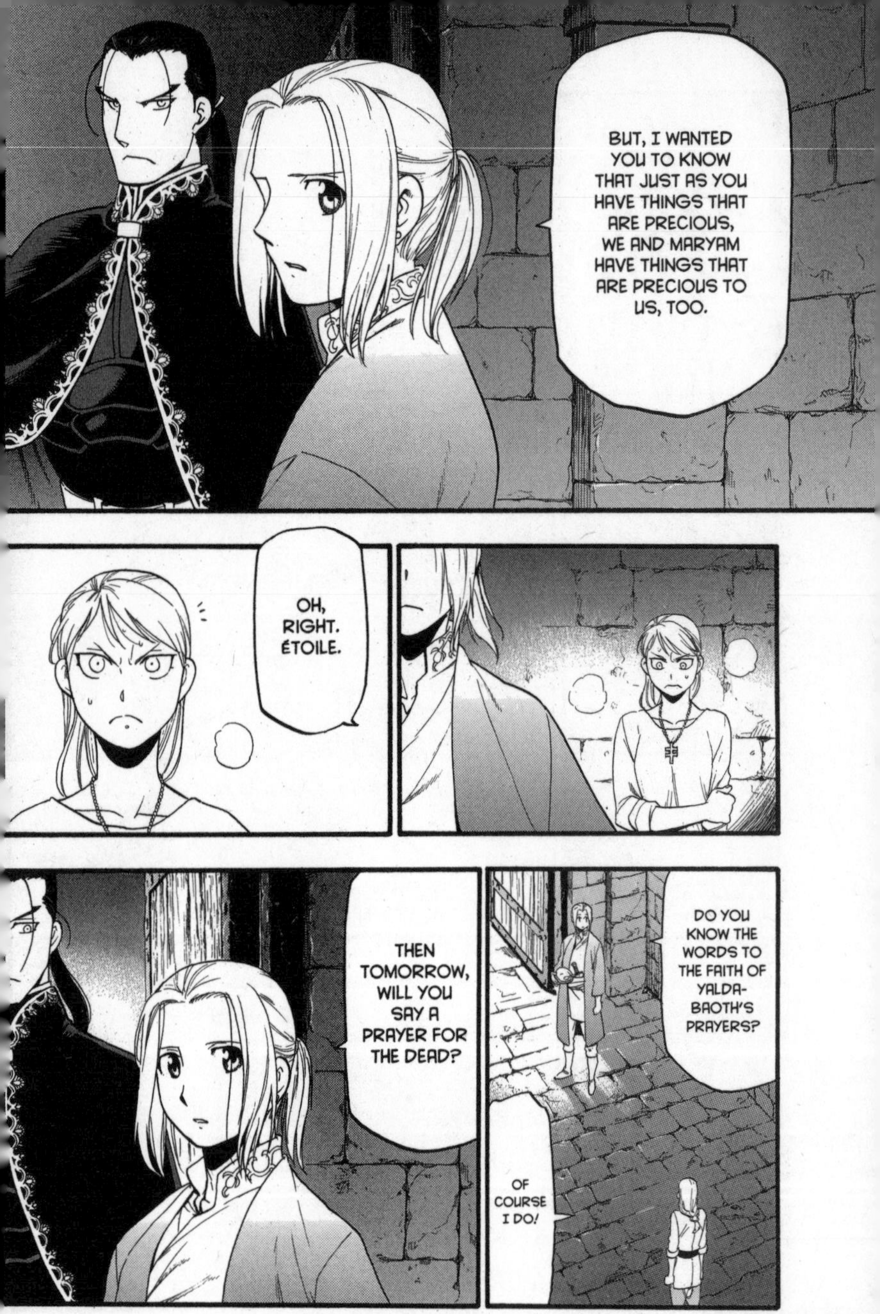
BUT, I WANTED YOU TO KNOW THAT JUST AS YOU HAVE THINGS THAT ARE PRECIOUS, WE AND MARYAM HAVE THINGS THAT ARE PRECIOUS TO US, TOO.
OH, RIGHT. ÉTOILE.
DO YOU KNOW THE WORDS TO THE FAITH OF YALDA-BAOTH'S PRAYERS?
OF COURSE I DO!
THEN TOMORROW, WILL YOU SAY A PRAYER FOR THE DEAD?

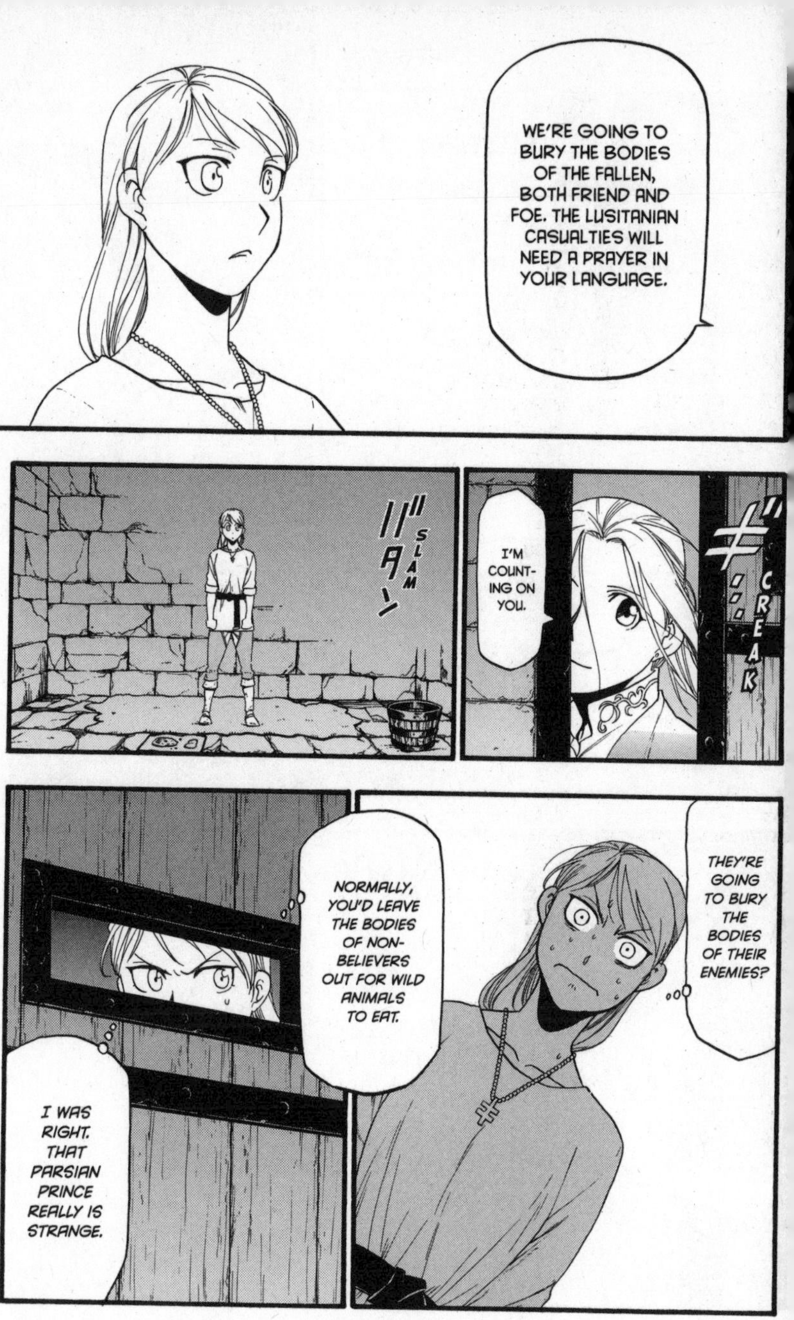
WE'RE GOING TO BURY THE BODIES OF THE FALLEN, BOTH FRIEND AND FOE. THE LUSITANIAN CASUALTIES WILL NEED A PRAYER IN YOUR LANGUAGE.
I'M COUNTING ON YOU.
CREAK
SLAM
THEY'RE GOING TO BURY THE BODIES OF THEIR ENEMIES?
NORMALLY, YOU'D LEAVE THE BODIES OF NON-BELIEVERS OUT FOR WILD ANIMALS TO EAT.
I WAS RIGHT. THAT PARSIAN PRINCE REALLY IS STRANGE.

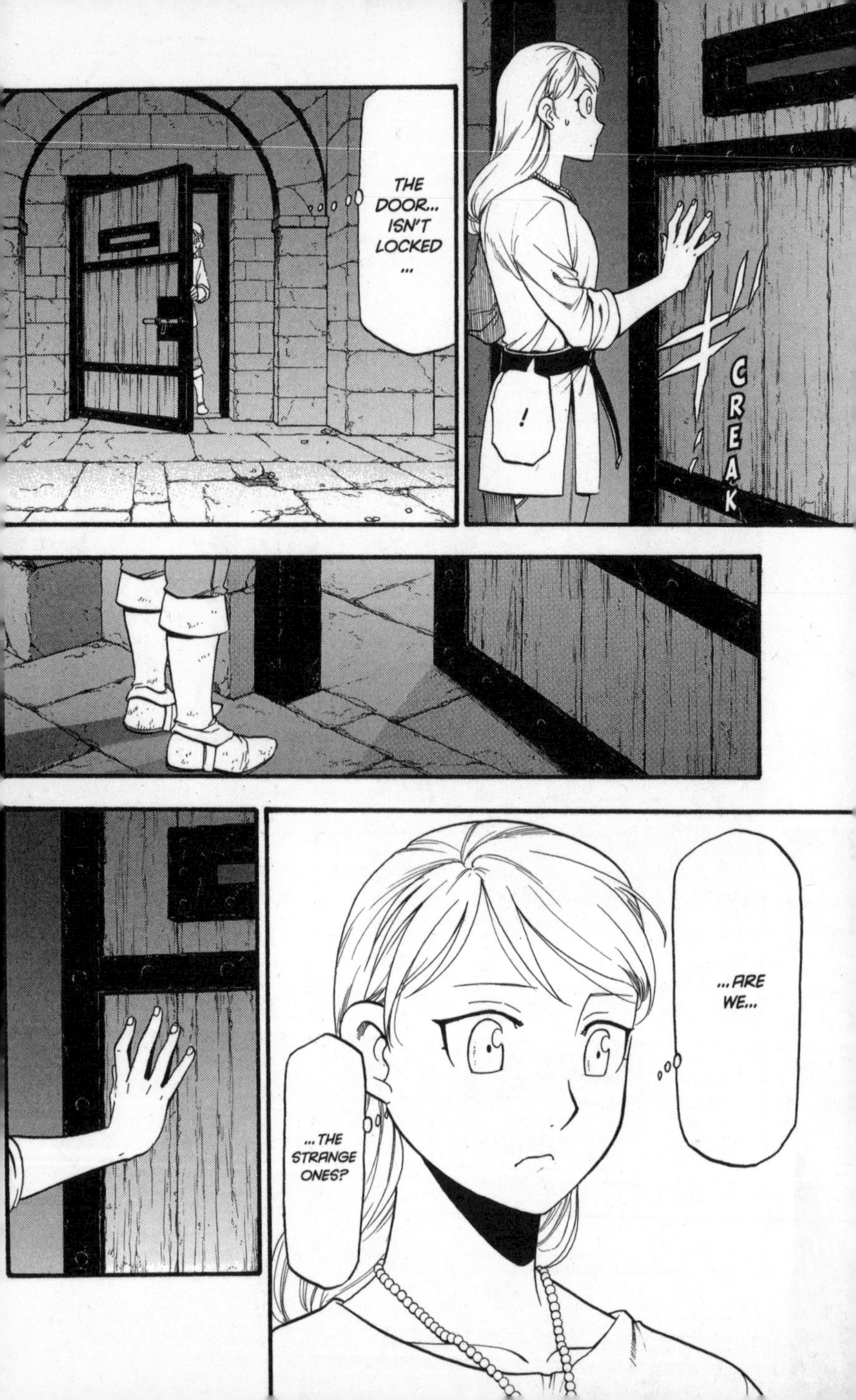
CREAK
!
THE DOOR... ISN'T LOCKED ...
...ARE WE...
...THE STRANGE ONES?

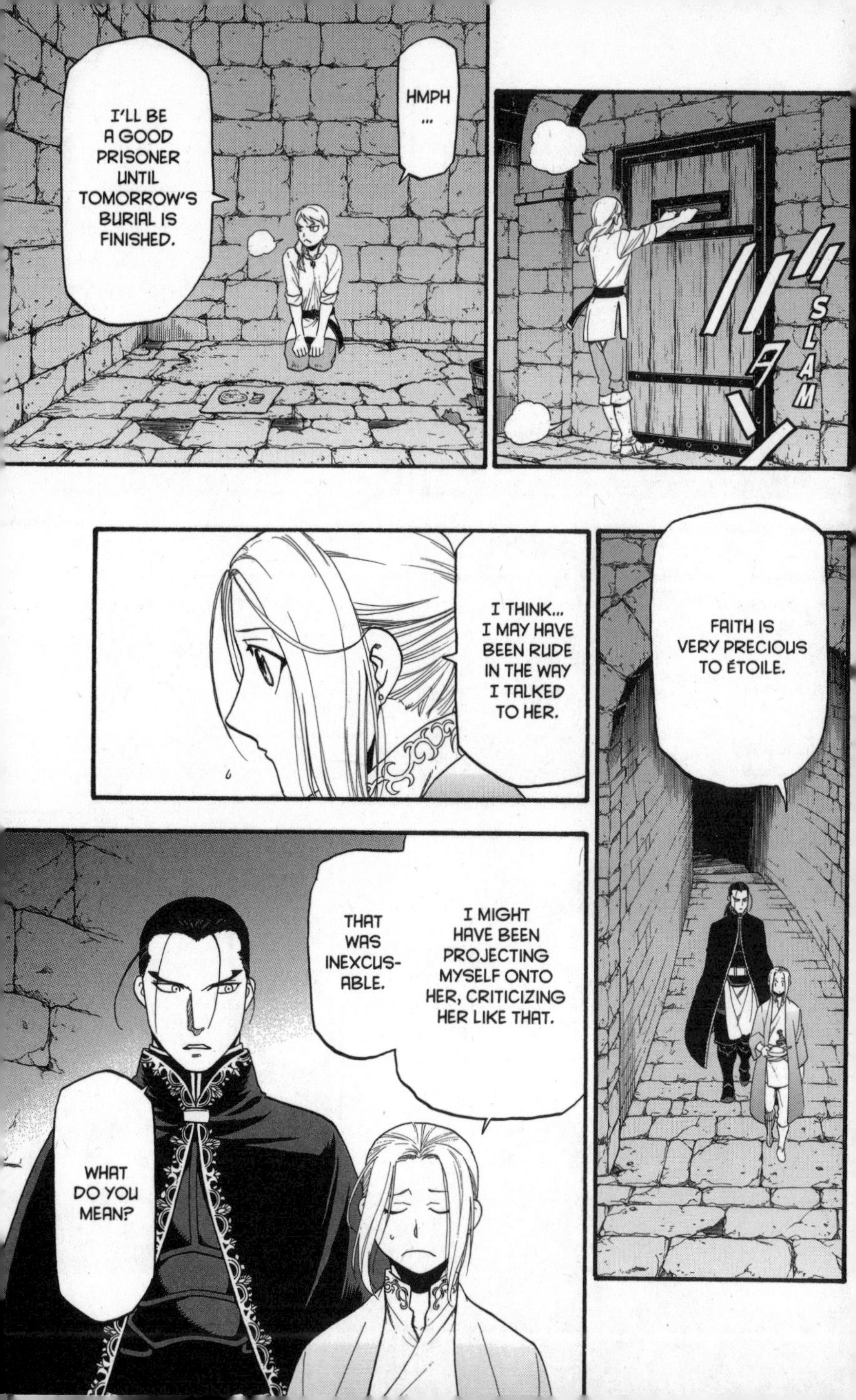
SLAM
HMPH ...
I'LL BE A GOOD PRISONER UNTIL TOMORROW'S BURIAL IS FINISHED.
FAITH IS VERY PRECIOUS TO ÉTOILE.
I THINK... I MAY HAVE BEEN RUDE IN THE WAY I TALKED TO HER.
I MIGHT HAVE BEEN PROJECTING MYSELF ONTO HER, CRITICIZING HER LIKE THAT.
THAT WAS INEXCUS-ABLE.
WHAT DO YOU MEAN?

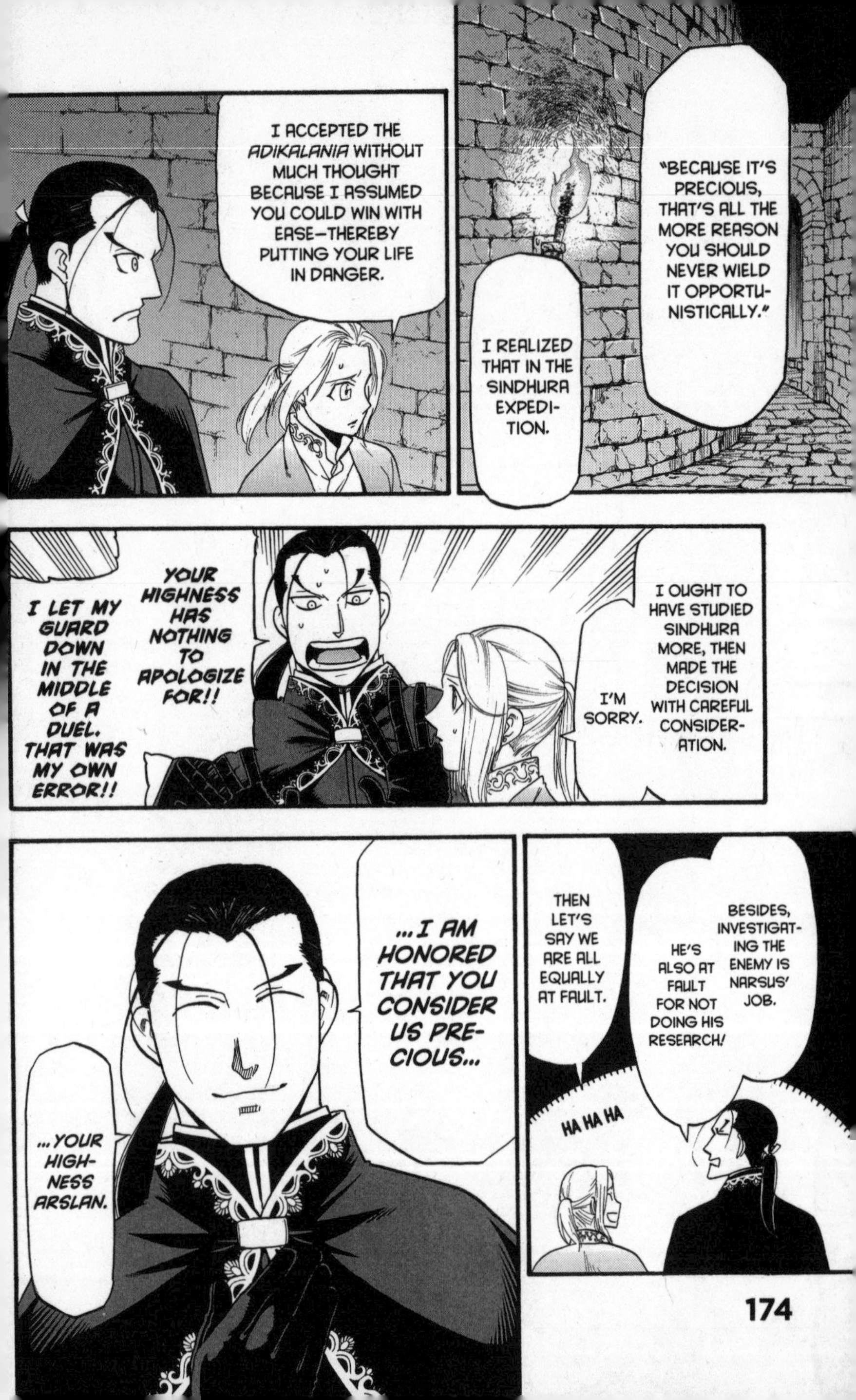
"BECAUSE IT'S PRECIOUS, THAT'S ALL THE MORE REASON YOU SHOULD NEVER WIELD IT OPPORTUNISTICALLY."
I REALIZED THAT IN THE SINDHURA EXPEDITION.
I ACCEPTED THE *ADIKALANIA* WITHOUT MUCH THOUGHT BECAUSE I ASSUMED YOU COULD WIN WITH EASE—THEREBY PUTTING YOUR LIFE IN DANGER.
I OUGHT TO HAVE STUDIED SINDHURA MORE, THEN MADE THE DECISION WITH CAREFUL CONSIDERATION.
I'M SORRY.
YOUR HIGHNESS HAS NOTHING TO APOLOGIZE FOR!!
I LET MY GUARD DOWN IN THE MIDDLE OF A DUEL. THAT WAS MY OWN ERROR!!
BESIDES, INVESTIGATING THE ENEMY IS NARSUS' JOB.
HE'S ALSO AT FAULT FOR NOT DOING HIS RESEARCH!
THEN LET'S SAY WE ARE ALL EQUALLY AT FAULT.
HA HA HA
...I AM HONORED THAT YOU CONSIDER US PRECIOUS...
...YOUR HIGHNESS ARSLAN.

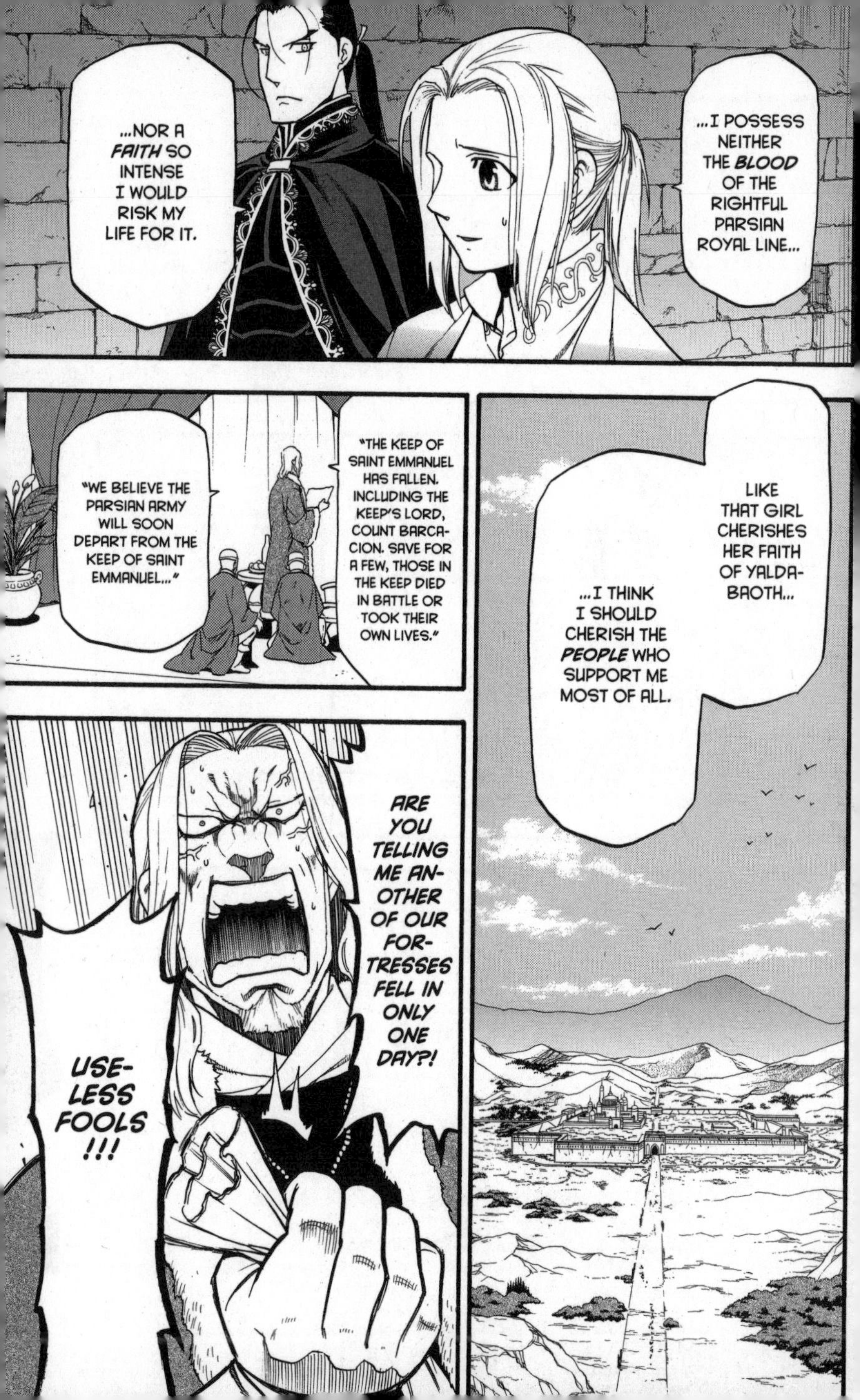
...I POSSESS NEITHER THE *BLOOD* OF THE RIGHTFUL PARSIAN ROYAL LINE...
...NOR A *FAITH* SO INTENSE I WOULD RISK MY LIFE FOR IT.
LIKE THAT GIRL CHERISHES HER FAITH OF YALDA-BAOTH...
...I THINK I SHOULD CHERISH THE *PEOPLE* WHO SUPPORT ME MOST OF ALL.
"THE KEEP OF SAINT EMMANUEL HAS FALLEN. INCLUDING THE KEEP'S LORD, COUNT BARCA-CION. SAVE FOR A FEW, THOSE IN THE KEEP DIED IN BATTLE OR TOOK THEIR OWN LIVES."
"WE BELIEVE THE PARSIAN ARMY WILL SOON DEPART FROM THE KEEP OF SAINT EMMANUEL..."
ARE YOU TELLING ME AN-OTHER OF OUR FOR-TRESSES FELL IN ONLY ONE DAY?!
USE-LESS FOOLS !!!

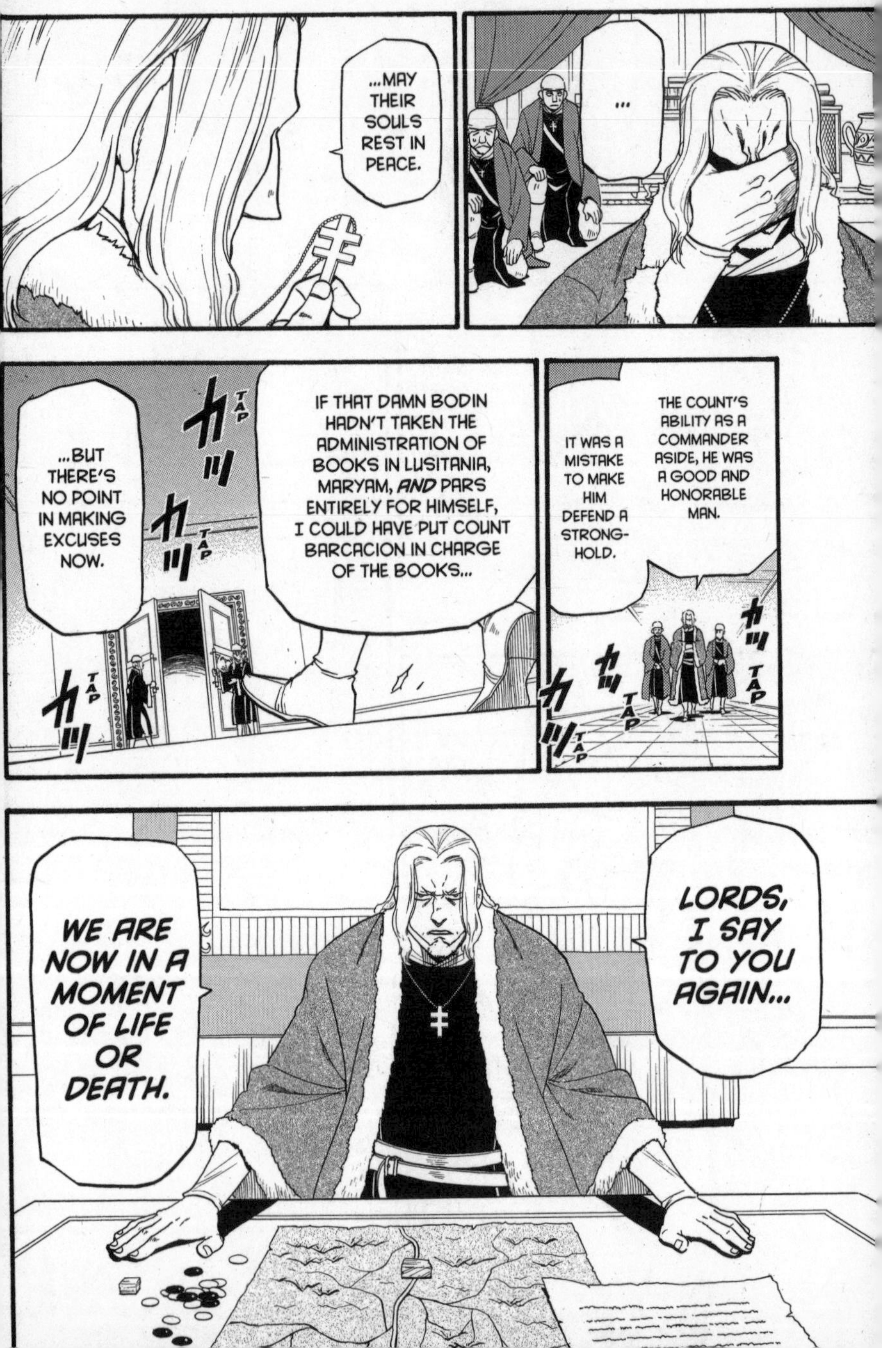
...
...MAY THEIR SOULS REST IN PEACE.
THE COUNT'S ABILITY AS A COMMANDER ASIDE, HE WAS A GOOD AND HONORABLE MAN.
IT WAS A MISTAKE TO MAKE HIM DEFEND A STRONGHOLD.
カッ TAP
カッ TAP
カッ TAP
カッ TAP
IF THAT DAMN BODIN HADN'T TAKEN THE ADMINISTRATION OF BOOKS IN LUSITANIA, MARYAM, *AND* PARS ENTIRELY FOR HIMSELF, I COULD HAVE PUT COUNT BARCACION IN CHARGE OF THE BOOKS...
カッ TAP
カッ TAP
...BUT THERE'S NO POINT IN MAKING EXCUSES NOW.
カッ TAP
LORDS, I SAY TO YOU AGAIN...
WE ARE NOW IN A MOMENT OF LIFE OR DEATH.

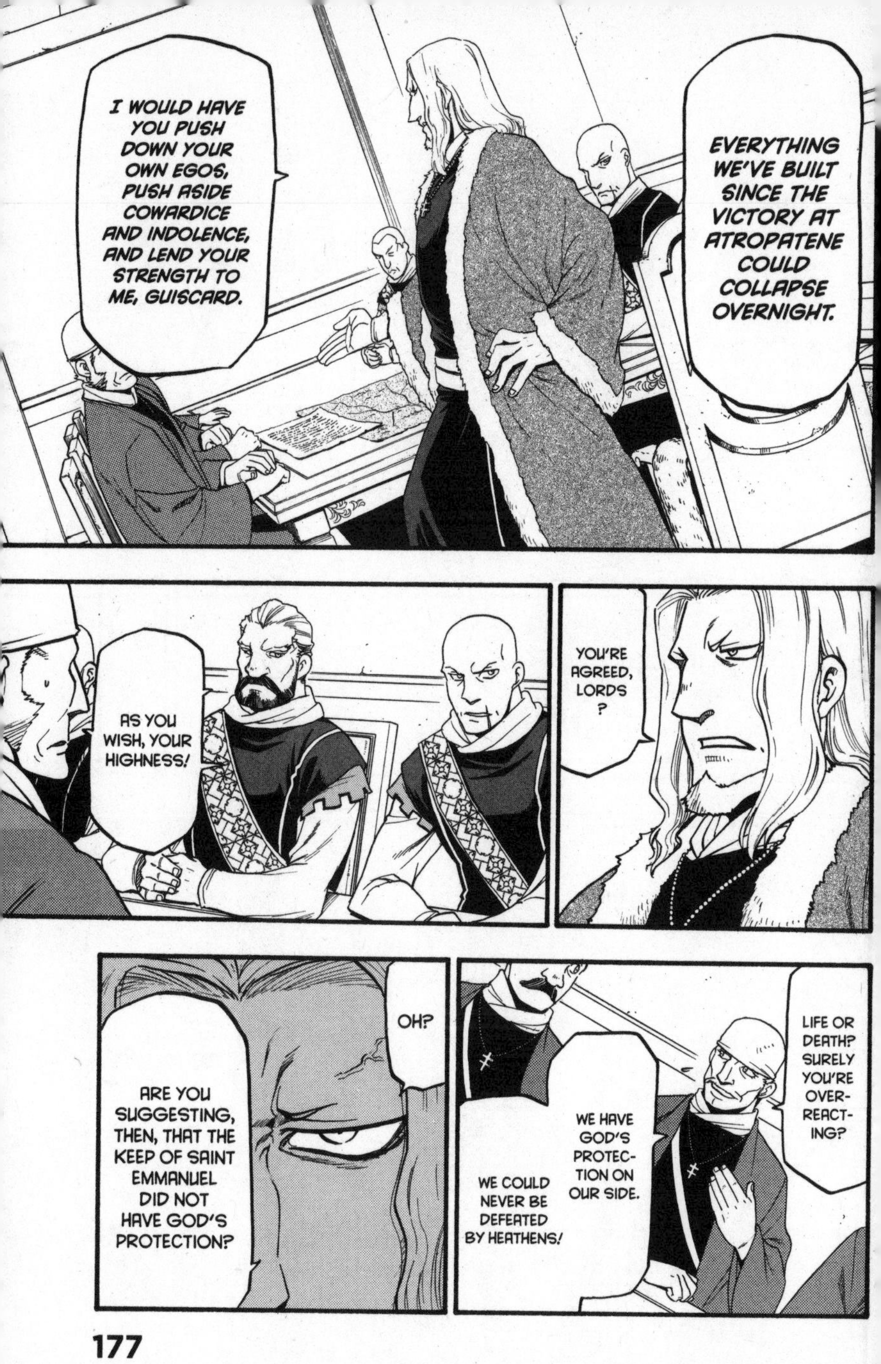
EVERYTHING WE'VE BUILT SINCE THE VICTORY AT ATROPATENE COULD COLLAPSE OVERNIGHT.
I WOULD HAVE YOU PUSH DOWN YOUR OWN EGOS, PUSH ASIDE COWARDICE AND INDOLENCE, AND LEND YOUR STRENGTH TO ME, GUISCARD.
YOU'RE AGREED, LORDS?
AS YOU WISH, YOUR HIGHNESS!
LIFE OR DEATH? SURELY YOU'RE OVER-REACT-ING?
WE HAVE GOD'S PROTEC-TION ON OUR SIDE.
WE COULD NEVER BE DEFEATED BY HEATHENS!
OH?
ARE YOU SUGGESTING, THEN, THAT THE KEEP OF SAINT EMMANUEL DID NOT HAVE GOD'S PROTECTION?

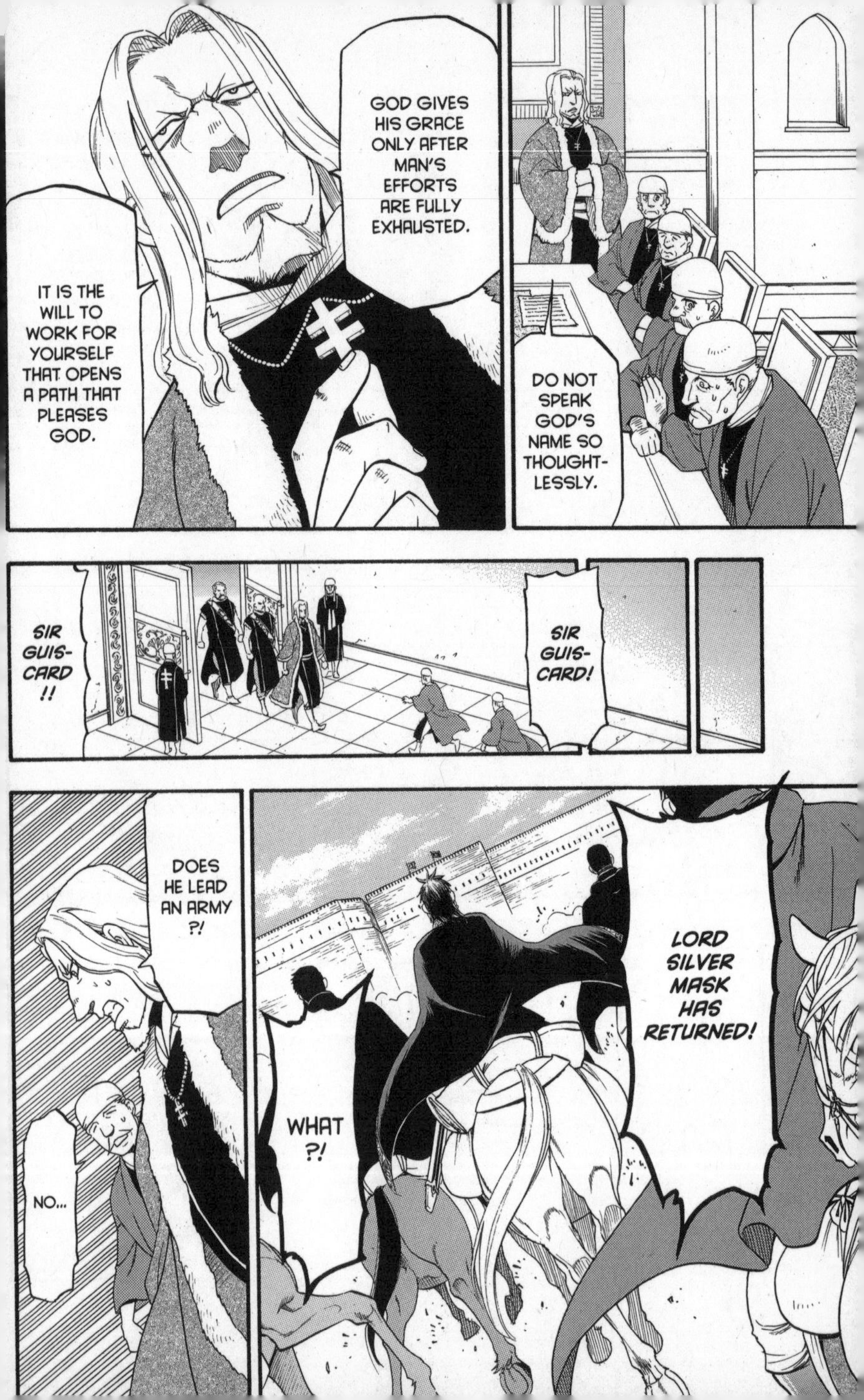
DO NOT SPEAK GOD'S NAME SO THOUGHTLESSLY.
GOD GIVES HIS GRACE ONLY AFTER MAN'S EFFORTS ARE FULLY EXHAUSTED.
IT IS THE WILL TO WORK FOR YOURSELF THAT OPENS A PATH THAT PLEASES GOD.
SIR GUISCARD!
SIR GUISCARD!!
LORD SILVER MASK HAS RETURNED!
WHAT?!
DOES HE LEAD AN ARMY?!
NO...

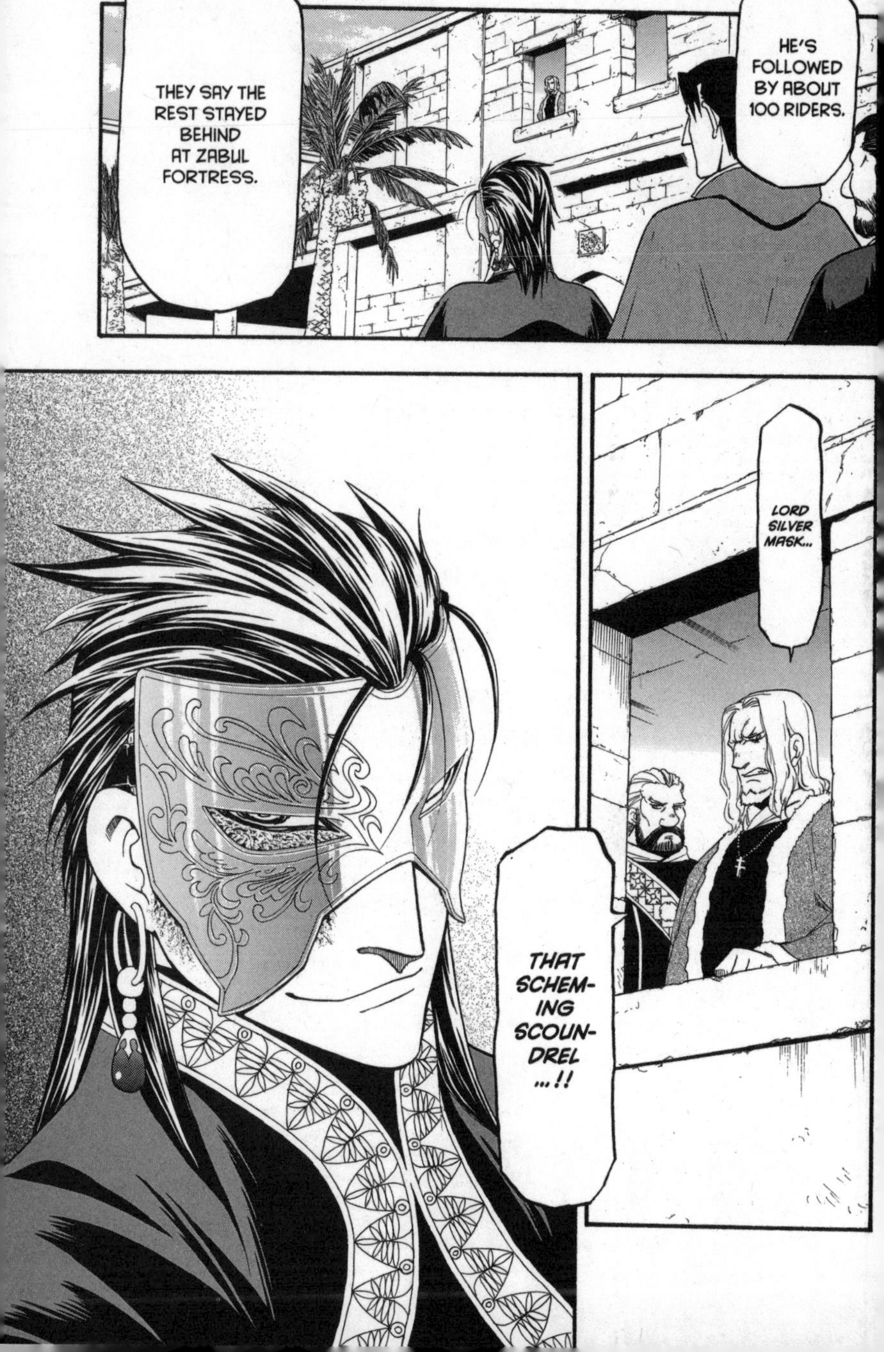
HE'S FOLLOWED BY ABOUT 100 RIDERS.
THEY SAY THE REST STAYED BEHIND AT ZABUL FORTRESS.
LORD SILVER MASK...
THAT SCHEMING SCOUNDREL ...!!

Map of Current Locations for Major Characters

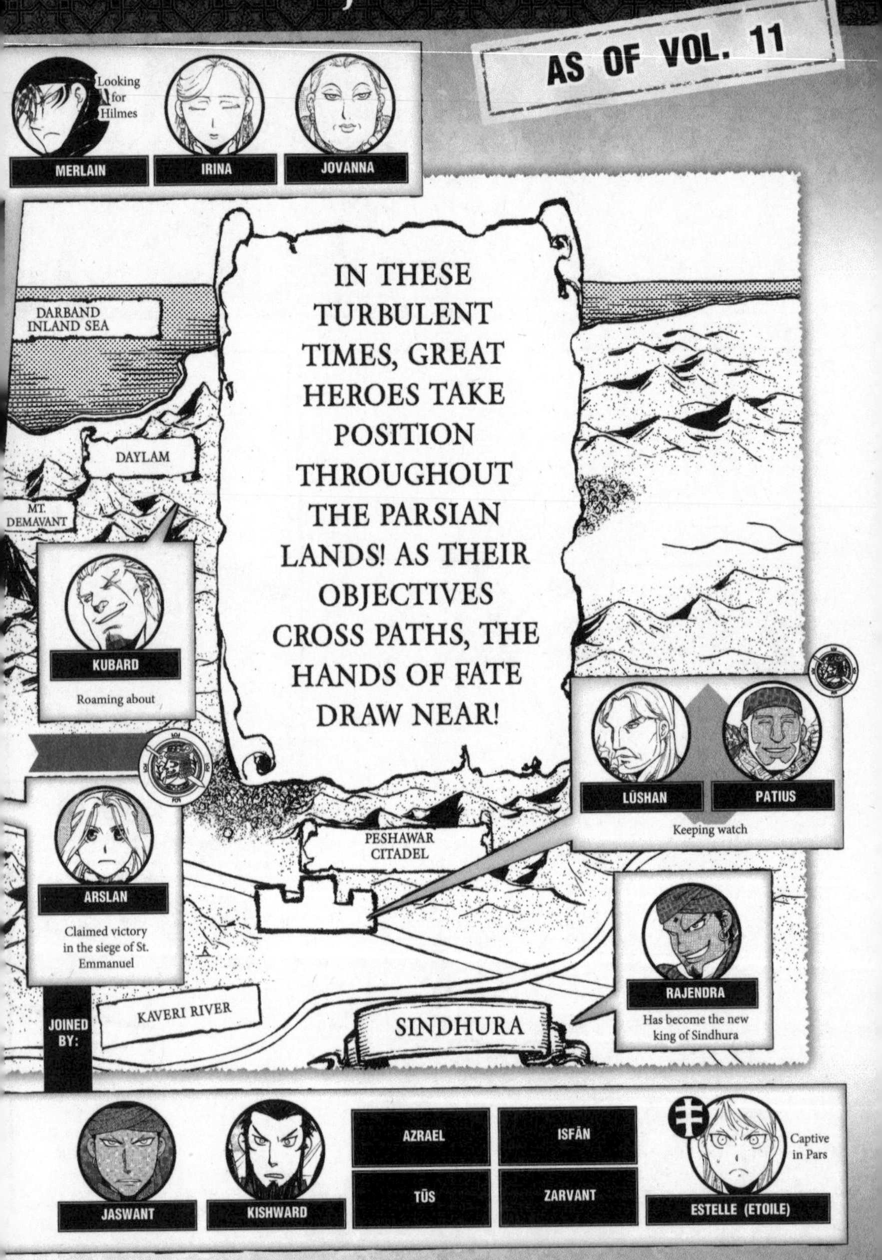
AS OF VOL. 11
Looking for Hilmes
MERLAIN
IRINA
JOVANNA
IN THESE TURBULENT TIMES, GREAT HEROES TAKE POSITION THROUGHOUT THE PARSIAN LANDS! AS THEIR OBJECTIVES CROSS PATHS, THE HANDS OF FATE DRAW NEAR!
DARBAND INLAND SEA
DAYLAM
MT. DEMAVANT
KUBARD
Roaming about
LŪSHAN
PATIUS
Keeping watch
ARSLAN
Claimed victory in the siege of St. Emmanuel
PESHAWAR CITADEL
RAJENDRA
Has become the new king of Sindhura
KAVERI RIVER
SINDHURA
JOINED BY:
JASWANT
KISHWARD
AZRAEL
ISFĀN
TŪS
ZARVANT
Captive in Pars
ESTELLE (ETOILE)

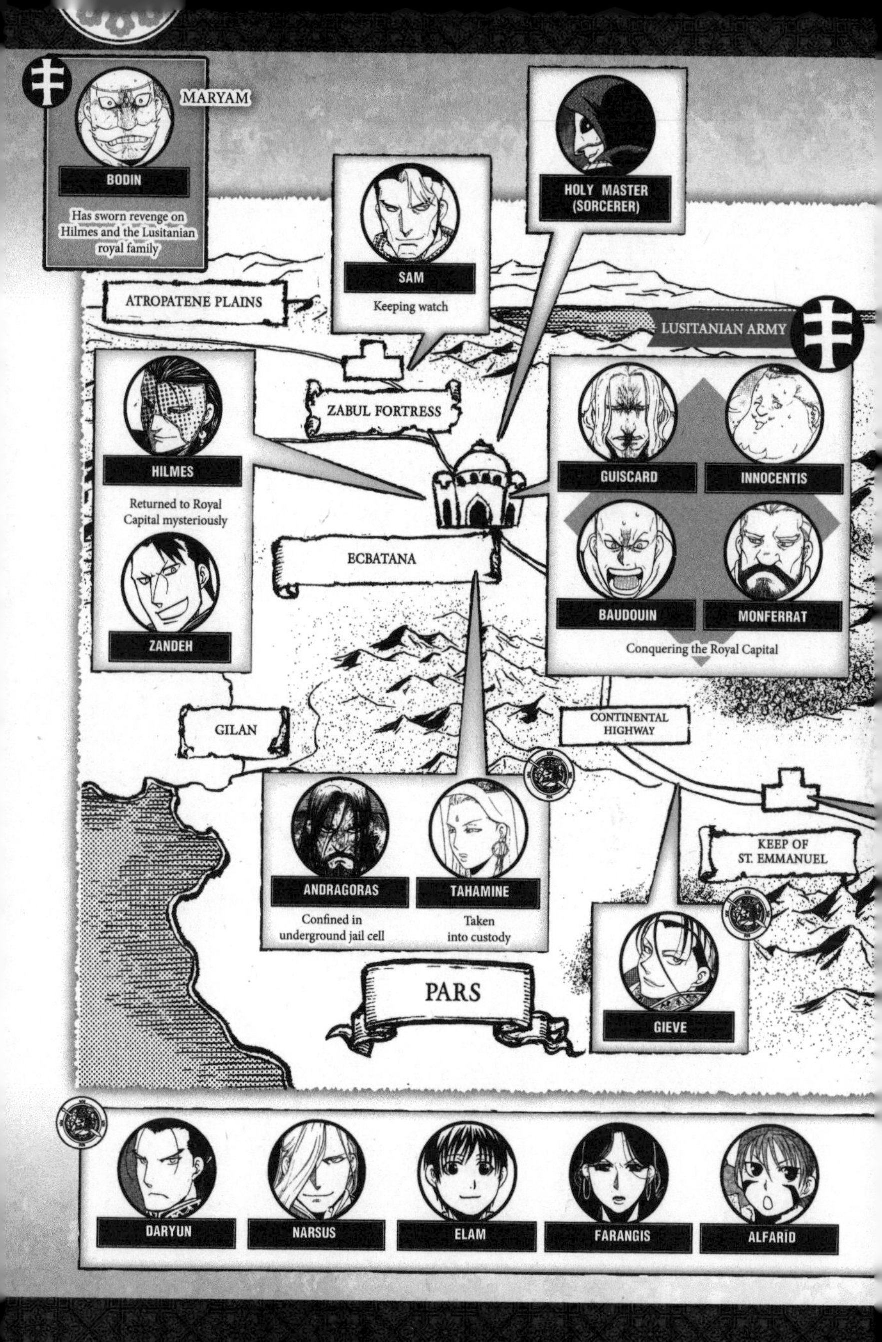
MARYAM
BODIN
Has sworn revenge on Hilmes and the Lusitanian royal family
SAM
Keeping watch
HOLY MASTER (SORCERER)
ATROPATENE PLAINS
LUSITANIAN ARMY
ZABUL FORTRESS
HILMES
Returned to Royal Capital mysteriously
ZANDEH
GUISCARD
INNOCENTIS
BAUDOUIN
MONFERRAT
Conquering the Royal Capital
ECBATANA
GILAN
CONTINENTAL HIGHWAY
KEEP OF ST. EMMANUEL
ANDRAGORAS
Confined in underground jail cell
TAHAMINE
Taken into custody
PARS
GIEVE
DARYUN
NARSUS
ELAM
FARANGIS
ALFARID

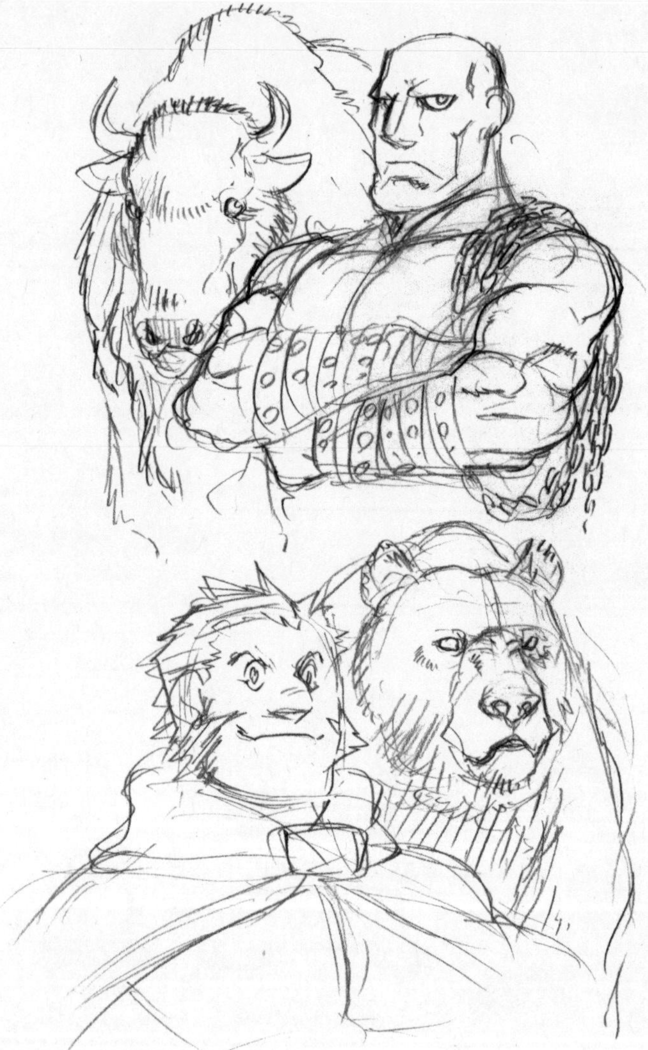

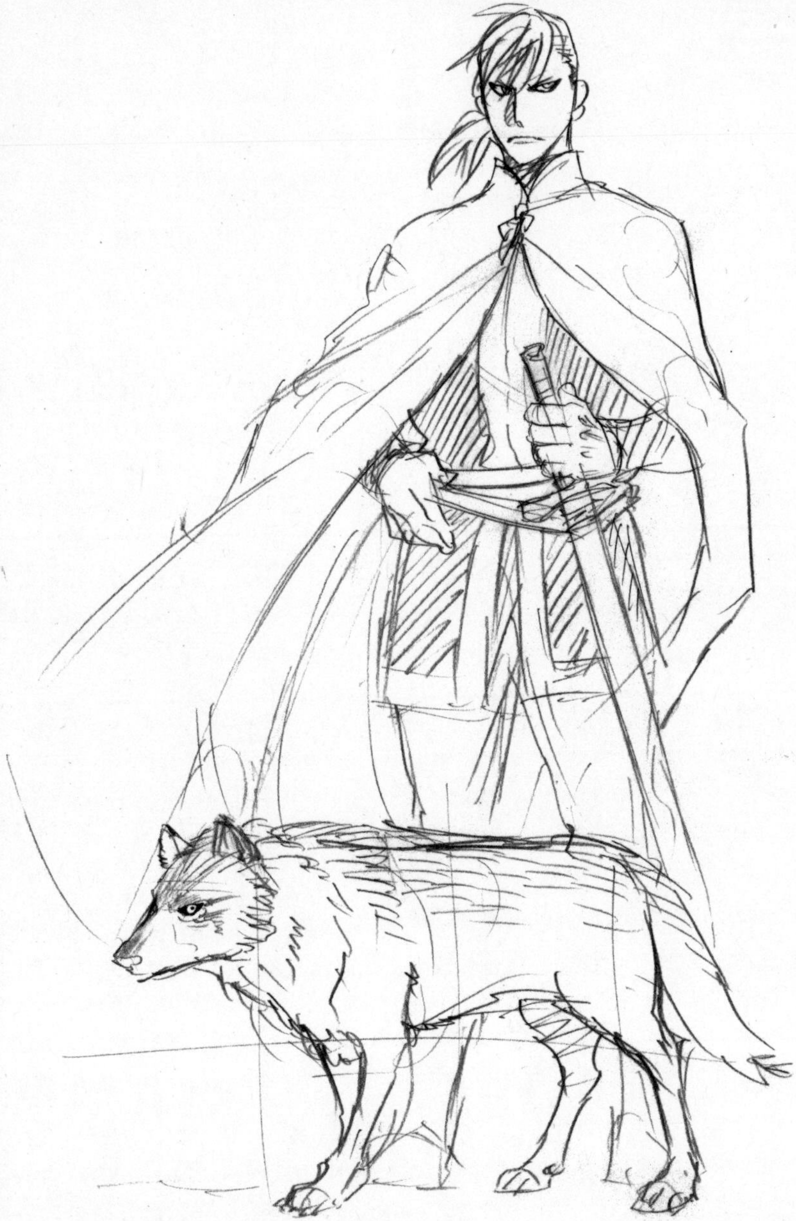

Japan's most powerful spirit medium delves into the ghost world's greatest mysteries!

Story by Kyo Shirodaira, famed author of mystery fiction and creator of *Spiral*, *Blast of Tempest*, and *The Record of a Fallen Vampire*.

Both touched by spirits called yôkai, Kotoko and Kurô have gained unique superhuman powers. But to gain her powers Kotoko has given up an eye and a leg, and Kurô's personal life is in shambles. So when Kotoko suggests they team up to deal with renegades from the spirit world, Kurô doesn't have many other choices, but Kotoko might just have a few ulterior motives...

IN/SPECTRE

STORY BY KYO SHIRODAIRA
ART BY CHASHIBA KATASE

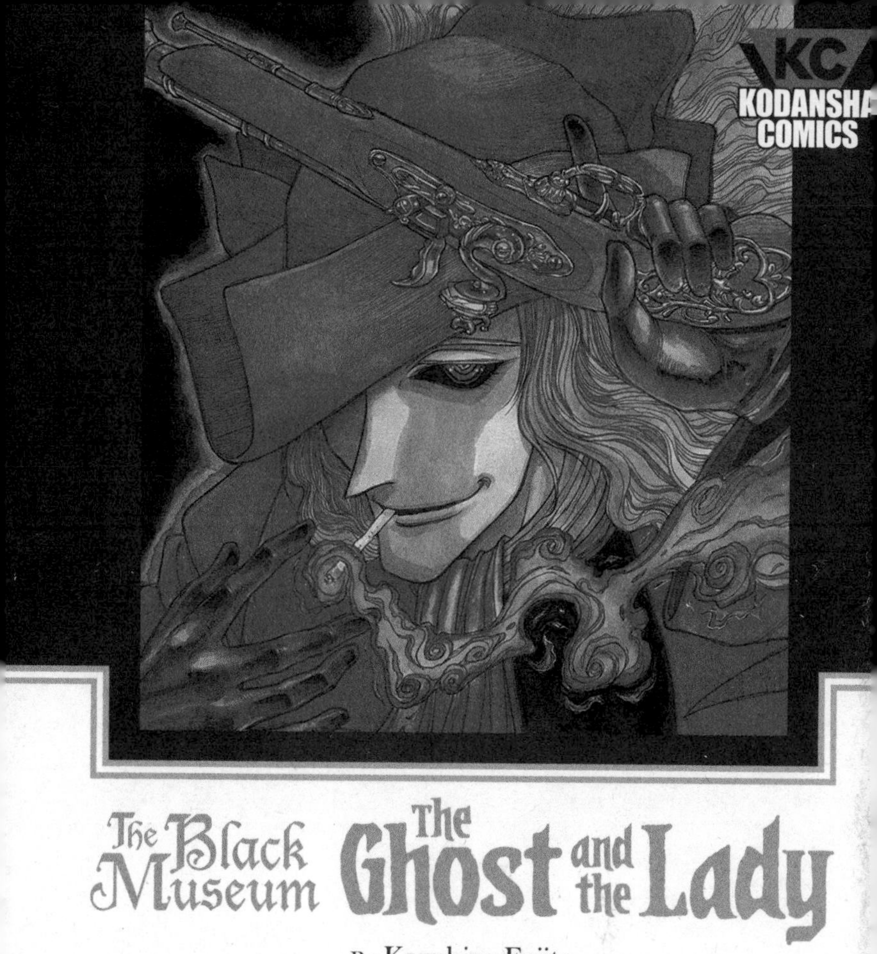
KC
KODANSHA COMICS

The Black Museum: The Ghost and the Lady

By Kazuhiro Fujita

Deep in Scotland Yard in London sits an evidence room dedicated to the greatest mysteries of British history. In this "Black Museum" sits a misshapen hunk of lead–two bullets fused together–the key to a wartime encounter between Florence Nightingale, the mother of modern nursing, and a supernatural Man in Grey. This story is unknown to most scholars of history, but a special guest of the museum will tell the tale of *The Ghost and the Lady*...

Praise for Kazuhiro Fujita's *Ushio and Tora*

"A charming revival that combines a classic look with modern depth and pacing... **Essential viewing both for curmudgeons and new fans alike.**" — Anime News Network

"**GREAT!** The first episode of *Ushio and Tora* captures the essence of '90s anime." — IGN

‹ KAMOME ›
SHIRAHAMA

Witch Hat Atelier

A magical manga
adventure for
fans of Disney
and Studio
Ghibli!

Witch Hat Atelier © Kamome Shirahama/Kodansha Ltd.

The magical adventure that took Japan by storm is finally here, from acclaimed DC and Marvel cover artist Kamome Shirahama!

In a world where everyone takes wonders like magic spells and dragons for granted, Coco is a girl with a simple dream: She wants to be a witch. But everybody knows magicians are born, not made, and Coco was not born with a gift for magic. Resigned to her un-magical life, Coco is about to give up on her dream to become a witch...until the day she meets Qifrey, a mysterious, traveling magician. After secretly seeing Qifrey perform magic in a way she's never seen before, Coco soon learns what everybody "knows" might not be the truth, and discovers that her magical dream may not be as far away as it may seem...

KC / KODANSHA COMICS

New action series from Hiroyuki Takei, creator of the classic shonen franchise Shaman King!

In medieval Japan, a bell hanging on the collar is a sign that a cat has a master. Norachiyo's bell hangs from his katana sheath, but he is nonetheless a stray — a ronin. This one-eyed cat samurai travels across a dishonest world, cutting through pretense and deception with his blade.

NekogaHara

STRAY CAT SAMURAI

By
Hiroyuki Takei

HAPPINESS

—ハピネス—

By Shuzo Oshimi

From the creator of *The Flowers of Evil*

Nothing interesting is happening in Makoto Ozaki's first year of high school. HIs life is a series of quiet humiliations: low-grade bullies, unreliable friends, and the constant frustration of his adolescent lust. But one night, a pale, thin girl knocks him to the ground in an alley and offers him a choice.

Now everything is different. Daylight is searingly bright. Food tastes awful. And worse than anything is the terrible, consuming thirst...

Praise for Shuzo Oshimi's *The Flowers of Evil*

"A shockingly readable story that vividly—one might even say queasily—evokes the fear and confusion of discovering one's own sexuality. Recommended." —The Manga Critic

"A page-turning tale of sordid middle school blackmail." —Otaku USA Magazine

"A stunning new horror manga." —Third Eye Comics

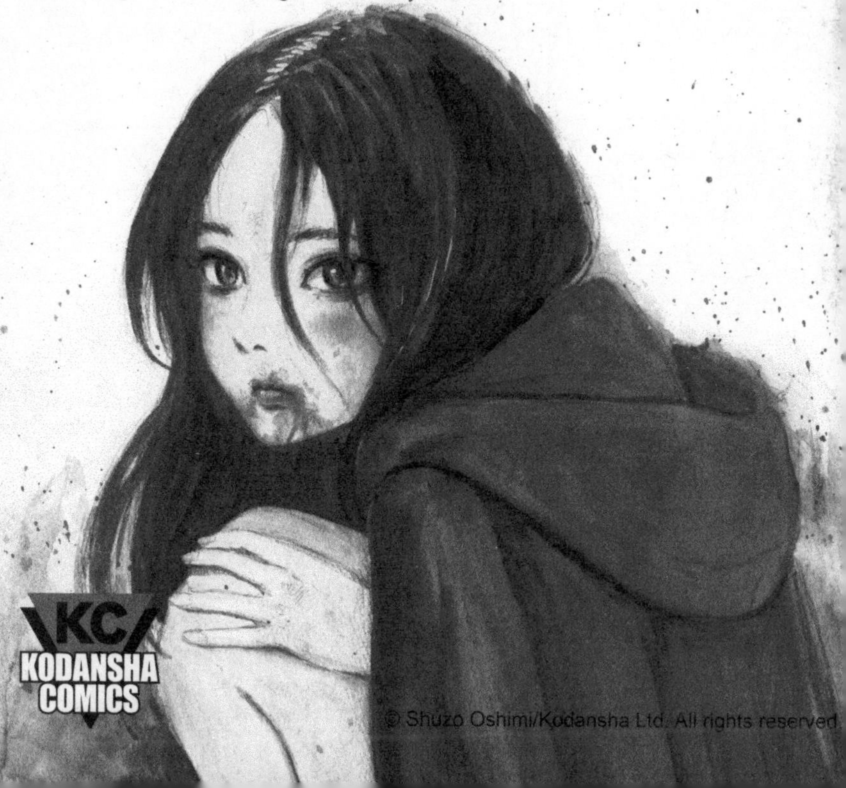
KC
KODANSHA COMICS

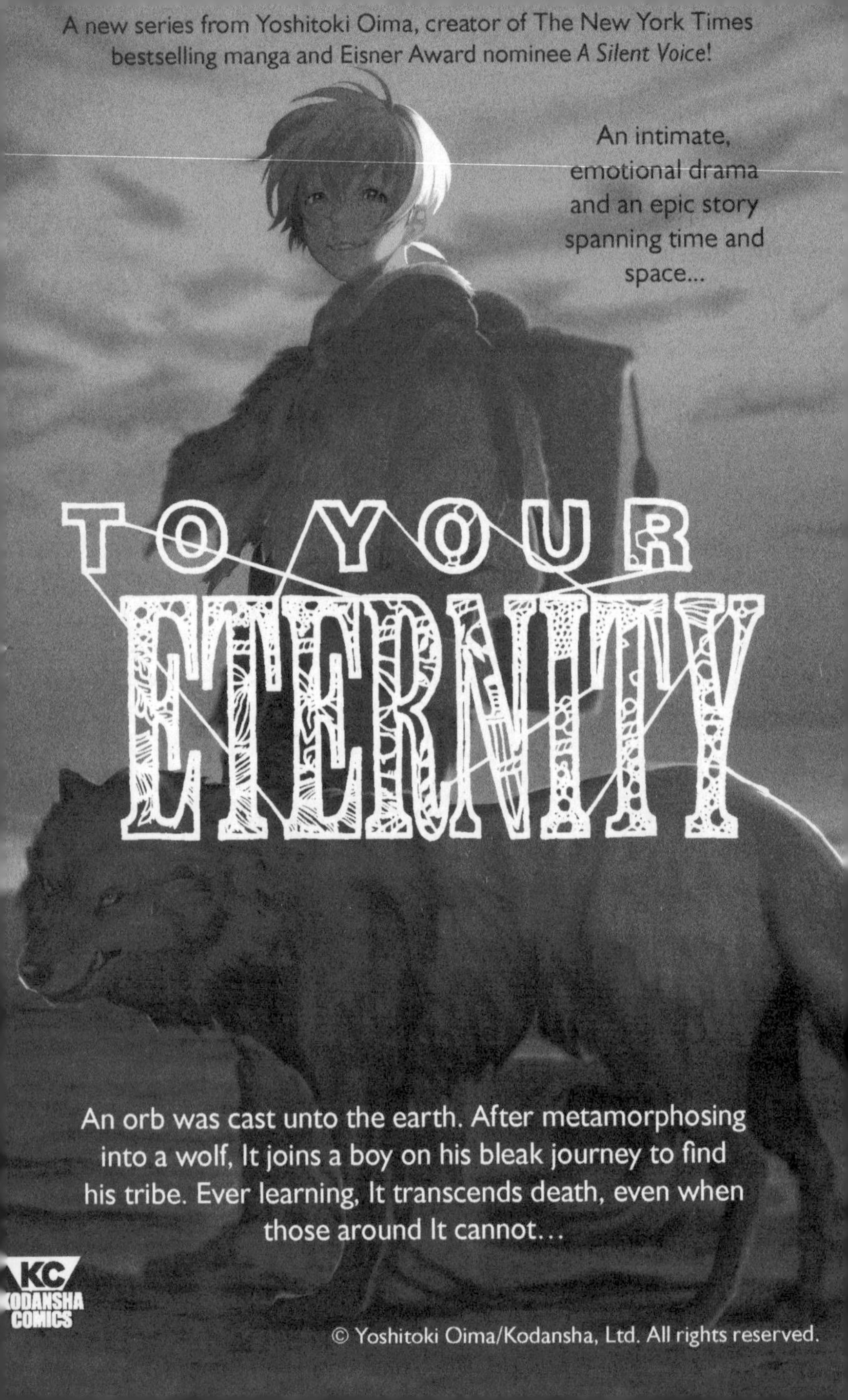
A new series from Yoshitoki Oima, creator of The New York Times bestselling manga and Eisner Award nominee *A Silent Voice*!
An intimate, emotional drama and an epic story spanning time and space...
TO YOUR ETERNITY
An orb was cast unto the earth. After metamorphosing into a wolf, It joins a boy on his bleak journey to find his tribe. Ever learning, It transcends death, even when those around It cannot…
KC KODANSHA COMICS
© Yoshitoki Oima/Kodansha, Ltd. All rights reserved.

DELUXE EDITION

BATTLE ANGEL ALITA

After more than a decade out of print, the original cyberpunk action classic returns in glorious 400-page hardcover deluxe editions, featuring an all-new translation, color pages, and new cover designs!

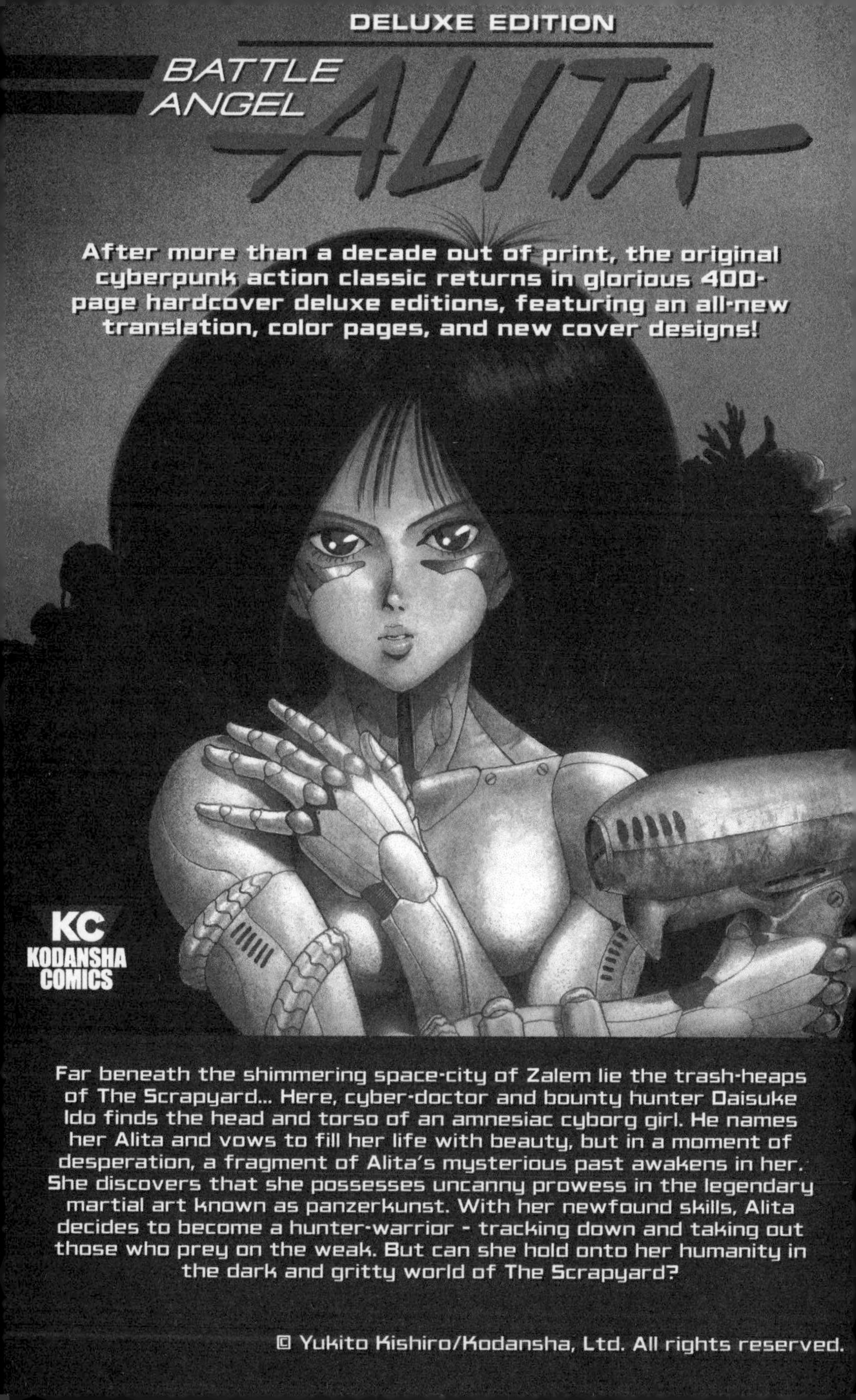

KC KODANSHA COMICS

Far beneath the shimmering space-city of Zalem lie the trash-heaps of The Scrapyard... Here, cyber-doctor and bounty hunter Daisuke Ido finds the head and torso of an amnesiac cyborg girl. He names her Alita and vows to fill her life with beauty, but in a moment of desperation, a fragment of Alita's mysterious past awakens in her. She discovers that she possesses uncanny prowess in the legendary martial art known as panzerkunst. With her newfound skills, Alita decides to become a hunter-warrior - tracking down and taking out those who prey on the weak. But can she hold onto her humanity in the dark and gritty world of The Scrapyard?

The Heroic Legend of Arslan volume 11 is a work of fiction. Names,
characters, places, and incidents are the products of the author's
imagination or are used fictitiously. Any resemblance to actual events,
locales, or persons, living or dead, is entirely coincidental.

A Kodansha Comics Trade Paperback Original.

The Heroic Legend of Arslan volume 11 copyright © 2019 Hiromu
Arakawa & Yoshiki Tanaka
English translation copyright © 2019 Hiromu Arakawa & Yoshiki Tanaka

All rights reserved.

Published in the United States by Kodansha Comics,
an imprint of Kodansha USA Publishing, LLC, New York.

Publication rights for this English edition arranged through Kodansha Ltd.,
Tokyo.

First published in Japan in 2019 by Kodansha Ltd., Tokyo, as Arslan
Senki volume 11.

ISBN 978-1-63236-856-0

Printed in the United States of America.

www.kodanshacomics.com

9 8 7 6 5 4 3 2 1

Translation: Amanda Haley
Lettering: James Dashiell
Editing: Ajani Oloye